The Concept of Divine Sovereignty in Micah

A Vision for the Fulfillment of the Abrahamic Promises

Colin Semwayo

MONOGRAPHS

© 2019 Colin Semwayo

Published 2019 by Langham Monographs
An imprint of Langham Publishing
www.langhampublishing.org

Langham Publishing and its imprints are a ministry of Langham Partnership

Langham Partnership
PO Box 296, Carlisle, Cumbria, CA3 9WZ, UK
www.langham.org

ISBNs:
978-1-78368-768-8 Print
978-1-78368-769-5 ePub
978-1-78368-770-1 Mobi
978-1-78368-771-8 PDF

Colin Semwayo has asserted his right under the Copyright, Designs and Patents Act, 1988 to be identified as the Author of this work.

All rights reserved. No part of this publication may be reproduced, stored in a retrieval system or transmitted, in any form or by any means, electronic, mechanical, photocopying, recording or otherwise, without the prior written permission of the publisher or the Copyright Licensing Agency.

Requests to reuse content from Langham Publishing are processed through PLSclear. Please visit www.plsclear.com to complete your request.

All Scripture translations in this work are the author's own.

British Library Cataloguing-in-Publication Data
A catalogue record for this book is available from the British Library

ISBN: 9781783687688

Cover & Book Design: projectluz.com

Langham Partnership actively supports theological dialogue and an author's right to publish but does not necessarily endorse the views and opinions set forth here or in works referenced within this publication, nor can we guarantee technical and grammatical correctness. Langham Partnership does not accept any responsibility or liability to persons or property as a consequence of the reading, use or interpretation of its published content.

Contents

Acknowledgements ix

Abstract xi

Abbreviations xiii

Tables and Figures viii

Chapter 1 1
   Introduction
      Need for This Study 1
      Concept of Divine Sovereignty 5
         Concept of Divine Sovereignty in the ANE Context 5
         Concept of Divine Sovereignty in the Old Testament 11
         Concept of Divine Sovereignty in Micah 14
      Purpose and Thesis Statement 17
      The Method of the Study 20
         A Biblical Theology for Micah 20
         The Task of Biblical Theology: A Definition 20
         A Structure of Biblical Theology: Covenantal Story/
            Metanarrative Approach 21
         A Method of Biblical Theology: Theological Exegesis 26
      Outline of the Investigation 26

Chapter 2 29
   Covenant Concept: A Theological Context for Micah
      Introduction 29
      Approaches to Biblical Covenants 30
         A Traditional Approach to Biblical Covenants 30
         An Alternative Approach to Biblical Covenants 35
         Abrahamic Covenant 39
         Mosaic Covenant 48
         Davidic Covenant 53
      Summary 61

Chapter 3 63
   Zion/Davidic Traditions: A Framework for Micah
      Introduction 63
         Definition of Zion/Davidic Traditions 67

    Approaches to Zion/Davidic Traditions..67
        Relationship between Zion and Davidic Traditions.....................67
        Motifs of the Zion/Davidic Traditions 68
    Analyzing Traditions in Micah 75
        Definitions 75
        Shared and Intended Contexts...77
        Criteria for Discerning Intertextual Allusions..............................79
        Putting It Together 85

Chapter 4 91

Divine Sovereignty and Mount Zion (Micah 1:2–4:8)
    Introduction 91
    Overview of Micah 1:2–4:8 92
        Unity of Micah 1:2–4:8 92
        Zion: A Key to Yahweh's Sovereignty in Micah 1:2–4:8 94
        Zion/Davidic Traditions Motifs in Micah 1:2–4:8 95
    Transformation of Zion 97
        Unbridled Sin: Idolatry and Social Injustice in Jerusalem............97
        Judgment: From Mountaintops to Mount Zion.......................105
        Restoration: The Exaltation of Zion...122
    Significance of Divine Sovereignty in Zion......................................128
        Zion as the Cosmic Mountain 128
        Yahweh as the Cosmic King...129

Chapter 5 131

Divine Sovereignty and the Davidic King (Micah 4:9–5:14)
    Introduction 131
    Overview of Micah 4:9–5:14 133
        Unity of Micah 4:9–5:14 133
        Zion/Davidic Traditions in Micah 4:9–5:14 135
    Transformation of Davidic Kingship..136
        Implied Sin Concerning Zion's King and Inhabitants 136
        Judgment upon Zion's King and Inhabitants.............................138
        Restoration of Zion's Former Dominion 151
    Significance of Davidic Kingship 167

Chapter 6 169

Divine Sovereignty and the New People of God (Micah 6:1–7:20)
    Introduction 169
    Overview of Micah 6:1–7:20 170
        Unity of Micah 6:1–7:20 170
        Zion/Davidic Traditions in Micah 6:1–7:20 172

  Transformation of the New People of God 177
    Yahweh Demands Covenant Recommitment 177
    Judgment upon the Wicked 187
    Transformation of the Righteous 192
  Conclusion 201

Chapter 7 203
  Covenantal Implications of Divine Sovereignty in Micah
  Introduction 203
  Zion/Davidic Traditions and the Abrahamic Traditions 204
  Restoration of the Abrahamic Promises 207
    Yahweh Restores the Land 207
    Yahweh Restores Kingship 208
    Yahweh Restores Israel's Status as a Great Nation 209
    Yahweh Restores a New Covenant Community 210
  Conclusion 210

Appendix 213
  Origins of the Zion/Davidic Traditions
  Introduction 213
  The Jebusite Theory 213
  The Shiloh Ark Theory 216
  The Davidic Court Theory 218

Bibliography 223

List of Tables and Figures

Table 2.1: Markers Connecting Obedience with Sinai Law 44

Figure 2.1: A Twofold Covenant Typology Model 32
Figure 2.2: An Embedded-Type Covenant Model 38
Figure 3.1: The Intended Context of Micah's Theophanic Tradition 88

Acknowledgements

To God be the glory in Christ Jesus! The long process of writing this dissertation has been a rewarding experience thanks to the numerous people who have each contributed in so many ways. As I reflect on the experience, I am reminded that such a project is a community endeavor. I acknowledge the impact the wider scholarly community had on this project. The numerous footnotes in this study testify to that.

First, I would want to thank my mentor and supervisor Dr Robert Chisholm Jr. for his guidance throughout this journey. From the inception of this project to my struggles as I wrestled with the book of Micah, Dr Chisholm has patiently walked along beside me. He has provided immeasurable scholarly guidance and insights. I am sincerely grateful for his mentorship. Next, I would like to thank Dr Richard A. Taylor for his learned stimulus. His composure in and out of class has been of a source of encouragement. Similarly, I want to express a debt of gratitude to Dr Greg W. Parsons who first instilled in me an appreciation of the Hebrew Bible when I was pursuing my master's degree in divinity. Dr Parsons encouraged me to pursue doctoral studies in Old Testament at Dallas Theological Seminary (DTS). It would be a travesty if I failed to thank the stimulating Old Testament faculty at DTS for their impact on my scholarship. Altogether, the praise in this present study reflects their scholarship, and any deficiencies are wholly mine. Finally, I would like to say thanks to the editorial staff at Langham Publishing for all their diligent work in putting together my manuscript for publication.

In closing, I would like to express my heartfelt thanks to my wife, Florence, who has followed the progress of this study with love, prayer, and indispensable support for the entire length of my seminary experience. I also sincerely thank my children, in birth order: Nyashadzashe, Dananai (both young adults now), Dadayinashe, and Itayinashe. I thank them for their love, patience, and understanding. I deeply love each one of them more than I can express here (Isa 8:18).

Abstract

Most scholars agree that although some parts of the book of Micah lack explicit cohesive links, there is sufficient thematic coherence in the final form of the book to encourage theological reflection. Perhaps the most likely example of thematic coherence is evident in Micah's treatment of the concept of Yahweh's sovereignty. Thus, the purpose herein will be to explore that coherence by analyzing how the reestablishment of Yahweh's sovereignty relates to the fulfillment of the Abrahamic promises. While the coherence is not perfect because of some residual discontinuities, Micah's use of the Zion/Davidic traditions may provide the needed reinforcement to build and develop this concept.

Methodologically, this study falls within the wider field of biblical theology. It puts forward a multiplex approach with Yahweh's sovereignty as a central theme and Israel's covenantal story as an encompassing metanarrative that frames the theme. The study structures its overall theological analysis and synthesis within a framework of the Zion/Davidic traditions. The traditions provide a ready-made framework for such an investigation because the three primary sub-themes that comprise the concept of Yahweh's sovereignty and the pattern that summarizes Israel's covenantal story are intrinsic to the Zion/Davidic traditions. More importantly, the traditions effectively reinterpret how the Abrahamic covenant is fulfilled for Micah's generation. It is possible then to carry out a theological analysis and synthesis of Yahweh's sovereignty in Micah under a single umbrella. Previous studies on the book of Micah have not yet adequately exploited this versatility of the Zion/Davidic traditions.

The theological analysis reveals that the reestablishment of Yahweh's sovereignty is achieved through the restoration of Zion as the throne of Yahweh's rule on earth and a Davidic king ruling as Yahweh's vicegerent at Zion with a new humanity properly serving as Yahweh's vicegerents worldwide. The divine intent is to restore the original order as at creation. A significant theological implication from our analysis is that Yahweh's ultimate intention is to fulfill the Abrahamic promises – land, kingship, Israel's status of honor as a great nation, and a new covenant community. Micah is extending those past promises to his eighth-century audience.

Abbreviations

ANE	Ancient Near East
ANET	*Ancient Near Eastern Texts Relating to the Old Testament.* Edited by James B. Pritchard. 3rd ed. Princeton: Princeton University Press, 1969.
AT	Annales Theoligici
BDB	Brown, F., S. R. Driver, and C. A. Briggs. *A Hebrew and English Lexicon of the Old Testament.*
COS	*The Context of Scripture.* Edited by William W. Hallo. 3 vols. Leiden: Brill, 1997–2002.
CTA	*Corpus des tablettes en cunéiformes alphabétiques découvertes à Ras Shamra-Ugarit de 1929 à 1939.* Edited by Andrée Herdner. Paris: Geuthner, 1963.
CTH	*Catalogue des textes hittites.* Emmanuel Laroche. Paris: Klincksieck, 1971.
GKC	*Gesenius' Hebrew Grammar.* Edited by Emil Kautzsch. Translated by Arthur E. Cowley. 2nd ed. Oxford: Clarendon, 1910.
HALOT	*The Hebrew and Aramaic Lexicon of the Old Testament.* Edited by Ludwig Koehler, Walter Baumgartner, and Johann J. Stamm. Translated and edited under the supervision of Mervyn E. J. Richardson. 4 vols. Leiden: Brill, 1994–1999.
IBHS	*An Introduction to Biblical Hebrew Syntax.* Bruce K. Waltke and Michael O'Connor. Winona Lake, IN: Eisenbrauns, 1990.

JM	Joüon, Paul, and T. Muraoka. *A Grammar of Biblical Hebrew*. Revised edition. Subsidia Biblica 27. Rome: Editrice Pontificio Istituto Biblico, 2006.
KAjr	Kuntillet ʿAjrud
NAC	New American Commentary
OTT	Old Testament Theology
RS	Ras Shamra

CHAPTER 1

Introduction

Need for This Study

If any theological themes can be said to stand at the center of Micah's seven chapters, one of them is certainly the sovereignty of Yahweh radiating from Zion.[1] In fact, the prophet's name itself is a question that hints at this. The name "Micah" (מיכה) (Mic 1:1) is short for "Micayah" (מיכיה) (Jer 26:18), which means "Who" (מי) is "like" (כ) "Yahweh" (יה)?[2] The name speaks of Yahweh's incomparability among the gods. Yahweh has no equal; he is the great king and he rules supremely. At the close of the book, the prophet also asks a related question, "Who is a God like you?" (מי־אל כמוך) (Mic 7:18). Evidently, it appears that the theme of Yahweh's incomparability frames the whole book. So how does Yahweh demonstrate his sovereignty between these frames? How does Micah flesh out this theme? How do the various oracles of doom and hope in the book relate to it? These questions deserve answers.

Although Yahweh's sovereignty is a major theme in the book of Micah, a moderate reading of its oracles "makes clear that there is a logical and more detailed line of argumentation that is not so easy to grasp."[3] Prior to the nineteenth century, biblical scholars credulously regarded the book of Micah as authentic. However, in the last third of the nineteenth century, scholars laid down severe skepticism concerning various aspects of the book. For instance, some scholars observed the abrupt changes from doom to hope

---

1. Begerau, "Micah, Prophet of Hope," 69; Barker, "Micah," 37.
2. All Scripture translations in this work are the author's own.
3. Begerau, "Micah, Prophet of Hope," 67.

oracles (2:1–11, 12–13; 3:9–12; 4:1–5), one topic to another (7:1–7, 11–13), and, even more so, the shifts in person and gender (1:10; 6:16: 7:15–19).[4]

As a result, some scholars conclude that Micah's book has no discernible structure; that is, Micah's oracles superficially connect to one another. Keil and Delitzsch consider Micah's style to be somewhat "rough and rugged."[5] H. W. Wolff regards the book of Micah as too intricate to untangle. He remarks, "This complicated meshwork, not so easily transparent, makes more difficult our understanding of the history of the book's formation."[6] Because of such alleged compositional fragmentation, others contend that the book's message appears veiled. D. R. Hillers expresses the difficulty even more sharply. He writes:

> A much more serious problem is an apparent incoherence of thought which must impress the reader who approaches the book for the first time, and which is not necessarily alleviated by a prolonged study. It is difficult to understand how Micah hangs together in a logical, systematic, or historical way.[7]

The foregoing paragraphs underscore the typical experiences of many scholars who have critically read the book over the past century. Surprisingly, such experiences of despair have motivated other scholars to set aside questions about the redaction or structure of Micah in order to understand the book's theological message. More recently, most scholars agree that even though some parts of Micah lack explicit cohesive markers, there is sufficient thematic coherence in the final form of the book to encourage theological reflection.[8] Perhaps the most likely example of thematic coherence is evident in Micah's treatment of Yahweh's sovereignty. While the coherence is not perfect

---

4. Keil and Delitzsch, *Twelve Minor Prophets*, 1:421. For helpful discussions on the history of criticism on Micah, see Willis, "Fundamental Issues," 80, and Jeppesen, "How the Book of Micah Lost Its Integrity," 101–131. For helpful introductions, see Harrison, *Introduction to the Old Testament*, 919–925; Cate, *Introduction to the Old Testament*.

5. Keil and Delitzsch, *Twelve Minor Prophets*, 1:421. For various proposals on the organization of Micah, see Jacobs, *Conceptual Coherence*, 13–43; Cuffey, *Literary Coherence*, 53–71.

6. Wolff, *Micah*, 18.

7. Hillers, *Micah*, 1.

8. Cuffey, *Literary Coherence*, 79–103.

because of some residual discontinuities,[9] Micah's use of the Zion/Davidic traditions may provide the needed reinforcement to build and develop this theme.[10] As will become clear shortly, these traditions offer a ready-made framework for analyzing the concept of divine sovereignty. This is so because sub-themes and other features that define the concept are intrinsic to the Zion/Davidic traditions.

In a recent theological commentary on Micah, Philip Peter Jenson has given some attention to the theological theme of Yahweh's sovereignty as an organizing principle for Micah. In fact, Jenson suggests that the theological dissonance between Yahweh as the sovereign God and his covenant relationship with a sinful community "is the reason why the language, the form and theology of Micah is so complex."[11] Jenson's summary of Micah implicitly suggests that the relationship between the hope and judgment oracles in Micah contributes to the challenges in reading Micah.

What is more, Jenson's overall understanding of Micah's theology is somewhat akin to how Roberts construes Isaiah's vision for Zion's future.[12] For Roberts, the framework for understanding such a vision is to attend to a twofold schema: divine king and human community. Two paradigmatic passages that adumbrate this schema are Isaiah 32:1–8 and 33:10–16, respectively.[13] For our purposes, Roberts's take on the role of the people in the future era provides an indispensable lens for our treatment of Micah 6:1–7:20. He aptly writes:

> If Zion is once again to be known as the faithful city of righteousness (Isa 1:26), this drastic change in Judean society must demand something of God's people as well as its leaders. Just as radical purging of corrupt officials and their replacement by righteous judges appears as a prerequisite for the unfolding of the age of salvation, so the rest of society must also experience the purging effect of God's judgment.[14]

---

9. McFadden, "Micah and the Problem of Continuities," 127–146.
10. Cuffey, *Literary Coherence*, 338.
11. Jenson, *Obadiah, Jonah, Micah*, 99.
12. Roberts, "Divine King," 127–136.
13. Roberts, 130–134, 134–36.
14. Roberts, 134.

Both strategies by Jenson and Roberts are the kind of motivation this study needs in order to reexamine Micah's concept of divine sovereignty under a covenantal framework. Such a framework can be helpful in exploring Micah's rich theological message. However, as I will discuss in a subsequent section, Jenson's actual analysis is inconsistent with his foregoing claim.

Most recently, a handful of scholars have also turned towards the theological importance of the Zion/Davidic traditions in the book, arguing that the prophet's central concern is for the restoration and eventual exaltation of Zion and her fortunes.[15] Frederik Poulsen's and Rick R. Marrs's studies are noteworthy in this regard. In discussing the Zion traditions in the prophets, Poulsen introduces the notion of the dynamic Zion tradition. In chapter 3, we will have more to say about this strand of the Zion traditions, but, for now, it is sufficient to say that Poulsen understands it as the development and transformation of Zion; that is, from judgment to restoration. For him, the dynamic Zion tradition proceeds in three phases: the destruction and the exile, the return, and the restoration of a new Zion.[16] Marrs also agrees with the two diametric poles of Zion in Micah: a Zion that experiences transformation through divine judgment and restoration.[17]

While these studies are commendable, several vistas for further research in Micah lie before us. A penetrating and significant observation stemming from our study of Micah is that the prophet utilizes key features from the Zion/Davidic traditions to underscore the concept of divine sovereignty. A search of scholarly literature shows that the Zion/Davidic traditions in Micah have received little scholarly attention in the past decades as a relevant framework for discussing the concept of divine sovereignty. To my knowledge, Micah studies have not yet adequately developed the Zion/Davidic traditions in Micah in order to surface the theological concept of divine sovereignty and its implication for the fulfillment of the Abrahamic promises. Since the concept of divine sovereignty serves as bookends to Micah's book (i.e., the concept is expressed in terms of Yahweh's incomparability [1:2; 7:18]), scholars have yet

---

15. Poulsen, *Representing Zion*, 55–56; Timmer, *Non-Israelite Nations*, 90–115; Biddle, "Dominion Comes to Jerusalem," 253–267; Zapff, "Perspective on the Nations," 301–303.

16. Poulsen, *Representing Zion*, 190.

17. Marrs, "Back to the Future," 82–83, 91–93.

to develop the connection between the concept and the Abrahamic covenant to its logical conclusion.

Therefore, a significant question that will serve as a polestar for the synthesis portion of our study is: How does the concept of divine sovereignty in Micah relate to the fulfillment of the Abrahamic promises (7:18–20)? The foregoing observations and the several questions raised thus far warrant a reassessment of Micah's portrayal of the concept of divine sovereignty. The present study is an attempt to answer these questions. However, before we can spell out our purpose and thesis statement in detail, we find it fitting to give a working definition of the concept of divine sovereignty.

Concept of Divine Sovereignty
Concept of Divine Sovereignty in the ANE Context

As is generally the case with many other topics in the ancient Near East (ANE) and in biblical studies, the concept of divine sovereignty is a vast subject.[18] In discussing the concept, one must acknowledge, without bias, its variegated expressions in the various cultures. If we exclude the reality of these variations, we erroneously eviscerate the theological dynamism the concept offered in the eyes of its authors and patrons. In this respect, Bernard F. Batto's characterization of the concept provides an appropriate starting point for our discussion.

Batto avers that in the ANE, "the concept of divine sovereignty had reference to the absolute and universal rule of the chief deity over heaven and earth."[19] Batto proceeds to note that the concept varied along geographical and chronological lines and reflected developments mainly in the earthly political realm.[20] Daniel I. Block perceptively adds that the chief gods – that is, the primordial cosmic gods who served as heads of the pantheons – exercised

---

18. The topic has attracted numerous studies. See, for example, Willis, *Dissonance*, 5–19; Batto, "Divine Sovereign," 143–186; Block, *Gods of the Nations*, 75–92; Schneider, *Introduction to Ancient Mesopotamian Religion*, 34–65; Fretheim, "Suffering God," 31–56; Seow, "Rule of God," 219–246; Labuschagne, *Incomparability of Yahweh*; Miller, "Sovereignty of God," 129–144; McCann, *Creation and the Sovereignty of God*; Moore, *Moving Beyond Symbol and Myth*; Cogan, *Imperialism and Religion*; Gibson and Biggs, *Organization of Power*.

19. Batto, "Divine Sovereign," 144.

20. Batto, 162; Walton, *Ancient Near Eastern Thought*, 93–94; Schneider, *Introduction to Ancient Mesopotamian Religion*, 51–52.

universal sovereignty.[21] In other words, the concept of divine sovereignty in the ANE assumed that the chief deity was a creator god.

As a first impression, Batto's claim for absolute or universal sovereignty sounds dubious given the polytheistic nature of ANE cultures. While this is a valid objection, there is other evidence to consider. Before we present the evidence, we should mention that our more developed theology should not impinge on what the ancient authors believed about their supreme gods. It would also be a travesty to impose ancient Israel's notion of divine sovereignty on its neighbors. Divine sovereignty took various forms, based mainly on each culture's view of its pantheon. Israel had no pantheon, so sovereignty took a significantly different form. No gods served as Yahweh's viceroys, whereas in other ANE cultures some gods served in this capacity. Yet even in such cases, where some of the gods in the pantheon served as vicegerents in governing parts of the cosmos,[22] ultimate authority resided in the hands of the supreme deity. He alone could issue unchallenged decrees.

In any event, a closer examination of the evidence from Mesopotamia substantiates the claim that Marduk exercised absolute or universal sovereignty. While the Mesopotamian pantheon is complex,[23] scholars discern a pattern in its evolution that runs from the fourth down to the first millennium BC.[24] In the initial stages, divine power was distributed among many gods who were basically associated with powers of nature.[25] However, in the later stages, the number of major gods shrank and the pantheon became more structured.[26] As such, more power concentrated on fewer deities, the cosmic gods.[27]

---

21. Block, *Gods of the Nations*, 19. Niehaus points out that in the ancient world the creator god was always suzerain over his creation. Niehaus, *Ancient Near Eastern Themes*, 35n4.

22. The present study utilizes the terms vicegerent and viceroy interchangeably.

23. Black and Green, *Gods, Demons and Symbols*, 147. As they state, "There is a sense in which it is impossible, in connection with ancient Mesopotamia, to speak of a pantheon (the deities of a people collectively). This is because under the (geographically ill-determined) heading Mesopotamia, at least 3,000 years of history are included, incorporating three main people (Sumerian, Babylonians and Assyrians)."

24. Schneider, *Introduction to Ancient Mesopotamian Religion*, 54.

25. Schneider.

26. Batto, "Divine Sovereign," 162; Schneider, *Introduction to Ancient Mesopotamian Religion*, 54–57.

27. Schneider, *Introduction to Ancient Mesopotamian Religion*, 54; Block, *Gods of the Nations*, 19.

With the rise of Babylon's imperial hegemony over the ancient world in the latter part of the second millennium BC,[28] the Epic of Creation portrays an evolution of political power from a pantheon of equals deliberating policy to an absolute king proclaiming policy for the whole pantheon and the universe.[29] As the evidence indisputably suggests, Marduk, after his victory over Tiamat, became the absolute and universal sovereign of heaven and earth, as all the gods in the pantheon ceded their powers to him.[30] The fact that all these gods granted Marduk sovereignty should not erode the absolute or universal character of that sovereignty. The authors/theologians of this epic sincerely believed that their god, Marduk, was a creator god, who ruled over all creatures and could pronounce immutable decrees without the consent of the other gods.

A. R. George has also reached a similar conclusion. As he puts it, "The business of the assembly after Marduk's enthronement is the decreeing of destinies: in the myth the gods decree absolute sovereignty for Marduk."[31] In a fascinating and multifaceted study on creation, William P. Brown also adds: "By unanimous consent, Marduk is made the one and only sovereign deity."[32]

In Assyria, Ashur simply supplanted Marduk as the absolute sovereignty.[33] Just as the poet of the *Epic of Creation* utilized themes used to exalt Ninurta in the Anzu myth and assigned them to Marduk,[34] "Neo-Assyrian theologians

---

28. Dalley, *Myths from Mesopotamia*, 228–230; Black and Green, *Gods, Demons and Symbols*, 182–184; Jacobsen, *Treasures of Darkness*, 21.

29. Foster, *From Distant Days*, 9.

30. For example, an excerpt from the Epic of Creation, tablet VI, lines 95–105, reads, "Then the great gods convened, They made Marduk's destiny highest, they prostrated themselves. They laid upon themselves a curse (if they broke the oath). . . . They granted him exercise of kingship over the gods, They established him forever for lordship of heaven and earth. . . . When he speaks, we shall all do obeisance, At his command the gods shall pay heed. His word shall be supreme above and below, The son, our champion, shall be the highest. His lordship shall be supreme, he shall have no rival." "Epic of Creation," translated by Benjamin R. Foster (*COS* 1.111:VI:95–105). Also see Frankfort, *Kingship and the Gods*, 220; Engnell, *Studies in Divine Kingship*, 21; Foster, *From Distant Days*, 10; Black and Green, *Gods, Demons and Symbols*, 147; Schneider, *Introduction to Ancient Mesopotamian Religion*, 54; Dalley, *Myths from Mesopotamia*, 228–230; Jacobsen, *Treasures of Darkness*, 21.

31. George, *Babylonian Topographical Texts*, 287; Oshima, *Babylonian Poems*, 44–45.

32. Brown, *Seven Pillars of Creation*.

33. Holloway, *Aššur Is King!*, 76; Schneider, *Introduction to Ancient Mesopotamian Religion*, 62–63.

34. Foster, *From Distant Days*, 10.

appropriated this myth of divine sovereignty for their own national god simply by substituting everywhere the name of Ashur in place of Marduk."[35] A catalyst for such an adaptation by the Neo-Assyrian theologians was the political ascendency of Assyria as a world power.

As we move west to Ugarit, the evidence contradicts the basic contention that Baal shared equal status with El in governing the cosmos. Admittedly, the mythological texts from Ugarit revolve around the exploits of Baal, the storm god (*CTA* 1–6).[36] The action centers primarily on the conflict between Baal and the other gods (i.e. Yamm and Mot) in their quest for domination in the cosmos but not for El's throne *per se*.[37] The wise El stood above these battles and intervened only when necessary. Thus, the seemingly passive role of the compassionate El in these conflicts need not suggest that he shared supremacy with Baal or any other lesser god.[38]

First, the mythological texts from Ugarit portray El as the creator of the gods.[39] He is referred to as "Creator of creatures" (*CTA* 4:II:11; 4:III:32; 6:III:5, 11). In the *Birth of the Gracious and Beautiful Gods*, El fathers the gods Dawn and Dusk (*CTA* 23:31-64).[40] Besides the Ugaritic texts, other sources show that El was the creator of heaven and earth. E. Theodore Mullen Jr. and others draw attention to the Karapate inscription and a Hittite fragment that show that El was viewed as a creator god.[41] Thus, the ancient clergies at Ugarit consistently viewed El, their primordial god, as the father of the gods and creator of heaven and earth.[42] As such, he was suzerain and owner of the universe.

---

35. Batto, "Divine Sovereign," 147.

36. Unless otherwise noted, all references to *CTA* texts in this study are from "The Ba'lu Myth," translated by Dennis Pardee (*COS* 1.86).

37. Sparks, *Ancient Texts*, 333; Handy, *Among the Host of Heaven*, 101–102.

38. L'Heureux, *Rank among the Canaanite Gods*, 10.

39. It suffices though to mention that the Ugaritic texts mainly emphasize cosmology and not theogony. In the Sanchuniathon's theogony, El plays a prominent role. It is possible that a version of this theogony preceded the Baal Cycle. See Attridge and Oden, *Philo of Byblos*, 46–55; Baumgarten, *Phoenician History of Philo of Byblos*; Paas, *Creation and Judgement*, 123–128.

40. "The Birth of the Gracious and Beautiful Gods," translated by Dennis Pardee (*COS* 1.87).

41. Mullen, *Assembly of the Gods*, 14–17.

42. Mullen, 17.

As the creator god, he was king over his creation, and absolute ruler of the gods (cf. *CTA* 1:III:23–24; 2:III:5; 3:V:15–16; 4:IV:23–26).[43]

Second, while El may appear to play a secondary role in the Ugaritic texts, he still held absolute sway over all the gods, including Baal. As the ultimate ruler, El established spheres of jurisdiction in the cosmos. Only by his decree were the younger gods appointed to govern particular realms.[44] El decreed that Yamm attain kingship (*CTA* 1:IV:11, 13, 17–18, 20). El commanded Kôṯaru-wa-Ḫasīsu to build a temple for Yamm, thus, pronouncing him king (*CTA* 2:III:6–11).[45] Besides establishing kingship for the other gods, El could also remove the younger gods from their assigned dominions. Šapšu emphatically made clear to ʿAṯtaru that El would dethrone him.[46] Similarly, the same threat was expressed to Mot as he was about to vanquish Baal (*CTA* 6:VI:22–20).[47] In these lines, we read that Mot was afraid of losing his rule.

In the case of Baal, the text clarifies that El established Baal's kingship.[48] Only by El's decree did Baal attain a temple, a symbol of his kingship (*CTA* 4:IV:58–V:63). In addition, the subordination of Baal's rule to the authority of El is evident in *Ug* 5 2.1 (RS 24.252 *recto*) and *Ug* 5 2.2 (RS 24.252 *verso*).[49] According to Conrad E. L'Heureux, *Ug* 5 2.1 "contains Baal's prayer to be confirmed as El's shepherd, that is, El's vice-regent for Ugarit."[50] Likewise, Lowell K. Handy adds, "Baal served in a position subordinate to EL."[51] If L'Heureux and Handy are correct, then the notion of vicegerency does not diminish El's sovereignty. In fact, the notion is consistent with divine sovereignty. Simply put, vicegerency in the cosmic realm complements divine sovereignty, just as the human king does in the earthly realm.

---

43. Mullen, 22–25.

44. L'Heureux, *Rank among the Canaanite Gods*, 10. As Mullen quips, El is the dispenser of kingdoms. Mullen, *The Assembly of the Gods*, 35; Handy, *Among the Host of Heaven*, 99–102.

45. Mullen, *The Assembly of the Gods*, 38–39.

46. A portion of the threat reads, "Surely he would pull up [the foundations of your] seat, overturn [the throne of] your kingship, break the staff of your rulership" (*CTA* 2:III:17).

47. L'Heureux, *Rank among the Canaanite Gods*, 11.

48. The text reads, "he [Baal] does cry out to the Bull, his father 'Ilu, to the king who established him" (*CTA* 3:V:43).

49. L'Heureux, *Rank among the Canaanite Gods*, 169–170, 181–182.

50. L'Heureux, 11.

51. Handy, *Among the Host of Heaven*, 101.

It is within the context informed by the foregoing evidence that this study understands El as the absolute sovereign at Ugarit. Unfortunately, Frank Cross concludes otherwise. For him, El's sovereignty was anything but absolute, since the chief god cowed when Yamm demanded the council to hand over Baal. However, Cross's conclusion is not as strong as it appears. Apparently the opening scene in the Baal Cycle recounts El and Yamm conspiring the death of Baal (CAT 1.1.V).[52] Thus, El had no reason to reject Yamm's demands, since he was involved in the plot to attack Baal in the first place. Against Cross, his dissertation advisor at Harvard University, Mullen also presents a persuasive case to correct the misconception that Baal was equal to El.[53] As he rightly concludes, "El's function as king reveals that he alone is the supreme power in the pantheon. He sits enthroned over the gods and rules them from a position of supreme power."[54]

Furthermore, a related feature in the concept of the divine sovereign in the ANE was that a deity earned the status of divine sovereignty following the battle against, and victory over, hostile and chaotic forces. For instance, pharaohs in Memphite theology, Marduk in Babylon, Asshur in Assyria, and Baal in Ugaritic are all depicted as warrior gods. The underlying belief here is that the pharaohs, Marduk, Asshur, and Baal each became king of the gods and cosmos because they fought the chaos that threatened order in society and in nature. Following their victory, the victor gods had a new temple/palace built for them from which they were acclaimed kings.[55] Batto goes on to clarify that "one of the functions of the divine sovereign was to bring order into the midst of chaos, to establish the conditions under which meaningful existence was not only possible but even guaranteed."[56]

Another valuable dimension in the concept of the divine sovereign in the ANE was that the human king ruled the earth on behalf of the gods. For instance, in Egypt, the pharaoh was the embodiment of Horus and Osiris in life and in death, respectively.[57] The pharaoh issued decrees, which had the

---

52. Parker, "Baal Cycle," 87–88.
53. Mullen, *Assembly of the Gods*, 12–45.
54. Mullen, 25–26.
55. Batto, "Divine Sovereign," 147–149; Miller, "Sovereignty of God," 130.
56. Batto, "Divine Sovereign," 162.
57. Batto, 149–150.

force of the divine will.⁵⁸ Similar conceptions prevailed in Ugarit, whereby King Kirta served as El's earthly regent.⁵⁹ Batto also presents iconographic evidence from the Neo-Assyrian period, which depicts the various kings as viceroy of the divine sovereignty.⁶⁰ For example, wall reliefs in the palace of Ashurnasirpal II (883–859 BC) depict the Assyrian king's action almost exactly as those of an anthropomorphic god placed in winged sundisk.⁶¹ According to Batto, the winged sundisk "is an expression of the power of the king as the nexus between heaven and earth wherein peace, security and the weal of the kingdom are accomplished."⁶²

Concept of Divine Sovereignty in the Old Testament
Yahweh as creator

Although the foregoing concept of divine sovereignty was widely shared among ANE cultures, Israel's conceptualization of Yahweh's sovereignty differed significantly, especially in its image of Yahweh as creator. For instance, the standard Mesopotamian cosmology is completely silent on the creation of the material cosmos.⁶³ In Israel, however, the concept of divine sovereignty has roots in the fact of the creation of the physical cosmos (Gen 1:1; cf. Jer 10:10-12).⁶⁴ Batto remarks that the concept of divine sovereignty "was the most transcendent characterization of God available."⁶⁵ Patrick D. Miller avers that the concept of Yahweh's sovereignty is the foundational stone of the Old Testament.⁶⁶

These accolades from Batto and Miller are on target. The concept of divine sovereignty is evident in that only God "created" (ברא) the heavens and the earth (Gen 1:1). The Qal form of the verb ברא only occurs with God as the subject and lacks any other agent – false gods or humans. Only Yahweh

---

58. Batto, 149.
59. Parker, "Kirta," 9–11.
60. Batto, "Divine Sovereign," 149–163; Keel, *Symbolism of the Biblical World*, 216–217; Klingbeil, *Yahweh Fighting from Heaven*, 260–267.
61. Batto, "Divine Sovereign," 153; Klingbeil, *Yahweh Fighting from Heaven*, 261.
62. Batto, "Divine Sovereign," 161.
63. Walton, *Ancient Near Eastern Thought*, 179.
64. Fretheim, *God and World*, 14, 46.
65. Batto, "Divine Sovereign," 144.
66. Miller, "Sovereignty of God," 129.

has this power. The comprehensiveness of Yahweh's creation undercuts all other claims to divinity.[67] Yahweh created everything, which implies there is nothing for the false gods to do. Furthermore, it is also precisely this lack of human referents for ברא, which underscores Yahweh's incomparability.[68] Eugene H. Merrill concurs:

> The first and perhaps grandest of the descriptions that characterize the God of the Old Testament in the Genesis record is that of his sovereignty. Upon this facet of his nature rest all subsequent description of him and in our understanding, the whole edifice of Old Testament theology. This is implicit in both his work as Creator ("In the beginning God," Gen 1:1) and in the mandate he issued to mankind to have dominion over all things as God's own image (Gen 1:26–28).[69]

Jon D. Levenson also plows the same field as Merrill. He cogently remarks:

> We can capture the essence of the idea of creation in the Hebrew Bible with the word "mastery." The creation narratives, whatever their length, form, or context, are best seen as a dramatic visualizations of the uncompromised mastery of YHWH, God of Israel, over all else. He alone is "the Lord of all the earth," [97:5] and when the cosmogonic events are complete, his lordship stands beyond all doubt. He reigns in regal repose, "majestic on high," [93:4] all else subordinate to him."[70]

Kenneth A. Mathews makes an important point concerning the nature of ברא, which will be germane to our present study. According to Mathews, the verb "conveys the idea of a special activity accomplished only by deity that results in newness or renewing. Also *bārā'* always refers to the product created and does not refer to the material of which it is made."[71] Levenson takes this insight even further. For him, "the point of creation is not the production of matter out of nothing, but rather the emergence of a stable community in

---

67. Brown, "Theological Interpretation," 402.
68. Brettler, *God Is King*, 159.
69. Merrill, *Everlasting Dominion*, 42.
70. Levenson, *Creation and the Persistence of Evil*, 3.
71. Mathews, *Genesis 1–11:26*, 128.

a benevolent and life-sustaining order."[72] This appears to be the case in Isa 41:20 whereby the prophet uses ברא to portray Yahweh transforming nature.

Yahweh as the great king
Alongside Yahweh as creator, another theme that frequently expresses the concept of Yahweh's sovereignty is his kingship. Ludwig Köhler maintains that a fundamental theme in Old Testament theology is that *"God is the ruling Lord. . . . Everything else derives from it. Everything else leans upon it. Everything else can be understood with reference to it and only to it. Everything else subordinates itself to it."*[73] Simply put, Yahweh is the king over all creation (e.g. Pss 10:16; 44:4–5; 74:12–17).[74] By virtue of being the creator God, Yahweh is king (Pss 29:10; 93:2; 95:3–5). Yahweh's kingship also relates to his role as a warrior (Pss 2; 10:16; 24:7–10; 44:4; 47:2–3). Moreover, Yahweh's kingship cooperates with his just rule (Pss 96:10; 99:4) since his throne was founded upon "justice and righteousness" (צדק ומשפט) (Ps 97:1–3).

Earthly king as vicegerent of the divine sovereign
Because of his transcendent nature, Yahweh does not rule the earthly realm directly. Adam and Eve exercised dominion over the earthly creatures as God's viceroys (Gen 1:26–28). As Richard Middleton puts it, "the writer of Genesis 1 portrays God as king presiding over 'heaven and earth,' an ordered and harmonious realm in which each creature manifests the will of the creator and is thus declared 'good.' Humanity is created like the God, with the special role of representing or imaging God's rule in the world."[75] Yahweh was not relinquishing the right of rule that belonged to him as creator. Rather, he assigned to humanity the role of viceroy in the earthly realm or agent king in his stead.[76] By doing so, God maintained his transcendence and kept the boundary between heaven and earth intact. It should not come as a surprise then that the same thought of vicegerency extends to the human king. The

---

72. Levenson, *Creation and the Persistence of Evil*, 12.
73. Köhler, *Old Testament Theology*, 30. Italics are original.
74. Merrill, *Everlasting Dominion*, 278.
75. Middleton, *Liberating Image*, 26.
76. Beale, *New Testament Biblical Theology*, 30–31.

ideal image of the king derived from the image of God.[77] Put differently, to be created in the "image of God" suggests royal status.

As Merrill correctly observes, the most potent expression of the concept of Yahweh's sovereignty, beyond Genesis, occurs in the enthronement psalms (Pss 47, 93, 95–100) and the royal psalms (Pss 2; 9; 10; 18; 20; 21; 45; 72; 89; 101; 110; 132; 144).[78] Most scholars agree that the central theological idea in these Psalms revolves around the concept of Yahweh's sovereignty (he rules as the great king), its exercise in a future Davidic king, and the place of Zion as the center of the universe.[79] As the Psalter articulated, the Davidic king, as the son of Yahweh, served as his viceroy in Zion and owed Yahweh everything (Pss 2:2–8; 21; 89:27; 110:3).[80] We will say more about the responsibilities of the Davidic king following our discussion of the Zion/Davidic traditions in chapter 3. In any event, these Psalms and many others aid us to understand the connection between the divine rule, human rule, and Zion. With all that said, perceptive readers will notice right away that these three themes (divine rule, human rule, and Zion) are the major tenets of the Zion/Davidic traditions. As such, it is possible to discuss the concept of Yahweh's sovereignty within a framework of the Zion/Davidic traditions.

Concept of Divine Sovereignty in Micah

In Micah, the concept of Yahweh's sovereignty dominates the whole book and serves as the backbone of the entire book. Carol J. Dempsey captures well this view of Micah in her recent commentary. She cogently writes, "Divine sovereignty is a core theological theme in the book of Micah."[81] The first implicit hint of the concept occurs in the opening summons. Yahweh's message concerning the destinies of the two capital cities, Samaria and Jerusalem, affects the whole nation of Israel (Mic 1:1b) and the whole world (v. 2a). The opening vocatives, "O peoples, all of them" (עמים כלם) and "O earth and all

---

77. Preuss, *Old Testament Theology*, 2:34.
78. Merrill, *Everlasting Dominion*, 44, 570–575; Roberts, "Enthronement of Yhwh and David," 676; McCann, *Theological Introduction to the Book of Psalms*, 41–50. Mays proposes that the organizing center of the Psalms is the sentence: "Yahweh reigns." Mays, *Lord Reigns*, 13. Also see, Stulman, *Jeremiah*, 30–31; Goldingay, *Theology of the Book of Isaiah*, 131–134.
79. Merrill, *Everlasting Dominion*, 570; Miller, "Ruler of Zion and the Hope of the Poor," 187–188; Grant, "Psalms and the King," 101–103; Eaton, *Kingship and the Psalms*.
80. Miller, "Sovereignty of God," 135–136.
81. Dempsey, *Amos, Hosea, Micah, Nahum, Zephaniah, Habakkuk*, 79.

that is in her" (ארץ ומלאה), establish a worldwide scope of Yahweh's influence (v. 2). Also, the mention of ארץ and "from his holy temple/palace" (מהיכל קדשו) (v. 2b) constitutes a merism denoting cosmic rule.[82] Allen comments, "Micah's God is no provincial deity but the universal Overlord to whom all nations must render account."[83] Hillers captures the pervasiveness of this concept well:

> This oracle [1:2–7] announces a number of themes of the book, including the fundamental idea, the rule of God. This irresistible rule first appears in its destructive force, in conformity with another fundamental idea: rebellion within mankind, especially the people of God, calls forth divine fury. This strikes at the central symbol of authority, the capital city.[84]

Such fronting of the theme effectively sets the tone of the entire book.

Another expression that explicitly suggests Yahweh's sovereignty appears in the divine appellation "Sovereign Lord" (אדני יהוה) (1:2). Barker understands אדני as sovereign.[85] For him, Yahweh's sovereignty means he exercises universal rule.[86] The third construct for divine sovereignty is "the Sovereign Lord of all the earth" (לאדון כל־הארץ) (Mic 4:13; cf. Zech 4:14). A fourth epithet, "the Lord of hosts" (יהוה צבאות), expresses Yahweh's cosmic rule following the restoration of Zion together with the ensuing idyllic peace (Mic 4:4; cf. Gen 2:1). James Swanson comments that these divine epithets emphasize a ruler's authority and majesty, while "also implying a relationship based on promise, covenant, or other relational factors (Gen 15:2)."[87]

---

82. See Allen, *Books of Joel, Obadiah, Jonah and Micah*, 269; Begerau, "Micah, Prophet of Hope," 69.

83. Allen, *Books of Joel, Obadiah, Jonah and Micah*, 269.

84. Hillers, *Micah*, 18.

85. Barker, "Micah," 49; Allen, *Books of Joel, Obadiah, Jonah and Micah*, 269.

86. Barker, "Micah," 49.

87. Swanson, *Dictionary of Biblical Languages*, §151. Although Swanson has the Abrahamic covenant in view, his general conclusion that Yahweh relates to humanity or the nations through some form of covenantal relationship has merit. Humanity is in a covenant relationship with Yahweh. Yahweh's covenant with Noah supports such a view (Gen 9:16–17). As such, the covenant with Noah is also an expression of Yahweh's sovereignty over his creation. What this means is that Yahweh always relates to humanity through some form of relationship, whether humanity is aware of it or not. Thus, since humanity has a relationship with Yahweh, it is untenable to conclude that Yahweh is sovereign over creation without a covenant. Such a scenario does not exist. Yahweh is eternally bound in a covenant relationship with creation.

Micah emphatically closes with a rhetorical question, "who is God like you?" (מִי־אֵל כָּמוֹךָ) (Mic 7:18), to affirm Yahweh's incomparability.[88] Yahweh's incomparability is an attribute of Yahweh as the cosmic creator, king, and judge. He has no equal and rules over other gods (Ps 89:7). In our target passage (Mic 7:18), the rhetorical question clearly suggests the uniqueness of Yahweh.[89] Yahweh's incomparability is seen through his forgiving love and grace.[90]

It is equally important to recognize that the incomparability of Yahweh is connected to his covenantal fidelity to the Abrahamic covenant (v. 20). By strategically concluding his book with a reference to Yahweh as the incomparable God (Mic 7:18–19) and the Abrahamic covenant (Mic 7:20),[91] the prophet makes a theological statement about the fulfillment of Abraham's blessings.[92] We believe that Yahweh's intent for Zion harkens back to the ancestral ideal embodied in the Abrahamic covenant. Yahweh's faithfulness to the Abrahamic covenant is the basis for future restoration (Gen 12; 15; 17; 28; 35). In this context, Micah's theological message finds its focal point in the Abrahamic covenant. Jenson makes this point in sharper terms. He writes,

> The book ends with a reference to Israel's first beginnings with God, sealed by gracious promises that had never been fully realized and had so often been frustrated, not least in Micah's day. But God is faithful and true, so these promises now become the grounds of hope for a future day when they will finally become a wonderful and joyful reality, not just for Israel but also . . . for the nations as well [cf. 4:1–5].[93]

Another expression of Yahweh's sovereignty is self-evident from the fact that he is creator of the universe. David VanDrunen contends that the covenant of creation and the covenant with Noah are foundational in understanding Yahweh's worldwide sovereignty under the natural law. VanDrunen, *Divine Covenants and Moral Order*, 13–14. For instance, Fretheim connects the sovereignty of God to creation theology. Fretheim, "Suffering God," 33.

88. Labuschagne, *Incomparability of Yahweh*, passim.
89. McComiskey and Longman, "Micah," 551.
90. Barker, "Micah," 134.
91. Leclerc, *Introduction to the Prophets*, 202.
92. Andersen and Freedman, *Micah*, 600; Sweeney, *Twelve Prophets*, 414. Begerau also observes that the reestablishment of Yahweh's sovereignty in Zion also speaks of Yahweh's covenant fidelity (Mic 7:18–20). Begerau, "Micah, Prophet of Hope," 67.
93. Jenson, *Obadiah, Jonah, Micah*, 189.

What we observe is that, at every turn, Micah stamps his message with the concept of Yahweh's sovereignty. From the foregoing discussion, we believe that Yahweh's sovereignty provides an appropriate theological center for the book (1:2; 7:18–20).[94] The theme gives us the ultimate reason for what motivates Yahweh's actions in the book. Despite the twists and turns in the book, Yahweh's ultimate goal is to fulfill his promises to Abraham.

It is our contention then that the rest of the book of Micah fleshes out the essence of the concept of divine sovereignty. In other words, Yahweh demonstrates his sovereignty in deeds. Willis presents a valuable analysis of the outworking of Yahweh's sovereignty. Her suggestion that the concept of sovereignty is a dramatic act is on target. As she argues, instead of being a mere assertion, the affirmation of Yahweh's sovereignty is a dynamic process, which meanders through a narrative pattern "that unfolds and builds to a crisis and then must be resolved before it can be asserted."[95] Willis's insight rings true for Micah. The book unfolds with Yahweh descending from his heavenly temple because of "sin" (חטא) (1:5). Throughout the book, Yahweh will deal with sin (e.g. 1:13, 3:8, 6:7, 13; 7:9). Yahweh defeats idolatry in the natural realm (1:3–4) and in the earthly realm (e.g. 1:6–7; 3:12). The issue is finally resolved at the close of the book as Yahweh confines חטא into the depth of the sea (7:19). Such a spatial movement of the text (heaven, mountains, earth, sea) also underscores the cosmic nature of Yahweh's sovereignty.

Purpose and Thesis Statement

In light of the foregoing discussion, this study seeks to elucidate Micah's portrayal of Yahweh's sovereignty in relation to the transformation of Zion and the fulfillment of the Abrahamic promises. Thus, the study contends that Micah reestablishes Yahweh's sovereignty by utilizing key features of the Zion/Davidic traditions in order to effect the fulfillment of the Abrahamic promises. The Zion/Davidic traditions are a symbol of future hope that reinterprets how the Abrahamic covenant is fulfilled for Micah's generation.[96] While our thesis seems clear enough, it needs a brief explanation and qualification.

---

94. Begerau, "Micah, Prophet of Hope," 70.
95. Willis, *Dissonance*, 19; Levenson, *Creation and the Persistence of Evil*, 3.
96. Jin, *Back to Jerusalem with All Nations*, 42.

Let us consider four related issues that arise from our thesis statement and which will eventually inform the outline of our investigation. First, on a definitional note, three primary sub-themes encapsulate the concept of Yahweh's sovereignty – Yahweh as the great king, the exaltation of Zion, and the restoration of Davidic kingship. Yahweh's sovereignty in Zion also implies that Zion's inhabitants must be fit to dwell in Yahweh's presence. They should observe and practice social justice and moral righteousness (cf. 6:8).[97] Only a righteous remnant will become the new people of God.

Second, Yahweh descends from heaven to reestablish his sovereignty. By saying that Yahweh reestablishes his sovereignty, we refer to the reinstatement of the originally intended order for the earth.[98] Because of the fall (Gen 3), the original order on earth gave way to disorder and humanity lost its vicegerency. As a result, sin in all its forms constantly challenges Yahweh's sovereignty. Specifically, unbridled sin on earth disorders those places, institutions, persons, or rituals that theologically mediate Yahweh's presence on earth (e.g. Zion, the temple, leadership, kingship, torah, worshipers).[99] Hence, the reestablishment of Yahweh's sovereignty is simply the restoration of the original order as it existed at creation with humanity properly serving as Yahweh's vicegerents on earth.

As we will explain in the next chapter, the reinstatement of humanity's vicegerency began with Yahweh's covenant with Abraham. Because of his covenantal faithfulness to Abraham, Yahweh's ultimate purpose is to transform the mediatorial pillar promises stipulated in the Abrahamic covenant (i.e. land, king, Israel's status as a great nation, and a new people of God). Specifically, Yahweh will transform Zion's temple (Mic 1:2–4:7), Zion's kingship (4:8–5:14), and a new covenant community (6:1–7:20). Each of these promises undergoes a radical transformation that involves judgment for sin and eventual restoration. For instance, in order to transform Zion's temple, Yahweh destroys illicit worship places and exiles the nation away from the land for idolatry and injustice, but, eventually, he will rebuild Zion's temple, reestablish his kingship, and restore a remnant. In the main, the book of

---

97. Roberts, "Enthronement of Yhwh and David," 685; Roberts, "Davidic Origin," 94.
98. McCartney, "Ecce Homo," 2; Alexander, *From Eden to the New Jerusalem*, 75–79.
99. Willis, *Dissonance*, 25.

Micah recounts how Yahweh's sovereignty is reestablished and extended throughout the universe.

Third, this study falls within the wider field of biblical theology. It puts forward a multiplex approach with Yahweh's sovereignty as a central theme and Israel's covenantal story as an encompassing metanarrative that frames the theme. The underlying metanarrative unfolds with Yahweh descending from his heavenly temple because of sin (Mic 1:5). He defeats idolatry in the natural realm (1:3–4), in the earthly realm (e.g. 1:6–7; 3:12), and finally confines sin into the depth of the sea (7:19). Such a spatial movement of the text (heaven, mountains, earth, sea) underscores the cosmic nature of Yahweh's sovereignty. In broadest terms, three words summarize Israel's covenantal story in Micah: sin, judgment, and restoration. The pattern repeats several times with variation as Yahweh restores Zion's fortunes.

Fourth, the study structures its overall theological analysis and synthesis within a framework of the Zion/Davidic traditions. The traditions provide a ready-made framework for such an investigation because the three primary sub-themes that comprise the concept of Yahweh's sovereignty, and the pattern that summarizes Israel's covenantal story, are intrinsic to the Zion/Davidic traditions. As we previously stated, observant readers will easily recognize that the three sub-themes that define Yahweh's sovereignty, and their related implications for Zion's future inhabitants, are also central to the Zion/Davidic traditions. Hence, these elements from the Zion/Davidic traditions provide a relevant framework for analyzing the concept of Yahweh's sovereignty in Micah. As such, it is possible to carry out a theological analysis and synthesis of Yahweh's sovereignty in Micah under a single cultural umbrella.

Thus, a significant theological implication from our entire study is that Yahweh's ultimate intention is to fulfill the Abrahamic promises – land, kingship, Israel's status of honor as a great nation, and a new covenant community. The prophet, we believe, is extending those past promises to his eighth-century audience. Finally, in our opinion, the concept of Yahweh's sovereignty in Micah, read within a framework of the Zion/Davidic traditions, subtly reveals a latent thematic coherence in Micah's two major sections (Micah 1–5; 6–7).

The Method of the Study

A Biblical Theology for Micah

This study falls within the wider field of biblical theology. Most biblical scholars understand the difficulties involved in biblical theology.[100] The critical issues are vast and the field is complex. Like any other topic in biblical studies, scholars hardly agree on how to approach the discipline. The discipline lacks a standard understanding of its definition, task, methods, or content. As J. L. McKenzie points out, "Biblical Theology is the only discipline or sub-discipline in the field of theology that lacks generally accepted principle, methods and structure. There is not even a generally accepted definition of its purpose and scope."[101]

Such uncertainty has resulted in a diversity of scholarly opinions and a plethora of proposals, which in itself adds to the confusion. As D. A. Carson quips, "Everyone does that which is right in his or her own eyes, and calls it biblical theology."[102] In any case, space and focus make it impossible for this present study to survey or even engage that larger debate. The methodological complexities of biblical theology are well known and this study does not need to rehearse them. However, it is prudent that we delineate our approach with clarity.

The Task of Biblical Theology: A Definition

Although the primary purpose of this study is to elucidate Micah's conceptualization of Yahweh's sovereignty, in the end, our ultimate aim is to understand Micah's theological message. Along these lines, Brian S. Rosner describes the task of biblical theology as follows:

> Biblical theology is principally concerned with the overall theological message of the whole Bible. It seeks to understand the parts in relation to the whole and, to achieve this, it must work with the mutual interaction of the literary, historical, and theological dimensions of the various corpora, and with the

---

100. For helpful surveys on the various approaches and critical issues involved in biblical theology, see Klink and Lockett, *Understanding Biblical Theology*, passim; Merrill, *Everlasting Dominion*, 1–33, 641–651; House, *Old Testament Theology*, 11–57.

101. McKenzie, *Theology of the Old Testament*, 17.

102. Carson, "Systematic Theology and Biblical Theology," 91.

inter-relationships of these within the whole canon of Scripture. Only in this way do we take proper account of the fact that God has spoken to us in Scripture.[103]

While we agree with Rosner that there is a normative aspect to doing theology, space and focus will not allow us to delve into this territory.

James Barr provides another definition for the task of biblical theology, which also seems adequate for our overall study. As he stressed almost two decades ago, Barr believes that biblical theology "is concerned with the vital central 'message' of biblical texts, with the interrelations of ideas that link one text with another, and with the deep underlying convictions that inspired the texts and united them as a composite and yet unitary 'witness' to the ultimate theological truth."[104]

A point that we need to emphasize in Barr's remark is the intertextual nature of the discipline. Waltke affirms Barr's conceptualization and captures this aspect well. He points out that intertextuality is essential for writing a biblical theology because it enables exegetes to explicate an author's message and to trace thematic developments within texts.[105] Consequently, we will consider other biblical sources and ANE literature, since these provide further background material that may illuminate our study.

A Structure of Biblical Theology: Covenantal Story/Metanarrative Approach

In light of the problems mentioned in the preceding paragraphs, how should we structure the study of Micah's theological concept of Yahweh's sovereignty? This study presupposes that biblical theology, Old Testament theology (OTT) in particular, seeks to identify and understand what the Old Testament says concerning God and God's relation to all creation, particularly to humanity through Israel. As such, Israel's covenantal story is a suitable OTT in its own right "because it is a pervasive theme throughout the Old Testament."[106] Simply put, the covenantal story states that covenant violations lead to

---

103. Rosner, "Biblical Theology," 3.
104. Barr, *Concept of Biblical Theology*, 7.
105. Waltke, *Old Testament Theology*, 113.
106. Pate et al., *Story of Israel*, 13, 23.

judgment, but genuine repentance assures divine forgiveness and restoration.[107] This covenantal story functions as the Argentinosaurus's backbone that carries the Old Testament's redemptive story in history. The covenantal story approach to OTT seeks to elucidate the biblical authors' understanding of the events and their implications within the unfolding contexts in which they are embedded.

Hence, this study adopts and adapts the argument of those scholars in favor of understanding Micah's theological message in terms of a covenantal story/metanarrative approach.[108] The story of Israel is encapsulated by the three-fold covenantal pattern of sin, judgment, and restoration.[109] C. Marvin Pate, J. Scott Duvall, J. Daniel Hays, E. Randolph Richards, W. Dennis Tucker Jr., and Preben Vang believe that a covenantal pattern that recurs consistently in the pre-exilic prophets, Micah in particular, is the theme of sin, judgment, and restoration. Thus, the concept of divine sovereignty theologically interweaves strands of sin, judgment, and restoration.[110]

Earlier, we mentioned Jenson as one who takes this covenantal story approach to Micah's theology. However, his analysis outline is inconsistent with the covenantal pattern he claims underlies Micah.[111] Two issues need highlighting. While judgment (Micah 1–3) and hope (Micah 4–5) are part of his outline, Micah 6–7 stands as an orphan. These last two chapters appear under a different rubric: "From Reproof to Praise."[112] This is a departure from the threefold covenantal pattern. An even more troubling issue for us is his sweeping conclusion that Micah 4–5 is a hope section. Such generalization takes lightly the theological significance of exile (4:9–10) and the loss of kingship in Zion (4:9, 14). Despite the short length of these verses, the catastrophes they speak of are of such a theological magnitude that we must call them what they actually are: judgments. Admittedly, as reasonable as

---

107. Pate et al, 18–21; Hays, *Message of the Prophets*, 63.

108. Pate et al., *Story of Israel*, 91; Hamilton, *God's Glory*, 47–51; Cuffey, *Literary Coherence of the Book of Micah*, 217–218; Miller, *Sin and Judgment in the Prophets*. Also see, Goldingay, *Old Testament Theology*; Dempster, *Dominion and Dynasty*; Routledge, *Old Testament Theology*; Alexander, *From Eden to the New Jerusalem*; Ciampa, "History of Redemption," 254–308; Routledge, "Is There a Narrative Substructure?," 183–204.

109. Pate et al., *Story of Israel*, 22.

110. Pate et al, 91.

111. Jenson, *Obadiah, Jonah, Micah*, 102.

112. Jenson, 102.

Jenson's explanation may appear, it does not necessarily change the sense of a threat into an oracle of hope.

Marrs proposes a somewhat similar overarching schema for the book of Micah as Jenson. He posits that the final form of the book of Micah "provides a theological exposition of Isaiah's vision in 1:21–26."[113] For him, Isaiah portrays the present dismal conditions of Zion. Zion is riddled with rampant sin. However, despite the rampant sin and infidelity, Zion will once again have a future; a future rooted in the past glories of the former Davidic empire.[114] Marrs then goes on to claim that Micah utilizes this past, present, and future schema from Isaiah as a template that underlies his own book. For him, Micah 1–3 portrays present Zion and Micah 4–5 captures the events of the transition from present to future.[115] In a footnote, he mentions in passing that Micah 6–7 treats the past.[116] However, he does not fully explain what that past entails or how it fits into his schema. Taking a more concessive tone, he concludes, "Although not without difficulties, in some way the book of Micah is organized largely around oracles treating the present (chaps. 1–3), the future (chaps. 4–5), and the past (chaps. 6–7)."[117]

However, trying to fit the whole of Micah into such a straitjacket as Marrs suggests is mistaken. Perhaps, by relegating Micah 6–7 to a footnote reference, Marrs is hinting at the difficulties one faces in organizing a theology for the book of Micah. For instance, Micah 4–5 notoriously alternates between the present and future several times, such that to label it a future passage is an overstatement. As Pate and others candidly put it, "Outlines of the prophetic books, however, are normally useless. As anthologies, they focus on a few major themes that they repeat over and over, so there is quite a bit of repetition."[118]

Furthermore, Marrs does not actually present an argument for how Micah relates to Isaiah 1:21–26. It is highly doubtful that Micah uses Isaiah 1:21–26 as a template for organizing his book. Just because a similar pattern to Isaiah 1:21–26 appears in Micah does not necessarily mean that Micah borrowed

---

113. Marrs, "Back to the Future," 92.
114. Marrs, 92.
115. Marrs, 93.
116. Marrs, 92n46.
117. Marrs.
118. Pate et al., *Story of Israel*, 91.

from Isaiah. In fact, the three-fold scheme of past, present, and future is nothing more than a rewording of the Pentateuchal pattern of sin, judgment, and restoration. Roy Ciampa provides an insightful analysis in which he shows that the covenantal pattern – creation/covenant, sin, exile, and restoration (CSER) – originated with the incident in Eden which resulted in the exile of Adam and Eve (Gen 3:23–24).[119] The rest of the biblical story seeks a resolution to the plight of humanity through Abraham and future Israel.[120] J. Daniel Hays agrees. He writes,

> the Scripture opens with two major story cycles. In the first story cycle, Genesis 3–11 presents the cosmic, worldwide story of sin and scattering (exile from the presence of Yahweh); Genesis 12:3 presents the hope of restoration (blessings for the scattered nations in Genesis 10–11). The other story runs from Genesis 12 to 2 Kings 25 and is about Israel. It parallels the first story and follows the same pattern of sin, exile, and promised restoration. The remarkable theological contribution of the prophets is that they wed these two stories together.[121]

Paradigmatically, the storyline is that present sin leads to judgment, but repentance will bring about a future restoration and that restoration involves a fulfillment of the past covenant blessings (e.g. Lev 26:15–44; Deut 30:1–10).[122] This archetypical pattern appears in most prophetic books.

In this light, we organize the concept of divine sovereignty in Micah 1–5 following the path Ciampa and Pate et al. chart. Rather than apply the covenantal pattern to the whole of Micah in one swoop, it is best to apply it to various sections of the book. In Micah, the covenantal pattern does unite large sections, but it is not as tight as modern scholars would desire.[123] Fortunately, the pattern repeats in these large sections and this aids us in discerning the central themes.[124] Thus, we organize the concept of divine sovereignty in Micah 1–5 around two central themes: Yahweh reestablishes his kingship in

---

119. Ciampa, "History of Redemption," 258.
120. Ciampa, 258.
121. Hays, *Message of the Prophets*, 63.
122. Pate et al., *Story of Israel*, 40–42, 47–48; Hays, *Message of the Prophets*, 63–64.
123. Pate et al., *Story of Israel*, 91.
124. Pate et al., 91.

Zion (1:2–4:7) and the Davidic king as the divine vicegerent restores Zion's former glory (4:8–5:14).

In both of these large sections, Micah develops each theme following the covenantal pattern of sin, judgment, and restoration. Like an electrocardiogram waveform (EKG), this pattern is the rhythm – that is, the spikes and dips on the theological spectrum – which traces the concept of Yahweh's sovereignty. Furthermore, we will demonstrate that each central theme has both a national and a universal dimension. In our opinion, our strategy offers a reasonable starting point for a theology of Micah without introducing much distortion to his message. Our strategy does not dislocate texts from their immediate context nor does it bring foreign categories to headline its organization. Rather, it allows our target sections to dictate their own natural flow. Merrill informatively proposes, "Ideally biblical theology should yield its own structure and categories."[125]

Concerning the later section of Micah, Yahweh's sovereignty has implications for the new covenant community and for Yahweh's faithfulness to the Abrahamic covenant (Micah 6–7). The thought flow of Micah 6–7 departs from the straightforward covenantal pattern of sin, judgment, and restoration as delineated for Micah 1–5. Of course, we are not suggesting that these three elements are missing from that section (6:1–7:20). Rather, the pattern subtly appears in this later section of Micah in a manner that differs markedly from Micah 1–5. Unlike Micah 1–5, whereby restoration comes through judgment, in Micah 6–7, the restoration of a new people of God comes through forgiveness for the repentant. As the just judge of all the earth (6:1–3), Yahweh discriminates between the unrepentant (wicked) and the repentant (righteous). Only the wicked are doomed (6:9–7:6), while the righteous are restored. Thus, Yahweh transforms the righteous remnant into a new covenant community not through judgment but through forgiveness and purging sin on their behalf (7:7–20). This remnant will inherit the Abrahamic blessings. Altogether, Micah puts a strong emphasis on Yahweh's resolute initiative to restore divine sovereignty in Zion (Micah 1–5) and on human responsibility (Micah 6–7). Yahweh demands obedience (6:6–8) and

---

125. Merrill, *Everlasting Dominion*, 31; Routledge, *Old Testament Theology*, 41n75.

repentance (7:9) as the primary prerequisites for the individual to become part of a new people of God.

A Method of Biblical Theology: Theological Exegesis

How does the synthesis between a descriptive theology and exegesis relate in practice?[126] The present study proposes theological exegesis as our hermeneutical tool for analyzing and elucidating Micah's concept of divine sovereignty. James K. Mead understands theological exegesis "as the reading of biblical texts with a view towards their theological content."[127] Mead further states that this view of theological exegesis "is very close to the concerns of biblical theology, but theological interpretation/exegesis, as it is used in contemporary scholarship, carries some distinct connotations."[128] For instance, the scope of theological exegesis is not in examining the Bible as a whole, but individual passages, since it aims to discern their theological message.[129] Likewise, Kevin J. Vanhoozer states, "The strongest claim to be made for theological interpretation is that only such reading ultimately does justice to the subject matter of the text itself."[130]

Without startling our audience, theological exegesis does observe the steps involved in grammatical-historical analysis. However, theological exegesis presupposes and is built on the foundation of sound "micro-exegesis."[131] An abbreviated exegetical analysis of selected passages will suffice to elucidate Micah's concept of divine sovereignty. In our opinion, theological exegesis offers a holistic and focused theological understanding of Micah's concept of Yahweh's sovereignty.

Outline of the Investigation

The study will argue and defend its thesis in seven chapters. Following this introductory chapter, chapters 2 and 3 will discuss contextual matters that

---

126. Allen, *Theological Approach to the Old Testament*, 3.
127. Mead, *Biblical Theology*, 11; Vriezen, *Outline of Old Testament Theology*, 4.
128. Mead, *Biblical Theology*, 11.
129. Mead, 11.
130. Vanhoozer, "Introduction," 22.
131. For a sound treatment of theological exegesis and a relevant example, see Brown, "Theological Interpretation," 387–390; Scobie, *Ways of Our God*, 387–390.

are foundational to the concept of Yahweh's sovereignty. Chapter 2 discusses key features of the Abrahamic, Mosaic, and Davidic covenants. Chapter 3 sets forth major themes from the Zion/Davidic traditions. Chapters 4, 5, and 6 are the major analytical chapters of this study. Chapter 4 will investigate the reestablishment of Yahweh's sovereignty in relation to the restoration of Zion (Mic 1:2–4:8). Chapter 5 explores the restoration of Davidic kingship in Micah 4:9–5:14. As Yahweh's vicegerent, the Davidic king rules the earth on Yahweh's behalf. In chapter 6, the study addresses Micah's adaptation of an important subsidiary motif from the Zion/Davidic traditions. Yahweh's choice of Zion meant that the inhabitants of Zion should be righteous.[132]

Chapter 7 concludes the whole study by synthesizing the overall covenantal implications of Yahweh's sovereignty. Yahweh's sovereignty in Micah makes statements about Yahweh's faithfulness to the Abrahamic covenant. Yahweh's ultimate goal is to restore four pillar promises of the Abrahamic promises (i.e. land, king, Israel's status as a great nation, and a new people of God). Finally, we conclude the whole project with an appendix, which briefly surveys and summarizes the debate on origins of the Zion/Davidic traditions.

---

132. Roberts, "Enthronement of Yhwh and David," 685.

CHAPTER 2

Covenant Concept: A Theological Context for Micah

Introduction

The reestablishment of Yahweh's sovereignty on earth entails the restoration of the Edenic order for the earth, with humanity exercising dominion as Yahweh's vicegerents. With the fall of Adam and Eve, humanity lost its vicegerency (i.e. dominion over the earth [Gen 1:28]). In response to the plight of humanity, Yahweh set off a series of divine initiatives intended to restore humanity's vicegerency. Apparently, following the disaster and the curse from Adam to Babel (Gen 3–11), Abraham is the solution to the plight of humanity (Gen 12:1–3). In other words, Yahweh's covenant with Abraham initiated Yahweh's plan for the restoration of humanity's vicegerency. As will become clearer in later sections, Yahweh's promises to Abraham of nationhood (i.e. land and descendants), great name, and the blessings for all nations (Gen 12:1–3, 7) are rooted in his intention to restore humanity's dominion over the earth.[1]

With the Abrahamic covenant established, subsequent covenants partially fulfilled key aspects of the Abrahamic promises. Specifically, in the Mosaic covenant, Israel became a great nation dwelling on their land (e.g. Deut 26:5; Josh 21:45; 23:14). In the Davidic covenant, the Davidic kings imperfectly

---

1. The creation mandate initially issued to Adam (Gen 1:28) finds expression at various points in the Patriarchal narratives (Gen 13:16; 15:5; 16:10; 17:20; 22:16–18; Exod 1:7). We should also not miss the language of dominion and ruling (Gen 22:17; Exod 1:7). Neither should we ignore the rhetoric of the "seed" language (Gen 3:15; 22:17). It is apparent that the author of Genesis deliberately wants his readers to see an "Adam" in Abraham.

29

served as Yahweh's vicegerents in Zion (2 Sam 7:14–16). Even though Israel failed to maintain the land and the Davidic dynasty failed to attain world domination, the divine intent to restore order on earth is evident. In light of the foregoing considerations, it is prudent to allocate some space to lay the foundation for the discussions that will follow in the subsequent chapters. Thus, this chapter sets forth key features of the Abrahamic, Mosaic, and Davidic covenants.

Approaches to Biblical Covenants
A Traditional Approach to Biblical Covenants

George E. Mendenhall, David N. Freedman, and Moshe Weinfeld inaugurated what most scholars regard as the traditional approach to biblical covenants. These three scholars posit that against their ANE backdrop, biblical covenants comprise two types: unconditional and conditional covenants. In his groundbreaking study, Mendenhall suggests that the formal structure in the Mosaic covenant (Exod 19–24) and Joshua 24 follow the Hittite suzerainty treaties of 1400–1200 BC.[2] He characterizes the Mosaic covenant as conditional because Israel unilaterally took an oath to obey the Decalogue (Exod 19:8; cf. 24:3–8).[3] Conversely, he treats the Abrahamic and the Davidic covenants as unconditional because only Yahweh unilaterally swore to fulfill the covenant promises and did not impose any explicit stipulations on the human partners.[4] Surprisingly, he views circumcision in the Abrahamic covenant not as a stipulation (Gen 17:10–14, 23–27) but as a mere sign like the rainbow in the Noahic covenant (9:12–17).[5] Thus, Mendenhall concludes that the Mosaic covenant patently differs from both the Abrahamic and Davidic covenants.[6]

---

2. Mendenhall identifies six formal elements found in the Hittite treaty texts: (1) preamble; (2) the historical prologue; (3) the stipulations; (4) provision for deposit in the temple for periodic public reading; (5) the list of gods as witnesses; and (6) the blessings and curses formula. Mendenhall, "Covenant Forms in Israelite Tradition," 58–60. For an informative treatment of similar treaties from the Neo-Assyrian period, see Wiseman, "Vassal-Treaties of Esarhaddon," 1–28.

3. Mendenhall, "Covenant Forms in Israelite Tradition," 61–62. For comprehensive and cogent discussions of the topic, see Kitchen and Lawrence, *Treaty, Law and Covenant*; Kline, *Treaty of the Great King*.

4. Mendenhall, "Covenant Forms in Israelite Tradition," 61–62.

5. Mendenhall, 62.

6. Mendenhall, 62.

A decade after Mendenhall's publication, David N. Freedman called attention to two types of divine covenants in the Hebrew Bible, namely, the covenant of human obligation and the covenant of divine commitment.[7] According to Freedman, the covenant of human obligation has formal affinities with Hittite treaties of the second millennium BC and, as its name suggests, Yahweh imposed obligations upon the human partner.[8] Notable examples of a human-obligation covenant include the Mosaic covenant (Exod 19–24) and its related covenant restoration texts (e.g. Deut 29–31; Josh 24).[9] Freedman also characterizes the covenant of human obligation as conditional because its maintenance depends on the human partner.[10]

In the second type (i.e. the covenant of divine commitment), Freedman insists that Yahweh imposed certain obligations upon himself.[11] Thus, it is unconditional in the sense that its maintenance depends not on the human partner but wholly on Yahweh.[12] Earlier, Freedman understood the Abrahamic and Davidic covenants as classical examples of the divine commitment covenant. More recently, Freedman and Miano have reclassified the Davidic covenant as a suzerainty-vassal treaty because of the human obligations which Yahweh explicitly imposed (cf. Ps 132).[13] Freedman's two categories may be represented as mutually exclusive sets as shown in figure 2.1. For him, Genesis 15 and 17 are examples of divine commitment covenants, while Exodus 19–24 and 2 Samuel 7 are examples of human obligation covenants.[14]

In one of his seminal papers, which scholars rightfully consider to be an epoch-making conclusion in covenant scholarship, Moshe Weinfeld discerns two types of covenants found in the Old Testament and in various ANE texts – namely, the obligatory and the promissory types.[15] For Weinfeld, the Mosaic covenant represents the obligatory type and shares many affinities with ANE

---

7. Freedman, "Divine Commitment," 420.
8. Freedman, 420.
9. Freedman, 420.
10. Freedman, 428.
11. Freedman, 428.
12. Freedman, 420–421, 425.
13. Freedman and Miano, "People of the New Covenant," 13–14.
14. Freedman, "Divine Commitment," 420–422; Freedman and Miano, "People of the New Covenant," 13.
15. Weinfeld, "Covenant of Grant," 184.

suzerain treaties, while the Abrahamic and Davidic covenants represent the promissory type.[16] Unlike Freedman, who considers the covenant of divine commitment as unique to Israel, Weinfeld observes that the promissory type parallels ANE royal grants.[17] Like Freedman, Weinfeld characterizes the Abrahamic and Davidic covenants as unconditional since they were "gifts bestowed upon individuals who excelled in loyally serving their masters."[18]

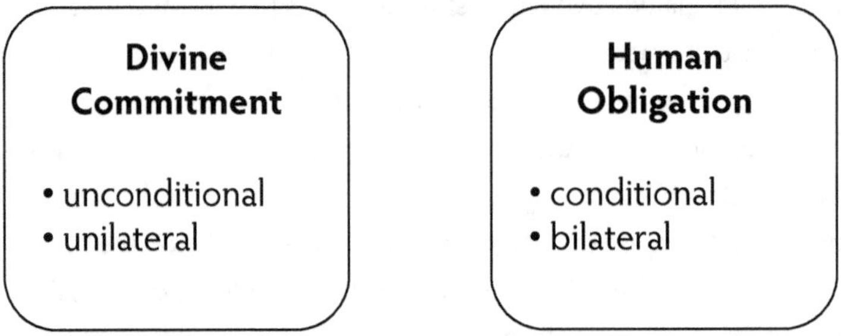

Divine Commitment
- unconditional
- unilateral

Human Obligation
- conditional
- bilateral

Figure 2.1: A Twofold Covenant Typology Model

Over the decades, scholars have adopted and adapted Weinfeld's conclusion such that discussing covenants in terms of conditional and unconditional still reverberates in certain circles. For instance, Irvin A. Busenitz characterizes every bilateral covenant as conditional and every unilateral covenant as unconditional.[19] Such a rigid bifurcation of biblical covenants is an integral feature of his formulation. However, this is not necessary. Classifying covenants as mutually exclusive fails to wrestle with the relationship inherent in them. Following Bruce K. Waltke and other scholars, this study rejects Busenitz's characterization. His rigid classification fails to grasp the complementary relationship that exists between the terms *conditional* and

---

16. Weinfeld, 184.

17. Weinfeld, 184–185. Here Weinfeld has in view the Syrian, Hittite, and Old Babylonian royal grants of the second millennium BC, and the Assyrian royal grants of the first millennium BC.

18. Weinfeld, 184–184, 189.

19. Busenitz, "Introduction to the Biblical Covenants," 180. For Busenitz the unilateral covenants are the Noahic, Abrahamic, Priestly, Davidic, and the New. See also Williamson, *Sealed with an Oath*, passim; Alexander, *From Paradise to the Promised Land*, 173–182; McComiskey, *Covenants of Promise*.

unconditional.[20] Gentry and Wellum concur with our conclusion. They argue that "dividing up the biblical covenants in terms of unconditional versus conditional is not correct. Old Testament covenants blend both aspects in an unfolding way."[21] In another place, they point out that "the Old Testament covenants comprise unconditional (unilateral) and conditional (bilateral) elements blended together."[22]

Some scholars have largely failed to heed or have ignored Weinfeld's explicit acknowledgment that not all royal grants were unconditional.[23] As he unequivocally notes, unconditional Hittite royal grants were an exception and most grants were actually conditional.[24] He further acknowledges that the suzerain could actually repossess the gift bestowed on the servant for covenant breach.[25] By his own admission, Weinfeld warns that a rigid classification is not in keeping with the mutual nature inherent in royal grant covenants. Mutuality in biblical covenants does not trump the notion that Yahweh is the sole grantor of the covenant nor does it impinge upon his grace.[26] Instead, it realizes that both Yahweh and the human partner have a role to contribute, regardless of their degree of participation. Biblical covenants exhibit a mutual relationship that renders the traditional categorizations passé.

Dividing divine covenants along conditional/unconditional lines poses a deeper problem for traditionalists. The approach fails to adequately answer questions about conditionality within the Abrahamic and Davidic covenants. The Abrahamic covenant comprises unconditional (Gen 15:9–21) and conditional passages (e.g. Gen 17:1–2, 9–14; 18:18–19; 22:14–18). After the near sacrifice of Isaac (Gen 22), the covenant becomes irrevocable. Similarly, the Davidic covenant includes unconditional (2 Sam 7:8–16) and conditional passages (2 Sam 23:1–7; 1 Kgs 2:3–4; 8:25–26; Pss 89:30–32; 132:11–12). The question that immediately confronts the exegete is how to reconcile

---

20. Waltke, "Phenomenon of Conditionality," 124.

21. Gentry and Wellum, *Kingdom through Covenant*, 120. Similarly, Kenneth J. Turner observes that "the language of 'conditional' and 'unconditional' proves unhelpful in understanding the relationship between the covenants." Turner, *Death of Deaths*, 239.

22. Gentry and Wellum, *Kingdom through Covenant*, 609.

23. Weinfeld, "Covenant of Grant," 191–195.

24. Weinfeld, 193.

25. Weinfeld, 194–195.

26. McCarthy, *Old Testament Covenant*, 3.

the unconditional and conditional features exhibited in these grant-type covenants.[27] Weinfeld sees the tension but surmises that the Deuteronomist reinterpreted the unconditional features in both the Abrahamic and Davidic covenants by inserting conditional features.[28] For him, the various calamities that the nation suffered called for theological reflection and reformulation of the covenant relationship. He speculates that:

> The exile of Northern Israel and the destruction of Jerusalem and disrupting of the dynasty refuted, of course, the claim of the eternity of the Abrahamic and Davidic covenants and therefore a reinterpretation of the covenants was necessary which was done by putting in the condition, i.e. the covenant is eternal only if the donee keeps his loyalty to the donor.[29]

Weinfeld is also cognizant of the antiquity and conditional features found in Psalm 132. However, such a juxtaposition of unconditional and conditional elements in an archaic text contradicts Weinfeld's Deuteronomist theory.[30] While Weinfeld's formulation somewhat tempers the tension between conditional and unconditional elements in grant covenants, it does so in an unsubstantiated manner.[31] His source-critical approach, as reasonable as it might appear, is speculative.[32] Rather than speculate on possible sources or

---

27. Recently, Gordon H. Johnston has convincingly demonstrated that it is not necessary to make a rigid dichotomy between unconditional and conditional features found in grant covenants. See Johnston, "Critical Evaluation"; idem "'Unconditional' and 'Conditional' Passages."

28. Weinfeld, "Covenant of Grant," 195.

29. Weinfeld, 195.

30. Weinfeld hesitantly reasons, "It is indeed possible that alongside the conception of unconditional promise of the dynasty there were also in existence the concept of a conditional promise. The conceptions of conditionality might have especially developed after the division of the kingdom. However, this ambiguous approach could not have been maintained after the fall of Judah. The Deuteronomist who was active at the time of the destruction and Exile therefore turned the conditionality into a dogma and built his ideology around it." Weinfeld, "Covenant of Grant," 196.

31. For a detailed critique of Moshe Weinfeld's thesis, see Knoppers, "Ancient Near Eastern Royal Grants," 670–697; Johnston, "Critical Evaluation," passim.

32. Contemporary scholars have offered various proposals in an attempt to reconcile the apparent tension between the conditional and unconditional features in the Abrahamic covenant and the Davidic covenant. See, for instance, Heideman, "Promissory and Obligatory Features," 150–285; McKenzie, *Covenant*, 77–79; Cross, *Canaanite Myth and Hebrew Epic*, 244–245, 260–261, 272–273; Alexander, *From Paradise to the Promised Land*, 173, 182; Williamson, *Sealed with an Oath*, 84–90; Gentry and Wellum, *Kingdom through Covenant*, 276–280; McComiskey, *Covenants of Promise*, 60–64, 145–147, 150; Hahn, *Kinship by Covenant*, 37–42, 197–198, 335;

attempt to reconstruct the data as evident in Weinfeld's formulation, what is required is to deal with the data as is, in its final form.

An Alternative Approach to Biblical Covenants

To grasp the continuity among the three major biblical covenants requires an alternative conceptualization of biblical covenants. In addition, the conceptualization should seriously attend to the dynamic and organic relationship that exists among the three major divine-human covenants (i.e. Abrahamic, Mosaic, and Davidic).

Although the traditional model emphasizes absolute separation among biblical covenants, several studies recognize their unitary nature.[33] Gordon H. Johnston's comparative studies on the Abrahamic and Davidic covenants have illuminated the unitary nature of biblical covenants. Johnston wrestles with and extends McCarthy's conclusions by probing more closely the correspondences between the Alalakh tablets and the Abrahamic covenant.[34] He makes a plausible case that Genesis 15, like the Hittite royal grant (*AT* 1), is a first-generation promissory land grant bestowed upon a loyal servant for faithful service to his master.[35] Such first generation land grants, Johnston observes, lack explicit human obligations. He also perceives that subsequent passages in the Abrahamic covenant (e.g. Gen 17:1–2; 18:18–19; 26:2–5.) correspond to the second-generation grant treaty (*AT* 456), which spells out the covenant obligations.[36]

As previously mentioned, Mendenhall concluded that the Mosaic covenant is unilateral and conditional. Contrary to Mendenhall's over-generalized

---

Kalluveettil, *Declaration and Covenant*, 132–133; Cross, *From Epic to Canon*, 3–21; Segal, *Rebecca's Children*, 7–9; McCarthy, *Old Testament Covenant*, 32–33.

33. Hultgren, *From the Damascus Covenant*, 470; Waltke, "Phenomenon of Conditionality," 125. See McCarthy, *Treaty and Covenant*; Knoppers, "Ancient Near Eastern Royal Grants."

34. Johnston, "'Unconditional' and 'Conditional' Passages," 1. McCarthy, in his analysis of the Alalakh tablets, had earlier observed that besides the suzerain-vassal treaty and the first generation royal grant (*AT* 1), some second generation texts are of a mixed form, namely, a grant treaty. According to McCarthy, *AT* 456 is an example of a grant treaty, which combines both features of the classical suzerain-vassal treaty and the typical royal grant forms. McCarthy, *Treaty and Covenant*, 86. The Alalakh tablets comprise "Abbael's Gift of Alalakh," translated by Richard S. Hess (*COS* 2.127) and "Land Grant," translated by Richard S. Hess (*COS* 2.137), which are known as *AT* 1 and *AT* 456, respectively.

35. Johnston, "'Unconditional' and 'Conditional' Passages," 7–8.

36. Johnston, 8–10.

conclusion, the Hittite covenants include self-subjugation treaties in which a king volunteers for vassalage.[37] Amnon Altman and F. Charles Fensham mention that in these treaties not only are obligations imposed upon the vassal king but the Hittite great king, the sun, swore an oath to protect his vassal against any military threats.[38] In the prologues of *CTH* 46 and *CTH* 53, as Altman states, "the would-be subordinate king asks explicitly for military help in return, and the prologue gives a detailed account of the steps taken by the Hittite king to fulfill this request."[39] Evidently, similar protection clauses appear in the Mosaic covenant, which shows Yahweh obligating himself to protect the new nation (Exod 23:22; 34:11; cf. Deut 3:8). Another biblical parallel is the self-imposed vassalage of King Ahaz of Judah to King Tiglath-Pileser for military assistance (2 Kgs 16:5–9).

Besides these first-generation constitutive treaties, there also existed second-generation follow up and modificative treaties that were "intended to reinforce an older subjugation treaty . . . *CTH* 41.I, 47, 62, 76, 92."[40] Like the Hittite vassal treaties, a generational typology is at play among the Sinai (Exod 19–34), Moab (Deut 1–28; cf. 29:1), and Shechem covenants (Josh 24). The Sinai covenant corresponds to the first-generation treaty type, while the Moab and Shechem covenants correspond to the second-generation treaties. Moreover, the Sinai and Moab covenants focus on the Mosaic law, while the Shechem covenant emphasizes the centrality of dwelling in the promised land under that law.

Scholars, for the most part, have consistently regarded the Abrahamic covenant as a royal land grant, but the Davidic covenant has received mixed views. As we previously stated, Freedman and Miano reclassified the Davidic

---

37. For instance, see *CTH* 46; *CTH* 49; *CTH* 51; *CTH* 52; *CTH* 53 translated by Beckman, *Hittite Diplomatic Texts*, 34–58. See also "Treaty Between Šuppiluliuma and Aziru," translated by Itamar Singer (*COS* 2.17A) and "Treaty Between Muršili and Duppi-Tešub," translated by Itamar Singer (*COS* 2.17B).

38. Altman, *Historical Prologue*, 64–65, 222; Fensham, "Clauses of Protection," 134–140.

39. Altman, *Historical Prologue*, 222, 223–229. Fensham writes: "One of the most humane stipulations in the Hittite treaties is the promise of protection of the vassal against enemies. This protection might have been promised to safeguard the head partner's kingdom, but still was a most encouraging experience for the vassal. There was no enemy [sic] to fear. Under such conditions small kingdoms could prosper and times of peaceful co-existence could develop." Fensham, "Clauses of Protection," 140.

40. Altman, *Historical Prologue*, 61.

covenant as a suzerainty-vassal treaty because of a greater number of conditional features in it.[41] However, others have vigorously challenged this classification. Gary N. Knoppers rejects classifying the Davidic covenant as a land grant.[42] Knoppers observes the tension (i.e. conditional versus unconditional) among the various Davidic covenant texts. He comments that the "contents and terms of covenants and alliances were shaped and modified to reflect the wishes of the partner(s), the reality of local circumstances, and anticipated exigencies."[43] Johnston believes that a generational typology also prevails among the various Davidic covenant texts. He argues that the political exigencies that gave rise to the Hittite royal throne grants (i.e. *CTH* 106a, *CTH* 106b.1, *CTH* 106b.2, and *CTH* 106b.3) appear to be at play in the Davidic covenant as well.[44] Johnston's and Knoppers's analyses demonstrate that the Davidic covenant texts fit the Hittite generational model (cf. 1 Sam 7:8–16; 1 Kgs 2:3–4; 3:14; 6:11–13).

No one conceptual model encompasses the covenant idea as described in the Old Testament. However, unlike the traditional models discussed earlier, it seems that Altman's conclusion on the Hittite suzerainty-vassal treaties demonstrates the inadequacy of classifying the Mosaic covenant as conditional. Similarly, Johnston and Knoppers offer a reasonable model that resolves the tension inherent in the seemingly unconditional Abrahamic and Davidic covenants and their subsequent clarifications which explicitly

---

41. Freedman and Miano, "People of the New Covenant," 7–9; See also Freedman, "Divine Commitment."

42. Knoppers, "Ancient Near Eastern Royal Grants," 695.

43. Knoppers, 696.

44. According to Johnston, *CTH* 106a is the original throne grant, which was composed as a promissory note and lacks explicit obligations. However, the follow-up document *CTH* 106b.1 is an edict that explicitly details specific obligations for the vassal king to obey. The third document (*CTH* 106b.2) is the official version, which is of a mixed form, blending both the promissory features from the original grant (*CTH* 106a) and obligatory features of the follow-up edict (*CTH* 106b.1). The fourth document (*CTH* 106b.3), Johnston argues, is a second-generation document, drawn-up by a new heir to the throne following the death of the suzerain king. The new document (*CTH* 106b.3) recaps various aspects from the previous official document (*CTH* 106b.2) and contains amendments which warn the vassal king that defection from the Hittite suzerain would incur the destruction of the vassal's dynasty. Johnston, "Critical Evaluation," 11. See Beckman, *Hittite Diplomatic Texts*.

stress the obligation of obedience.[45] Johnston, Knoppers, and many others have corrected Weinfeld's conclusions, and, for this reason, the present study affirms and builds upon their conclusions.[46] As J. J. M. Roberts points out, Weinfeld's traditional model should be abandoned.[47]

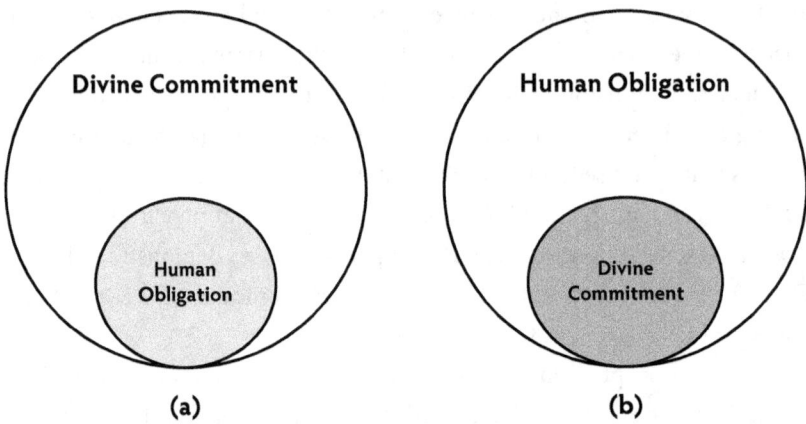

Figure 2.2: An Embedded-Type Covenant Model

An immediate consequence of the foregoing paragraphs is that each divine-human covenant comprises at least two parts: divine commitment and human obligations as depicted in figure 2.2. Figure 2.2(a) portrays the nature of the Abrahamic and Davidic covenants. These two covenants stress the divine commitments, whereas the human obligations are deemphasized. Conversely, figure 2.2(b) depicts the Mosaic covenant. Here the human obligations (law) are more prominent than the divine commitments.

The model highlights the organic relationship which exists among the three covenants in a way that preserves their unity. The Mosaic and Davidic covenants each fulfill portions of the Abrahamic promises. Each covenant has a blend of promises and obligations in varying degrees. Knoppers's conclusions also anticipate our suggested model and lend us support. He notes

---

45. For the Abrahamic covenant, contrast the initial passage (Gen 15) and subsequent passages (Gen 17:1–2, 9–14; 18:18–19; 22:14–18; 26:5b). For the Davidic covenant, see 2 Sam 7:8–16 and 2 Sam 23:1–7; 1 Kgs 2:3–4; 3:14; 6:11–13; Ps 132:11–12.

46. Johnston, "'Unconditional' and 'Conditional' Passages," 11. Also see Waltke, "Phenomenon of Conditionality," 123–139; Knoppers, "Ancient Near Eastern Royal Grants," 670.

47. Roberts, "Davidic Covenant," 209.

that covenants may be symmetric or asymmetric.[48] In other words, different covenants blend promissory and obligatory elements in different shades. Moreover, the unbalanced nature of covenants does not warrant "a typology of two diametrically opposed kinds of covenant" as in the traditional approaches.[49]

Abrahamic Covenant

Although the particulars of the Abrahamic covenant must be reconstructed from several passages scattered throughout Genesis 12–22, it is best to visualize the covenant as one, since the reality of the Old Testament evidence regards it as such. Viewed as a unit, the Abrahamic covenant comprises a blend of divine commitments and human obligations in varying degrees.[50] In fact, that the divine commitments are in the foreground and reverberate louder than the human obligations does not weaken the mutual nature inherent in the covenant.[51]

Divine commitment

That Yahweh is fully committed to fulfilling the Abrahamic covenant may be seen in several ways, but the most conclusive and persuasive way is to attend to the solemn oaths in Genesis 15 and 22. First, Yahweh's calling and dealings with Abraham suggest his intention to bring blessings to all humanity through Abraham and his descendants. His promises to Abraham of nationhood (i.e. land and descendants), great name, and the blessings for all nations (Gen 12:1–3, 7) are firmly "rooted in his intention to restore creation and to bring about redemption."[52] Carol M. Kaminski wisely observes that Yahweh's promises to Abraham guarantee the continuation of creation despite human sin.[53] Thus, the series of Yahweh's promises to Abraham in Genesis

---

48. Knoppers, "Ancient Near Eastern Royal Grants," 696.
49. Knoppers, 696.
50. Gen 24:7; 26:3–5; 35:9–12; Exod 2:24; 6:3–4; Lev 26:42; Deut 1:8, 35; 4:31; 6:10; 2 Kgs 13:23; 1 Chr 16:16; Ps 105:9. See Youngblood, "Abrahamic Covenant," 32; Grüneberg, *Abraham, Blessing and the Nations*, 222–235, 242.
51. Waltke, "Phenomenon of Conditionality," 123.
52. Gentry and Wellum, *Kingdom through Covenant*, 635.
53. Kaminski, *From Noah to Israel*, 108. Similarly, Gentry and Wellum point out that Yahweh "will keep his promise regardless of what Abraham does." Gentry and Wellum, *Kingdom through Covenant*, 635.

12 already mark his steadfast commitment to bless all nations via Abraham and his future descendants.

Second, the promise that Abraham would become a great nation with land and innumerable descendants is solemnized by oath into a covenant (Gen 15:18). The mysterious animal ritual (Gen 15:9–11), which, in essence, is Yahweh's response to Abraham's appeal for a confirmation of the promises, functions as a covenant oath, among other things. This fact alone (i.e. Yahweh turning the promises into a covenant relationship) is by itself indicative of his steadfast commitment. Gordon Paul Hugenberger defines an oath as "any solemn declaration or enactment which invokes the deity to act against the one who would be false to an attendant commitment or affirmation."[54] Hugenberger makes the definition even more compelling. For him, "it appears that such a ratifying oath may well be the *sine qua non* of covenant precisely because it invokes the deity to act against any subsequent breach of the covenant."[55] Weinfeld is also on target in stating that an "oath gives the obligation its binding validity."[56] To say that an oath plays an important role in ratifying covenants is not an overstatement (e.g. Gen 26:28; Deut 29:12, 14). However, caution should be exercised because biblical writers may include an oath or they may not.[57]

Hugenberger also argues that an oath should not be limited to verbal self-maledictions but should include symbolic acts or even oath-signs.[58] Apparently, the nature of an oath is a significant issue because an oath often intertwines elements of both blessings and curses.[59] An example of this twofold nature of an oath may be seen in Genesis 15 whereby the blessings are verbalized in promises (Gen 15:13–16, 18–20) and the curses are ritually dramatized (vv. 9–10).[60] A similar situation occurs in Genesis 17 where

---

54. Hugenberger, *Marriage as a Covenant*, 193.
55. Hugenberger, 184, 215.
56. Weinfeld, "ברית Berîth," 255–256.
57. McCarthy, *Treaty and Covenant*, 169.
58. Hugenberger, *Marriage as a Covenant*, 168, 185–214; Williamson, *Sealed with an Oath*, 43.
59. Hahn, *Kinship by Covenant*, 53. Hahn's schema on the twofold nature of an oath is reasonable and informative. Nonetheless, his conclusion that the animal ritual chiefly signifies Yahweh's self-malediction is unconvincing (Gen 15:9–11; Jer 34:8–22).
60. Hahn, 53.

the blessings are verbalized (Gen 17:4–8, 15–16) and the curse is ritualized in circumcision (vv. 11–14). Furthermore, Genesis 22 has a similar schema. The blessings are explicitly verbalized (Gen 22:16–18), whereas the curses are ritually implied in the near sacrifice of Isaac (vv. 14–19).[61] Consequently, a covenant breach does not necessarily nullify the covenant per se but invokes the curses spelled out or implied at the initiation of the covenant.[62] On the other hand, a covenant restoration following a breach occasions the restoration of the blessings.

Turning back to Genesis 15, one is on firmer ground, we believe, in positing that the mysterious ritual and the revelatory dream portray a covenantal oath (Gen 15:9–18).[63] Even though the ritual's finer details elude us, what is clear is that Yahweh provided Abraham with the needed assurance he sought (v. 8).[64] Weinfeld supports this view by stressing that the animal ritual (vv. 9–11), together with the flaming torch and the smoking oven (v. 17), symbolizes God's oath as suzerain committing himself to keep his promise to Abraham.[65] He presents invaluable evidence from various ANE treaties, stemming from the third and second millennia, which substantially strengthens this position.[66] Sacrifices were a means of ratifying treaties (cf. Jer 34:18–20).[67]

Space and focus do not allow for an exhaustive contextual exposition of the animal-slaughter ritual, the symbols of smoke and fire, and the subsequent revelatory dream. However, it is reasonable to conclude that, among other things, the animal-slaughter ritual (Gen 15:9), the ensuing revelatory dream (vv.12–16), and the imagery of the smoking oven and fiery torch passing

---

61. Hahn, 53.
62. Hahn, 53.
63. See Williamson, *Sealed with an Oath*, 43, 86–87; Hahn, *Kinship by Covenant*, 102.
64. Freedman, "Divine Commitment," 423.
65. Weinfeld, *Deuteronomy*, 102.
66. Weinfeld, 102.
67. Weinfeld lucidly notes: "Though the torch and the oven are usually held to be related to the theophany, it seems that in this particular context they have a different meaning. In the ancient Near Eastern Šurpu documents we read about an oath taken by holding a torch or about the oath of furnace or stove. In the same series of texts, we find the oath of the slaughtered sheep and the touching of its wound. It therefore stands to reason that like the cutting of the animals so the torch and the oven are part of the procedure of taking the oath. . . . A later Alalaḫian covenantal text tells us about an offering and a brazier in connection with the oath that the parties had taken which reminds us of the offerings and the oven and torch in Gen. XV." Weinfeld, "Covenant of Grant," 197–198.

between the pieces (v. 17) function as an oath that ratifies a bilateral covenant and not a unilateral covenant. The ritual demonstrates Yahweh's unwavering commitment to Abraham and his future descendants.[68]

The *Akedah* test marks the pinnacle of Yahweh's commitment to Abraham (Gen 22). The Abrahamic cycle opens with Yahweh's promises to Abraham (Gen 12:1–3). Next, Yahweh ratifies the promises to an implicit contingent covenant (Gen 15:9–21). An explicit obligatory covenant reiteration follows. It expands Yahweh's commitment to bless Abraham (Gen 17:3–8, 15–16, 19–21) and imposes obligations on Abraham and his descendants (vv. 1–2; 9–14). Finally, the covenant culminates with Yahweh's climactic verbal oath (Gen 22:15–18).[69] Chisholm cogently sums up the developing relation between Yahweh and Abraham:

> At the beginning of the story, God chooses Abraham to be his covenant partner; the arrangement is comparable to the suzerain-vassal relationship that we see in the ancient Near East. By the end of the story, Abraham has proven his loyalty (see

---

68. Some scholars contend that the symbol of the smoking oven and the fiery torch passing between the slaughtered animal pieces depicts Yahweh by himself initiating a completely unilateral covenant (Gen 15:17; cf. Exod 13:21; 19:18; 20:18). Such a mysterious symbol, they surmise, evinces Yahweh's absolute unilateral commitment. Gentry and Wellum emphatically insist that the "fact that only God passes between the pieces is quite remarkable and shows that the promise depends upon him and him alone." Gentry and Wellum, *Kingdom through Covenant*, 251. Williamson senses the enigmatic meaning of the symbols, but, unfortunately, he too views the rite as evidence for an absolute unilateral covenant. Williamson, *Sealed with an Oath*, 86. Briefly, the foregoing views have a fissure and are partially correct. To suppose that the smoking oven and the fiery torch exclusively symbolize Yahweh's presence is an assumption fraught with problems and remains a matter plagued with uncertainty. There may, nonetheless, be more to the symbolism than just Yahweh's presence. For instance, in several passages the symbols of oven and fire appear not as divine symbols but as human symbols (Lam 5:10; Hos 7:4, 7; Zech 12:6). In fact, Johnston aptly distinguishes several literary and thematic correspondences between Genesis 15:17 and Zechariah 12:6, which suggest that the former passage might be construed as a prophetic vision anticipating Israel's future conquest of Canaan. Johnston, "Oven and Torch," 21. In this regard, the smoking oven and the flaming torch symbolize Yahweh leading Israel into victory against the Canaanites. Mathews comments that by "the passing of the firepot through the severed pieces, the Lord's presence with enslaved Israel symbolically ensures the preservation and deliverance of Abram's descendents." Mathews, *Genesis 11:27–50:26*, 172. J. Gerald Janzen even suggests that the smoking oven and the flaming torch may represent Yahweh and Abraham. Janzen, *Abraham and All the Families*, 40. While scholars may differ in pinpointing exactly what the symbols may represent, most agree that the ceremony involved two parties rather than Yahweh alone. As a corollary, this view suggests that the mysterious ritual is not unilateral but bilateral.

69. Hahn, *Kinship by Covenant*, 10–11; Williamson, *Sealed with an Oath*, 90.

especially Gen 22:12, 15-18) by obeying God's commands (cf. Gen 26:5). God has elevated the patriarch to the status of a favored vassal who now possessed an unconditional royal grant from the great King himself.[70]

Similarly, Keith N. Grüneberg aptly observes that Genesis 22:16–18 is the confluence of Yahweh's promises to Abraham; the only place where the promises other than land are sealed by a divine oath.[71] Following the *Akedah* test, Yahweh, by means of a verbal oath, committed himself to fulfill the promises he made to Abraham (Gen 22:16–18; cf. 26:2–5; Exod 32:13; Deut 7:12; 13:18; 28:9). In explicit terms, Yahweh swears by his own name (Gen 22:16) and makes certain his commitment to Abraham as suggested by the cognate infinitive absolute constructions in the promises: "I will surely bless you" (ברך אברכך) and "I will surely multiply" (והרבה ארבה) (Gen 22:17). Gentry and Wellum observe that Genesis 22 presents "the strongest statement of a guarantee by God."[72] The emphatic nature of Yahweh's verbal oath shows undeniably his steadfast commitment to Abraham and his future descendants, which essentially renders the Abrahamic covenant irrevocable. Future Israel may act treacherously against Yahweh and forfeit the blessings, but the covenant will still stand.

Yahweh fulfilled his commitment to Abraham concerning innumerable descendants in Egypt (Exod 1:7). By his own confession, Pharaoh feared that the rapid rate at which Abraham's descendants multiplied threatened the very existence of his kingdom (Exod 1:9–10). Even Moses notes at several points that Yahweh had immensely increased Israel (Deut 1:10; 10:22; 26:5). Thus, these evaluative notices of Israel's population increase signal Yahweh's initial fulfillment of the promise of progeny.

Human obligation

Although several texts contain imperatives (e.g. Gen 17:1–2; 18:19), the human obligations in the Abrahamic covenant are not so much communicated by divine imperatives as by Abraham's obedience.[73] Scholars have long

---

70. Chisholm, "Divine Uncertainty and Discovery," 9.
71. Grüneberg, *Abraham, Blessing and the Nations*, 228.
72. Gentry and Wellum, *Kingdom through Covenant*, 285.
73. Levenson, *Death and Resurrection*, 141; Pate et al., *Story of Israel*, 18, 23, 24, 40.

observed that the idea of obedience in the Old Testament is so pervasive that even the Sinai law itself builds upon it.[74] C. H. Bullock aptly observes that "the virtue of obedience became the criterion" by which Abraham's character and that of future Israel is measured.[75] The idea is enshrined in the term שמר regarding Adam's vocation (Gen 2:5).[76] Unlike Adam, Abraham does obey Yahweh's commandment: "and you shall keep my covenant" (ואתה את־בריתי תשמר) (Gen 17:9). In fact, from its inception, the fulfillment of the promises depends on Abraham's obedience to the divine imperatives: "You go" (לך) (Gen 12:1) and "so you might be" (והיה) a blessing (v. 2). Thus, the implied human obligations in Genesis 15 find explicit expression in at least five subsequent passages as shown in table 2.1 (Gen 17:1–2, 9–14; 18:18–19; 22:15–18; 26:5). With the exception of Genesis 17:1–2, the key terms which mark Yahweh's demands and Abraham's obedience are שמר and שמע, respectively. Exodus 19:5 shows that Yahweh's demands for Abraham extend to Israel.

Table 2.1: Markers Connecting Obedience with Sinai Law

Imperatives	Obedience	
הִתְהַלֵּךְ לְפָנַי וֶהְיֵה תָמִים		Gen 17:1–2
אֶת־בְּרִיתִי תִשְׁמֹר		Gen 17:9
וְשָׁמְרוּ דֶּרֶךְ יְהוָה		Gen 18:19
	עֵקֶב אֲשֶׁר שָׁמַעְתָּ בְּקֹלִי	Gen 22:18
וַיִּשְׁמֹר מִשְׁמַרְתִּי	בְּקֹלִי... עֵקֶב אֲשֶׁר־שָׁמַע	Gen 26:5a–b
וּשְׁמַרְתֶּם אֶת־בְּרִיתִי	אִם־שָׁמוֹעַ תִּשְׁמְעוּ בְּקֹלִי	Exod 19:5

In the first half of Genesis 17, Yahweh imposes demands on Abraham to govern the relationship (Gen 17:1–2). Most likely Abraham's lapse of faith in Genesis 16 prompted Yahweh to renew the covenant. Among other things, the restoration appended explicit imperatives as conditions to fulfill the covenant promises (Gen 17:1–2). For instance, the two imperatives function

---

74. See, for example, Barrick, "Mosaic Covenant," 215; Kaiser, *Toward Rediscovering the Old Testament*, 152–153.

75. Bullock, "Ethics," 195.

76. Rendtorff, "'Covenant' as a Structuring Concept," 39.

as commands to administer the covenant.⁷⁷ Yahweh expects Abraham to continue on a path of moral and ethical obedience in order to realize the covenant promises he initiated in Genesis 15:18. Weinfeld notes that the expression התהלך לפני corresponds to the language used in Assyrian grants and conveys the idea of a loyal servant serving perfectly.⁷⁸

In the second half of Genesis 17, Yahweh also demands Abraham and his household be circumcised (Gen 17:9–14). Yahweh's command to Abraham to "keep" (תשמר) the covenant (17:9) entails the circumcision of Abraham and every male in his household (v. 10b).⁷⁹ As table 2.1 shows, verbal affinities connect Genesis 17:9 to the Sinai law (Exod 19:5): (את־בריתי תשמר) // (ושמרתם את־בריתי). Faint echoes from these passages also reverberate in the expression "keep my charge" (וישמר משמרתי) (Gen 26:5b). These intertextual patterns put circumcision on par with the Sinai stipulations (cf. Lev 26:15, 41; Gen 26:5).⁸⁰ Presumably, circumcision portends Israel's commitment to obey the law. However, disobedience meant covenant "breach" (הפר), for which Yahweh will excommunicate the culprit from the covenant community (Gen 17:14).⁸¹

Taken as a whole, Yahweh's injunction of circumcision (Gen 17:9–14) is sandwiched between Yahweh's promises of land (vv. 2, 4–8a), of a special relationship with future Israel (v. 8b), and of a royal descendant (v. 16). The location of this injunction indicates that Yahweh's promises (12:1–3) and his

---

77. The two imperatives are "continue to walk before me" (התהלך לפני) and "be blameless" (והיה תמים) (Gen 17:1). In addition, the syntactical construction and context suggest contingency. Imperatives "continue to walk before me and be blameless" (התהלך לפני והיה תמים) (Gen 17:1), followed by a cohortative with a simple ו "so that I may establish my covenant between me and you" (ואתנה בריתי ביני ובינך) (Gen 17:2) marks purpose/result. Although an indirect cohortative is used mainly after a direct volitive mood (*GKC*, §108d-f; *IBHS*, §34.6a), volitive forms with a ו are ambiguous. Only context may ascertain the exact nuance (*JM*, §116a-b). At any rate, the maintenance of the covenant and the realization of its provisions depend on Abraham's obedience to the covenant obligations.

78. Weinfeld, "Covenant of Grant," 186.

79. "Circumcise every male belonging to you" (המול לכם כל־זכר). The second person imperfect verb (תשמר) has the force of a command. In addition, the Niphal infinitive absolute (המול), "shall be circumcised," functions as an imperative and expresses a command in the second person. *GKC*, §113y-bb.

80. Bernat, *Sign of the Covenant*, 26. For various views on the debate, see Gentry and Wellum, *Kingdom through Covenant*, 272–275; Thiessen, *Contesting Conversion*, 30–39; Wenham, *Genesis 16–50*, 23–24.

81. "That [soul] person shall be cut from his people" (ונכרתה הנפש ההוא מעמיה).

initial covenant (15:18) must be understood within the context of human obligation. This strongly supports the conclusion that Yahweh's relationship with Abraham had implied obligations from the very beginning.

Genesis 18 provides further evidence that Yahweh's initial covenant promises had obligations attached to them as Yahweh spells out the condition for realizing the promises (Gen 18:18; cf. 12:1–3; 15:1–5).[82] Yahweh elected Abraham so he could "command" (יצוה) his children to obey the Lord. Such obedience is referred to figuratively as "to keep the way of Yahweh" (ושמרו דרך יהוה). The subsequent infinitive construct with a prefixed ל (i.e. ל of manner) functions epexegetically to clarify the metaphor.[83] To keep the way of Yahweh means "to do righteousness and justice" (לעשות צדקה ומשפט). The significance of the demand to practice צדקה ומשפט as a condition to maintain the covenant and to receive its provisions is not an exaggeration. The pair (i.e. צדקה ומשפט) stands at the core of the covenant relationship and is a shorthand for human obligations (cf. Amos 5:7, 24; 6:12; Isa 1:21; 5:7; 9:7; 10:2).[84] The incident at Sodom and Gomorrah underscores the principles involved in this word pair. The unfolding episode of Sodom and Gomorrah is somewhat a case study of divine righteousness and justice in the midst of judgment (Gen 18–19). Subtly, Yahweh instructs Abraham on the topic so that he, in turn, may teach his descendants likewise (Gen 18:19). Yahweh showed and revealed his demands to Abraham.

Genesis 22 attributes the fulfillment of the covenant promises to Abraham's obedience. In reiterating his promises to Abraham after the *Akedah* test, Yahweh unequivocally points to Abraham's obedience as the catalyst for his commitment: "because you have obeyed my voice" (עקב אשר שמעת בקלי) (Gen 22:18). One observation to note is that this causal clause forms the other

---

82. "He may command his sons and his household after him to keep the way of the Lord" (יצוה את־בניו ואת־ביתו אחריו ושמרו דרך יהוה) (Gen 18:19).

83. *GKC*, §114 o-p

84. Allen, *Theological Approach to the Old Testament*, 75. For James L. Mays, the idea behind צדקה is that of "the quality of life displayed by those who live up to the norms inherent in a given relationship" and "the rightness that belongs to those who fulfill their responsibilities which their relationship to God creates." Mays, *Amos*, 92–93, 103.

part of the expression alluded to in Genesis 26:5. Grüneberg's appraisal on Abraham's obedience is on target.[85]

The notion of obedience as a human obligation in the Abrahamic covenant and beyond comes into sharp relief as Yahweh renews the covenant with Isaac (Gen 26:1–5). Since this is a covenant restoration text, it comes as no surprise that Genesis 26:1–5 conflates several Genesis promises associated with the Abrahamic covenant. These include blessings (Gen 26:3b; cf. 12:2), land (26:3c; cf. 12:17; 15:18; 17:8), the oath (26:3d; cf. 22:16–18), numerous descendants (Gen 26:4a; cf. 15:5; 17:6; 22:17), and universal blessings (26:4b; cf. 22:18). Yahweh extends the promises to Isaac because of Abraham's obedience as established by the causal clause (Gen 26:5).[86]

First, we draw attention to this causal clause. The versatility of this causal clause rests precisely in its twofold function of binding the law to both Yahweh's promises and to human obedience. What we observe is that Abraham's obedience is tantamount to observing the law, since the clause is juxtaposed to forensic terms associated with the law at Sinai: (וישמר משמרתי מצותי חקותי ותורתי).[87] Evidently, this strongly suggests that Abraham's obedience is foundational to the Mosaic law.

---

85. Grüneberg comments that "Abraham's obedience is not blind, a matter merely of outward performance or of submission to arbitrary divine whims. It rather stems from his relationship with a God who does provide (v. 14) and remain faithful to his promises (vv. 16–18), who is working for good even when demanding something painful or puzzling.... Human obedience does not enable something other than can come from God's promise; rather Abraham's actions became a further grounding for the promise alongside God's free decision." Grüneberg, *Abraham, Blessing and the Nations*, 224, 226.

86. "Because Abraham obeyed my voice and he kept my obligation: my commandments, my statutes, and my instructions" (עקב אשר־שמע אברהם בקלי וישמר משמרתי מצותי חקותי ותורתי) (Gen 26:5; cf. Deut 11:1). The forensic terms (מצותי חקותי ותורתי) and their combinations are abundantly intimated in the Mosaic Covenant (e.g. Exod 18:16, 20; Lev 18:5, 26; 19:37; 20:22; 25:18; 26:3, 15, 43, 46; Deut 4:1, 40, 45; 5:1; 6:1; 7:11; 12:1).

87. The presence of forensic terms in Genesis 26:5, which explicitly suggest that Abraham kept the law before Sinai, has both perplexed scholars and generated diverse views. For instance, Claus Westermann, as well as Gerald J. Janzen, adamantly views it as pure anachronism. Westermann, *Genesis 12–36*, 425; Janzen, *Abraham*, 100. David A. Bernat, in line with the Documentary Hypothesis, sees the presence of the forensic terms as evidence for a late date of the Pentateuch. Bernat, *Sign of the Covenant*, 40n41. On the other hand, James K. Bruckner, Terence E. Fretheim, and others argue that although the patriarchs did not have the technical codifications of the Sinai law, they had implied law, which was somewhat akin to it; in fact, the patriarchs' life experiences and concrete struggles were foundational to the formulation of the Sinai law. Bruckner, *Implied Law*, 32, 218; Fretheim, "Book of Genesis," 529. More recently, Brian Neil Peterson argues that parts of Genesis serve as case law. For him, the author of Genesis "sought to present specific instruction on key legislative aspects of the Torah. In other

Second, we draw attention to the intertextual patterns tabulated in table 2.1. An interesting observation to note is that Exodus 19:5 alludes to Genesis 26:5a. Such a twofold link of the causal clause through juxtaposition (i.e. to forensic terms associated with the law at Sinai) and literary allusion effectively underscores the role obedience plays towards the fulfillment of the covenant promises.[88] The human obligation in the covenant relationship is inextricably linked to the demand of obedience to Yahweh's voice. As Mathews rightly suggests, "By employing covenant terminology, the author depicts the complete obedience of Abraham as the ideal for Israel in the land who must observe the provisions of the Sinaitic covenant (e.g. Lev 26:3; Deut 4:40; 30:16)."[89]

In summary, the Abrahamic covenant comprises a blend of divine commitments and human obligations. Obedience to Yahweh's voice, rather than the imposition of divine imperatives per se, is the key that characterizes Abraham's obligations. Most important is that the ideas of election, promissory blessing, and righteousness are contingent upon Abraham's accomplishing his obligation.[90]

Mosaic Covenant

The characterization of the Mosaic covenant as a suzerain-vassal treaty is a well known fact. Comparative analysis between ANE treaties and the Mosaic covenant texts convincingly confirms this conclusion.[91] The traditional approach emphasizes the difference between the Abrahamic and Mosaic covenants. However, we have objected to this characterization of the covenants, arguing instead for the unitary nature of covenants. That is, all biblical covenants comprise a blend of divine commitments and human obligations.

---

words, the author appears to have wanted to show what certain laws actually looked like in a 'real life' setting." Peterson, *Genesis as Torah*, viii. See also Carmichael, *Law and Narrative in the Bible*; Carmichael, *Origins of Biblical Law*; Carmichael, *Spirit of Biblical Law*; Adamczewski, *Retelling the Law*.

88. Youngblood, "Abrahamic Covenant," 40.

89. Mathews, *Genesis 11:27–50:26*, 405.

90. Mathews, 223.

91. For a comprehensive discussion on the topic, see Kitchen and Lawrence, *Treaty, Law and Covenant*. For similarly cogent studies on the subject, see Kline, *Treaty of the Great King*; Mendenhall, "Covenant Forms in Israelite Tradition"; Won, "Examination of the Relationship," 202–239.

Apparently, the unitary nature of covenants clears a path to investigate continuities among covenants. Several scholars have sensed such continuity among biblical covenants. John J. Mitchell insists that the Mosaic covenant and other covenants that develop from the foundation laid by the Abrahamic covenant.[92] R. E. Clements holds that the Mosaic covenant is the democratization of the Abrahamic promises to Israel.[93] Allen correctly suggests that the Mosaic covenant "inaugurates the fulfillment of the promises given to the patriarchs."[94] Although the two covenants differ at several points, we concur with the assessments of these scholars and would go on to state that the model depicted in figure 2.2(b) best captures the essence of the Mosaic covenant. The model stresses human obligations on the part of Israel, because of her new socio-religious environment in Canaan. Therefore, in keeping with our commitment to the unitary nature of covenants, in the following two sections we will stress the continuity between the Abrahamic and Mosaic covenants.

Divine commitment

Waltke opens his discussion of the Mosaic covenant by suggesting that the covenant requires "Israel to pledge herself to Him [Yahweh] without obligating Him by a like pledge to Israel."[95] For the most part, this study has followed Waltke's views at many turns. However, in this instance, we disagree with his conclusion because the data suggests otherwise. Repeatedly, Yahweh's promises to Abraham have his descendants in view as well (see Gen 12:7; 15:18; 17:7–10; 21:12–13; 24:7). After Abraham had separated from Lot, Yahweh assured him that his descendants would possess the land "forever" (עַד־עוֹלָם) (Gen 13:15). In addition, part of the covenant formula – "to be God to you" (לִהְיוֹת לְךָ לֵאלֹהִים) – shows Yahweh commits not only to be Abraham's God (Gen 17:7b) but to be the God of his descendants also (v. 7c). Furthermore, formula C, the expanded covenant formula, occurs in a key text which anticipates Yahweh's deliverance of Israel from Egypt (Exod 6:2–8).[96] Israel's

---

92. Mitchell, "Abram's Understanding of the Lord's Covenant," 45n43.
93. Clements, *Abraham and David*, 75–78.
94. Allen, *Theological Approach to the Old Testament*, 56.
95. Waltke, "Phenomenon of Conditionality," 132–133.
96. In his seminal study on the covenant formula, Rolf Rendtorff has shown that the covenant formula – the verb היה + the double (לִהְיוֹת לְךָ לֵאלֹהִים) – takes three forms. Formula A: I will be your God; Formula B: You will be my people; Formula C = A + B: I will be your

groaning, because of Egyptian bondage, triggers events that are about to change the course of history for Abraham's descendants as Yahweh reassures Moses of the imminent future. He will fulfill his promises by delivering Israel from bondage (v. 6), making Israel his people (v. 7), and then giving them the land of Canaan (v. 8; cf. v. 4). Allusions to Genesis 17:7 and to the rest of the Abrahamic promises are clear. Thus, Yahweh's pledge in the expanded covenant formula demonstrates his commitment to Israel, just as he was committed to Abraham. Such collocation of the covenant formula and the Abrahamic promises shows that Yahweh is obligated or committed to Israel.

The bilateral nature of the Mosaic covenant is well known. It suffices to stress, however, that on the grounds of Abraham's obedience, Israel's future was firmly guaranteed. Throughout Moses's era and during the conquest, Yahweh fulfilled his promises for Israel, all except kingship. Hence, the major patriarchal promises of progeny and land receive concrete and expanded treatment in the Mosaic covenant.[97]

Human obligation

A well-known feature of the Mosaic covenant is the Sinai law. Joseph Blenkinsopp's informative statistics highlight one way to construe the importance of the law in the Mosaic program. In his words:

> One of the most anomalous features of the Pentateuch read as a literary work is a narrative tempo. The Israelite camp in the wilderness of Sinai en route from Egypt to Canaan occupies from start to finish about a third of the total length of the Pentateuch (Exod 19:1–Num 10:28; 1, 987 verses out of 5,848), yet it lasts less than one year out of the 2,706 from creation to the death of

---

God and you will be my people. Rendtorff, *Covenant Formula*, 13.

97. The promises included the following: Israel becoming a great nation (Gen 12:2; 17:4–6; 18:18; cf. Exod 19:5–6; Deut 4:6–8, 32–34; 7:6–8; 28:1); Israel inheriting the land of Canaan (Gen 12:7; 13:14–17; 15:7–21; 17:8; 26:2–4; 28:13–15; 35:12; cf. Exod 6:3; 23:20–33; 33:1–3; Num 14:20–38; Deut 1:7–8; 4:1; 7:1; 8:1, 7–10; 11:22–25); Israel being multiplied (Gen 13:16; 15:4–7; 17:4–21; 22:17; 26:4, 24; 28:14; 35:11; cf. Exod 1:12; 32:13; Num 23:10; Deut 1:10; 6:3); Israel being a blessing to the nations (Gen 12:3; 18:18; 22:18; 26:4; 28:14; cf. Deut 4:6–8, 32–40; 28:9–10); and Yahweh being their God and/or Israel being his people (Gen 17:7–8; 26:3, 24; 28:15; cf. Exod 6:7; 19:5–6; Lev 11:45; 26:12, 45; Deut 26:18; 28:9; 29:18–19; 32:8–9). These promises are an essential feature of the covenant.

Moses. This narrative anomaly indicates the transcendent value assigned to law in the life of Israel.[98]

However, a less well-known observation is that the roots of Sinai law trace back to the narratives in Genesis. Until recently, scholars had given little attention to the canonical context of law in Genesis as a precedent to Sinai law. Thanks to the perceptive and pioneering studies by James K. Bruckner and others, it is now clear that "Genesis is full of references that are of interest to procedural law: commercial law, treaties and covenants and juridical procedure."[99]

To explicate implied law in Genesis "requires focused attention on the voices of the characters that accuse, plead, describe evidence, argue, and render judgments."[100] Bruckner goes on to connect implied imperatives in Genesis to analogous Sinai laws. For instance, the seventh commandment on adultery (Exod 20:14; Deut 5:18) and its corollary, the tenth commandment – covetousness of another man's wife (Exod 20:17; Deut 5:21) – have precedents in the accusations against Abimelech on Abraham's wife, Sarah (Gen 20).[101] Bruckner further observes that the various laws against injustices, especially towards widows, orphans, and aliens (Exod 22:21–24), developed from the judicial narrative of Sodom and Gomorrah (Gen 18–19).[102]

Walking along a similar path as Bruckner, Jo Ann Davidson adds a number of other examples. For example, the Sabbath day stands as the climax of the creation account (Gen 2:1–3) but receives codification at Sinai (Exod 20:8–11; Deut 5:12–15).[103] Cain's grievous murder of Abel (Gen 4:3–16) informs the command against murder (Exod 20:13; Deut 5:17), and Rachel's stealing of her father's household gods (Gen 31:19) lies behind the eighth commandment against stealing (Exod 20:16; Deut 5:19).[104] Jacob's urging of his household

---

98. Blenkinsopp, "What Happened at Sinai?," 155.

99. Bruckner, *Implied Law in the Abraham Narrative*, 27; See Davidson, "Decalogue Predates Mount Sinai," 61–81.

100. Bruckner, *Implied Law in the Abraham Narrative*, 20–21.

101. Bruckner, 217–218.

102. Bruckner, 218.

103. Davidson, "Decalogue Predates Mount Sinai," 64.

104. Davidson, 65–68, 74–75.

to put away their idols (Gen 35:1–4) anticipates the prohibition against idol worship (Exod 20:4–6; Deut 5:8–10).[105]

Davidson presents a plausible case, concluding that, in one form or the other, the implied law is attested throughout Genesis. In light of these attestations, Yahweh's acclamation of Abraham as he extends the covenant to Isaac is particularly impressive (Gen 26:5; cf. Lev 26:1–13; Deut 6:1–4; 8:1; 10:18; 11:1; 16:19–20; 26:17; 28:1–14). As we stated earlier, the triad of forensic vocabulary in Genesis 26:5 shows that there is greater continuity in the human obligations Yahweh imposed in both the Abrahamic and Mosaic covenants than the proponents of the traditional approach acknowledge.[106] As Kaiser comments, "The very terms used for Abraham's obedience were the ones that would later come to denote the whole Mosaic law."[107] Abraham's obedience to implied law serves as a motivation for the nation to do the same. Moses expresses this fact by prefacing the revelation of Yahweh at Sinai (Exod 19:16–25), the giving of the law (Exod 20:1–23:33), and the ratification of the covenant (Exod 24:1–33) with obedience to Yahweh's voice (Exod 19:5; cf. Gen 17:9; 26:5).

A significant goal of the Mosaic covenant was the establishment of a special nation through which Yahweh would realize his plan for all humanity. To be such a nation, Israel had to obey the principal obligations spelled out in the Decalogue (Exod 20:1–17) and contextualized in the book of the covenant (Exod 20:22–23:33). The law served to secure and maintain the patriarchal promises for each successive generation, to guarantee Israel's holiness by pointing out sin (Exod 23:20–33; Lev 18:24–29), and to reveal Yahweh's nature and character to Israel and to the nations (Deut 4:6–8). With regard to the realization of the Abrahamic promises, William D. Barrick observes that "the fulfillment of the promises and blessings of any of the covenants for any particular individual or generation was dependent upon their obedience to God's revelation. Disobedience annulled the blessings of God for that individual or generation in his/her/its own time, but disobedience did not invalidate the unconditional terms of the covenant."[108] Contrary to popular

---

105. Davidson, 76.
106. Youngblood, "Abrahamic Covenant," 42–44.
107. Kaiser, "Images for Today," 126.
108. Barrick, "Mosaic Covenant," 222.

opinion, obedience to the law is not a vehicle to bring Israel into a covenant relationship with Yahweh. Instead, the law defines the means to maintain a previously established relationship so that blessings could flow.[109]

In summary, the Mosaic covenant focuses on the covenant relationship between Yahweh and Israel, which in essence fulfills the promise embedded in the covenant formula (Gen 17:7; Exod 6:7) to which Israel would give assent as the narrative unfolds (19:5, 8). Another focus of the covenant, that Israel would possess the land of Canaan, receives treatment in Numbers 10:11–Josh 24.[110] The book of Joshua makes abundantly clear that Yahweh fully realized the land promise when Israel conquered Canaan (Josh 21:43–45). Taken together, the picture presented not only demonstrates the continuity between the Abrahamic and Mosaic covenants but also stresses the steadfast nature of Yahweh's ongoing commitment to both the patriarchs and Israel, a commitment anchored solely in Yahweh's resolve and on his great name (2 Sam 7:23; Ps 106:7–8; Isa 48:9–11; Ezek 39:25).[111]

Davidic Covenant

Most scholars regard the Davidic covenant as the most complicated and controversial of the covenants; its principal passage (i.e. 2 Sam 7) is the most endlessly argued text.[112] For instance, the literary history of Nathan's oracle and its messianic nature are hotly debated (2 Sam 7:19; cf. 1 Chr 17:17).[113] Moreover, scholars disagree a great deal on the oracle's influence and role in the pre-Deuteronomistic Jerusalem royal ideology and in late post-Deuteronomistic redactions.[114] Speaking of its Deuteronomistic nature, McCarter notes, "It is

---

109. Broyles, "Traditions, Intertextuality, and Canon," 191.
110. Dick, *Reading the Old Testament*, 147–152.
111. Rendtorff, *Covenant Formula*, 29.
112. Collins and Collins, *King and Messiah as Son of God*, 25–28; Gakuru, *Inner Biblical Exegetical Study*, 1–9; Hwang, *Hope for the Restoration*, 8–19.
113. Steinmann, "What Did David Understand?," 22–27.
114. Kasari, *Nathan's Promise in 2 Samuel 7*, 5–7, 15–19. Worthy of note here is that royal ideology concerns the wedding of ideas of the dynasty and the building of a temple for the gods. Close ANE analogies to 2 Sam 7 include the Assyrian Royal Building inscriptions from the third and second millennia down to 859 BC. From such inscriptions, Antti Laato has ably discerned five themes associated with the concept of dynasty. These include a genealogy of the king, which covers 3–7 generations; legitimation of the king by the gods; dedication of a building project, particularly temples of the gods; a prayer of the king or an expression of hope connected with the foundation ceremony of the temple; and blessings and curses demanding that the

clear that 2 Samuel 7 expresses certain important Deuteronomistic ideas, for which it stands as a primary point of reference in the larger history," and that "the present form of the text is built largely of Deuteronomistic rhetoric."[115] However, legitimating kings by oracular decree is well attested in various ANE parallels, and it is highly likely that the kings of Judah would also avail themselves to such means in order to validate their claims to the throne.[116] It is reasonable to suppose that the Deuteronomistic author/redactor used an older tradition.[117] As such, it suffices to note that Nathan's oracle was not a late composition of the Deuteronomist.

What is more, the lack of the term ברית in Nathan's oracle complicates discussions of the Davidic covenant. This raises questions about the nature of the divine promise: Is it a legal text describing a covenant or is it simply a prophecy?[118] Notwithstanding the foregoing, a pressing issue for our immediate needs is to clarify and reiterate that the Davidic covenant is best characterized in terms of divine commitment and human obligation rather than reverting to the traditional model (i.e. unconditional [grant-type] and conditional [treaty-type]). To insist on the traditional model because of a lack of an explicit oath by David or his heirs, as Scott Hahn does, ignores the obligatory aspects of the covenant, which are explicitly stated in subsequent passages that allude back to Nathan's original oracle.[119] Without belaboring

---

monumental inscriptions be restored. In other words, those who restore the buildings will be blessed, while those who fail to do so will be cursed. See Laato, "Second Samuel 7," 248–49.

115. McCarter, *II Samuel*, 220–221.

116. Laato, "Second Samuel 7," 263. He concludes that the texts "from the ancient Near East which we have presented . . . indicate that there is no prima facie reason to regard the central idea in 2 Samuel 7 – the promise of an eternal dynasty to David – as an anachronistic element in the account of the reigns of David and Solomon. On the contrary, we have shown that the Akkadian royal ideology remained a constant line of thought throughout the centuries and that nothing indicates that the idea of an eternal dynasty was limited to either an early or a late period."

117. Collins and Collins, *King and Messiah as Son of God*, 27; Schniedewind, *Society and the Promise to David*, 35–36.

118. Avioz, *Nathan's Oracle*, 25.

119. Hahn, *Kinship by Covenant*, 177–178. It appears Hahn selectively puts a lot of emphasis on subsequent passages that allude to 2 Samuel 7 to build and prove his grant model. His model includes these five features: (1) Divine oath sworn to David (Ps 89:3); (2) God blesses David but curses his enemies (Ps 89:20–23); (3) God binds himself unconditionally to David by taking covenant obligations (2 Sam 7:9, 11–12, 16); (4) God undertakes obligations, which are extended to David's descendants (Ps 89:4; cf. 2 Sam 7:12–16; Ps 110:4); and (5) David's exceptional virtue and loyalty to God are the reasons for the divine grant (2 Sam 22:21–26).

the point, it suffices to mention that the Abrahamic and Davidic covenants are essentially similar to the Mosaic covenant.

Divine commitment

Nathan's original oracle offers David several divine promises, none of which is dependent on explicit obedience. Waltke and several other scholars point out that Yahweh's promises divide into two parts – those that are directed to David during his lifetime (2 Sam 7:8–11a) and those that pertain to David's future descendants, after his death (2 Sam 7:11b–16).[120] First, Yahweh promises David a great name (v. 9), a secure place for the nation (v. 10), and rest from his foes (v. 11a). These promises pertain directly to David. What is interesting here is that overtones of the Abrahamic promises can hardly be missed as Yahweh promises to make David's name great (Gen 12:2; 2 Sam 7:9). David's ensuing international battles and victories over the various nations appear to underline his greatness (2 Sam 8; 10:3–18). Accordingly, Israel was firmly planted in her own land and enjoyed her rest as the defeated nations made peace with them (2 Sam 10:19). Thus, one can begin to observe a close relationship between the Abrahamic covenant and the Davidic covenant. Such a close relationship underlines the unitary nature of covenants.[121]

Second, Yahweh promises to give David's future descendants an everlasting dynasty (2 Sam 7:11b), kingdom (v. 12), and throne (v. 13). These three promises are summarized and reiterated in verse 16 and obviously pertain to a time after David's death. With regard to Yahweh's promise of an everlasting dynasty, Yahweh stresses that the Davidic covenant is irrevocable, despite the future sin of David's descendants (vv. 14–15). Although verse 15 explicitly stresses Yahweh's commitment to the Davidic dynasty, verse 14 also makes certain that Yahweh demands obedience from David's descendants. Using an

---

Evidently, there is a methodological flaw. Further, what Hahn insists are also tell-tale signs of a grant covenant appear in treaty types as well. For instance, adoption, servanthood, and father/son imagery, which underlie his Davidic covenant schema, are attested in vassal treaties as well. As Knoppers has demonstrated, grant covenants contain pledges of allegiance by vassal kings to their overlord masters just as in treaty type covenants. See Knoppers, "Ancient Near Eastern Royal Grants," 677–678.

120. Waltke, "Phenomenon of Conditionality," 130; Gentry and Wellum, *Kingdom through Covenant*, 394; Grisanti, "Davidic Covenant," 237–240.

121. For instance, John Bright regards the Davidic covenant as a renewal and an extension of the Abrahamic covenant. See Bright, *Covenant and Promise*, 71.

evocative father-son metaphor, which is an adoption formula reminiscent of the covenant formula, Yahweh "restates the Torah's teaching that the Lord would punish disobedient covenant people with the instrumentality of human oppressors (cf. Lev 26:25; Deut 28:25, 49–52)."[122] Evidently, apostasy on the part of the Davidic rulers may threaten the throne for that particular ruler, but the covenant was irrevocable. Waltke's remark captures this sense well. As he puts it, "The beneficiaries' darkest crimes do not annul the covenants of divine commitment."[123]

A relevant question that scholars often raise is whether Yahweh fulfilled the covenant promises during David's lifetime. On the one hand, Robert D. Bergen holds that Yahweh did not fulfill the Davidic promises during David's lifetime.[124] On the other hand, Clements maintains that the three major promises to Abraham of land, a great nation, and blessing to the nations all find fulfillment in the era of David.[125] Clements goes on to state that "the importance of the ancient covenant with Abraham was to be found in its foretelling the rise of the Davidic state and Kingship."[126] Both Bergen's and Clements' positions are inadequate. As we tried to highlight in the preceding paragraphs, the initial signs of that fulfillment are already at work. While we agree that a close relationship between the Abrahamic covenant and the David covenant exists, the absolute fulfillment of the Abrahamic promises was never attained during David's lifetime. For instance, the promise of being a blessing to the nations was hardly fulfilled. David's kindness towards the Ammonite king brought war instead of blessings (2 Sam 10:1–4).

At any rate, while the eschatological fulfillment awaits the second coming of Christ, the historical realization of Yahweh's promises to both Abraham and David reached their zenith during Solomon's reign. For instance, the population of Judah and Israel reached vast numbers (1 Kgs 4:20; cf. Gen 13:16; 22:17), the land boundaries extended beyond Canaan (1 Kgs 4:21, 24; cf. 2 Sam 7:10; 8; Gen 15:18; Num 24:17; Deut 11:24; Josh 1:4), and the

---

122. Bergen, *1, 2 Samuel*, 341.
123. Waltke, "Phenomenon of Conditionality," 131.
124. Bergen, *1, 2 Samuel*, 339.
125. Clements, *Abraham and David*, 52–60.
126. Clements, 60.

land attained unprecedented peace (1 Kgs 4:20b, 25; cf. 2 Sam 7:9).[127] As Solomon reflected on Yahweh's faithfulness, he acknowledged that Yahweh had indeed fulfilled some of his promises to David (1 Kgs 8:15–24, 56). What is more, Solomon's assessment and paraphrase of the divine promises links the Davidic covenant to the Mosaic covenant (1 Kgs 8:56–61). His benediction mentions Moses as the channel of divine promises – particularly, rest from enemies (1 Kgs 8:56; cf. Deut 12:10). In addition, the passage explicitly demands obedience to torah (1 Kgs 8:58, 61).

Human obligation

While there is an ongoing debate among scholars on the overall nature of the Davidic covenant, few would deny the presence of human obligations attached to it in subsequent passages which allude to Nathan's original oracle. Avraham Gileadi mentions that "the fate and welfare of the nation hinged on the king's loyalty to YHWH."[128] In that light, the first piece of evidence demonstrating that Yahweh's original promise to establish David's throne perpetually had obligations attached to it is the demand for a king who rules in righteousness (2 Sam 23:3–5).[129] As David reflected on Nathan's oracle, he recognized that ideal kingship was rooted in a covenant relationship (2 Sam 23:5);[130] a relationship marked by the fear of Yahweh as expressed in the king's righteous rule (vv. 3–4). As the narrator notes, soon after Nathan's oracle (2 Sam 8:1), David

---

127. Waltke, *Old Testament Theology*, 539.

128. Gileadi surmises that a unique feature of the Davidic covenant from other biblical covenants is the concept of protection. According to Gileadi, the protection clause in ANE treaties was principally dependent on the relationship between the suzerain and vassal. Gileadi, "Davidic Covenant," 159.

129. Bergen, *1, 2 Samuel*, 466; Avioz, *Nathan's Oracle*, 66.

130. As Avioz has convincingly shown, the poem in 2 Samuel 23:1–7 is replete with verbal allusions to Nathan's oracle (2 Sam 7). Avioz, *Nathan's Oracle*, 64. This poem contributes immensely to the theological development of the Davidic covenant. Besides its articulation of the concept of royal ideology, the poem is the earliest text to read Nathan's oracle specifically as a covenant. Even though the term ברית is attested in 2 Samuel 23:5, McKenzie contends that the passage is part of a section of 2 Samuel 21–24 "widely regarded by scholars as a later addition to the Deuteronomistic History." See McKenzie, *Covenant*, 68. However, the incipient words in the superscription, "the last words of David" (2 Sam 23:1), need their due consideration and should be taken seriously. This inscription suggests that the poem dates at least three decades or so after Nathan's dynastic oracle (cf. 2 Sam 5:4–5). To date the poem on the basis of vocabulary is not persuasive because it assumes that words attested in Late Biblical Hebrew were not available to pre-exilic writers. This is fallacious, since vocabulary deemed late is actually present in pre-exilic texts. For a detailed exploration of the problem involved in linguistic dating of biblical texts, see Young, Rezetko, and Ehrensvärd, *Introduction to Approaches and Problems*.

established moral righteousness and social justice over all Israel (2 Sam 8:15; 1 Kgs 10:9; Ps 72:1). Even more significant is the thematic link the passage shares with Yahweh's expectations of Abraham. David's exemplary administration of justice over all Israel (2 Sam 8:15) traces back to Abraham as a role model and teacher of justice and righteousness (Gen 18:19).[131] David's act of extending "kindness" (חסד) to Mephibosheth (2 Sam 9) underscores, in bold relief, David as the ideal embodiment of kingship, whose major responsibility was to establish and to administer justice and righteousness in the land (2 Sam 8:15; 1 Chr 18:14; cf. Gen 18:19; 1 Kgs 10:9; 2 Chr 9:8; Ps 72:1; Jer 22:3, 15; 23:5; 33:15). David's righteousness became the norm for evaluating future Davidic rulers (Pss 35:6–7; 72:1–4; 2 Kgs 14:3; 18:3; 22:2). Solomon will be endowed with wisdom in order to promote social justice in all Israel (1 Kgs 3:6, 9). No wonder Absalom attempted a *coup d'état* on the pretext of being able to administer justice for the people (2 Sam 15:2–7). While much more could be said about David's poem (2 Sam 23:1–7), it suffices to mention that although the king expressed confidence in Yahweh's faithfulness to realize the covenant promises (v. 5), he also recognized that Yahweh would punish disobedient rulers (vv. 6–7).

In his groundbreaking study of Psalm 89, Nahum M. Sarna has shown that this psalm interprets Nathan's oracle (2 Sam 7).[132] The psalm explicitly reads Nathan's oracle as a covenant (Ps 89:4), and it mentions that Yahweh will definitely punish David's future descendants for violating torah (vv. 31–33). One can hardly miss the Deuteronomistic overtones in the passage. Gentry and Wellum note that Psalm 89:31 "relates directly to Deuteronomy 17 and emphasizes that the Davidic king must know and keep Torah in order for this to be the basis of his rule of the nation.... While the emphasis is on the faithfulness of Yahweh, the need for Torah-keeping on the part of the king is duly noted."[133] Gakuru holds that Psalm 89 views the Davidic covenant as

---

131. Smith, *Fate of Justice and Righteousness*, 42–56, 70–73. Smith perceptively discusses 2 Samuel 8:15 in light of a common shared ANE ideology and moral tradition regarding kingship, חסד, and the establishment of justice and righteousness.

132. Sarna, "Psalm 89," 30–31. Besides similarities in ideas and motif, Gakuru lists several verbal parallels between Ps 89 and 2 Sam 7:1–17. Gakuru, *Inner Biblical Exegetical Study*, 126.

133. Gentry and Wellum, *Kingdom through Covenant*, 403. See also Grisanti, "Davidic Covenant," 245; Kasari, *Nathan's Promise in 2 Samuel 7*, 237–238.

unconditional.[134] For him, punishment against a disobedient Davidic son does not affect the throne of David, but only the son. Apparently, Gakuru understands the term "unconditional" to mean the lack of human obligations. This is not quite correct. As discussed earlier, the term generates an unnecessary tension with other passages that see explicit human obligations as an integral part of the covenant (e.g. 1 Kgs 2:3–4; 8:25–26; 11:38). Furthermore, it fosters a false perception that Yahweh's promise of an everlasting throne is open-ended and does not demand obedience from the Davidic rulers. What is even more troubling is Gakuru's mixed view on this issue. In his own words, the sin/punishment relationship (2 Sam 7:14; Ps 89:30–32), "shows that strictly speaking the promise is not totally condition-free."[135]

With that said, another psalm that is crucial for an understanding of Nathan's oracle is Psalm 132. Laato dubs it "a *crux interpretum* in the reconstruction of the development of the Jerusalemite/Israelite royal ideology."[136] First, the psalm interprets Nathan's oracle as a sure oath,[137] which hints at the certainty of Yahweh's commitment (Ps 132:11). Second, Yahweh's exhortation to the Davidic rulers in the next conditional clause suggests that the divine promise is contingent upon obedience (v. 12).[138] Since the expression "keep my covenant" (ברית תשמר) alludes to both the Abrahamic (Gen 17:9) and Mosaic covenants (Exod 19:5), it is not farfetched to suggest that the future Davidic rulers are to obey torah. Scholarly opinion is divided concerning the meaning of "and my testimony" (Ps 132:12a; cf. Ps 25:10).[139] Regardless of the various opinions, many scholars acknowledge the conditional aspect of the covenant.[140] Speaking of Psalm 132:11, 12, Gentry and Wellum insist that "once more, the promises of God undergird and support on both sides the need for a faithful, obedient son."[141]

---

134. Gakuru, *Inner Biblical Exegetical Study*, 130.
135. Gakuru, 148.
136. Laato, "Psalm 132," 49.
137. Koehler, Baumgartner, and Stamm, *Hebrew and Aramaic Lexicon*, 69
138. "If your sons will keep my covenant and my testimonies" (אם־ישמרו בניך בריתי ועדתי). The particle, (אם), signals a conditional clause. See *GKC*, §159lv, dd.
139. For a brief survey of the various opinions, see Gakuru, *Inner Biblical Exegetical Study*, 114–115.
140. Collins and Collins, *King and Messiah as Son of God*, 33.
141. Gentry and Wellum, *Kingdom through Covenant*, 395.

Besides 2 Sam 23:1–7 and the two Psalms (i.e. 89 and 132), other passages in the books of Kings and Chronicles further clarify the nature of Nathan's oracle by making the human obligations explicit. For instance, in his last charge to Solomon, David reminds him of his moral obligation and of his responsibility to obey torah in order for Yahweh to fulfill the dynastic promise (1 Kgs 2:1–4; cf. 1 Chr 22:6–13; 28:1–10). Likewise, as Solomon prepared to build the temple, Yahweh guaranteed him that he would fulfill the promise to David if and only if Solomon obeyed torah (1 Kgs 6:12). Furthermore, Yahweh assured him that he would indwell the temple and would not forsake the nation (v. 13). Worthy of mention here is that David appears to have understood Nathan's original promises concerning Solomon as being conditioned on Solomon's obedience.

Finally, after Solomon had completed the building of the temple (1 Kgs 9:1–3; 2 Chr 7:17–22), Yahweh himself appeared in response to Solomon's prayer and reminded him that obedience to torah is an absolute prerequisite for Yahweh to establish an enduring throne for him (1 Kgs 9:4–5).[142] Paul R. House states that "Solomon's obedience, however, must be motivated by 'integrity of heart,' not by a mere external observance of God's word."[143] Conversely, if Solomon and his sons disobey through idolatry (v. 6), they will not only forfeit the throne, but Yahweh will exile the people from the land and devastate the temple (vv. 7–9; cf. Lev 26:27–39; Deut 28:36–37).

In summary, the Davidic covenant builds upon and develops the Abrahamic promise of kingship (Gen 17:6, 16). Like all Israel, the Davidic rulers are to obey the Mosaic stipulations in general and the law pertaining to Israel's kings in particular (Deut 17:14–20). Above all, they are required to model social justice and moral righteousness (2 Sam 8:15; 1 Kgs 10:9). Furthermore, it is their responsibility to sponsor Yahweh's cult by building and maintaining the temple/palace in Zion (see Deut 12). A point which the biblical passages stress is that the original divine promises to David are irrevocable, yet their fulfillment in any generation, and hence the perpetuity

---

142. The "if . . . then" (יִ . . . אִם) construction in v. 4 and v. 5, which marks the conditional nature of the promise, can hardly be missed. A similar construction occurs between v. 6 and v. 7, which stresses the consequences of disobedience.

143. House, *1, 2 Kings*, 151.

of the covenant, is contingent upon the obedience of David's royal heirs.[144] Apostasy by any king would result in divine judgment, but, regardless of the extent of that judgment (e.g. exile), the door for future restoration was left open (see Jer 33:17). Like Joshua (Josh 21:43–45), Solomon also reflected on Yahweh's faithfulness by noting that Yahweh had indeed fulfilled his promises to David (1 Kgs 8:20) and to Moses (1 Kgs 8:56).

Summary

The purpose of this background chapter was to lay out a covenantal context because it is foundational to the reestablishment of Yahweh's sovereignty. We endeavored to underscore the unitary nature of the covenants by showing how the Mosaic and Davidic covenants essentially build on and develop the Abrahamic promises. With the covenantal background at hand, the next chapter provides an overview of the Zion/Davidic traditions. Key themes from these traditions inform the concept of Yahweh's sovereignty in Micah.

---

144. Bateman, Bock, and Johnston, *Jesus the Messiah*, 69–70.

CHAPTER 3

Zion/Davidic Traditions: A Framework for Micah

Introduction

Since the early twentieth century, critical scholarship has come to appreciate the function ancient traditions played in shaping prophetic messages. Borrowing from Craig C. Broyles's definition, a tradition is a complex of religious ideas associated with a community's beliefs, customs, symbols, persons, institutions, rituals, and events.[1] Broyles suggests that a variety of Old Testament traditions include creation, ancestor, exodus, wilderness and conquest, Yahweh's war, judges, divine kingship, and the day of Yahweh.[2] He also notes that some traditions were used in the cult for worship; these include the ark, tabernacle, temple, festival, sacrifices, liturgies, and Levites.[3]

Nowadays, many Old Testament scholars agree that the prophetic literature is replete with references to ancient traditions and comes to us adorned in ancient garb.[4] John Bright deemphasized the creativity and originality of

---

1. Broyles, "Traditions, Intertextuality, and Canon," 44, 159.
2. Broyles, 159.
3. Broyles, 159.
4. For insightful introductions, which demonstrate that Hebrew prophets drew from ancient traditions, see Fishbane, *Biblical Interpretation in Ancient Israel*; Knight, *Tradition and Theology*; Gowan, *Theology of the Prophetic Books*, 51; Tucker, "Prophecy and Prophetic Literature"; Clements, *Prophecy and Tradition*; Day, "Inner-Biblical Interpretation," 230–246. Alongside these general treatments on the subject, studies that demonstrate a prophet's interaction with earlier biblical traditions include Davies, *Prophecy and Ethics*; Winkel, *Jeremiah in Prophetic Tradition*; Tull, *Remember the Former Things*; Kim, "Intertextual Reading," 113–124. For illustrations of how a central and paradigmatic biblical tradition, viz. the exodus traditions,

the prophets' message, contrary to what his predecessors had once suggested. He argued that the prophets were not innovators but reformers who reshaped ancient traditions for their own message.⁵ Shortly after Bright's publication, Gerhard von Rad succeeded in what might be termed one of the most important undertakings, the search for the specific traditions behind the prophets' message. He found traditions in the broader complexes of ancient election traditions which were connected with the exodus, Zion, and David.⁶ Walking along the same path as Bright, Rad also concluded that "the prophets were never as original, or as individualistic, or in such direct communion with God.... As we now see, they were in greater or lesser degree conditioned by old traditions which they re-interpreted and applied to their own times."⁷

Without rejecting the prophets' indebtedness to tradition, G. Fohrer objected to the view that the prophets preached exclusively from tradition. Instead, he stressed that "they [the prophets] were primarily charismatic, not the elaborators of tradition or cultic officials. They themselves lay claim to preaching the living word of God as they received it and not to proclaiming a tradition. Therefore they are not bound to a tradition nor rooted in it, but they utilized it as an instrument for their message."⁸ However, R. E. Clements insisted that the prophets were the "voices of covenant tradition" and that their message is best understood within a covenantal context.⁹

As one moves to the investigation of particular prophetic books, while keeping the preceding discussion in perspective, it becomes apparent that the general conclusions of these illustrious scholars have merit. A cursory reading of the extant book of Micah reveals that it is a skillfully interwoven theological reflection of a Judean prophet on the impending crises befalling

---

meanders throughout the Old and New Testaments, see a collection of essays in R. Michael Fox, ed., *Reverberations of the Exodus in Scripture*.

5. Bright, *History of Israel*, 264. For example, Wellhausen, speaking of the prophets, had earlier postulated that "they do not preach on set texts; they speak out of the spirit which judges all things and itself is judged of no man. Where do they ever lean on any other authority than the truth of what they say; where do they rest on any other foundation than their own certainty? It belongs to the notion of prophecy of true revelation." See Wellhausen, *Prolegomena to the History of Israel*, 398–399.

6. Rad, *Old Testament Theology*, 2:117.

7. Rad, 2:4.

8. Fohrer, "Remarks," 314.

9. Clements, *Prophecy and Covenant*, 23.

Samaria and Jerusalem because of Israel's covenant breach at the close of the eighth century. The book contains a substantial number of literary allusions and echoes of antecedent theological traditions of ancient Israel. Thomas L. Leclerc aptly observes that

> Micah's familiarity with several Israelite traditions is impressive. Some of the more prominent traditions upon which he draws are the following . . . theophany (1:2–4) . . . the mercy of God (7:18–20) . . . the exodus (6:3–5; 7:15) . . . the promises to Abraham and Jacob (7:20). . . . In calling attention to Micah's use of these, it becomes clear that the prophet is firmly rooted in the history of his people. He is a converser and conveyor of the people's collective story. But he preserves and recounts the tradition in dialogue with the present state of his people. He thus uses the past to address the present. In so doing, he demonstrates that the God who acted on their behalf in the past continues to be present to the people, demonstrating justice in punishing sin, and showing mercy in preparing a better future.[10]

Without compromising his individuality or originality, perhaps Micah drew from the old wells of ancient Israelite traditions either through social interactions with other communities or through religious affiliations.[11] In any case, such familiarity with established traditions afforded Micah a starting base from which to argue his case but then arrive at a new application of those traditions.[12]

For our present purposes, a complex of prominent traditions that Micah adopts and uses is the Zion/Davidic traditions, whose key themes and implications permeate his oracles. Most recently, several scholars have turned towards the theological importance of the Zion/Davidic traditions in the book, arguing that the prophet's central concern is for the restoration and eventual exaltation of Zion and her fortunes.[13] In his stimulating article on

---

10. Leclerc, *Introduction to the Prophets*, 201–202.
11. Clements, *Prophecy and Tradition*, 5.
12. Rad, *Old Testament Theology*, 2:179.
13. Poulsen, *Representing Zion*, 55–56; Timmer, *Non-Israelite Nations*, 90–115; Marrs, "Back to the Future," 82–96; Biddle, "Dominion Comes to Jerusalem," 253–267; Zapff, "Perspective on the Nations," 301–303; Levenson, *Sinai and Zion*, 197–200.

Zion in Micah, Marrs captures the essence of one of the most fascinating features in the book of Micah – the unraveling drama of Zion's fate (i.e. Zion under judgment and restoration). He rightly observes that "Zion appears not solely as it currently exists but as an object of divine intent. . . . Zion undergoes transformation. This transformation, although envisioned as a future event, in actuality captures Yahweh's *original* intent for Zion and its inhabitants. Ultimately, Zion has a future, but it is a future embodied in her past."[14]

Apparently, these proven Zion/Davidic traditions contribute immensely to the concept of divine sovereignty. The three pillar motifs from the traditions – Yahweh as the great king, the election of the Davidic dynasty as Yahweh's viceroy, and the election of Zion – are foundational to our discussion of the concept of divine sovereignty. Furthermore, a key implication of these three pillar motifs – which is also a crucial part of our discussion – is that Yahweh's presence in Zion calls for human responsibility. Yahweh insists on obedience prior to restoration. Specifically, the covenant community must observe social justice and righteousness as prerequisites for dwelling in Yahweh's presence and for inheriting the Abrahamic promises. In this respect, the three key motifs from the Zion/Davidic traditions and their implication present a ready-made cultural framework for studying the concept of Yahweh's sovereignty in Micah.

Hence, Micah utilizes certain aspects of the Zion/Davidic traditions to offer hope to a seemingly powerless remnant and to the obedient nations through the reestablishment of Yahweh's kingship in Zion, the restoration of Zion's temple, and the promise of a new Davidic king. Moreover, as part of Micah's cultural context, the Zion/Davidic traditions evoke familiar dramatic events and socio-religious settings in the minds of Micah's audience and thus facilitate both coherence and interpretation of the text.[15]

Ultimately, it is our aim to demonstrate that Micah fleshes out the concept of Yahweh's sovereignty by adapting themes from the Zion/Davidic traditions. Therefore, our primary purpose in this chapter is to introduce the various strands of the Zion/Davidic traditions. We will do so by briefly discussing scholarly approaches to the traditions and their basic motifs, and by offering

---

14. Marrs, "Back to the Future," 82. (Italics are original.)
15. Renz, "Use of the Zion Tradition," 78–79.

criteria for their identification. However, before the study proceeds to these matters, a clarification of what we mean by *Zion/Davidic traditions* is in order.

Definition of Zion/Davidic Traditions

Broadly speaking, the phrase *Zion/Davidic traditions* speaks of a host of multifaceted expressions, key ideas, metaphors, eschatological beliefs, and related motifs that focus on the three-way relationship between Yahweh, Zion, and the Davidic dynasty.[16] An immediate consequence of this complex triad of interrelated theological and political beliefs is that it functioned as a means to justify and legitimate the rule of the Davidic king as Yahweh's vicegerent on earth.[17]

Besides the definition and its importance, we also need to explain the relationship between the Zion and Davidic traditions and to clarify the plural term *traditions*. At this point, it suffices to say that these two traditions are distinct but inextricably related. We will revisit this issue shortly.

The plural term indicates that there is no fixed understanding regarding Zion in the Old Testament.[18] The use of the plural term stems mostly from criticism against studies that conceived of a Zion tradition with a fixed set of ideas, especially the inviolability of Zion.[19] As we will spell out shortly, nowadays scholars focus on the twofold perception of the Zion traditions – namely, the classical and the dynamic.[20] For instance, Broyles points out that at times traditions develop "through Israel's changing circumstances, and fluctuating faithfulness, and through Yahweh's progressive revelation."[21]

Approaches to Zion/Davidic Traditions

Relationship between Zion and Davidic Traditions

As expected, the relationship between the Zion traditions and the Davidic tradition is a matter of scholarly debate. Some scholars argue that the two

---

16. Monson, "Temple of Solomon," 6–8.
17. Chalmers, *Interpreting the Prophets*, 76; Allen, *Theological Approach to the Old Testament*, 119–120.
18. Tan, *Zion Traditions*, 24; Dow, *Images of Zion*, 26; Poulsen, *Representing Zion*, 14; Groves, "Zion Traditions," 1019; Levenson, "Zion Traditions," 1098.
19. McConville, "Jerusalem in the Old Testament," 28.
20. Poulsen, *Representing Zion*, 14.
21. Broyles, "Traditions, Intertextuality, and Canon," 164.

traditions are independent of each other. As Ollenburger contends, "David and Zion are the central symbols of two different traditions and cannot simply be identified, or the one reduced to the other."[22] In his view, the Zion traditions are associated with the ark and are independent of the Davidic tradition, which is mainly concerned with the legitimation of the Davidic dynasty.[23] He contends that the Zion Psalms (Pss 46; 48; 76) speak of a relationship between Zion and Yahweh's kingship, not with the Davidic king.[24] Likewise, Renz also argues that the Zion tradition is able to stand without support from the Davidic tradition. He states, "The priority and sufficiency of the Zion tradition is, however, evident in those psalms which give expression to Zion without any reference to the Davidic kingship (see Pss. 46, 48, and 76)."[25]

Without plunging deeply into the long-standing and still inconclusive debate, in our opinion the two traditions are distinct, but related. Though the evidence is slight, there is enough to show that a relationship exists between the two traditions. For instance, the account in 2 Samuel 5–7 shows a close relationship between the Zion traditions and the Davidic tradition.[26] David's transportation of the Ark of the Covenant to the city of David (Zion) buttresses the connection (2 Sam 6). In addition, several passages juxtapose Yahweh's election of David to that of Zion (e.g. 1 Kgs 11:13, 32; Pss 2:6; 78:68–70).

Motifs of the Zion/Davidic Traditions

Classical Zion tradition

The classical Zion tradition presents a static image of Zion as the last stronghold because Yahweh defends Zion from foreign enemies.[27] Despite the attack on the land of Israel by foreign enemies, Zion is inviolable and remains

---

22. Ollenburger, *Zion*, 59.
23. Ollenburger, 59–60.
24. Ollenburger, 60–62.
25. Renz, "Use of the Zion Tradition," 85.
26. Willis, "David and Zion," 139. The Davidic tradition mainly refers to the establishment, legitimation, and succession of the Davidic throne.
27. Primary biblical texts foundational to the concept of the classical Zion tradition include the following (to name a few): Isaiah 8:5–10; 17:12–14; 24:21–23; 25:6–12; 26:1–7; 30:27–33; 33:5–6, 14–24; 37:33–38; 60–62; 65:17–25; Psalms 2; 46; 48; 65; 76; 84; 87; 95–99; 110; 112; 125; 128; 132. Some significant secondary studies on the subject include Strong, "Zion"; Batto, "Divine Sovereign"; Roberts, "Zion," 331–347; Vaughn and Killebrew, *Jerusalem in Bible and Archaeology*; Hess and Wenham, *Zion, City of Our God*; Levenson, *Sinai and Zion*; and Hayes, "Tradition of Zion's Inviolability."

standing with a remnant of survivors.[28] Edzard Rohland wrote one of the pioneering works on the classical Zion tradition and it remains the basic work on the subject. Based on three Zion psalms (Pss 46:7; 48:5–7; 76:4, 6–9), Rohland identified a cluster of motifs that are often connected with the Zion tradition. These are:

1. Zion is the peak of Zaphon, the highest mountain (Ps 48:3);
2. The river of paradise flows from Zion (46:5);
3. Yahweh battled and defeated the chaotic flood waters of Zion (46:3);
4. Yahweh defeated the kings and nations at Zion (46:7; 48:5–7; 76:4, 6–7);[29]
5. The nations make a pilgrimage to Zion.[30]

For Rohland, the central feature of the tradition is the fourth motif, the *Völkerkampf* motif: "war of the nations." In the *Völkerkampf*, Yahweh defeats earthly kingdoms that besiege Zion's gates.[31] His victory comes through terror (Ps 48:4–6) or reproach (Pss 46; 76:7) and ultimately puts an end to war as he destroys military weapons (Ps 76:4).[32]

Like any topic in biblical studies, some scholars have vehemently leveled criticism against Rohland's conclusions from several fronts. For instance, Poulsen complains that the data set Rohland utilized to enumerate the motifs is insufficient (i.e. the number of texts: Pss 46; 48; 76).[33] He suggests we expand the data space to include the dynamism of the tradition in the prophetic literature.[34] Ollenburger also notes that "these [Pss 46; 48; 76] are not the only texts in which Zion functions as a symbol, and these Psalms are not . . . systematic expositions of a theological doctrine."[35] Renz observes that Rohland's list only includes motifs connected with the divine mountain

---

28. Poulsen, *Representing Zion*, 32.
29. Rohland, "Die Bedeutung der Erwählungstradition Israels," 141–142.
30. In his 1957 article, Hans Wildberger followed Rohland's list but added a fifth element, the Völkerwallfahrt, (the pilgrimage of the nations to Zion). Wildberger, "Die Volkerwallfahrt zum Zion," 62–81.
31. Rohland, "Die Bedeutung der Erwählungstradition Israels," 142.
32. Rohland, 142.
33. Poulsen, *Representing Zion*, 11.
34. Poulsen, 11.
35. Ollenburger, *Zion*, 17.

from Canaanite texts and neglects those from earlier Israelite traditions.[36] He thus concludes that the list "does not reflect the historical nature of the election of Zion."[37] Despite the criticism, Rohland's motifs are still invaluable as foundational elements of the Zion traditions.

Besides Rohland's motifs, J. J. M. Roberts has presented his own definition of the Zion tradition. In his influential article, Roberts claims that the two fundamental features of the tradition are that Yahweh is the great king (e.g. Pss 46:5; 48:3; 47:3) and that Yahweh chose Zion as his dwelling place (e.g. Ps 78:68–69; Isa 14:13; 28:16).[38] He further enumerates several subsidiary motifs associated with these fundamental conceptions of the Zion tradition. Some of these subsidiary themes associated with Zion are: Mount Zion is the highest of all mountains and the source of blessings (Pss 46:4; 48:12–14; 78:68-69; 132:13–18; 133:1–3; 147:12–20); Yahweh's presence ensures the security of Zion (Pss 48:3–7; 76:1–12; 96:6); nations will make pilgrimage to Zion to pay tribute to the great king (Ps 76:11–13); Zion's inhabitants must be fit to live in Yahweh's presence (Pss 15; 24:3–4; 101:8).[39] For our purposes, the last subsidiary motif concerning the fitness of Zion's inhabitants informs our understanding of Micah 6–7.

Similarly, Levenson offers three theological motifs in his treatment of the Zion tradition – namely, the enthronement of Yahweh after victory, the election of Zion and David, and the visions of peace.[40] Renz also provides a list of motifs associated with the Zion tradition. However, his list focuses on particular designations concerning Yahweh and motifs from the ark traditions, rather than Zion. His list includes the designation of Yahweh as יהוה צבאות and as "(El) Elyon," the connection of Yahweh with the cherubim, the portrayal of Yahweh as king, Yahweh's כבוד, and Yahweh's footstool.[41]

Recent studies reject the foregoing narrow views of a Zion tradition as a fixed concept of ideas with a fixed content. Poulsen challenges this limited view and argues that we ought to look at the defeat of Zion as well, rather

---

36. Renz, "Use of the Zion Tradition," 80–81.
37. Renz, 81.
38. Roberts, "Zion," 332.
39. Roberts, 338–343.
40. Levenson, "Zion Traditions," 1099–1101.
41. Renz, "Use of the Zion Tradition," 82–83.

than just focusing on Zion's inviolability and its victories.[42] Lois K. Fuller Dow shares a similar concern. She states:

> In most of these studies, not enough emphasis is given to the fact that Jerusalem/Zion has a dual role in the Old Testament of being *both* inviolable cosmic mountain of God *and* capital city of sinful people vulnerable to God's judgment. The tendency is always to concentrate on one aspect or the other. The interplay of these two roles shapes the theology of the city that emerges when Israel contemplates the exile. According to the prophets, their seeming incompatibility will finally be resolved by a divine transformation of human nature.[43]

Dynamic Zion tradition

In contrast to the classical Zion tradition, which mainly draws from a limited set of Psalms, the dynamic Zion tradition demands that we expand the context to include the entire prophetic corpus. As Ollenburger points out:

> Interpretation of the Zion symbol cannot be restricted only to those texts that display the principal motifs of what has been identified as the "Zion tradition," nor can it be restricted to those texts which explicitly mention Zion or Jerusalem. It must rather be expanded to a range of texts which form the network of relationships within which Zion functions as the central symbol.[44]

The expansion of the context to include the prophets brings the central claim of the dynamic Zion tradition into sharper relief. The prophets indicted Jerusalem (Zion) of its sins and pronounced its defeat and destruction (e.g. Amos 2:4–5; Isa 3:1, 8; 5:3; Jer 1:3, 15–18). Such a view was in concert with the covenantal relationship between Yahweh and Israel. Yahweh had made demands upon his people, which carried consequences for disobedience. Because the prophets understood that Yahweh did not guarantee protection to an immoral people, they challenged and contradicted their audience's popular misconceptions about the inviolability of Zion. However, despite

---

42. Poulsen, *Representing Zion*, 72.
43. Dow, *Images of Zion*, 27.
44. Ollenburger, *Zion*, 20.

Zion's destiny, the hope for a restored and glorified Zion was not lost. It is this nexus of judgment and restoration of Zion that stands as an important organizing concept of the dynamic Zion tradition.[45] In short, the dynamic Zion tradition constitutes a confluence of different theologies or traditions regarding the destruction, restoration, and maintenance of Zion.

In his investigation of the image of Zion in the prophetic literature, Poulsen notices "two main perceptions of Zion, which stand in structural tension with each other: Zion as the last bastion and Zion as a place which is destroyed and rebuilt."[46] Of course, the former image is the classical Zion tradition, while the latter is what he calls the dynamic Zion tradition: "It is destroyed and abandoned, yet eventually rebuilt and repopulated."[47] Unfortunately, Stansell only recognizes the judgment aspect of the dynamic Zion tradition because he limits his analysis to what he deems the authentic text of Micah (Micah 1–3).[48]

The schema Poulsen charts fits well the covenantal pattern of sin, judgment, and restoration stemming from the Pentateuch. In fact, one can make a strong case that the two main perceptions of Zion, which Poulsen promotes, are effectively an application of Levitcus 26 to Zion.[49] Pate and others note, "In Leviticus the paradigm of sin-exile-restoration is clearly presented."[50] Specifically, Levitcus 26 correlates obedience and disobedience to blessings and curses, respectively. Yahweh threatens Israel with total destruction of their cities and high places as well as exile from the land for persistent violations of their covenant obligations (Lev 26:30–33). However, judgment is not the whole story. Yahweh also promises to restore the nation back to the land upon genuine repentance (Lev 26:40, 42, 44). This is in keeping with his faithfulness to the Abrahamic and Mosaic covenants (vv. 42–45).[51]

Kaiser concurs. He states, "The programmatic statements found in Leviticus 26 and Deuteronomy 28 are useful for interpreting all the prophets. Both of these chapters clearly lay down the alternative prospects: increased

---

45. Tan, *Zion Traditions*, 24–25.
46. Poulsen, *Representing Zion*, 189.
47. Poulsen, 189.; Marrs, "Back to the Future," 82–83, 91–93.
48. Stansell, *Micah and Isaiah*, 40–52.
49. Pate et al., *Story of Israel*, 18–23; Hamilton, *God's Glory*, 49–51; Kaminski, *Was Noah Good?*, passim.
50. Pate et al., *The Story of Israel*, 42.
51. Pate et al., 42

degrees of blessing or judgment."[52] Mark F. Rooker also agrees. He writes, "The wellbeing of the nation of Israel at any given time in their subsequent history would be defined in the terms of the teaching of Leviticus 26 and Deuteronomy 28."[53] For our purpose, the application of Levitcus 26:15-44 to Zion is essentially the dynamic Zion tradition. In particular, the defeat and restoration of Zion for idolatry and injustice (e.g. Mic 1:5, 9, 12; 3:9-4:5) – in fulfillment of the covenant curses in Levitcus 26:14-45 – is essentially what Poulsen calls the dynamic Zion tradition.

Davidic tradition

While the foregoing discussions on the classical and dynamic Zion traditions are commendable, an obvious gap remains. For the most part, the studies focus only on the election of Zion and the city's relationship to Yahweh. However, the Zion traditions also need to take into account the election of David and his relationship to both Zion and Yahweh. Roberts, with regret, confesses that "the one glaring gap that I see in my earlier treatment of the Zion tradition is a failure to treat adequately the position of the Davidic monarch with that tradition."[54] Without proposing another category for the Zion traditions, we accept Robert's modification and include the election of David as one of the major components of the classical Zion tradition.

In any event, the Zion/Davidic tradition is the classical Zion tradition modified to include the election traditions about David and his descendants as Yahweh's vicegerents (e.g. Pss 2:6; 89:29; 132:10-13). According to Hayes, the election of David and that of Zion "were taken up immediately at the royal court and proclaimed as part of the redemptive Heilsgeschichte and royal ideology."[55] This was done to provide divine explanation for David's rise to power (1 Sam 16:14-2 Sam 5:12) and his dynasty's succession story (2 Sam 6:23-20:26; 1 Kgs 1-2).[56] Just as Zion is described in lofty language, so too is the Davidic king. For instance, Yahweh promises to make him his firstborn

---

52. Kaiser, *Toward Rediscovering the Old Testament*, 195.
53. Rooker, *Leviticus*, 319.
54. Roberts, "Solomon's Jerusalem," 165; Roberts, "Zion," 332-343; Humphreys, *Crisis and Story*, 55-64.
55. Hayes, "Tradition of Zion's Inviolability," 420.
56. Hayes, 420.

and "the highest among the kings of the earth" (עֶלְיוֹן לְמַלְכֵי־אָרֶץ) (Ps 89:27), just as Yahweh is עֶלְיוֹן (Gen 14:19; Pss 18:13; 46:4).[57]

Furthermore, the Davidic king is also described as the son of God (Ps 2:7). In this context, Yahweh's decree of sonship is an act of adoption. It signifies the king's unique status as Yahweh's earthly viceroy, which meant that he participated in the divine rule on earth. This act of adoption was confirmed on the day of the king's coronation.[58] What is more, the king's unique status had certain privileges. For instance, the son is able to request divine blessings and protection (Ps 21).[59] Yahweh would put off any opposition to the king, whether from within the kingdom or from without (e.g. Ps 2:2–8; 89:27; 110:3).[60] Anyone who dared challenge the Davidic king was challenging Yahweh's sovereignty (1 Sam 24:7, 11; 26:9, 11, 16). As Roberts insightfully observes, "such theological claims could be used in self-serving ways to legitimate abusive and unjust exercise of such power."[61]

On the other hand, the unique position from which the Davidic king benefited had certain obligations. Because of his privileged position, the Davidic ruler was required to sponsor, construct, and maintain Yahweh's temple (e.g. 2 Sam 7:13). Furthermore, Yahweh expected the Davidic kings to promote social justice and righteousness in the land (Pss 72:1–4; 101:1–2; 1 Kgs 10:9),[62] because the sovereign king himself was righteous and just (Ps 89:14; 99:4).[63] As Roberts points out, "One of the king's primary roles, according to this ideal, was, like God, to deliver the poor and oppressed from the hand of the powerful oppressor (Ps 72:12-14)."[64]

Alongside these tasks, a major responsibility for the Davidic king was to participate in the nation's military campaigns in order to maintain Yahweh's land (e.g. Pss 2:9–12; 89:21–38) and to extend his kingdom to "the ends of the earth" (e.g. Pss 2:8; 72:8). Some passages describe the military campaigns of the Davidic king in mythological terms. For instance, Yahweh assists the king

---

57. Chalmers, *Interpreting the Prophets*, 83.
58. Chalmers, 83.
59. Chalmers, 83.
60. Roberts, "Enthronement of Yhwh and David," 682.
61. Roberts, 682.
62. Roberts, 683.
63. Chalmers, *Interpreting the Prophets*, 84.
64. Roberts, "Enthronement of Yhwh and David," 683.

by putting David's hand on the sea and the rivers, Yahweh's two cosmogonic foes (Ps 89:26).[65] This should not startle our modern sensibilities because some theophanic passages identify enemy kings and hostile nations with primeval chaos (e.g. Ps 46:3–7; Isa 17:12–13). Viewed as such, "the victories of the Davidic king are simply a participation in and reinstatement of God's primeval victories."[66] These militaristic aspects of Yahweh as the divine warrior and of the Davidic king will inform our reading of Micah 1:2–5:14 in the subsequent chapters.

Analyzing Traditions in Micah

Definitions

We close the chapter by highlighting how we will identify and analyze the Zion/Davidic and related traditions in Micah. One of the more prominent modes of comparative studies involves intertextuality, a catchall term used for various tactics for reading texts in relation to other texts.[67] Jonathan Culler cautions that intertextuality "is a difficult concept to use because of the vast and undefined discursive space it designates."[68] We share Culler's concern. A survey of some biblical studies on intertextuality shows that the field lacks unanimity regarding a universally acknowledged set of definitions, terminology, and methodology.[69]

Despite these concerns, a subfield of intertextuality that has been recently dominating biblical studies is literary allusions. Earl Miner understood an allusion as a "tacit reference to another literary work."[70] In the 1970s, other

---

65. Roberts, 679–680.

66. Roberts, 679.

67. Kelly, "Intertextuality and Allusion," 1–4; Broyles, "Traditions, Intertextuality, Canon," 167.

68. Culler, *Pursuit of Signs*, 109.

69. Without trying to add more confusion to an already muddled field, it is beyond the extent of the present study to attempt a detailed exploration of the phenomenon of intertextuality. Fortunately, in studying the topic of intertextuality, I have benefited from the introductory study by Graham Allen, *Intertextuality*; see also Still and Worton, "Introduction," 1–45; Plett, "Intertextualities," 3–29; Juvan, *History and Poetics of Intertextuality*; Clayton and Rothstein, *Influence and Intertextuality*; Fewell, *Reading Between Texts*; Barton, "Déjà Lu," 1–16; Tull, "Intertextuality and the Hebrew Scriptures," 59–90; Miller, "Intertextuality in Old Testament Research," 283–309.

70. Miner, "Allusion," 18.

influential literary theorists reformulated the study of allusions.[71] Unsatisfied with Miner's formulation of an allusion as an indirect, casual, or brief reference, Ziva Ben-Porat argued that a

> literary allusion is a device for the simultaneous activation of two texts. The activation is achieved through the manipulation of a special signal: a sign (simple or complex) in a given text characterized by an additional larger referent. This referent is always an independent text. The simultaneous activation of the two texts thus connected results in the formation of intertextual patterns whose nature cannot be predetermined.[72]

Porat's influential definition has been adapted and utilized in studies of innerbiblical exegesis and allusion. In these studies, some scholars confine the literary allusion exclusively to the alluding text and the evoked text (often a unique text).[73] Furthermore, the marker element in these studies is usually a clear-cut verbal expression of the marked element. To be sure, this approach to allusions and its criteria for discerning them holds its prideful place in most biblical studies. However, from the perspective of our present needs, the approach is inadequate for analyzing allusions to cultural traditions, which comprise a constellation of texts. The activation of only two texts according to Porat's schema is not a viable hermeneutic for allusions to traditions.

The observations above draw attention to yet another leading literary theorist, Carmela Perri. Perri, like Perot, also challenged and rejected Miner's formulation of an allusion as a tacit reference. Yet, unlike Porat, Perri aptly argued that the alluding marker activates "one or more texts outside its context."[74] Perri's more nuanced definition does not limit the connection in an allusion to just two texts. Her formulation suggests that from its early conception the study of allusions was not limited to the activation of only two texts. More importantly, her understanding of the marker as polyvalent opens a welcome path suitable for studying allusions to cultural traditions.

---

71. In this study, we use literary allusion and allusion interchangeably.

72. Ben-Porat, "Poetics of Literary Allusion," 107–108.

73. For example, Sommer, *Prophet Reads Scripture*, 6–31; Kelly, "Intertextuality and Allusion," 132; Jauhiainen, *Use of Zechariah in Revelation*, 29–32.

74. Perri, "On Alluding," 295.

Some biblical scholars are beginning to note that literary allusions to cultural traditions work differently than what we might have been accustomed to. In a recent publication, Abner Chou has voiced concern in the way biblical scholars approach literary allusions. In his words, studies in inner-biblical exegesis "fall somewhat short since they often imply a one to one textual correlation as opposed to the fact that a text could be interwoven with a network of texts."[75] For him, the prophets in particular did not only allude to a single passage but rather to multiple texts and also to the main ideas of a tradition in a set of texts.[76]

Therefore, based on the formulations of Perri and the insightful encouragement of Chou, an allusion to cultural traditions is an attempt by an author to direct his readers to time-honored texts, "knowledge of which contributes to the meaning for the reader."[77] Thus, when Micah used cultural traditions, he was not necessarily alluding to a unique text but to a set of scattered texts that preserve themes and motifs of a particular tradition. As shown earlier, key themes of the Zion/Davidic traditions appear in several texts and not in a single text.

Shared and Intended Contexts

At this juncture, it is prudent that we introduce the notions of shared and intended contexts: notions we find germane to the discussion of allusions to cultural traditions. The constellation of texts that comprises a tradition provides a context for interpreting the alluding text. When both the author and the audience are aware of this context, we refer to it as the shared context. Besides the shared context, we can also speak of the author's intended context. According to Harriet Hill, the intended context is the context that the audience believes is shared and the author actually shares.[78] It is the intended context that helps elucidate the author's intended meaning. Later on, we will detail how the intended context may be constructed from the shared context.

Since effective communication within a culture requires a stable body of established terminology (common words, phrases, and concepts), the

---

75. Chou, *Hermeneutics of the Biblical Writers*, 21n44.

76. Chou, 39–40, 53–58.

77. Hughes, *Scriptural Allusions and Exegesis*, 52; Broyles, "Traditions, Intertextuality, Canon," 159.

78. Hill, *Bible at Cultural Crossroads*, 27–29.

question we need to address is whether Micah and his audience shared the same cultural assumptions. In general, it is not far-fetched to assume that both the biblical authors and their audience were aware of their cultural traditions. For instance, Psalm 78 – a protracted recounting of ancient Israel's cultural traditions[79] – shows that some traditions were handed down through the generations orally (vv. 3–4, 6). Since the traditions were to some extent disseminated orally, we can assume that the majority of the common people within ancient Israel knew of these traditions.

As a result, where authors assume that they share the same intended context with their audiences, they do not communicate everything in detail. They only write enough to stimulate in their audiences' minds some information they think the audiences has. For the audience to understand fully the authors' messages, they infer the meaning from the assumed context. For instance, Micah's interlocutor mentioned that the Lord was in their midst, to which Micah inferred that it pointed to the standing temple (3:11). In other words, Micah's interlocutor did not exactly specify what the Lord's presence entailed, but Micah knew that it referred to "the mountain of the house" (הר הבית) (3:12). Both Micah and his interlocutor shared the assumption about the temple tradition which held that the standing temple was a sign of Yahweh's presence among his people. Hence, Yahweh's presence meant security.

In other cases, where the authors think their audiences lack or have forgotten the contextual background, they remind their audience and direct them to the correct intended context. For example, Yahweh reminded Judah's leaders that they ought to know the proper way to administer justice (Mic 3:1; cf. Deut 17:3–7, 8–13). Yahweh also exhorted Israel to remember the wilderness traditions about King Balak (Mic 6:5; cf. Num 22–24). The assumption here is that Yahweh expected Israel to know about these traditions. On another occasion, a worshiper thought that a large quantity and a special quality of burnt offering were enough to appease Yahweh (Mic 6:6–7). Yahweh had to remind the misguided worshiper that genuine worship is only possible in an environment marked by justice, kindness, and humility (v. 8). As these examples demonstrate, authors have a specific context in mind, and they

---

79. The cultural traditions discussed in the psalm include the exodus (Ps 78:11–13; 42–53), wilderness traditions (vv. 14–40), conquest/settlement traditions (vv. 54–67), and Zion/Davidic traditions (vv. 68–72).

design their messages in a way that guides the audience to that intended context. From these examples, we may safely assume that Micah's audience knew the cultural traditions of ancient Israel.

Criteria for Discerning Intertextual Allusions

Crucial for our purposes is the nature of the marker element that directs readers to the shared context or alludes to aspects of a cultural tradition.[80] Because the marker element evokes a constellation of texts, it takes a different form from a marker used in allusions to a unique text. In allusions to cultural traditions, the marker does not have to match the marked elements in the evoked texts precisely. As we will demonstrate shortly, the marker and marked elements take various forms (e.g. synonymous terms, stereotypical language, and formulaic expressions). This kind of language is the language of cultural traditions.

With that said, a fundamental issue at hand is the recognition of potential allusions to traditions. How does one identify and validate an allusion to cultural traditions when one lives centuries after an author? What constitute sufficient indicators of an allusion? Should precise verbal parallels be the sole determiner of an allusion? Should we ignore similar structures, patterns, or combinations of conceptual ideas lacking in precise vocabulary?[81] Thus, a brief discussion of the ongoing scholarly debate on criteria for identifying allusions may sharpen our understanding of the nature of the marker.

Although there is a healthy and ongoing proliferation of studies attending to allusions, a consensus on the criteria for identifying potential allusions is lacking. Over the centuries, scholars have offered a plethora of criteria, but still disagreements on what constitute an allusion hamper progress.[82] The task lacks scientific argumentation, and, as a mere human art, what one scholar deems an allusion another demurs.[83] Rather than argue for a one-size-fits-all criteria for allusions, Joseph R. Kelly recommends that scholars should devise

---

80. Jael, "Sociorhetorical Intertexture," 153; Walton, *Ancient Near Eastern Thought*, 19–22; Middleton, *Liberating Image*, 62–65.

81. Hughes, *Scriptural Allusions and Exegesis*, 46.

82. See Hays, *Echoes of Scripture*, 29–32; Thompson, *Clothed with Christ*, 31–36; Paulien, "Elusive Allusions," 40–43; Leonard, "Identifying Inner-Biblical Allusions," 246.

83. Hutton, "Isaiah 51:9–11," 277.

specific criteria aimed at particular texts and adapt general criteria from other scholars only as initial guides.[84]

On these suggestions, the present study proposes criteria specifically tailored to Micah's use of cultural traditions by critically drawing from Sommer, Paulien, Hays, and Leonard.[85] Since their criteria are somewhat redundant, we could refine them. A profitable place to start is to streamline Hays's influential criteria in accordance with Pattemore's approach. Pattemore observes the redundancy in Hays's criteria and astutely narrows them to just two – namely, accessibility and contextual effects. An overarching criterion to intertextuality is that accessibility of a shared context determines the strength of an allusion.[86] Accessibility leads to an optimally valid interpretation. In this light, we identify the cultural traditions in Micah using verbal, thematic/conceptional, and contextual parallels between the alluding text and the evoked texts.

Verbal parallels

A marker that is indispensable to Micah's allusions to tradition is shared vocabulary or verbal parallels. Hill and Leonard concur that the entry point for identifying an allusion is shared vocabulary.[87] Its attractive feature is its ability to soothe the sting of subjectivity to some degree. Even though scholars may split hairs over the number of words in a marker or phrase that count as a valid marker, most would agree that shared vocabulary is the most important marker towards establishing a potential literary allusion.

So, what features in shared vocabulary should one look for? For instance, how many parallel terms are necessary to validate claims of an allusion? Sommer points out that the marker element "may be a poetic line or sentence or phrase, or it may consist of a motif, a rhythmic pattern, an idea, or even the form of the work or its title."[88] In the example of Wordsworth's poem that he discusses, Sommer explains that markers may include words, images, setting,

---

84. Kelly, "Intertextuality and Allusion," 155.

85. Paulien, "Covenant in the Old and New Testaments," 42–43; Sommer, *Prophet Reads Scripture*; Hays, *Echoes of Scripture*, 29–32; Leonard, "Identifying Inner-Biblical Allusions," 246.

86. Pattemore, "Relevance Theory," 47; Hill, *Bible at Cultural Crossroads*, 32–35. Also see Furlong, "Relevance Theory and Literary Interpretation," 196.

87. Hill, *Bible at Cultural Crossroads*, 32–33; Leonard, "Identifying Inner-Biblical Allusions," 246.

88. Sommer, *Prophet Reads Scripture*, 11.

and theme.[89] In a recent study, Jonathan G. Kline argues that even consonantal paronomasia (i.e. soundplay) can function as a marker of literary allusion to earlier traditions.[90] What Sommer and Kline, as well as Broyles, are hinting at is that markers come in various forms and lengths, and can be simple or complex. As such, interpreters must be alert to any marking elements in the specific texts they are working with. Simply stated, each text has its own unique markers and must be approached on a case-by-case basis. As such, it does not necessarily follow that criteria developed for allusions to a unique text work for allusions to cultural traditions.

With regard to the number of terms required to declare something an allusion, Beth L. Tanner is content with a single word whereas Paulien suggests that a minimum of two words is necessary.[91] Thompson suggests that, as a rule, the more the number of shared terms between two texts, the higher the likelihood for an allusion.[92] From a cultural tradition standpoint, the number of words in a marker is not a pressing issue. Hays assumes that a quotation, an allusion, or an echo each lie along a continuum on the intertextual plane, which moves from the explicit to the subliminal.[93] As such, the weaker the shared context the louder the marker becomes.

In other words, if an audience has a weak awareness of a cultural tradition then an author will employ a quotation, because it "requires a more substantial introduction to guide the reader towards optimal relevance."[94] The converse is equally true. If people share a strong awareness of a cultural tradition, then the author utilizes an allusion with only a few keywords. As Pattemore concludes:

> Thus, whether the relationship of a statement to a previous text is an "informal quotation," an "allusion" or an "echo" is scarcely important. What is important is whether the author has made manifest only the assumptions expressed by the statement . . .

---

89. Sommer, 11.
90. Kline, *Allusive Soundplay*, 1–17.
91. Tanner, *Book of Psalms*, 41.
92. Thompson, *Clothed with Christ*, 31.
93. Hays, *Echoes of Scripture*, 23.
94. Perry, "Relevance Theory and Intertextuality," 218.

and those entailed by the immediate context, or in addition, the assumption that he used a particular source for his language.[95]

For our purposes, Perri's, Chou's, and Pattemore's nuanced understandings of the flexibility of a marker are appropriate for the identification of traditions in Micah. A keyword or phrase is enough to evoke a tradition. For instance, when Micah mentions the simple word "my people" (עַמִּי) (e.g. Mic 3:2, 3, 5; 6:3, 5), he is using more than a term of endearment. Rather, he is using a shorthand for the covenant formula, which alludes to the covenantal traditions comprising several texts and not necessarily to a unique text (e.g. Gen 17:7; Exod 6:7).

Consider also Micah's accusation of Judah's rich elites. The single keyword "covet" (חמד) (Mic 2:1) is enough to trigger the contextual framework of the Sinai tradition's prohibition against covetousness (e.g. Exod 20:17; Deut 5:21). Because this aspect of their cultural context is well-known, it is easily accessible with little processing effort.[96] As a result, Micah's accusation achieves a valid interpretation. For a people in a covenantal relationship, a possible effect for Micah's audience is an awareness of covenant breach, which contradicts their present course of action. Hence, the length of a marker is not a limiting factor in identifying a tradition in the book of Micah.

In another place, Broyles notes that "a tradition may be identified by a constellation of motifs (e.g. recurring phrases) that center on notable persons, events, places, institutions, symbols, or rituals."[97] Thus, Micah's mere mention of "Bethlehem" (בית־לחם) (Mic 5:2) evokes the Davidic traditions – specifically, the roots of David (1 Sam 16:1; cf. Ruth 4:11). By emphasizing the place name of the origins of David, Micah is essentially saying that the future ruler of Judah will be David *redivivus*.

In addition, a point we need to reemphasize is that the form of the marker and marked elements does not have to be precise and can be of varying lengths. Michael A. Lyons makes a valid case in his studies of Ezekiel's allusions to the holiness code (Lev 17–26). He points out that inversion, splitting, or redistribution of the marker elements are valid techniques an author may

---

95. Pattemore, "Relevance Theory," 52.

96. On Micah's audience's awareness of the traditions, see our section on "Shared and Intended Contexts" on pages 77–79.

97. Broyles, "Traditions, Intertextuality, and Canon," 159.

utilize to aid readers in recognizing an allusion.⁹⁸ In our case, some scholars may likely agree that the rhetorical question, "Who is a God like you?" (מִי־אֵל כָּמוֹךָ) (Mic 7:18a), parallels "Who is like you among the gods, O Lord?" (מִי־כָמֹכָה בָּאֵלִם יְהוָה) (Exod 15:11). There is enough in the marker element for Micah's audience and readers to recognize that the prophet has the exodus traditions in mind. Altogether, it is evident that identifying allusions to ancient traditions in Micah is not as stringent as one might think at first blush.

Contextual parallels

Hill argues that shared vocabulary is only an address, an entry point into a network of assumptions.⁹⁹ Even after the audience has discerned potential shared vocabulary and before the analysis proceeds, a prerequisite is to determine the specific intended context the utterance suggests. This is particularly crucial in instances where the literary marker is polyvalent; that is, the marker points to a plethora of different contexts. Tradition, with its stereotypical language, has such polyvalent markers. In such instances, the search for a relevant interpretation guides us towards the intended context beginning with the most accessible shared context.

Take, for instance, Micah's behavior of walking barefoot and naked as he laments the disaster befalling Samaria and Jerusalem (Mic 1:8). Miller identifies the passage as a funeral lament.¹⁰⁰ In his own words, Miller further suggests that the term "naked" (עָרוֹם) (Mic 1:8) "evokes the condition of the primeval man and woman in Eden (Gen 2:25; 3:7, 10, 11)."¹⁰¹ Contrary to Miller, the contextual assumptions suggest that the prophet places this act not within a simple funeral lament but a city lament genre. That is, the prophet is lamenting the doom of Samaria and that which is about to befall the towns of Judah and Zion (Mic 1:9–16).¹⁰²

---

98. Lyons, "Marking Innerbiblical Allusion," 245.
99. Hill, *Bible at Cultural Crossroads*, 33; Jodłowiec, *Challenges*, 38–39.
100. Miller, "Micah and Its Literary Environment," 103, 222.
101. Miller, 205.
102. Hillers, *Micah*, 22; Also see Carr, *Formation of the Hebrew Bible*, 229–234. F. W. Dobbs-Allsopp argued that ancient Israel had a city lament genre that was comparable to but independent of the Mesopotamian city lament. Some shared themes in the genre include the destruction of cities, destruction of temple and sanctuaries, destructive divine power and abandonment, taunting of the passerby, disturbance of social order, and exile. For Dobbs-

Furthermore, Micah's symbolic act of walking naked and barefooted most likely parallels Isaiah's act rather than the nakedness of Adam and Eve. Both prophets used similar phrases to describe their symbolic actions – namely, "barefoot and naked" (שׁילל וערום) (Mic 1:8) and "naked and barefoot" (ערום ויחף) (Isa 20:3). What is more, note that the terms do not have to be precise in order to declare a valid allusion to a shared tradition (a symbolic act that speaks of an imminent exile following judgment).[103] The prophets employed synonyms for "barefoot" (i.e. שׁילל and ויחף). The term ערום also appears in inverted order. As this example demonstrates, there is more to an allusion than precise vocabulary.

In short, the recovery of the intended context (i.e. the city lament genre rather than a funeral lament) allows Micah's audience to infer that the symbolic act points to the coming captivity with very little effort.[104] Here, the context allows the explicit sense of the symbolic act from Isaiah to flow and fill the interpretive gap in Micah. Towards the close of this chapter, we will revisit this important issue of selecting Micah's intended context from the wider shared context.

Thematic parallels

Besides verbal and contextual parallels, texts are also connected via thematic or conceptual elements.[105] Although shared vocabulary or phrases make the evocation of a previous text more certain, one must broaden the search to include other elements or complexes of elements in a given text that may act as markers to a referent text. In the main, thematic parallels among texts involve ideas or concepts that go beyond specific verbal parallels. Of course, in cases where verbal parallels are certain, thematic parallels may play a supportive role. On the other hand, when dealing with stock or metaphoric vocabulary,

---

Allsopp, Amos 5:1–3, 16–17, and possibly 18–21 are examples of the city lament genre. Dobbs-Allsopp, *Weep, O Daughter of Zion*, 143–146; Greenstein, "Lamentation and Lament," 67–84.

103. Note that cultural practices, rituals, customs, and beliefs are all part of a cultural tradition. See our definition of tradition on page 63. Furthermore, it is not quite correct to argue that this cultural practice is a mourning rite. On the contrary, in times of mourning, people dress in sackcloth rather than walk around naked (e.g. Gen 37:34; 1 Kgs 21:27; Joel 1:8, 13).

104. Hillers, *Micah*, 23.

105. Paulien, "Covenant," 41–42.

it is often difficult to pinpoint a specifically evoked text.[106] In such cases, the vocabulary might suggest a theme belonging to the larger ancient tradition that an author might be evoking.[107]

For instance, the phrase "and the people will stream to it" (ונהרו עליו עמים) (Mic 4:1–2) may seem strange to modern readers who may be unfamiliar with ancient Israel's traditions. However, for those familiar with the ancient traditions, in particular Micah's audience, the phrase figuratively speaks of the pilgrimage of the nations to a restored Mount Zion. This is a common theme in the Zion/Davidic traditions (e.g. Ps 84:5–7).[108] An audience familiar with how the ancient divine warrior's script works can easily discern from the immediate context (i.e. Mic 3:12; 4:1–5) that, following the warrior's victory and the rebuilding of the temple, pilgrims march to the temple to pay homage to the victor king (e.g. Exod 15:17–18).

Putting It Together

The lucid guidelines by Broyles and Chalmers, which describe a three-stage process of analyzing traditions, are adequate and adaptable for the present project.[109] First, we will identify the marker in the alluding text. In particular, we will attend to several key themes, loaded words, and phrases that speak of Yahweh as the great king, Yahweh's choice of Zion, and Yahweh's choice of the Davidic dynasty. In addition, we will also pursue language that speaks of Zion's future inhabitants in relation to Yahweh's demand for justice. Because we are dealing with tradition, on most occasions the marker element (i.e. the

---

106. Here we need to be careful, because we might be dealing with idioms that have no allusive function.

107. As Donna N. Fewell has ably illustrated, one way to construe the book of Esther is to attend to thematic links it shares with the book of Exodus: For instance, the human protagonists in both texts are foreigners adopted into the royal family, who hesitantly turned into redeemers. In addition, in both texts, an oppressed people receive deliverance. Following their deliverance, the people observe a religious celebration (Passover and Purim), which becomes a written tradition to be observed by future generations. Yahweh's hand is ever present at every turn in the exploits of Moses and Aaron in the exodus narrative. By contrast, in Esther, Yahweh's absence does not deter Mordecai's and Esther's determination to liberate their people. Fewell, "Introduction," 12–13. Also see Miller, "Intertextuality in Old Testament Research," 295–296. Miller gives other examples of thematic connections between texts in cases where verbal correspondences are lacking. For instance, Psalm 1 and Deuteronomy 30 share thematic connections and so do Genesis 22 and Judges 11.

108. Roberts, "Zion," 332, 342.

109. Broyles, "Traditions, Intertextuality, and Canon," 159; Chalmers, *Interpreting the Prophets*, 85.

trigger word[s] that point to the tradition) will be polyvalent, serving as an address to a network of contextual assumptions (i.e. a mutual cultural context that is built on many texts).[110] As we will see shortly, on some occasions Micah guides us towards his intended context.

Besides these themes or motifs, we will also pay particular attention to the recurring dynamic Zion tradition pattern. This pattern is at the core of Micah's rhetorical strategy. Micah's rhetorical strategy is the crude but reshaped pattern adopted from the dynamic Zion tradition: the introduction of a major object (theme) → delay of its fate → judgment on the object → restoration/renewal of the object.[111] Micah unmistakably accuses Zion (introduction of the object/theme) of being the "high places" (במות) of Judah (1:5), delays Zion's fate (1:6–3:11), and pronounces judgment on Zion (3:12). However, Yahweh will eventually rebuild Zion and its temple (4:1). As we will see, Micah skillfully utilizes this pattern of the transformation of Zion (Mic 1:5; 3:12; 4:1) paradigmatically to argue for the transformation of Zion's kingship as well (4:9–5:14).

The second step involves the evaluation of the cultural environment from the first step in order to construct a shared context between author and audience. In the first place, we concern ourselves with accessibility. The advantage of the idea of a shared context is that an audience does not have to search everywhere for contextual assumptions. Rather, they have access to that appropriate context which an author intends and can access it with little effort.[112] On this basis, the accessibility of contextual assumptions guides the audience towards the author's intended context.[113] There is then an attempt to establish

---

110. Chalmers, *Interpreting the Prophets*, 86.

111. Recall that Poulsen divides the dynamic Zion tradition into three stages: destruction, exile, and the return and new Zion. Poulsen, *Representing Zion*, 135. As we have already stated, Jenson suggests that the whole book of Micah follows a pattern of sin → judgment → restoration. Jenson, *Obadiah, Jonah, Micah*, 99; Pate et al., *The Story of Israel*, 91; Dow, *Images of Zion*, 99–100.

112. Chalmers explains that access to pertinent contexts was natural because the prophets and their audience had a "common frame of reference, a common way of viewing the world and a shared body of knowledge." Consequently, the existence of such shared knowledge suggests communication was possible without the need for specifying every detail. Hence, the marker element could be as simple as a single keyword. According to Chalmers, "Their mere mention would have triggered off a wealth of associations in the minds of the original hearers." Chalmers, *Interpreting the Prophets*, 85.

113. Hill, *Bible at Cultural Crossroads*, 32.

a shared context to guide both author and audience. For instance, here we will ask whether Micah had access to the theophanic tradition (Mic 1:3–4). The stereotypical nature of the theophanic tradition and Micah's knowledge of mountains as the abode of Yahweh (3:12–4:1) suggest that the prophet had access to the tradition. What about Micah's audience; did they have access to the tradition too? Micah's rejoinder to his interlocutor implies that they shared the same knowledge with Micah about the mountain motif (3:11).

In the second place, we will then attempt to construct and describe the intended context applicable for that particular utterance "because traditions are usually multidimensional [polyvalent], and the prophet may wish to evoke only part of these."[114] As Hill stresses, "Selecting the intended context is critical to understanding the intended meaning of an utterance. Although the context is not stated explicitly, it is not random. Speakers have a specific context in mind, and they design their message in a way that leads the hearer to that context."[115]

For instance, Micah's use of military terms in the theophanic imagery guides us towards the divine warrior tradition (1:3–4). As Micah provides more clues (or "contextual bridges," as Hill calls them), an interpreter may limit the context even further. For instance, Micah speaks of mountains melting at the advent of the divine warrior (1:4). By using the imagery of melting mountains, Micah effectively distinguishes his divine warrior tradition from those in which nature responds differently at the warrior's presence (e.g. Exod 15:8; Ps 77:16–18).

As depicted in figure 3.1, it is evident that Micah's intended context for the utterance in Micah 1:3–4 is a sub-subset of the mutual cultural environment. The context construction funnels from the wider theophany tradition to the divine warrior tradition and narrows to the mountain motif. Contrary to popular views, it is not quite correct to say that Micah's intended context is the general theophanic tradition. Instead, it is the divine warrior viewed in light of the mountain motif.

---

114. Chalmers, *Interpreting the Prophets*, 86.
115. Hill, *Bible at Cultural Crossroads*, 24, 27–34.

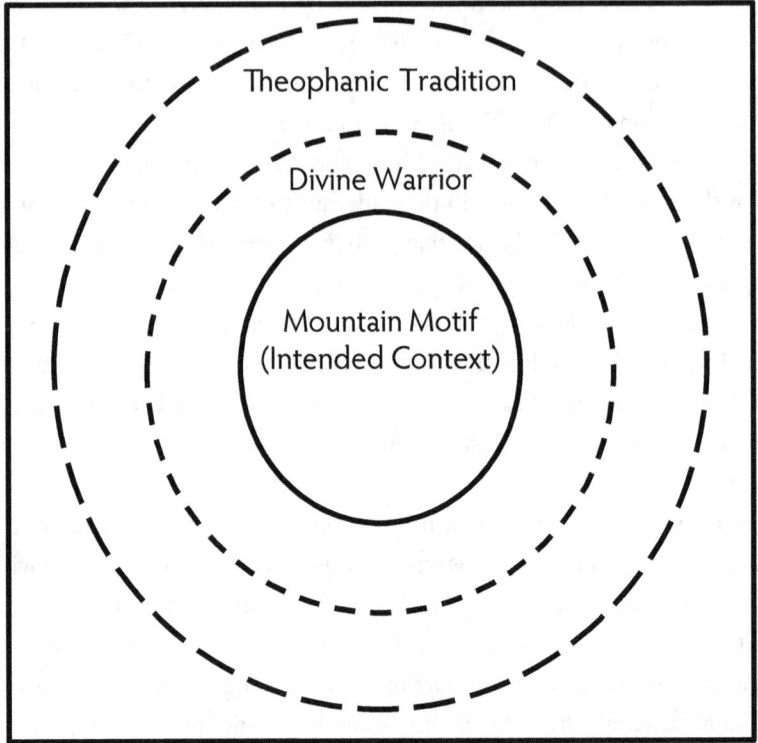

Figure 3.1: The Intended Context of Micah's Theophanic Tradition

In the third step, we identify how the prophet uses and develops the tradition.[116] This step involves interpreting the alluding text by reading it in the light of the intended context from the second step. We apply theological exegesis to the alluding marker to elucidate its major theological theme. Similarly, we will also elucidate a common theme from the evoked context (e.g. from those texts linked to the intended context). We will then attend to the cultural effects that may flow from the context to the alluding text. Chalmers mentions three such cultural effects. First, the prophet could conform to the

---

116. Chalmers, *Interpreting the Prophets*, 89.

tradition without considerable developments or alteration.[117] An example of this practice is Micah's allusion to the exodus and wilderness/conquest traditions (Mic 6:4–5). The prophet is simply trying to contrast Yahweh's faithfulness to the covenant relationships to Judah's unfaithfulness (6:1–8). Second, the prophet could continue the tradition but may recontextualize it to his context.[118] For instance, Micah alludes to the defeat of pharaoh's armies at the Red Sea. However, Micah reshapes the tradition and uses it to depict Yahweh's defeat of sin (7:19). Such usage underscores Micah's reshaping of a tradition to create his own unique message.[119] Finally, the prophet could contradict the tradition.[120] Broyles notes, "After identifying a tradition presupposed by a passage, we may discover that the tradition has been transformed or given a distinct twist from its regular, cultural usage."[121] For instance, Micah pronounces a scathing judgment on Zion (3:12). The long-standing assumption was that the temple, a symbol of Yahweh's presence among his people, guaranteed Zion's security. Micah's pronouncement clearly contradicts the classical traditions about Zion's inviolability (e.g. 3:11b).

According to Chalmers, "such changes are often important for discerning the prophet's message . . . [as such] we need to consider three related questions."[122] First, how has the prophet contradicted the traditional material? Second, what are the implications of such transformation? An implication of Micah's judgment against Zion is to convince the people to repent in order to avert disaster. If Yahweh can destroy his own temple, definitely he will not spare sinners. Third, what is the purpose of altering the traditions? For instance, what is the theological purpose of the divine warrior's devastation of the whole land including Zion (Mic 1:2–7, 3:12)? Apparently, Yahweh is actualizing the curses for covenant breach (Lev 26:14–39). As a result, this has implications for the fulfillment of the Abrahamic covenant (see Mic 7:20; Lev 26:42).

---

117. According to Chalmers, "Such use of the traditional material may be a means of establishing the veracity and/or authority of what the prophet is trying to communicate, as he or she is essentially drawing on well-established and generally accepted ideas." Chalmers, 89.

118. Chalmers, 90.

119. Chalmers, 90

120. Chalmers, 90

121. Broyles, "Traditions, Intertextuality, and Canon," 162.

122. Chalmers, *Interpreting the Prophets*, 90–91.

CHAPTER 4

Divine Sovereignty and Mount Zion (Micah 1:2–4:8)

Introduction

Bearing in mind the conclusions of the previous two chapters, the present chapter explores the multifaceted themes and motifs of the Zion/Davidic traditions that inform the concept of divine sovereignty in Micah 1:2–4:8. Two crucial themes towards this end are Yahweh as the great king and his choice of Zion. These two themes serve as vehicles for portraying Yahweh's sovereignty in Zion. Although Yahweh rules over creation from his holy temple in heaven, he chose to dwell in Zion and exercise his kingship in and through the sacred city.[1]

Inextricably related to the reestablishment of Yahweh's sovereignty is the transformation of Zion. According to Batto, at "critical junctures when his creation is threatened God emerges from his transcendent abode amid awesome clouds to (re)impose order over chaos and to (re)establish a kingdom befitting this majestic divine sovereign."[2] Batto's conclusion fittingly encapsulates our main concern in this chapter – namely, the transformation of Zion as the course of action for reestablishing divine sovereignty in the royal city.

Put differently, Yahweh's sovereignty on earth is linked to Zion's spiritual condition. In the subsequent pages, we will show that idolatry and injustice pollute Zion. In response to the rampant sin on earth (Zion in particular),

---
1. Tan, *Zion Traditions*, 30.
2. Batto, "Combat Myth," 185–186; Dunn, *Sanctuary in the Psalms*, 45.

Yahweh descends from heaven as the Divine Warrior in purifying judgments to rid the land of sin.[3] However, judgment is not the whole story. Because of his covenantal commitment to maintain Zion eternally as his earthly abode (Ps 132:13–14), Yahweh will restore the sacred city and her temple. The restoration of the sacred city signals the restoration of Yahweh's kingship in Zion. Thus, the rebuilding of the temple in Zion is an entry point into the discussion of Yahweh's sovereignty.

In this vein, the present chapter contends that Micah portrays Yahweh as the Divine Warrior on a mission to reestablish his sovereignty in Zion. He does so through purifying judgments focused on Zion. Towards this goal, the chapter has three main sections. Following this introductory section, the chapter will show that the transformation of Zion is a central and unifying theme of our target unit (Mic 1:2–4:8). At this point, we will also present evidence for the presence of motifs from the Zion/Davidic traditions in our target unit. The bulk of the chapter will then flesh out the transformation of Zion in relations to the dynamic Zion tradition pattern of sin, judgment, and restoration. The chapter will close with a discussion of the polemical significance of Yahweh's sovereignty in Zion. As we hope to demonstrate, Yahweh's sovereignty in Zion serves polemical ends against pagan worship. Zion's exaltation shows her sacred status above other rival sacred mountains. Yahweh's kingship in Zion is also a polemic against pagan deities. Only Yahweh is the cosmic ruler.

Overview of Micah 1:2–4:8

Unity of Micah 1:2–4:8

On a broader scope, the macro-structure of the book of Micah as a whole is still a matter of ongoing scholarly debate. With few exceptions, the dominant structures in much of current scholarship are variants of the doom/hope

---

3. There is a long-standing consensus among commentators that Micah adapted the divine warrior tradition. See Barker, "Micah," 50; Jacobs, *Conceptual Coherence*, 81; Stansell, *Micah and Isaiah*, 6; Luker, "Doom and Hope, 166–170; Niehaus, *God at Sinai*, 310; Cross, *Canaanite Myth and Hebrew Epic*, 174–175; Barrick, *BMH as Body Language*, 47; Ortlund, *Theophany and Chaoskampf*, 263.

pattern based on the summons "hear" (שמע).⁴ Since the arguments of these studies have been treated extensively elsewhere, a rehearsal of the survey is unnecessary at this point.⁵ In line with our methodological goals, we find a thematic approach to the book of Micah to be a profitable direction that extends the frontiers of research beyond the doom/hope pattern.

Besides the superscription (1:1), Micah divides thematically into three major units (1:2–4:8, 4:9–5:14, and 6:1–7:20) based on the prophet's animation of key strands from the Zion/Davidic traditions. In the first division (1:2–4:8), the prophet reanimates two central strands: Yahweh as the great king and Yahweh's choice for Zion. Evidently, these come into focus by paying particular attention to a dominant theme that runs steadily throughout the gamut of this major unit, the transformation of Zion.

By the transformation of Zion, we mean Zion's destruction and future restoration. The theme of transformation is so dominant that a clear development of the plot is evident. The theme moves from accusation (1:5) to judgment (3:12) and culminates in the restoration of the temple and Yahweh's enthronement as the great king (4:1–8). As a result, the theme integrates all the parts of this major unit. In addition, perceptive readers will also notice that the Divine Warrior is the only agent of transformation in this unit. No

---

4. Over the past decades, scholars have offered several proposals to demarcate the book's major units. In his redactional analysis of the arrangement of Micah's oracles, John T. Willis contends that Micah's book follows a threefold arrangement: 1–2; 3–5; 6–7. Each division opens with the summons to hear (1:2; 3:1; 6:1), followed by doom oracles (1:2–2:11; 3; 6:1–7:6), and finally closes with hope oracles (2:12–13; 4–5; 7:7–20). Willis, "Structure, Setting, and Interrelationships," 122–123, 136. Like Willis, Waltke sees a three-fold division, which alternates between doom and hope oracles. Each section begins with the imperative "hear" (1:2; 3:1; 6:1) and the hope oracles contain the motif of shepherding (2:12; 4:8; 5:3; 7:14) and, more significantly, the mention of the remnant (2:12–13; 4:6–7; 5:6–7; 7:8). Waltke, *Commentary on Micah*, 15. David G. Hagstrom offers a plausible two-fold structure (1–5; 6–7) signaled by the summons to hear (1:2; 6:1). The other occurrences of the summons (3:1, 9; 6:1, 9) serve as focusing markers rather than macro-structural dividers. Hagstrom, *Coherence*, 22–27. Following a similar macro-structure as Hagstrom, yet depending on conceptual coherence, Jacobs views the book of Micah as "Yahweh's disputes with Israel concerning Israel's fate." Jacobs, *Conceptual Coherence*, 65. Wolff traces an elaborate redactional history of the book and suggests a four-fold macro-structure (1–3; 4–5; 6:1–7:7; 7:8–20). Wolff, *Micah*, 25–6. Shaw sees six rhetorical units (1:2–16; 2:1–13; 3:1–4:8; 4:9–5:14; 6:1–7:7; 7:8–20) based on an investigation of the historical setting of the book. Shaw, *Speeches of Micah*, 224–225.

5. For a recent evaluation of the various proposals of the coherence of the book of Micah, see Cuffey, *Literary Coherence*, 120–212.

human agency appears in this unit. This observation gives the passage its uniqueness and may serve as a structural delimiter.

In the second unit (4:9–5:14), Micah revives the theme of Yahweh's choice of David as his earthly viceroy. We will discuss the details of the second unit in chapter 5. However, it suffices to point out a plain distinction between the first two major units. In Micah 1:2–4:8, Yahweh alone metes out judgment whereas in the second unit Yahweh employs human agency as a means to restore Zion's former dominion. Micah describes Yahweh fighting alongside a militarized remnant (4:11–13) and equipping the new Davidic king for war (5:3–4).

Finally, in the third unit (6:1–7:20), Micah reinvigorates a subsidiary theme from the Zion/Davidic traditions, which stipulates that Yahweh's choice of Zion has implications for Zion's inhabitants. Zion's inhabitants must be fit to dwell in Yahweh's presence. As Roberts aptly states, "only those who meet God's righteous standards can live in his presence (Isa 33:13–16; Ps 24:3–4)."[6] Micah 6:1–7:20 emphasizes righteousness as a prerequisite for the new people of God to maintain covenant relations with Yahweh. We will revisit the issue of unity of the third major section in chapter 6.

Zion: A Key to Yahweh's Sovereignty in Micah 1:2–4:8

Zion is a crucial concern of our target unit. It is the seat of Yahweh's earthly rule and the "the center of political and religious life for the people."[7] Its fate is a key to Yahweh's sovereignty. In the present, sinful Zion appears as an object of Yahweh's righteous wrath (1:5; 3:1–12), but, in the future, a restored Zion will serve as the center of Yahweh's idyllic reign (4:1–8). In sum, Zion's restoration signals the reestablishment of Yahweh's sovereignty.

The explicit references to Zion indicate its significance to the prophet's overall argument in Micah 1:2–4:8. The term "Zion" (צִיּוֹן) is abundantly utilized in the book of Micah, with six occurrences in Micah 1:2–4:8, three in Micah 4:9–5:14, and none in Micah 6:1–7:20. Such an uneven frequency distribution hints at the term's importance in Micah 1:2–4:8. By manner of its grammatical distribution in our target passage, Zion appears three times

---

6. Roberts, "Zion," 332, 342.
7. Hillers, *Micah*, 20.

in the absolute state (3:10, 12; 4:2) and three times in the construct state – "Daughter Zion" (בת־ציון) (1:13; 4:8) and "on Mount Zion" (בהר ציון) (4:7).

Zion is also closely associated with "Jerusalem" (ירושלם). Jerusalem is referenced eight times in the book of Micah. All occurrences appear exclusively in our target unit (1:1, 5, 9, 12; 3:10, 12; 4:2, 8). Of these occurrences, it appears four times in synonymous parallelism with Zion (3:10, 12; 4:2, 12). Once again, this amplifies our contention that Zion is a significant theme in Micah 1:2–4:8. The considerable occurrences of the term promote the internal coherence of our pericope.

Although Micah does not explicitly mention Zion in Micah 2:1–13, this silence does not lessen its importance. Other contextual indicators strongly suggest that Zion is still a focal point. For instance, the motif of "gate" (שער) functions in such a role (1:9, 12; 2:13). In its first two occurrences, it refers to the gate of Jerusalem (1:9, 12). Hagstrom makes a case that שער also refers to Jerusalem in the third instance (i.e. 2:13).[8] He reasons that this last reference is the climax of the motif, which shows that the "destruction has already reached the gate of Jerusalem; now the people are led out through the gate to meet their fate."[9]

Hagstrom's conclusion assumes that Micah 2:12–13 is a doom passage and speaks of a looming exile. Nevertheless, despite the nature of the oracle, the general conclusion that the passage has Zion as its focal point still holds. Assuming that it is a hope passage, one can still argue that Micah 2:12–13 implies a new exodus destined for Zion. In this scenario, the destruction occurs at a gate of an enemy's town. Yahweh then leads a remnant out of the breached gate toward Zion (cf. 4:6–7).

Zion/Davidic Traditions Motifs in Micah 1:2–4:8

Mic 1:2–4:8 drips with motifs from the Zion/Davidic traditions. In the opening verses, Micah shows that he has the Zion traditions in mind as evident from his appeal to the divine warrior theophany. Micah's portrayal of Yahweh as the divine warrior is in line with the Zion/Davidic traditions. The simile in Micah's theophany (Mic 1:4) has an unmistakable affinity to a similar simile

---

8. Hagstrom, *Coherence*, 96–97.
9. Hagstrom., 97.

in the Zion enthronement psalm (Ps 97:5).[10] Levenson reckons that the divine warrior tradition, and his enthronement following his victory, is one of the motifs of the Zion/Davidic traditions.[11]

In the main, Psalm 97 emphasizes the establishment of Yahweh's kingship in Zion (vv. 1–2, 8). Yahweh's kingship often connects to his martial arts as divine warrior (e.g. Exod 15:3, 18; Ps 24:8–10).[12] Thus, by drawing from Psalm 97, Micah is already hinting that Yahweh is coming to restore his sovereignty in Zion.[13]

Another allusion to the Zion/Davidic traditions in our target passage is seen in the epithet "Yahweh of Hosts" (יהוה צבאות) (Mic 4:4).[14] The epi-

---

10. The statement "mountains will melt . . . like wax before the fire" (ונמסו ההרים . . . כדונג מפני האש) (Mic 1:4) parallels "mountains melt like wax before the Lord" (הרים כדונג נמסו מלפני יהוה) (Ps 97:5; cf. Pss 18:7; 46:6; 68:3). Although there are differences in word order and morphology between Mic 1:4 and Ps 97:5, these are not enough to invalidate the correspondences. Evidence for shared expressions is clear. Besides the intervening terms and the transposition of terms, a strong verbal correspondence exists between the marker and marked expressions. Several commentators have likewise correctly discerned the lexical similarities between the imagery in Micah and in the evoked passages. For instance, Smith-Christopher, *Micah*, 53; Waltke, *Commentary on Micah*, 49; Marrs, "Micah and a Theological Critique," 190n11; Barrick, *BMH as Body Language*, 48. Furthermore, the recent publication of an improved decipherment of the Kuntillet ʿAjrud corpus provides extra biblical evidence for the pervasiveness of the divine warrior theme in ancient Israel. The same marker in Micah 1:4 shares lexical and thematic parallels with the Kuntillet ʿAjrud wall inscription:]r. wymsn. hrm. wydkn. pbnm["mountains melted and the highlands crushed" (KAjr 4.2.2). The inscription describes the melting of mountains at the coming of El in language reminiscent of Micah's theophany. Despite the inscription's fragmentary nature, its stereotypical language is akin to Micah's imagery. "Kuntillet ʿAjrud: Plaster Wall Inscription," translated by P. Kyle McCarter (*COS* 2.47D:173). Aḥituv, Eshel, and Meshel, "Inscriptions," 111. Presumably, the verb form is likely a Niphal imperfect of מסס. For brief discussions on the verb form see Naʾaman, "Inscriptions of Kuntillet ʿAjrud," 309–310; Weinfeld, "Kuntillet ʾAjrud Inscriptions," 108; Aḥituv, *Echoes from the Past*, 235.

11. Levenson, "Zion Traditions," 1099–1101; Petersen, *Royal God*, 16.

12. Generally, that ancient kings often connected their kingship to military prowess as a means to legitimate their throne has long attracted scholarly attention. Longman, "Psalm 98," 270. Trimm surmises that within their first year of ascendency, new kings frequently embarked on a military expedition to demonstrate to their subjects that the gods had decreed their kingship. Trimm, *"YHWH Fights for Them!,"* 37. Wright eloquently writes, "One of the reasons why ancient kings were so fond of depicting themselves as great warriors is that their power-base commonly viewed victories on the battlefield as divine confirmation of the king's rule." Wright, "Military Valor and Kingship," 38. A classical example in this regard is found in 2 Samuel 5, which underscores David's military victories following his enthronement as king over all Israel.

13. Ortlund, "Intertextual Reading," 276.

14. In an effort to accentuate Yahweh's sovereignty, Barker suggests that the epithet be rendered "Yahweh who rules over all." Barker, "Micah," 86.

thet belongs to the ark-cherubim tradition (e.g. 1 Sam 4:4).[15] Apparently, the ark-cherubim tradition is related to the Zion/Davidic traditions (2 Sam 6:2; Pss 46:8; 48:9).[16] In addition, the mention of "Gath" likely alludes to the tradition about David's lament over the death of Saul and Jonathan (Mic 1:10; cf. 2 Sam 1:20). Furthermore, the reference to "Adullam" also alludes to difficult times in David's life (Mic 1:15; cf. 1 Sam 22:1; 2 Sam 23:13).

More importantly, there are indicators that Micah was aware of the classical Zion traditions. Some notable motifs include the inviolability of Zion (Mic 3:11; cf. Pss 46:6; 48:4; 76:3–6); Zion as a place of pilgrimage for the nations (Mic 4:2; cf. Pss 24; 22:28–31; 84:6–8); and Zion as a place of peace and security, where weapons of war are no more (Mic 4:3–4; cf. Pss 76:1–3; 46:8–11).[17] In Zion, people will peacefully sit under their vines and worship Yahweh (Mic 4:4–5). In short, Micah conforms to the Zion/Davidic traditions as a way to communicate to his audience that he is essentially drawing from well reputed and generally acknowledged concepts.[18]

Transformation of Zion

The first installment towards the reestablishment of Yahweh's sovereignty on earth calls for the transformation of Zion and her temple. As we have stated in chapter 1, rampant sin in the land disorders those places, institutions, or rituals that theologically mediate Yahweh's presence among his people (e.g. Zion, the temple, leadership, Davidic kingship, torah, worshipers). The other two promises, kingship and the new people of God (worshippers), will be discussed in chapters 5 and 6, respectively.

Unbridled Sin: Idolatry and Social Injustice in Jerusalem
Yahweh accuses Jerusalem of idolatry

Although the superscription is grammatically removed from the material in the rest of the book, it presents the prophet's vision as one that "concerns Samaria and Jerusalem" (על־שמרון וירושלם) (Mic 1:1). Thus, the main subjects

---

15. For a detailed study of the epithet, see Mettinger, *In Search of God*, 123–150.
16. Jamie A. Grant surmises that Ps 97 belongs to the complex of psalms associated with the cherubim-ark tradition. Grant, "Psalms and the King," 150–151.
17. Tan, *Zion Traditions*, 30.
18. Chalmers, *Interpreting the Prophets*, 89.

of the vision are limited to the sacred capital cities of Samaria and Jerusalem, which metonymically stand for Israel and Judah, respectively.[19] However, the next verse within the incipient prophetic judgment speech (v. 2),[20] broadens the scope of Yahweh's concern by summoning all the nations of the earth to attend to the cosmic judgment scene.[21] From here onwards the announcement of judgment funnels down from the whole earth (v. 2), to the mountains (vv. 3–4), to Samaria (vv. 6–7), and finally to Zion (3:12). Such funneling shows that the sins of Samaria and Zion affect the whole earth. More importantly, the funneling also shows that Zion is Yahweh's ultimate target.

Because of covenant breach (i.e. rampant idolatry and injustice) wrought in the capital cities of Samaria and Jerusalem (1:5), Yahweh descends from his heavenly abode as the divine warrior to unleash covenant curses upon the nation. In the opening judgment speech (1:2–7), Micah accuses Zion of idolatry (v. 5). Calling Jerusalem "the high places" (במות) of Judah (v. 5) is an indictment on idolatry. Several passages in the Torah associate במה with illicit worship centers (Lev 26:30; Num 33:52; Deut 33:29).

Patrick H. Vaughan asserts that high places were originally sacred space constructed to incubate a theophany.[22] Later on, these simple structures developed from being mere cultic platforms to include the sanctuary itself.[23] Moreover, the verbal parallel between "heights of the earth/mountain tops" (במותי ארץ) (1:3; cf. Amos 4:13) and "high places" (במות) (v. 5),[24] likely

---

19. Sweeney, *Twelve Prophets*, 2:345.

20. In this atypical oracle, Micah inserts his theophanic imagery cast in the form of a judgment speech (Mic 1:2-7): summons (v. 2); divine warrior theophany (vv. 3–4); accusations (v. 5); judgment (vv. 6–7). The precise genre or Gattung of the passage (i.e., Mic 1:2-7) is still a debatable issue. Earlier scholars – for instance, Fohrer – speak of this passage, including vv. 8–9, as a prophetic lawsuit speech. Fohrer, "Micha 1," 82. Similarly, Elliger identifies the passage as a lawsuit speech. Elliger, "Die Heimat Des Propheten Micha," 58n182. However, Stansell and others reject the view that the passage is a lawsuit. Stansell excludes v. 2 from consideration and finds vv. 5–6 to be the kernel of the passage, so identifies the passage (1:3-6) as a typical judgment speech. Stansell, *Micah and Isaiah*, 17–18. Sweeney takes the same path as Stansell. Sweeney, *Twelve Prophets*, 2:348–349. Despite Stansell's and Sweeney's efforts the tide is receding to the earlier view. Most recently, Juan Cruz and others believes the passage is a lawsuit. Cruz, "Who Is Like Yahweh?," 88; O'Brien, *Restoring the Right Relationship*, 24; Petersen, *Prophetic Literature*, 193; Barker, "Micah," 48.

21. Barker, "Micah," 502.

22. Vaughan, *Meaning of "Bāmâ,"* 25.

23. Vaughan, 25.

24. The demonstrative pronoun "all this" (כל־זאת) is anaphoric (v. 5) and points back to the theophany (vv. 3–4). *GKC*, §126a-b; *JM*, §143b.

suggests that the melting mountains are illicit worship places associated with pagan gods (v. 4).[25] It follows then that the reason for the destruction of the mountain tops was idolatry perpetrated on them. Pagan gods, the embodiment and source of sin, had their shrines on these mountain tops. In short, the opening lawsuit indicts Samaria and Zion for idolatry.[26]

Yahweh accuses Jerusalem of social injustice

Alongside the accusation against idolatry, Micah also indicts Zion of unbridled injustices (Mic 2:1–11; 3:1–12). In five scathing oracles (2:1–5, 6–12; 3:1–4, 5–8, 9–12), the prophet relentlessly wrestles with injustice to underscore its seriousness to the covenant relationship. First, Micah indicts the rich and powerful for swindling the poor of their land (2:1–3). Second, Micah disputes against those who rejected Yahweh's word of judgment (2:6–7), accuses some of injustices against women and children (vv. 8–9), and then indicts some people, or maybe some false prophets, of speaking lies (v. 11). Third, the prophet accuses the leaders of Israel of cannibal-like injustices (3:1–4). Fourth, he accuses greedy prophets who mislead the people (vv. 5–8).

---

25. Andersen and Freedman posit that במותי ארץ "is a tenacious mythological term . . . an ancient expression describing the rumpled surface of the earth consisting of both hills and valleys." Andersen and Freedman, *Micah*, 164.

26. Some scholars have challenged the idea that Micah's lawsuit denounces idolatry. In his classic article, Robert H. Pfeiffer's writes, "Micah, to the best of our knowledge, had nothing to say about idolatry." For him, Mic 1:7 is a gloss. Pfeiffer, "Polemic against Idolatry," 233. Likewise, Shaw denies that idolatry is the root cause for the divine warrior's destruction of Samaria. He understands Samaria's פשע as her political and economic treaties with foreign nations. For some unclear reasons, he renders במות in verse 5 as the "death" of Judah. Even more troubling is that Shaw, drawing from Amos and later Aramaic documents, remarks that the פסיליה and the עצביה refer not to idols or cultic objects but to carvings and hewn stones which adorn buildings or temples. It behooves us that Shaw appeals to external evidence, yet a few chapters later Micah uses פסיל to refer to cultic images, which the nation venerates (Mic 5:12). Shaw, *The Speeches of Micah*, 48–49. In a similar vein, Anthony Phillips emphatically insists that references to idolatry in the eighth-century prophetic books (i.e., Micah, Amos, and Isaiah) "must be regarded as redactional" because the prophets were not confronting cultic violations at all during that era; rather, they indicted the nation for injustices and for perversion of justice. As such, Phillips rejects that Micah's references to idolatry are a plea to the Decalogue or to the covenant. Phillips, *Essays on Biblical Law*, 170; Fritz, "Das Wort Gegen Samaria Mi 1:2–7," 329–331. However, the speculative nature of redactional theories makes their conclusions doubtful. The theories, let alone the number of reconstructions, show uncertainty. In fact, Phillips does not present any evidence to support his redactional conclusion. As Andersen and Freedman have argued, redactional theories are not very strong and they are difficult to validate for lack of textual support. Andersen and Freedman, *Micah*, 179.

The fifth oracle climaxes the ills of social justice in the book (3:9–12). Several scholars have weighed in on the importance of Micah 3:9–12. Hagstrom aptly points out that the resumption of the summons in 3:9 marks this passage as the climactic oracle of Micah 1:2–3:12.[27] For him, the intervening material (1:8–3:8) moves from the destruction of Samaria (1:6–7) and climaxes in 3:12 where Zion suffers the same fate.[28] Marrs writes that Micah 3:9–12 is the most notable passage in the book of Micah that presents the current dismal degradation of Zion.[29] Sweeney observes the Zion/Davidic traditions behind the text. He insists that this passage shows that Micah, unlike Isaiah, had no stake in the claims of the motif, from the classical Zion tradition, that Zion is inviolable.[30]

In any case, Micah 3:9–12 presents a typical judgment oracle. Formally, the oracle exhibits a typical structure: an introduction marked by the summons "hear" (שמעו) (v. 9a); a complex accusation, which states the reason for judgment (v. 9b) and then concretizes it in the following two verses (vv. 10–11); and the announcement of judgment, marked by "therefore" (לכן) (v. 12), closes the oracle. Unlike Micah 2:3, a messenger formula is lacking after the announcement of judgment.[31]

More importantly, the accusation directly addresses the rulers, the priests, and the prophets, but its ultimate focus falls unmistakably on Zion. Micah emphasizes or maintains this focus on Zion in several distinct ways. First, the parallel terms, "Jerusalem" (ירושלם) and "Zion" (ציון), both appear in the

---

27. Hagstrom, *Coherence*, 101. Poulsen agrees. He writes that Mic 3:9–12 culminates the judgment motif. Poulsen, *Representing Zion*, 136; Waltke, *Commentary on Micah*, 176; Barker, "Micah," 79. Jenson's comments are also noteworthy in this matter. In his theologically sensitive commentary, he writes, "The condemnation of evil deeds in ch. 2 leads to accusations that highlight the office of those who should have known how to behave in accordance with Israel's covenant law. In ch. 3 we find a well constructed set of three oracles of judgment of roughly equal length (vv. 1–4, 5–8, 9–12). The third brings to a climax the two by addressing the target of the first oracle (Israel's leaders, vv. 1, 9) and the second (the prophets, vv. 5–6, 11a). It also adds the third pillar of Israelite society, the priests (v. 11a)." Jenson, *Obadiah, Jonah, Micah*, 130.

28. Hagstrom, *Coherence*, 100.

29. Marrs, "Back to the Future," 83. In a footnote (n15), Marrs proceeds to argue that "Mic 3:1–4 treats the judicial abuses present in the courts; 3:5–8 decries the absence of justice in the ministry of the false prophets; 3:9–12 addresses the breakdown of justice throughout the governmental system."

30. Sweeney, *Prophetic Literature*, 195.

31. Stansell, *Micah and Isaiah*, 49.

accusation (Mic 3:10) and in the announcement of judgment (v. 12).[32] Second, the triad of feminine suffixes – "her leaders ... her priests ... her prophets" (ראשיה ... וכהניה .... ונביאיה) (11a) – further underlines the significance of Zion.[33] Third, while the culprits are the city's leadership, judgment falls against Zion itself rather than the leaders (v. 12).[34] This lack of correspondence of agency (i.e. the agent of sin is not the one punished) further buttresses the importance of Zion in this passage.[35] Finally, Micah headlines the sin of Zion in four different ways. To these, we now turn.

Zion's leadership perverts justice

In the opening accusation, Micah headlines the sin of Zion by showing that Zion's leaders had perverted and twisted the city's judicial system. With an almost exact repetition of 3:1, the addressees here are the "the heads ... and the rulers" (וקציני ... ראשי) (Mic 3:9a). The accused comprise the government itself. It includes all the institutions responsible for administering justice in the city – namely, the political, social, and judiciary leaders.

While Micah brings the status of the addressees into purview, his description of their deplorable actions, portrayed with a deep irony, underscores the gravity of the accusation.[36] The general accusation is that the nation's leaders are "the ones who abhor justice" (המתעבים משפט) (Mic 3:9).[37] Here, "abhor" (תעב) has an estimative (i.e. qualitative) sense of a continuous state of harboring hate or a very strong dislike of justice, implying contempt and a negative attitude toward the importance of justice.[38] In sum, the heads and rulers "make crooked all that is straight" (כל־הישרה יעקשו) (v. 9). They pervert all that is right by bending the rules, which undermines order in a just society.[39]

---

32. Stansell, 49; Jacobs, *Conceptual Coherence*, 136.
33. Stansell, *Micah and Isaiah*, 49.
34. Stansell, 49.
35. Wisely, Miller does not discuss 3:9–12 in his treatment of the correspondence between sin and judgment. He recognizes the lack of correspondence between sin and judgment. Miller, *Sin and Judgment*.
36. Reimer, "Prophet Micah and Political Society," 221.
37. The Piel participle, תעב, is variously used of things that are repulsive (Deut 7:26; Pss 5:7; 107:18; Amos 5:10; Job 9:31; 19:19; 30:10). Koehler, Baumgartner, and Stamm, *Hebrew and Aramaic Lexicon*, 1765–1766. IBHS, §24.2f-g.
38. Swanson, *Dictionary of Biblical Languages*, §9493.
39. Jacobs, *Conceptual Coherence*, 136; Jenson, *Obadiah, Jonah, Micah*, 138.

In short, Micah accuses these leaders of gross injustice. At the heart of injustice in Micah's days was a corrupt juridical system. As Barker cogently points out, "The 'establishment' was controlled by corrupt public officials who winked at (and even participated in) all the unjust and oppressive practices Micah has been condemning up to this point."[40] Although the indictment against idolatry focused on the threat to the vertical relationship (Mic 1:5), injustice threatened the horizontal one. The abuse of power by Israel's corrupt leaders (e.g. rich elites, civil and religious leaders) created a societal upheaval, which was contrary to the egalitarian ideals of the Sinai tradition.

Undeniably, when Zion's leaders ignore justice and allow the wicked to oppress the marginalized, it is not only the culprits that suffer but also the temple. The very institution that mediates Yahweh's sovereignty on earth is also threatened. Roberts's conclusion on the gravity of the cosmic consequences of injustice deserves mentioning. As he notes, "An Israel that perverted justice and oppressed the poor was just as much a threat to the stability of the created order as any other sinful nation; and thus Israel was just as much a potential object of divine judgment."[41]

Zion built on bloodshed

Another headline that underscores the sin of Zion is that Zion was a city built on bloodshed. In his elaboration of the accusation, Micah's indictment ironically illustrates the leaders' perversion of justice. This illustration is described through the imagery of building. The prophet connects the leaders' destructive actions (i.e. the perversion of justice) with the building of Zion: "build Zion with bloodshed and Jerusalem with injustice" (בנה ציון בדמים וירושלם בעולה) (Mic 3:10).[42]

The nature of the imagery is unforgettable, but its referent is unclear as the various scholarly proposals suggest. Some understand the indictment in terms of actual public building projects undertaken in Jerusalem under Hezekiah's reign.[43] For Wolff, "Micah's words probably refer not only to construction accidents with fatal consequences, but also, in light of his charges concerning

---

40. Barker, "Micah," 80.
41. Roberts, "Enthronement of Yhwh and David," 681.
42. Reimer, "Prophet Micah and Political Society," 222.
43. Wolff, *Micah*, 107; Jenson, *Obadiah, Jonah, Micah*, 138.

injustice, to the extreme mistreatment of laborers, or even to their death sentence."[44] Jacobs also adds, "The accusation leveled against the leaders is that they built Jerusalem by means of violence and cruelty. The specifics of this could be understood in light of the labor practices and taxation to which the populace was subjected in order to finance the building of Jerusalem."[45]

Others focus on the ritual aspects of bloodshed. Sweeney suggests that Micah's reference to blood calls to mind "the images of animal sacrifice that were normally made at the Temple" or "the many thousands who died as the Assyrians overran the nation."[46] Andersen and Freedmen reason that the sacrificial view points to human foundation sacrifices which often accompanied temple building rituals.[47] Against the sacrificial view, David J. Reimer surmises that the reference to bloodshed does not suggest a ritual sacrifice, but murder.[48]

Perhaps, the mention of bloodshed refers to the death penalty imposed upon unsuspecting innocent victims, who hoped for justice at the central court.[49] According to the law, the verdict of the death penalty was imposed by the central court upon those who challenged and appealed the lower court's decisions (cf. Deut 16:18–20; 17:8, 12–13).[50] After all, bribery at the central court favored the rich and disadvantaged the poor (Mic 3:4).

Zion built on bribes

What is more, Micah further emphasizes the sin of Zion by showing that Zion's leaders perform their duties for bribes (Mic 3:11a). In verse 11a, the prophet develops the accusation by clarifying some of its concrete aspects. Here, the "leaders" (ראש) seem to be associated with judiciary functions (v. 11aα), and the "rulers" (קצין) (v. 9) probably include both the "priests" (כהן) and "prophets" (נביא) (v. 11aβ). As Barker observes, "All classes of leaders are now included in Micah's scathing denunciation. Prophets, priests,

---

44. Wolff, *Micah*, 107.
45. Jacobs, *Conceptual Coherence*, 137.
46. Sweeney, *Twelve Prophets*, 2:374.
47. Andersen and Freedman, *Micah*, 382.
48. Reimer, "Prophet Micah and Political Society," 222.
49. Waltke, *Commentary on Micah*, 179.
50. Merrill, *Deuteronomy*, 263.

judges, and other governmental rulers alike betrayed their trust."[51] Despite their different offices, their sin is the same. Each of these leaders performed their prescribed duties for a "bribe" (שחד) (Mic 3:11a), which was a plain violation of the law (Deut 16:19).[52] Specifically, the priests corrupted their teaching ministry by charging a "fee" (מחיר). The false prophets profited from divinations by charging "money" (כסף).

Zion's false leaders are hypocrites

Finally, Micah emphasizes the sin of Zion by exposing the hypocrisy among Zion's leaders (Mic 3:11b). Marrs thinks that 3:11 is a cogent commentary on 2:6–11.[53] In this case, the prophet fittingly brings his accusation to a climax. Here Micah accuses the unjust leaders of falsely claiming to trust in Yahweh, "yet they claim to lean on Yahweh" (ועל־יהוה ישענו) (v. 11bα). The syntactical construction – על followed by ישענו – has the metaphoric sense of "depending on" or "supporting oneself on."[54] Swanson clarifies that "lean" (שען) connotes "trust and belief in an object to the point of being in jeopardy if the object of trust fails, as a figurative extension of leaning upon a physical object for support (Job 24:23; Prov 3:5; Isa 10:20; 31:1; 50:10)."[55]

Micah then goes on to quote the claim of these leaders, which apparently provides a false sense of security.[56] A rhetorical question opens their claim: "Is not the Lord in our midst?" (הלוא יהוה בקרבנו) (Mic 3:11bβ). A negative assertion then follows the rhetorical question, "disaster will not come against us" (לא־תבוא עלינו רעה). Presumably, their claim rested on a belief that Yahweh's presence guaranteed Zion's security. This was a misplaced belief in

---

51. Barker, "Micah," 80.

52. Clements's pointed description of the prophets' (including Micah's) attitude towards this aspect of injustice is on target. He writes, "An examination of the strictures of the prophets reveals that many of their strongest condemnations are for those whose responsibility it was to administer justice. It was not Israel's not knowing the law, but its leaders' and judges' unwillingness to administer it fairly, that had led to such a lamentable disregard of righteousness. The judges are blamed, not because they do not possess an adequate code of just laws, but because they do not use them justly." Clements, *Prophecy and Covenant*, 76–77; Pate et al., *Story of Israel*, 94–95.

53. Marrs, "Micah and a Theological Critique," 198n42.

54. Koehler, Baumgartner, and Stamm, *Hebrew and Aramaic Lexicon*, 1612.

55. Swanson, *Dictionary of Biblical Languages*, §9128.

56. The leaders rely on Yahweh, saying: "Is not the Lord in our midst? Disaster will not come against us" (הלוא יהוה בקרבנו לא־תבוא עלינו רעה) (v. 11bβ).

the motif of Zion's inviolability (cf. Ps 46:5–8; 48:4–8). Clements addresses the danger and harmful effects such a misplaced attitude posed. He points out that Jerusalem's temple "could become a token of a divine guarantee to bless Israel, irrespective of the people's conduct and loyalty to him."[57]

Thus, here we see that Micah polemicizes against leaders who falsely assumed that Yahweh would protect Zion unconditionally.[58] His opponents conformed to the classical Zion traditions. They reasoned that Zion as the city of the Great King was inviolable. Waltke points out that the standing temple on Mount Zion appeared to lend support to their view.[59] As a result, they perceived no contradiction between their words and their deeds. However, Micah's announcement of judgment poignantly contradicts this false assumption on the city's inviolability (Mic 3:12).

Judgment: From Mountaintops to Mount Zion
Zion punished for social injustice and idolatry

The incipient logical particle, "therefore" (לכן), signals the announcement of Zion's judgment (Mic 3:12). The reason for judgment is the immediate unbridled injustices (vv. 9–11, 12aα). However, from another perspective, the annihilation of the entire city is also the result of idolatry in Zion. Here we need to recall that Micah had initially accused Jerusalem of being a "high place" (במות) (1:5) but had deferred its judgment.[60]

Micah's use of intratextuality confirms that idolatry is also another cause for Zion's fate. As we have stated previously, the concrete penalties portraying Zion's destruction are reminiscent of the divine warrior's desolation of the mountains (Mic 1:3–4) and Samaria (1:6–7).[61] In addition, the references to "mountain" (הר) and "high place" (במות) (3:12bβ) recall similar terms used earlier – "high places" (במותי) (1:3, 5) and "the mountains" (ההרים) (1:4). Altogether, these verbal links and their strategic placement show a

---

57. Clements, *God and Temple*, 79.
58. Poulsen, *Representing Zion*, 56.
59. Waltke, *Commentary on Micah*, 189.
60. Cruz, "*Who Is Like Yahweh?*," 111–113.
61. The description of Samaria's desolation, לעי השדה למטעי, "a heap of ruins in the field, a planting place" (1:6), parallels that of Zion, עיין תהיה ... שדה תחרש, "will be plowed as a field . . . will become a heap of ruins (3:12aβ, 12bα).

continuation of the divine warrior's devastation from the mountaintops (1:3–4) to Mount Zion (3:12).

Therefore, Micah 3:12 signals the thematic climax of Micah 1:2–3:11 because it answers the long-deferred judgment upon Zion (1:5). In what, on the surface, appears to be a haphazard style and a clumsy argument, Micah 1:6–3:11 apparently delays the presentation of the climactic judgment (3:12).[62] By so doing, Micah skillfully builds suspense, which eventually climaxes with the total annihilation of present Zion. The future of Zion will hardly be like her past.

In this respect, we find it necessary to go a step beyond a merely isolated exposition of the judgment of Zion (Mic 3:12). A contextual exposition that takes into account the divine warrior's activities throughout Micah 1:2–4:8 allows us to trace the recurring judgment motif along the four-tiered cosmic paths, which the divine warrior traverses, to its climactic conclusion.[63] In the following, we shall trace the development of this motif by examining the devastation of the mountaintops (1:3–4), the destruction of Samaria (vv. 6–7), Judah (vv. 8–16), and finally Zion (3:12).

Yahweh battles false gods on the mountaintops

In order to initiate the purging program, Micah adapts the divine warrior tradition and casts Yahweh as the divine warrior battling false gods on the mountains. For Israel to continue her tenure on the land, Yahweh had explicitly commanded the nation to demolish Canaanite high places and all forms of idolatry upon possessing the land (e.g. Num 33:52; Deut 7:5, 25; 12:2–3). Unfortunately, Micah's generation had failed to live according to these torah demands (Mic 1:2–7; cf. 5:11–13; 6:16). In response, Yahweh appears as the

---

62. As Wagenaar states, "The opening lines of the oracle against Samaria and the last lines of the oracle against Jerusalem now prove to be direct parallels." Wagenaar, "Hillside of Samaria," 30.

63. The divine warrior descends from his heavenly realm (Mic 1:2), purges idolatry in the natural realm (vv. 3–4), on the earthly realm (vv. 5–16; 3:12), and finally, confines sin into the sea (7:19). Chapter 6 will discuss the divine warrior's act of purifying the people and confining sin into the sea.

divine warrior to unleash covenant curses upon the nations, starting with their false gods (1:3–4).[64]

That Micah has the defeat of the false gods in view is defensible based on the strategic placement of the divine warrior imagery within the opening judgment speech (Mic 1:2–7). Most noteworthy are the cosmic spheres Yahweh navigates. He originates from "his holy temple" (מהיכל קדשו) in heaven (v. 2), descends and straddles the "mountaintops" (במותי ארץ) in the natural realm (vv. 3–4), before he reaches Samaria and Jerusalem on earth (vv. 5–7; 3:12), and finally ends at the sea (7:19). Essentially, Micah is working with a hierarchical cosmology. Yahweh resides in heaven, the gods in the natural sphere, humans on earth, and sin belongs to the sea. Because of its placement, the theophany brings direct judgment against the gods residing in the natural realm – that is, on the idolatrous mountains. Thus, at this point in Micah's prophecy, the divine warrior directly targets the gods.

Second, a look at the mountain symbol illuminates the intricacies of the battle even further. Recent studies convincingly show that the topographical expression "mountain tops" (במותי ארץ) refers to mythological mountains associated with ANE imagery of the storm god and his battles. As we have hinted at briefly, the divine warrior tradition in Psalm 97 shows that the melting of mountains results in the overthrow of the gods. Similarly, the divine warrior tradition in KAjr 4.2 strongly attributes the melting of mountains and overthrow of the gods to a divine battle.[65] In fact, Old Testament prophets

---

64. Micah inserts his divine warrior imagery in an oracle cast in the form of a judgment speech (Mic 1:2–7): summons (v. 2); divine warrior theophany (vv. 3–4); accusations (v. 5); judgment (vv. 6–7). The insertion of the divine warrior imagery in a judgment speech context should not startle us. Yahweh's wars are inextricably connected to Israel's covenant obligation. Obedience leads to military victory (Exod 23:22–23; Lev 26:6–7; Deut 4:23–28; 28:7), whereas disobedience results in defeat (Lev 26:32–33; Deut 28:25, 47–52).

65. In an effort to leave no stone unturned, some scholars have offered explanations for the melting of mountains. Aloysius Fitzgerald, for instance, suggests that the image of the Divine Warrior's treading employed in Mic 1:3–4 shows Yahweh as the god of the dry sciroccostorm rather than Yahweh as a storm god who brings the rains. He further surmises that the Niphal form (מסס) of "melt" is usually used of mountains dissolving because of the super-hot sirocco winds, which can melt ore like wax. Fitzgerald, *Lord of the East Wind*, 108n82. Waltke surmises that the figurative images stem from volcanic eruptions and/or earthquakes. Waltke, *Commentary on Micah*, 48–49. However, J. C. L. Gibson argues that the rhetoric arose not from observing nature but from mythological motifs which were familiar to Israel. Gibson, *Language and Imagery*, 105. Along similar lines, Hillers wisely cautions: "It is misguided to look for a naturalistic explanation of the melting of mountains" because it is stereotypical imagery found in descriptions of theophany. Hillers, *Micah*, 20.

often pronounced judgment against the mountains because of idolatry. For example, Ezekiel's judgment oracle against the mountains of Israel – precisely because of the shrines Israel had erected – captures the same issue Micah dealt with in his generation (Ezek 6:1–7).[66] There is no reason to suppose that Micah departed from such a mythopoeic worldview concerning the relationship between mountains, idols, and the gods.[67] Rather than just pronounce an oracle against the mountains like Ezekiel, Micah poignantly presents mountains melting before the divine warrior's fiery presence. The melting of mountains in Micah's imagery, we contend, entails a divine battle. Andersen and Freedman also share this view. They note, "Yahweh comes out as warrior; and the combat is a reenactment of the old cosmic battle with the primal elements, here represented by 'mountains.'"[68]

At any rate, the mountaintops serve as the abode of the false gods and participate in illicit worship. Alberto R. W. Green presents iconographic data from Anatolia that depicts storm gods with battle maces and spears straddling the "mountaintops" (במותי ארץ).[69] McComiskey and Longman insightfully reason that these mountaintops were places of military advantage because of their height.[70] Any god in possession of the enemies' heights had conquered and brought them into vassalage (Deut 33:29; Ezek 36:2).[71] W. Boyd Barrick agrees with the conquest view. For him, the term (במותי ארץ) refers to the mythological mountains, "which the god surmounts in theophany, symbolically expressing his cosmic victory and sovereignty."[72]

That the "mountaintops" (במותי ארץ) are associated with the storm gods' battles brings the militaristic connotation of the expression "tread upon the mountaintops" (על־במ(ו)תי ודרך) into sharper focus (Mic 1:3). This expression

---

66. Cohn's remarks are on target as he states that the mountains themselves are culpable because of the high places erected upon them. Cohn, *Shape of Sacred Space*, 35. On the other hand, Habel's comment that the mountains metonymically stand for the people misses the contextual sense of the passage. Habel, "Silence of the Lands," 134–135.

67. Andersen and Freedman, *Micah*, 515.

68. Andersen and Freedman, 137; Also see Waltke, *Commentary on Micah*, 48; Ortlund, *Theophany and Chaoskampf*, 264; Smith-Christopher, *Micah*, 52–53; Middlemas, *Divine Image*, 110; Hillers, *Micah*, 19–21; Barrick, *BMH as Body Language*, 50.

69. Green, *Storm-God*, 116–117. See especially fig. 15 and 16.

70. McComiskey and Longman, "Micah," 503.

71. McComiskey and Longman, 503.

72. Barrick, *BMH as Body Language*, 109.

appears in two more passages which have a militaristic context (Job 9:8; Amos 4:13). In addition, based on internal evidence, the verb "tread down" (דרך) has militaristic undertones as evidenced by the Assyrian invaders who "tread down" (דרך) the nation's palaces (Mic 5:4–5; cf. Deut 33:29; Pss 60:12; 108:13). Some scholars also understand the verb in a militaristic sense.[73] Barker points out: "Treading the high places of the earth speaks of conquest."[74] Andersen and Freedman forcefully state, "This tradition gives Micah 1:3b a military connotation, an association not incompatible with the naturalistic phenomena . . . identified as divine warrior. Such convulsions take place in the battle with the monstrous forces."[75] Along a similar vein, Christopher J. H. Wright states that Yahweh's struggle with idolatry is essentially a battle against false gods.[76]

Yahweh devastates Samaria

Having purified the natural realm, the divine warrior descends to the human realm, with a focus on Samaria and Jerusalem (Mic 1:5). Micah most likely evokes the covenant curses spelled out in Levitcus 26:30–33. In this passage, Yahweh himself, in the first person, threatens three major catastrophes: (1) to destroy Israel's illegitimate cultic places and their idols (Lev 26:30); (2) to desolate Israel's cultic cities (vv. 31–32, 33b); and (3) to exile Israel from the land (v. 33a). In Micah 1:6–7, the divine warrior actualizes the first two threats in reverse order. First, he demolishes the city itself (Mic 1:6), then he ravages the idols (v. 7), and finally, he exiles the people (vv. 8–16). Such inversions are typical in literary allusions, and Micah uses the device in other places. For example, he alludes to the patriarch, exodus, and conquest traditions in reverse order (Micah 6–7).

Besides thematic similarities, remarkably, Micah and Leviticus share an indisputable constellation of vocabulary: "high place" (במה) (Lev 26:30; Mic 1:3, 5; 3:12); "idols" (גלולים) (Lev 26:30) and "idols" (פסיל) (Mic 1:7). In addition, both texts speak of cannibalism (Lev 26:29; Mic 3:1–4). The aftermaths

---

73. Pablo Richard argues that idolatry provokes Yahweh's intervention in the battle against false gods. Pablo Richard, "Biblical Theology," 1, 58. Crenshaw concludes that in Micah's theophany Yahweh "comes as conqueror of the mountain ranges, the sanctuaries thus succumbing to the intense heat of divine anger." Crenshaw, "'Wedōrēk 'al-Bāmŏtê 'āreṣ,'" 45.

74. Barker, "Micah," 50.

75. Andersen and Freedman, *Micah*, 164.

76. Wright, *Mission of God*, 177.

of the devastation are also similar: the divine warrior will "desolate" (שמם) the land and destroy idols (Lev 26:31; Mic 1:7). Furthermore, both texts speak of the people's exile (Lev 26:33; Mic 1:8–16). Cumulatively, there is enough evidence to suggest that Micah most likely had the covenant curses in mind as he announced judgment on Samaria.

Although the divine warrior utterly desolates the idolatrous city of Samaria (Mic 1:6), his ultimate goal is to purge Samaria of idolatry and revert the city to its natural state of agricultural verdancy (v. 6). The most important piece of evidence to support this assertion is the syntactical construction "will make ... into a ... into a" (שים ... ל ... ל) (v. 6a).[77] The term "make" (שים) occurs eight times in Micah and has a transformative sense, which means that the object of the verb will change states.[78] Smith-Christopher even points out that the "term ... is used to refer to 'creating,' 'making,' or setting up something. In the prophetic literature, it often refers to God's act of carrying out forceful judgment by transforming something into a ruin or a wasteland, a kind of 'de-creation.'"[79]

In addition, "make" (שים) followed by "into a heap of ruins" (לעי) transforms Samaria into a heap of ruins. At first blush, this might appear as if the divine warrior leaves Samaria as a wasteland. However, it is the second complement, "into a planting place" (למטעי), which actually determines the ultimate product of the divine warrior's intentions. Andersen and Freedman correctly observe that the two complements in parallel hint at two ideas of a useless ruin becoming a productive farmland.[80] For them, Micah's qualification of a heap of stones in a field and the parallelism of a vineyard imply that Samaria is not a wasteland but a well-planned vineyard.[81]

---

77. Noteworthy is the expression ושמתי שמרון לעי השדה למטעי כרם: "I will make Samaria into a heap of ruin in the open field, a place for planting vineyards" (Mic 1:6a). According to *GKC*, §117ii and §119t, the syntactical construction (שים ... ל ... ל) is an object-complement double accusative (see Gen 12:2; 27:9; Lev 24:5; 1 Kgs 18:32; Jer 9:10). In our target passage, Samaria is the object accusative, while the ל prepositions mark the object complements. The complements are the products of the verb, שים.

78. Mic 1:6, 7; 2:12; 4:7, 13, 14; 7:16. Brown, Driver, and Briggs, *Hebrew and English Lexicon*, 964.

79. Smith-Christopher, *Micah*, 55.

80. Andersen and Freedman, *Micah*, 177.

81. Andersen and Freedman, 177.

Furthermore, Hillers's informative study on treaty curses in the ANE and the Old Testament is invaluable to our argument. He aptly observes that for a place to become a ruin or a wooded height where something grows is actually the exact opposite of the ordinary curse or prophetic threat.[82] As he goes on to point out, "Usually the prophecy is that a place will become a waste where nothing grows, or that noxious weeds, *etc.*, will grow over it."[83]

Another piece of evidence to show that the divine warrior's ultimate intention is to transform Samaria from an idolatrous city into a useful and productive agricultural verdancy is the futility curse on agricultural fertility. Micah's imagery of the demolition of Samaria and the idea of planting vineyards recalls the futility curse:[84]

| למטעי כרם | into a place for planting vineyards | Mic 1:6 |
| כרם תטע | you will plant a vineyard | Deut 28:30; cf. Lev 26:16 |

According to the full futility curse, "You shall plant a vineyard, but you shall not enjoy its fruit" (כרם תטע ולא תחללנו) (Deut 28:30b). For Hillers, the form of the futility curse comprises a protasis, which describes the activity, and an apodosis, which states the frustration of the activity.[85] Micah departs from the typical form of the futility curse by omitting the apodosis, which is the essential element of the curse. Without the apodosis (i.e. the frustration), it is tenuous to argue that Samaria's transformation from an idolatrous city to a place for planting vineyards amounts to a curse. Had Micah intended to

---

82. Hillers, *Treaty-Curses*, 53.

83. Hillers, 53–54.

84. The concepts of building and planting are well-known and recurrent themes in the prophets. In many instances, the concepts stem from the Deuteronomistic curse. Several biblical authors allude to and adapt the curse for their own purposes (e.g. Amos 5:11; 9:14; Isa 5:1–17; Zeph 1:13; Jer 6:9–15; 29:5, 28; 31:4; Deut 20:5–6; 28:30; Isa 62:6–9; 65:21; Ezek 28:26; 36:36). Scholars have long observed that a military threat informs the curse. In a recent study, Jeremy D. Smoak demonstrates that Old Testament authors adopted and reshaped the imagery of building houses and planting vineyards as a wartime curse. He comments that it "is during wartime that the fulfillment of one's labors, such as the harvesting of a vineyard, is thwarted." He also points to Assyrian royal annals and iconography, which describe the destruction of houses followed by the destruction of viticulture after a successful siege, as potential sources behind the curses imagery. Smoak, "Building Houses," 20, 19–24. Also see Walsh, *Fruit of the Vine*; Smith-Christopher, *Religion of the Landless*; Anderson, *Blessing and the Curse*, 221–228.

85. The activity and the frustration may be expressed: You shall do X but Y shall happen. According to Hillers, the apodosis is often introduced by ולא ("but not"). Hillers, *Treaty-Curses*, 29.

pronounce a curse on Samaria, he could have utilized the full form, since he was well acquainted with it (cf. Mic 6:14–15).

Thus, the divine warrior's devastation of Samaria "into a place for planting vineyards" (למטעי כרם) is actually useful (1:6).[86] First, transforming the city into a verdant vineyard makes sense because, before Omri founded the city (1 Kgs 16:24), Samaria was located within a fertile agricultural basin suitable for the cultivation of wheat, barley, and vineyards for wine production.[87] One can hear faint echoes of a polemic against Baal as Samaria reverts to a vineyard. It was Yahweh who provided the produce of the land and not Baal.

Second, in contrast to Assyrian warriors who ravage houses and vineyards, making the land uninhabitable and unprofitable, the divine warrior's demolition of Samaria actually mirrors that of a farmer plowing the land in preparation for cultivation. This productive ruination of Samaria – that is, the transformation of ruins into a farmland for vineyards – is a characteristic feature of the divine warrior's advent (e.g. Joel 4:18; Ps 65:9–13). The agricultural fertility of the land is at stake, and the destruction of Samaria is a means towards restoring the produce of the land (cf. Lev 26:3–5; Deut 11:13–15).[88] Thus, Samaria as periphery land is still suitable for cultivation but without any religious status. It is a failed religious center. As will eventually become apparent with the restoration of Zion, Samaria's periphery status serves to promote Zion's supremacy as the chosen sanctuary city.[89]

In Micah 1:7, the divine warrior obliterates idolatrous objects with the goal of purging the land. Here Micah casts Samaria's idolatry as a replay of the destruction of the golden calf incident as he anchors his announcement to key Deuteronomic stipulations:

---

86. The noun מטע occurs six times in the Old Testament. Besides its metaphorical usage (Isa 60:21; 61:3; Ezek 31:4), the noun carries the common sense of a "planting place" (i.e., a piece of land for planting [Ezek 17:7; 34:29: Mic 1:6]). In an agrarian society like ancient Israel, fertile land for planting crops was economically crucial. Thus, it makes sense that Samaria would revert to its original purpose as an agriculturally verdant land. Clearly, such a reversion is beneficial for the people. In fact, Jeremiah would later make this very point. Although far removed from Micah's generation, Jeremiah explicitly anticipates a time when Samaria will once again revert to a fruitful vineyard plantation for the benefit of its citizens (Jer 31:5).

87. DeVries, *Cities of the Biblical World*, 224–226.

88. Gowan, *Eschatology in the Old Testament*, 98.

89. Hjelm, *Jerusalem's Rise to Sovereignty*, 255.

יכתו ... ישרפו באש	crushed ... shall be burned in fire	Mic 1:7a
ואשרף ... באש ואכת	I burned it ... in the fire and I crushed it	Deut 9:21

Despite the difference in form and word order, the affinities between the two texts are remarkable. It is important to observe that the evoked text recounts the story of Moses's destruction of the golden calf (Exod 32:20). Previous scholarship has generally overlooked this observation. Micah's literary allusion puts the divine warrior's destruction of the idols of Samaria squarely on par with Moses's destruction of the golden calf. Just as Moses purified the camp by destroying the golden calf, which eventually led to the renewal of the covenant (Exod 34:1–28), in Micah the divine warrior shares a similar concern. The divine warrior attempts to purify and restore the land so he might eventually renew the covenant with a remnant (Mic 7:8–20).

Ultimately, only when the idols and images are "crushed" (יכתו), "burned in fire" (ישרפו באש), and "made desolate" (אשים שממה) can the divine warrior restore the boundaries between Israel and the nations. When the verb "desolate" (שממה) takes the land as its object, it carries the sense of emptying the land of its inhabitants (Mic 7:13; cf. Lev 26:33). However, in this instance, the use of the adverbial accusative (שממה), with idols as an object, likely suggests a figurative sense; that is, the death of the idols or the gods they represent. Perhaps, the gods/idols are being emptied of their perceived potency.

In addition, the use of "they will return" (ישובו) suggests that purging is an effective way of separating the idolatrous objects from the land. Admittedly, the precise meaning of (ישובו) eludes us. Possibly, smelting the idols returns them to their natural state (i.e. into their constituent elements). Most likely is the idea that foreign soldiers will use the melted metals to hire prostitutes or that they will donate the metals to their patron gods.[90] Maybe the crushed particles of the metal will be scattered (cf. Exod 32:20; Deut 9:21).[91]

Yahweh devastates Judah

In Micah 1:8–16, the divine warrior exiles the people from the land. According to the Levitical covenant restoration program, the purification

---

90. Chisholm, *Handbook on the Prophets*, 418; Waltke, *Commentary on Micah*, 55.
91. Andersen and Freedman, *Micah*, 185.

of the land requires the removal of all forms of idolatry as well as the exile of the people (Lev 26:30–33). Having purified Samaria of idolatry, the divine warrior sets his eyes towards Jerusalem. Micah responds in a lament because he recognized that the destruction of Samaria portends a similar outcome for Jerusalem (Mic 1:8–9, 12, 13). As the divine warrior marches towards Jerusalem, he devastates the towns of Judah's Shephelah (vv. 10–16).[92] Andersen and Freedman reject the idea that a military campaign is in view in this passage because "there is very little language that suggests military activity."[93] Likewise, Shaw views the loss of the Shephelah not in terms of a

---

92. Micah 1:10–16 is one of the most difficult passages in the Old Testament. Textual corruption and obscure details pose difficulties in translation. See Hillers, *Micah*, 10, 24; Mays, *Micah*, 51. On the one hand, many scholars agree that the Shephelah functioned as a buffer zone or battle ground for Jerusalem. For instance, LaMar C. Berrett and D. Kelly Ogden comment that the "Shephelah was Judah's first line of defense; important fortress cities like Lachish guarded the hills from incursions by foreign enemies." See Berrett and Ogden, *Discovering the World*, 175. Berrett's and Ogden's view that Lachish featured a palace-fortress finds support in Micah's reference to Lachish's inhabitants harnessing their chariots and horses (Mic 1:13). Besides being a buffer zone for Jerusalem, Lachish receives the worst condemnation from Micah because it served as a cultic center (Mic 1:13). Archaeological evidence unearthed a ninth-century BC Israelite sanctuary together with a raised platform ("high place"), a Maṣṣebah (pillar), and Asherah at Lachish. Boyd, "Lachish," 526. On the other hand, there is a lack of consensus among scholars concerning the historical setting for the crises described in Micah's oracles, since most of the towns listed have not yet been identified. It is possible that the events depicted in Micah are closely tied to the sack of Samaria in 722 BC and to the Judean exile to Assyria in 701 BC (cf. Isa 11:12–16; Mic 1:16). For a cogent presentation on the historical issues in Micah – which includes detailed archaeological evidence – see Stohlmann, "Judean Exile," 147–175; Na'aman, "'House-of-No-Shade Shall Take Away Its Tax,'" 298–300; McFadden, "Micah and the Problem." Recently, Julia M. O'Brien has challenged the view that the passage reflects Sennacherib's military campaign of 701 BC. See O'Brien, *Micah*, 14–16. For a detailed dating schema of Micah's oracles see Shaw, *Speeches of Micah*. Shaw discerns six rhetorical units in Micah and proposes different historical settings for each. He assigns Mic 1:2–16 to the reign of Jotham before the death of Jeroboam II (747 BC); Mic 2:1–13 to the time of Menahem's coup; Mic 3:1–4:8 possibly reflects the time after Pekah's takeover of Samaria; Mic 4:9–5:14 most likely portrays the Syro-Ephraimite siege of Jerusalem, which took place just after Uzziah's death; Mic 6:1–7:7 may reflect the time prior of the arrest of Hoshea in 725 BC; Mic 7:8–20 is a message to the citizens of Samaria shortly after the first capture of the city in 722 BC. Shaw, *Speeches of Micah*, 224–225.

93. Andersen and Freedman reason that the geographical locations of the last four towns (i.e., Moresheth Gath, Achzib, Mareshah, and Adullam) are off the main path of advance. As such, the locations of these towns pose a challenge for an invading army marching from Lachish to Jerusalem. In other words, the army had to backtrack in order to reach these towns. Andersen and Freedman, *Micah*, 211. See also Nogalski, *Book of the Twelve*, 531. However, immediate problems that militate against Andersen's and Freedman's conclusion are the assumptions that ancient armies could only advance towards enemy towns in one campaign, attacking towns in a straight line of march, and that backtracking poses a problem for these armies. Their boldness to claim knowledge of ancient military strategies with such precision seems doubtful. In fact,

military invasion but rather as the towns revolting from Jerusalem on their own and taking "a course which is harmful and disloyal to Jerusalem."[94] Both of these claims fall short. As we will see shortly, the textual evidence supports a veiled military invasion in order to introduce the theme of exile. Mays is correct in observing that the "language gives the impression of composition while the invasion was in full movement."[95]

Among other things, the passage attenuates the violent details of the devastation of Judah's towns in order to introduce the theme of exile. The core statement of the theme is that the destruction of the land ultimately results in exile because of unbridled idolatry. Idolatry defiles the people, the land, and the sanctuary.[96] It fragments the triangular bond that exists among Yahweh, the people, and the land. That is, it first separates Yahweh from his land and consequently separates the people from the land. This idea of separating the people from the land stands at the core of the exile concept.

According to the Deuteronomistic formulation, the exile represents the ultimate covenant curse, which terminates the history of the people in the land (Deut 28:63–68). In contrast, the priestly formulation regards the exile as a purification of the land so that it can redeem its sabbaths, which it did not experience when Israel dwelt in it (Lev 26:32–35; 43). What is more, the exile does not mean the land will remain empty *ad infinitum*. The divine warrior will eventually deliver a remnant from exile and restore them to the purified land (Lev 26:44–45). Micah most likely had this impressive text in view in his conceptualization of the land and the exile. The introduction of the exile at this point in Micah is fitting because it is a natural outcome of a military campaign.

While we disagree with Rainer Albertz's redactional analysis, his conclusion that the divine warrior's judgment is an act of purification hits the target.[97]

Nadav Na'aman has shown that Assyrians armies often campaigned in several stages, which were often divided geographically and chronologically. Na'aman, "Sennacherib's Campaign," 64–65. Julia M. O'Brien somewhat concurs with the view of Andersen and Freedman but on the grounds of Micah's historicity. Assuming a Persian period for the book, she notes that the "literary artfulness of this unit raises questions about its historical precision." O'Brien, *Micah*, 16.

94. Shaw, *Speeches of Micah*, 40; Shaw, "Micah 1:10–16," 227.

95. Mays, *Micah*, 53–54.

96. For example, Lev 18:24–30; Deut 18:9–12; 2 Kgs 16:3; Ps 106; Jer 7:9–15; 16:18; 32:34; Ezek 5:11; 20:30–31.

97. Albertz, "Exile as Purification," 237–240.

Shaw's defection hypothesis (i.e. Judah's towns defected from Jerusalem) is flawed precisely at this point. Idolatry instead of defection is the main charge against Samaria, which results in exile. Also, the divine warrior's twofold restoration program of purifying the land is a military invasion (Mic 1:2–7) and exile (vv. 8–16).

Several pieces of evidence support the claim that the prophet is introducing the theme of exile in this section. Micah's response of walking barefooted and naked is not just a show of empathy on those suffering the divine warrior's judgments but also a sign-act, which foreshadows a military activity followed by an exile.[98] An appeal to a similar sign-act in Isaiah validates our observation: the expression "barefoot and naked" (שׁילל וערום) (Mic 1:8) has an affinity to "naked and barefoot" (ערום ויחף) (Isa 20:2, 3, 4), which has a military invasion and an exile in view (Isa 20:4). In times of mourning, a person usually wears sackcloth rather than going naked (see Gen 37:34; 1 Kgs 21:27; Joel 1:8, 13; Amos 8:10; Isa 22:12). Thus, it is reasonable to conclude that Micah's sign-act combines with the lamentation to communicate the status of a prisoner of war being led into captivity naked and barefoot.

Moreover, the reference to jackals and ostriches is not an ancient course in ethology (cf. Job 30:29; Isa 34:13; 43:20). The reference speaks of the wilderness-like conditions the divine warrior's wrath brings. The once inhabitable land turns into a wilderness. The idea of wild animals inhabiting desolated human settlements is part of a curse commonly found in judgment oracles (e.g. Isa 13:21; 34:13; 35:7; Jer 50:38; Ezek 13:4; Ps 44:19).[99] Jeremiah connects the imagery to an imminent military invasion and exile (Jer 9:11). Jeremiah probably alluded to Micah's imagery and made it explicitly clear that the imagery implied an exile.[100]

---

98. Kelvin Friebel's proposed communication theory, "Rhetorical Nonverbal Communication," provides an insightful point of departure for understanding prophetic sign-acts. Central to Friebel's theory is the idea that prophetic sign-acts were persuasive devices and had a similar function as the prophetic word itself. Friebel, "Hermeneutical Paradigm," 41. He writes, "When one views the nonverbal sign-actions as serving the same communicative and rhetorical functions as verbalized prophecies, then the distinctions between the two are not those of intentional function or of purpose, but merely the channel through which the communication takes place: the sign-acts employed the nonverbal channel, while oracles used the verbal channels of either vocalic verbal (i.e. oral speaking) or non-vocalic verbal (i.e. written form)."

99. Smith-Christopher, *Micah*, 65; McComiskey and Longman, "Micah," 506.

100. Smith-Christopher, *Micah*, 65.

Another piece of evidence that demonstrates that Micah introduces the coming exile is the reference to "Adullam" (עדלם) (Mic 1:15), which alludes to the days of David's exile as he and his army hid from Saul in the cave of "Adullam" (עדלם) (1 Sam 22:1; 2 Sam 23:13). Thus, the expression "the glory of Israel will enter Adullam" (עד־עדלם יבוא כבוד ישראל) probably refers to the leaders and elite citizens of Mareshah going into exile.[101] Finally, the language of mourning, weeping, rolling in the dust (Mic 1:9–10, 11b), humiliation (vv. 11a; 16a), and giving parting gifts (v. 14) is consistent with "an exile" (גלה) (v. 16).[102] Altogether, the people's continued disobedience led to the divine warrior's intervention. He will purify the land through judgments. In short, exile followed the great devastation.

Yahweh devastates Mount Zion

The divine warrior finally reaches his ultimate destination, the city of Jerusalem (3:12). The logical particle, "therefore" (לכן), which signals the announcement of judgment (3:12), is followed by a causal marker "because of you" (בגללכם), which states the reason for the judgment. Together, "therefore, because of you" (לכן בגללכם) emphasizes the strong connection between the wicked leaders and the looming judgment. Judgment is imminent because of injustice at the central court. On the surface, it appears as though the judgment is disproportionate to the accusation. How can the sins of a few leaders accused of injustice result in the utter annihilation of the entire city? However, upon closer examination, Micah is simply reflecting on and applying the

---

101. Barker, "Micah," 61; Chisholm, *Interpreting the Minor Prophets*, 136.

102. Smith-Christopher, *Micah*, 72. While the explicit mention of גלה strongly supports the view of an impending "exile" (v. 16), some voices have challenged this conclusion. Shaw thinks that the Qal form of the verb does not carry the later technical sense of going or being taken into exile but simply means "they have left you." Shaw, *Speeches of Micah*, 40. Mays's take on this issue is confusing. On one hand, he understands the passage as Sennacherib's military campaign along the eastern Mediterranean coast of 701 BC, which led to the devastation of the Shephelah towns, including the exile of the population. Just a few pages later, Mays writes that "v. 16, is like v. 13b, a later application of Micah's saying to Jerusalem after the city has fallen to the Babylonians." Mays, *Micah*, 53, 60. Arguably, the Babylonian exile (586–539 BC) looms large in the Old Testament; however, in recent years, biblical scholars are beginning to challenge this rigid view of the exile theme. Gudme and Hjelm mention that the major exiles in the Old Testament include the deportation of Israel (ca.722 BC, see 2 Kgs 17); the two waves of deportations to Babylon (ca.598/597 BC, see 2 Kgs 24:10–17; and ca. 587/586 BC, see 2 Kgs 25:1–21), and the voluntary flight to Egypt (ca. 582 BC, see Jer 52). Gudme and Hjelm, "Introduction," 1. Also, Stohlmann convincingly argues for the Judean exile of 701 BC (Mic 1:16; Isa 11:12–16). Stohlmann, "Judean Exile," 168–174.

theological principle of collective retribution (e.g. Deut 16:20). The principle states that the sins of a few results in the punishment of the many.[103]

Like that of Samaria, the devastation of Zion is graphic and comprehensive. Stansell points out that the imagery of doom "is not simply punishment of those groups accused, but total annihilation of the city, palace, temple, and all."[104] Micah captures the overwhelming devastation through three agricultural metaphors. In the first clause, "Zion will be plowed into a field" (ציון שדה תחרש) (Mic 3:12aβ). Against Waltke, here we understand "into a field" (שדה) as an accusative of product,[105] rather than an accusative of state.[106] Even though Waltke's option might achieve what he hails as "the striking effect,"[107] it profoundly attenuates the transformative effect inherent in the verb "will be plowed" (תחרש). Undeniably, some grammarians do agree that "plow" (חרש) is a verb of shaping.[108] As such, the product, "field" (שדה), is the result of the verb's transformative action. While the Niphal verb "will be plowed" (תחרש) is an incomplete passive, the identity of the agent of destruction is the divine warrior.[109] Metaphorically, like a farmer breaking and turning over the soil,

---

103. Morrow, *Introduction to Biblical Law*, 68.

104. Stansell, *Micah and Isaiah*, 52.

105. *GKC*, §117ii; §121d.

106. Waltke, *Commentary on Micah*, 182; cf. *IBHS* §10.2.1. According to Bill T. Arnold and John H. Choi, in an accusative of product, "the object did not exist prior to the verbal action, but is brought about by the action and is therefore the product or result of the action." Arnold and Choi, *Guide to Biblical Hebrew Syntax*, 15. Further support for taking שדה as an accusative of product comes from the transformative ellipsis formed by the parallel clauses: ל . . . תהיה (Mic 3:12b).

107. Waltke, *Commentary on Micah*, 182.

108. Gesenius, *Gesenius's Hebrew and Chaldee Lexicon*, 309–310. As Arnold and Choi clarify, an accusative of product is common with verbs of shaping, making, or preparing, which typically takes two accusatives. We should note that ציון is an object accusative, while שדה is an accusative of product. Arnold and Choi, *Guide to Biblical Hebrew Syntax*, 21. Also see Joüon and Muraoka, *Grammar of Biblical Hebrew*, 420, §125p.

109. The referential ambiguity created by the incomplete passive in 3:12 poses a challenge for interpreters as evident in their divergent solutions. Bruce K. Waltke senses the ambiguity and stops interpreting all together. Waltke, *Commentary on Micah*, 150. Luker insightfully argues for the divine warrior as the agent. Luker, "Doom and Hope in Micah," 173–174. Longman unambiguously writes, "God himself will destroy this proud city. The destruction will be so complete that nothing will be left. Even the temple, which was the pinnacle of the hope that God's presence in Jerusalem would spare it from destruction, will be utterly destroyed and abandoned so that weeds will overgrow it." Longman, "Micah," 655. Marrs writes, "Yahweh will destroy the base of that false trust (Zion) . . . Yahweh counters by returning Zion to a plowed field and heap of ruins." Marrs, "Back to the Future," 83–84. Some scholars, resort to historical agents. Marvin A. Sweeney sees the Assyrian army under Sennacherib as the agent. Sweeney,

the divine warrior will upend Zion. So complete will be the devastation that the whole land (i.e. the city and its temple) will revert to cultivation and to a haunt for wild animals.[110]

Micah continues his description of Jerusalem's catastrophic situation in the second clause: "Jerusalem will become a heap of ruin" (וירושלם עיין תהיה) (Mic 3:12bα). Swanson suggests that "a heap of ruin" (עיין) speaks of "a mound of building material in a random pile, as a result of destruction (Ps 79:1; Jer 26:18a)."[111] Concerning "will become" (תהיה) – the main verb in the clause – S. Amsler's insightful study stands out. Amsler observes that the prophets' use of "to be" (היה) stresses the spectacular, the unanticipated, the incredible, and yet the reality of the decreed events.[112] He even goes so far as to insist that היה does not necessarily describe a facile historical process but describes events embodying Yahweh's special intrusion into earthly affairs to manifest his absolute sovereignty.[113] He argues:

> By multiplying par[allel] statements with a plethora of images, but without thoroughly describing the process, the prophets indicate that their *hyh* is not meant to express the precise course of events, but essentially the sovereign intervention of Yahweh in its various manifestations. . . . This intervention, both in judgment and in salvation, remains a wonder transcending the

---

Twelve Prophets, 2:374–375. Kenneth L. Barker believes the agent is King Nebuchadnezzar's Neo-Babylonian army. Barker, "Micah," 81. Contrary to Sweeney and Barker, at this point in Micah's prophecy (1:2–4:8), the only active martial agent is the divine warrior. As much as we might want to ground the passage in history, the immediate context lacks authentic clues from Micah himself (i.e., the text) to pursue a convincing, clear-cut historical reconstruction. An intentional examination of the context – the nature of the action involved and the characteristic attributes of the potential agent – provides genuine clues that guide us towards a relevant solution of identifying the agent behind the Niphal verb, תחרש. Specifically, the divine warrior's actions and statements describing Samaria's devastation parallel those describing the destruction of Zion. Bicknell, "Passives in Biblical Hebrew," 46, 50, 129. Meir Sternberg also agrees with Bicknell. While Sternberg notes the active role a reader plays in gap-filling (i.e., inference), he states that it is not an arbitrary process. Rather, it depends on many factors (clues), such as actions and themes, which the text explicitly communicates. Sternberg, *Poetics of Biblical Narrative*, 189.

110. Hoppe, *Holy City*, 77.
111. Swanson, *Dictionary of Biblical Languages*, §6505.
112. Amsler, "היה," 362.
113. Amsler, 362.

normal course of events and demonstrating the effectiveness of divine decision.[114]

Finally, the prophet brings the judgment of Zion to its ultimate conclusion in the third clause: "the mountain of the house into a wooded high place" (והר הבית לבמות יער) (Mic 3:12bβ). Having used the two synonymous terms for the city (Zion and Jerusalem), Micah opts for a more cultic term, "the mountain of the house" (הר הבית), which is really an abbreviation of "the mountain of the house of Yahweh" (הר בית־יהוה) (4:1). The emphasis is on the religious character and significance of the city. The spatial movement of the text started from heaven, then descended to the natural realm, then to the earth, to Israel, to Zion, and to the temple (1:2–3:12). Apparently, Micah has the temple at Zion as the ultimate concern. He foresees the city as a religious unit with the temple at the heights of the mountain as its focal center.[115]

However, divine judgment will turn the temple mount "into a wooded high place" (לבמות יער) (3:12). Paul R. Gilchrist is probably correct in stating that the semantic range of "ruins" (יער) includes a dense forest and a habitation where wild animals roam freely (e.g. 2 Kings 2:24; Amos 3:4; Mic 5:7).[116] Figuratively, "ruins" (יער) refers to Yahweh's judgments. Gilchrist concludes that, in certain instances (e.g. Mic 3:12), "the figure of judgment is turned around so that rather than being cut down, it is pictured as allowed to grow into a wilderness forest."[117] Indeed, such an empty space is fit for wild beasts. Jenson's remarks on the expression "into a wooded high place" (יער לבמות) are right on target. He writes, "Whichever habitat we imagine, the threat is that what was regarded as the center of the Israelite political and religious universe will become a place of desolation, forsaken by God and people."[118]

Taken together, the three spatial metaphors of Zion's destruction suggest an end to the city's election status.[119] As a field, a heap of ruins, and a wooded

---

114. Amsler, 362.

115. Renaud, *La formation du Livre de Michée*, 141.

116. Gilchrist, "יער," 391.

117. Gilchrist, 391.

118. Jenson, *Obadiah, Jonah, Micah*, 141; Wolff, *Micah: A Commentary*, 108–109; Mays, *Micah*, 92.

119. Clements, *Prophecy and Covenant*, 50.

height, Zion is inappropriate for any sacred purpose.[120] Essentially, Zion had forfeited her sacred status as the deity's dwelling place. It was an unthinkable idea though that the divine warrior was destroying or abandoning his own temple. Such a notion contradicted a popular assumption that calamity would not come because of the presence of the temple. The warrior was supposed to protect Zion (e.g. Pss 46:1–7; 48:1–5). His presence meant that the city and its inhabitants were safe as Micah's interlocutor presumed (Mic 3:11; cf. Jer 7:4).[121] Micah intrepidly opposed this notion. Yahweh's presence in Zion was not absolute and the temple was not an adequate guarantee of Yahweh's favor.[122] The temple was unable to save a people plagued by unbridled sin.

What is more, the catastrophe on Zion is actually a historical fulfillment of Yahweh's unfailing word. As he had explicitly warned, persistent covenant breach would result in a military defeat (Lev 26:31). Yahweh himself, as the divine warrior, will be the instrument of destruction (Lev 26:32–33). In fact, the whole of Micah 1:2–4:8 fulfills this threat from Levitcus 26. Throughout our target passage, Yahweh is the sole agent of destruction.

Several theological and rhetorical implications stem out of Zion's destruction. Perhaps Micah's relentless emphasis on the divine warrior's activities had a polemical intent against false gods. Maybe the prophet sought to dispel any imagination among his audience that any other gods were responsible for Zion's fate.[123] As evident, Micah does not even hint at human agency or armies in the imagery of Zion's devastation. Furthermore, Micah's emphasis on the divine warrior's activities likely conjures up a theological awareness among the remnant that their fate rests exclusively in Yahweh.[124] Their distress should go beyond the physical reality of the temple's ruination but point to the theological realization of a strained covenantal relationship.[125]

More importantly, Micah likely had a persuasive intent as well. Probably, the prophet desired the remnant to conclude that if the divine warrior could destroy the temple, his earthly house, how much more would he be willing

---

120. Maier, *Daughter Zion*, 59.

121. Chalmers, *Exploring the Religion*, 79–84. Conversely, the absence of the deity brought disorder, injustice, defeat from enemies, and exile. Walton, *Ancient Near Eastern Thought*, 129.

122. Clements, *God and Temple*, 84.

123. Boase, *Fulfilment of Doom?*, 200.

124. Boase, 200.

125. Boase, 200

to punish disobedient leaders entrusted with authority (e.g. priests, prophets, false teachers, judges). Such a conclusion might elicit fear and lead to repentance (cf. Jer 26:18–19).

Restoration: The Exaltation of Zion

Even though judgment is a pervasive motif in Micah 1:2–4:8, it is not the whole story nor Yahweh's last word.[126] Yahweh will restore the temple and establish his kingship (4:1–8). Micah envisions a new exalted temple/palace emerging out of the once ruined mountain (Mic 4:1aα). Mount Zion will tower over the other mountains and become great again (Mic 4:1aβ; cf. Ps 97:8).[127] While this greatness has nothing to do with Mount Zion's geophysical reality, Mays remarks that Zion's exaltation speaks of the "universal disclosure of the true house of God."[128] Zion will once more be a harbinger of peace. The nations will flow to the sacred city to learn torah, and Yahweh, as the judge, will settle their disputes (Mic 4:2–5).

Yahweh restores Zion's temple

In promising the restoration of Zion (Mic 4:1), Micah here continues the divine warrior's activities and applies them to Zion. As we have already pointed out, there is a continuity of thought between Micah 1:2 and 4:8. This point requires reemphasis because failure to appreciate these connections may lead to some errors in interpreting the book of Micah. As we have previously stated, Wolff believes that Micah is a complex book.[129] His negative appraisal lies in part in his insufficient attention to the unitary message the theophanies communicate. He reads the initial divine warrior theophany (1:3–4) as distinct and divorced from its complementary theophany (4:1–5).

As many scholars observe, there is continuity between the two theophanies. Clifford points out that the two passages are two sides of a recurring drama that is often abstracted from such divine warrior theophanies.[130] This connection allows us to discuss the theme of restoration. Despite the divine warrior's ruination of the land and the deportation of the people (Mic 1:16;

---

126. Leclerc, *Introduction to the Prophets*, 199.
127. McComiskey and Longman, "Micah," 524.
128. Mays, *Micah*, 96.
129. Wolff, *Micah*, 18.
130. Clifford, "Roots of Apocalypticism, 7.

3:12), the victorious warrior will not leave Zion as a plowed field. In a great reversal, the mountain of the house of the Lord "will be established" (נכון) as the head of the mountains (4:1).[131] Here we encounter an important and persistent motif common to the divine warrior tradition – that is, the building of the temple/palace following his victory (cf. Exod 15:17). As Clifford reminds us, "The warrior-god's victory is symbolized by a palace and dedication feast for all the gods."[132] Similarly, Mays also emphasizes that the election of Mount Zion as the place of Yahweh's abode in Micah 4:1 is consistent with other ANE traditions regarding divine mountains (cf. Pss 46:4; 48:2).[133]

Micah envisions a new exalted temple rising from the once ruined mountain (Mic 4:1aα). Mount Zion will tower above the mountains (Mic 4:1aβ; cf. Ps 97:8).[134] While this greatness has nothing to do with Mount Zion's geophysical reality, Mays comments that Zion's exaltation speaks of the "universal disclosure of the true house of God."[135] Likewise, Wolff notes that Zion's exaltation above other mountains points to Zion's preeminent status as the center of the world.[136] He further remarks that such exaltation "presents a polemic against other divine mountains, known to us from Ugarit to Mesopotamia."[137] Evidently, the divine warrior will demote all other mountains and destroy all competing shrines (Mic 5:9–14).

Furthermore, Mount Zion will be the boundary between the divine and human realms as nations will pilgrimage to Zion to meet their Sovereign Lord (Mic 4:1b–2a).[138] Michael B. Hundley argues that since the temple structure marked the intersection of two otherwise separate realms, "it became a place of power, accomplishing specific functions and communicating specific

---

131. The Niphal verb נכון deserves a comment. When understood within the context of the divine warrior's victory, the use of the verb כון, "established," in close proximity with הר, suggests that the divine warrior himself is the rebuilder of his sanctuary (Exod 15:17; cf. Ps 65:6). Although Micah does not identify the rebuilder of the new temple on Mount Zion (Mic 4:1aα), Yahweh is likely the builder (cf. Ps 78:68–69).

132. Clifford, "Roots of Apocalypticism," 22.

133. Mays, *Micah*, 96.

134. McComiskey and Longman, "Micah," 524.

135. Mays, *Micah*, 96.

136. Wolff, *Micah*, 120.

137. Wolff, 120.

138. Cohn, *Shape of Sacred Space*, 39, 69.

messages."¹³⁹ Thus according to Hundley, the temple's importance depended on the divine presence and the ritual interactions between that presence and humanity.¹⁴⁰

What is more, the figurative use of "established" (כון) with Zion as the object hints at the special status of Zion.¹⁴¹ This special status is because Yahweh chose Zion as his place of residence (cf. Deut 12:5; Ps 48:3–4; 78:67–69; 132:12–15; Zech 1:17). Yahweh's abode in the temple at Zion speaks of his presence in the midst of his people, "which intimates that its resident [Yahweh] had a vested interest in his residence and the community around it."¹⁴² We should note though that the presence of Yahweh was more important than the exaltation of the temple itself.¹⁴³ Cohn informatively remarks

---

139. Hundley, *Gods in Dwellings*, 3.
140. Hundley, 3.
141. Andersen and Freedman, *Micah*, 402.
142. Hundley, *Gods in Dwellings*, 3.
143. For Wolff, such exaltation reflects the completion of the postexilic temple. In other words, the sense of נכון as understood here is that of the physical elevation of the temple mount. He explains that "Here the unshakable stability (נכון) and especially the towering grandeur of God's mountain is emphasized for it stands as the peak of the mountains." Wolff, *Micah*, 120. Furthermore, the LXX translation of this statement exacerbates the issue of the towering of the temple mount of Zion over all the mountains. The LXX rendering of this verse is problematic: ἐμφανὲς τὸ ὄρος τοῦ κυρίου, ἕτοιμον ἐπὶ τὰς κορυφὰς τῶν ὀρέων ("the mountain of the Lord will manifest, established upon the tops of the mountains"). The LXX of Micah expresses נכון twice as ἐμφανές and ἕτοιμον. The LXX of Isaiah might account for the doublets in Micah. In Isa 2:2, ἐμφανὲς is from נכון and appears in the same word-order as that of the MT of Isa 2:2 (contrast Isa 2:2 [LXX] – ἐμφανὲς τὸ ὄρος κυρίου –with Micah 4:1 [LXX] – ἐμφανὲς τὸ ὄρος τοῦ κυρίου, ἕτοιμον ἐπὶ τὰς κορυφὰς). Most likely, then, the LXX translated נכון twice, first as ἕτοιμον at the place it appears in Micah (MT) and then by ἐμφανές at the same position as in Isaiah. This plausibly explains the doublets in Micah (LXX). Hence, the LXX appears to be a conflation of Isaiah and Micah passages; thus the MT should be preferred. For a more detailed discussion and references, see Waltke, *Commentary on Micah*, 193–194; McKane, *Book of Micah*, 121–122; Hillers, *Micah*, 49. While the idea that Mount Zion will be on top of the mountains is abnormal, to understand נכון in a literal sense as the physical elevation of Mount Zion above the other mountains is to go beyond what the data suggest. In the first place, the use of the verb to describe building structures becomes important. BDB, in its entry of נכון correctly suggests a metaphoric sense rather than a literal one (Brown, Driver, and Briggs, *Hebrew and English Lexicon*, 465). *HALOT* does not view נכון as the elevation of the temple in height. Rather, *HALOT* views the periphrastic construction of the yiqtol copulative יהיה with the participle נכון to describe building structures as "enduring" or "to be permanent" (Koehler, Baumgartner, and Stamm, *Hebrew and Aramaic Lexicon*, 464). נכון often describes the endurance of the throne or the dynasty of David (see 2 Sam 7:16, 26; 1 Kings 2:45). At any rate, the abstract sense of נכון suggests that the Lord's mountain "will be [permanently] established" in contrast to the collapse of the mountains in Micah 1:4. It gained its preeminent status among other mountains because of God dwelling there (i.e., his throne is established there) not because of its physical grandeur.

that "it is not the inherent nature of Zion that makes it secure but Yahweh's dwelling in the city."[144] Clements also insists that the centrality of the temple lies "in the belief that, as his chosen dwelling-place Yahweh's presence was to be found in it, and that from there he revealed his will and poured out his blessing upon his people."[145]

The impact of the exalted status of Zion is that "the people will flow to it [Zion]" (ונהרו עליו עמים) (Mic 4:1d) and "many nations shall come" (והלכו גוים רבים) (v. 2a). The emphasis of these parallel clauses is on the universal scope of the nations as they pilgrimage to the temple to acknowledge Yahweh's sovereignty. The pilgrims exhort each other in Israel's cultic language as they are in the process of streaming to Zion. They are not concerned with bringing tribute or offering to the temple, rather their sole focus in this pilgrimage is to "learn" (תורה) the ways of Yahweh, (Mic 4:2; cf. Ps 60:3–7; Hag 2:7).[146] Ironically, in Micah 3:11, "teaching" (תורה) is associated with the priests (cf. Jer 18:18; Ezek 44:23; Hag 2:11–13) and could hardly achieve peace and justice (cf. Mic 3:7, 11). However, in Micah 4:2, Yahweh himself is the one doing the teaching. Here תורה alludes to the general divine instruction, which brings peace and justice.[147] In some respect, Mount Zion appears to take over from Mount Sinai. In the future, what Mount Zion will be for Gentile nations closely mirrors what Mount Sinai had been for Israel in the past.

---

144. Cohn, *Shape of Sacred Space*, 39.

145. Clements, *God and Temple*, 76. He further notes that the exodus and Sinai traditions informed the belief. In the same vein, Clifford notes that the tradition behind Mic 4:1–5 is in concert with the Canaanite tradition regarding cosmic mountains. Clifford, *Cosmic Mountain*, 156–158. Similarly, Jon D. Levenson observes that Zion inherited various motifs associated with the Sinaitic theophany tradition. These include the divine warrior's march from Sinai (Deut 33:2; Ps 68:8–9), Sinai as the abode of Yahweh, and Sinai as the place for promulgating the law. As he goes on to point out, the "transfer of the divine home from Sinai to Zion meant that God was no longer seen as dwelling in an extraterritorial no man's land, but within the borders of the Israelite community." Levenson, *Sinai and Zion*, 91. Andersen and Freedman also acknowledge that the language was meant to evoke concrete ideas in the minds of the audience about how some motifs of the Sinai traditions were transplanted to Jerusalem. For instance, they point out that the "combination of mountain and house achieves a synthesis of the Sinai tradition (where the model of the Tabernacle/Temple was revealed to Moses) and the Zion tradition, where Solomon's Temple (the 'house' of 3:12 and 4:1–2) was erected." Andersen and Freedman, *Micah*, 404.

146. Ben Zvi, *Micah*, 97.

147. Ben Zvi, 98.

Besides learning torah, the pilgrims will have their disputes settled (Mic 4:3). Here Micah depicts Yahweh as the judge. As Ollenburger observed, among the various ways that Micah depicts Yahweh's sovereignty on Mount Zion, the most prominent ones are Yahweh as the judge (Mic 4:3-4) and king (v. 7).[148] Trimm also connects the divine warrior theme with Yahweh as a just judge (Gen 18:25; Ps 82:1; 1 Sam 8:20; Joel 3:12; Pss 7; 110:6).[149] In short, Yahweh "will judge" (ושפט) and "he will mediate" (והוכיח) between the nations, which results in an idyllic era (Mic 4:2-5). Andersen and Freedman correctly state that "the instruction desired [by the pilgrims] is a resolution of international disputes when both parties unreservedly agree to abide by Yahweh's decision."[150]

Apparently, the same pair of verbs "judge/mediate" (יכח/שפט) occurs twice in Isaiah 11:3-4, with the Davidic "branch" as the judge. The two parallel *weqātal* verbs suggest the maintenance of peace. The nations will transform war instruments into agricultural tools (Mic 4:3b; cf. Joel 4:10). The fact that military weapons will become agricultural tools recalls the basic task of humanity and the blessings of Eden (Gen 2:15). The consequence of a demilitarized Zion is everlasting peace, as each man dwells under his vine and under his fig tree without fear (Mic 4:4a). That they will no longer fear echoes God's promise to Israel before they entered Canaan (Lev.26:6), implying the formation of a new Israel and new exodus/conquest.

Yahweh restores his kingship in Zion

What is more, the rebuilding of the temple/palace anticipates the divine warrior's enthronement as king (4:7). Trimm affirms that the divine warrior theme is inseparable from the concept of divine kingship since the latter entails the victory of the warrior's battle (see Exod 15:3, 18).[151] In fact, a fundamental issue at stake in the divine warrior tradition is kingship (see Exod 15:11; Ps 47:7-8) and the ensuing cosmic order that the victor king inaugurates (see Pss 89:16-19; 93:1-2).[152] Apparently, Micah 2:12-13 already

---

148. Ollenburger, *Zion*, 23.
149. Trimm, *"YHWH Fights for Them!,"* 38-39.
150. Andersen and Freedman, *Micah*, 405.
151. Trimm, *"YHWH Fights for Them!,"* 37.
152. Clifford, "Roots of Apocalypticism," 31-32.

anticipates the divine warrior's kingship as he delivered a remnant from exile and led them to Zion (see Exod 13:21; Deut 1:30–33). Evidently, a return from exile to the promised land was simply a return to Zion. Cruz captures well the return of the divine warrior to assume kingship in Zion. He writes:

> [Mic] 2:12–13 does not only announce the return of the remnant to their homeland, but also the return of Yahweh, who will lead them home and rule over them as king. The re-establishment of Yahweh's sovereignty is an important feature of the grand programme of the restoration of Israel, and will be made evident in the second pastoral-royal in 4:6–7.[153]

From this significant idea of the divine warrior as king in Zion (Mic 4:7), an important strand of thought proceeds; that is, only when the victorious warrior sits enthroned in Zion will blessings flow to the people. He will assemble those with physical infirmities (i.e. the lame, the cast-off, and the afflicted) and will restore them to form a strong nation (Mic 4:6–7; cf. Ps 97:10).[154] As McComiskey and Longman point out, the "emphasis is on the misery and helplessness of the exiles and forms a striking contrast to the "strong nation" (Mic 4:7) they are to become as a result of God's intervention in their behalf."[155] In keeping with his covenant obligations, the divine warrior will transform the fortunes of Zion and will eternally rule over a remnant on Mount Zion. Furthermore, in anticipation of the Davidic kingdom, daughter Zion will regain her former dominion (Mic 4:8). Altogether, Micah 1:2–4:8 participates in the unfolding drama of the divine warrior's advent to punish Israel for covenant breach (1:2–3:12), yet the ultimate goal is the nation's restoration (4:1–8). The building of the temple on the cosmic mountain (4:1) and the enthronement of the eternal king (4:7) signal Yahweh's absolute kingship!

---

153. Cruz, "*Who Is Like Yahweh?*," 198.
154. Sweeney, *Twelve Prophets*, 2:381–382; Poulsen, *Representing Zion*, 154.
155. McComiskey and Longman, "Micah," 525.

Significance of Divine Sovereignty in Zion
Zion as the Cosmic Mountain

Yahweh's sovereignty in Zion serves polemical ends against pagan worship. Zion's exaltation shows her sacred status above other sacred mountains. Yahweh's victory, just like Baal's victory, resulted in the establishment of his kingship at his new temple on Mount Zion, the cosmic mountain. The imagery of the cosmic mountain as the temple/palace of the gods is familiar from ancient Near Eastern mythology.

In Mesopotamia, Gudea's temple-building text specifies the temple's cosmic characteristics, "The temple . . . which grows between heaven and earth. . . . The beautiful mountain . . . which towers above the mountains" (Gudea Cylinder B: i. 1–7).[156] In Neo-Assyrian literature, Esarhaddon describes Esarra as "Ehursaggula, house of the Great Mountain. . . . Its lofty high head scraped the sky."[157] In Ugaritic literature, Baal established his temple on the cosmic mountain, Mount Zaphon, after his victory over Yamm.

Similarly, Mount Zion functioned as the divine mountain in Israel as a symbol of Yahweh's victory and a symbol of his universal kingdom (see Ps 68:15–18). In this light, Mount Zion serves as the center of the earth and will be established as the true place of worship in contrast to Mount Zaphon, its competitor.[158] Wolff himself suggests that the preeminence of Mount Zion serves as "an indirect polemic against other divine mountains, as they are known to us from Ugarit to Mesopotamia."[159]

In addition, the ultimate goal of the divine warrior's devastation of the mountains was not the destruction of the gods per se, but the restoration and reestablishment of cosmic order. Samuel Terrien correctly observes that worshipping pagan gods only brings chaotic confusion within the universe.[160] Subtly, the destruction of mountains is a means towards the restoration of order; their destruction essentially exalts Zion as the chief mountain. Accordingly, Zion's exaltation speaks of the reestablishment of Yahweh's earthly throne, which leads to the restoration of righteousness and justice

---

156. "The Cylinders of Gudea," translated by Richard E. Averbeck (*COS* 2.155: 429)
157. Hurowitz, *I Have Built You an Exalted House*, 245.
158. Waltke, *Commentary on Micah*, 194.
159. Wolff, *Micah: A Commentary*, 91.
160. Terrien, *Psalms*, 680.

(Mic 4:2). These twin themes are foundational to Yahweh's kingship and are harbingers of cosmic order. Hossfeld and Zenger conclude that a major role of the storm imagery is that it "undivinizes the gods" and restores divine rule, resulting in the nurturing of righteousness and justice on earth.[161]

Yahweh as the Cosmic King

Yahweh's kingship also serves as a polemic against pagan deities, which is a sign of his cosmic rule. Opening the book with the divine warrior tradition is a polemic against other gods, among other things. Specifically, the divine warrior tradition underscores the cosmic sovereignty of Yahweh in militaristic terms. Although the militaristic nature of Micah's theophany presents an incomplete picture of a battle scene for our modern sensibilities (e.g. lack of explicit mention of enemy gods actively wielding weapons), the vestiges that remain are not merely bare images depleted of their meaning. For Micah's idolatrous audience, the mention of melting mountains, fire, and other features was enough to evoke scenes of the storm-god warrior defeating enemies and marching triumphantly to take up kingship over the cosmos at the cosmic mountain.

Presumably, Micah adapted and transformed the divine warrior tradition into counter-myths, which he anchored firmly in history, to demonstrate "how all the powers and attributes of god that were claimed for pagan deities properly belong to Yahweh."[162] In fact, to acclaim Yahweh as king is a polemic against the divinity of all other deities in the ANE since Marduk and Baal were acclaimed as such.[163] Likewise, Yahweh's acclamation as king over the other gods delegitimizes their kingship (cf. Ps 97:7, 9).[164] Psalm 97 opens with the introit (יְהוָה מָלָךְ) "Yahweh reigns!" (v. 1), which celebrates his enthronement (cf. Pss 47; 93; 96; 99).[165] Indisputably, Yahweh is king because of his military prowess. Thus, Micah's use of the divine warrior tradition is polemical. To

---

161. Hossfeld and Zenger, *Psalms 2*, 473.

162. Boadt, "Mythological Themes," 217.

163. As Marduk battled Tiamat, the gods acclaimed him king: "Marduk is king!" Similarly, after defeating Yam, Baal is hailed king: "Baal shall be king!" Human, "Psalm 93," 158.

164. Human, 158.

165. On the basis of grammar, it is possible to translate the expression יהוה מלך as "Yahweh is king" or "Yahweh has become king" (see 1 Kgs 15:33; 2 Kgs 9:14). See Tate, *Psalms 51–100*, 472n1b; Howard, *Structure of Psalms 93–100*, 36.

convince the pagan idolaters of Yahweh's cosmic sovereignty, Micah depicts Yahweh descending from heaven to battle idolatry perpetuated by the gods in the natural realm. Religious polemics against pagan gods is another way to underscore Yahweh's sovereignty.[166]

---

166. Chisholm, "'To Whom Shall You Compare Me?,'" 64; Middlemas, *Divine Image*, 22–23.

CHAPTER 5

Divine Sovereignty and the Davidic King (Micah 4:9–5:14)

Introduction

In keeping with the general cultural assumptions of the ancient world concerning the concept of divine sovereignty, the Old Testament makes evident that Yahweh did not only choose a place from which to rule but also a human king as his earthly vicegerent (e.g. 2 Sam 7:7–16; Pss 2:7–12; 78:68–71; 89:5–18, 19–37). The divine vicegerent and Zion were together Yahweh's administrative provisions for the actualization of his reign throughout the earth (Ps 2:6).[1] As Batto points out, "The human king was the 'image' of the divine sovereign, his viceroy on earth, charged with perfecting the divine sovereign's work of creation by promoting right order, justice, and the human weal."[2] Walton also adds, "As in the ancient Near East, the Israelite king is the agent of the divine plan, concerned with the will of the deity, and representative of divine authority."[3] Dan G. McCartney makes a strong case that the reinstatement of the Davidic dynasty in Zion signals the arrival of the divine sovereignty on earth.[4] In other words, Yahweh exercises his sovereign rule on earth through his earthly vicegerent seated in Zion.

In light of the foregoing observations, this chapter investigates the reestablishment of Yahweh's sovereignty in Micah 4:9–5:14 in relation to the third

---

1. Mays, *Lord Reigns*, 19.
2. Batto, "Divine Sovereign," 163; Chalmers, *Interpreting the Prophets*, 83.
3. Walton, *Ancient Near Eastern Thought*, 284.
4. McCartney, "Ecce Homo," 2, 3; Alexander, *From Eden*, 91–94.

major claim of the Zion/Davidic traditions: Yahweh's choice of the Davidic king as his earthly viceroy. Evidently, the restoration of Yahweh's reign in Zion coincides with the restoration of the Davidic dynasty. Micah 4:7–8 clearly illustrates this situation. These two significant verses relate the reign of Yahweh to that of the Davidic king.

Immediately after Yahweh announced his reign over a restored remnant in Zion (Mic 4:7), the next verse promises the restoration of David's "former dominion" (הממשלה הראשנה) and "kingship" (ממלכת) (4:8bα).[5] As most scholars would agree, the promise recalls the glorious days of the Davidic kingdom. At its core, the promise also anticipates the coming of an ideal king who will restore Zion's dominion over the nations. Viewed as such, there can be no doubt then that the reestablishment of Yahweh's kingship in Zion inextricably dovetails with the restoration of his viceroy's kingdom.[6] In his recently published commentary on Micah, Stephen G. Dempster states, "The events described in this large unit [4:6–5:14] indicate the method by which Jerusalem's and the temple's glory will be achieved."[7]

Therefore, it is our contention in this chapter that the rest of Micah 4:9–5:14 fleshes out the promise made in 4:8. An immediate consequence of the promise is its assumptions.[8] It assumes that Zion has lost its former dominion and that Zion has not yet regained her former status.[9] These assumptions allow us to query what precipitated the loss of Zion's former dominion in the first place. What was Zion's sin, which resulted in the loss of her king and her former glory (4:9–14)? As we will show, the combined message of the three tumultuous oracles (Mic 4:9–10, 10–13, 14) underscores the ineffectiveness of Zion's present king and anticipates the transition of Zion's kingship from a theocracy (4:7) to an ideal dynastic monarchy (5:1).

Following our discussion of the fate of Zion's king (Mic 4:9–14), we will pick up the positive aspects of the promise, the restoration of Zion's former dominion. Two related themes central to this promise are evident. These include the restoration of the Davidic kingship and Zion's domination over

---

5. Jacobs, *Conceptual Coherence*, 150; Lee, *Intertextual Analysis*, 112.
6. Dempster, *Dominion and Dynasty*, 188–189.
7. Dempster, *Micah*, 132.
8. Luker, "Doom and Hope," 180.
9. Jacobs, *Conceptual Coherence*, 150.

the nations.[10] Thus, the coming Davidic king and the defeat of the nations take center stage and become the main attractions of our target passage. Towards these goals, we will organize our analysis of the transformation of Davidic kingship around the dynamic Zion tradition pattern of sin, judgment, and restoration. Finally, we will close the chapter with a discussion of the significance of Davidic kingship in Zion.

Overview of Micah 4:9–5:14

Unity of Micah 4:9–5:14

While Micah 4:9–5:14 coheres thematically around the concern for Zion's former dominion, the internal structure of Micah 4:9–5:14 poses a challenge for scholars, because the message alternates abruptly between scenes of defeat and humiliation (e.g. 4:9–10) and scenes of battle and victory (e.g. 4:11–13).[11] Cuffey observes a similar challenge. He notes that "in 4:9–5:14 it is much harder to decide which material should be grouped with which."[12] Richard A. Fuhr Jr. and Gary E. Yates also remark that the "chronology of the events that the prophet portrays is also difficult to determine because the prophet telescopes near and far events together in some confusing ways."[13] As a result, "Quite a number of competing readings of the structure of this section have been proposed."[14]

Despite the aforementioned challenges, Micah 4:9–5:14 comprises a distinct rhetorical unit from the previous one (1:2–4:8). Rhetorically, the adverbial particles "now" (עתה) mark the unit (4:9, 10, 11, 14). These particles underscore Zion's present distress because of the lack of an effective king. They markedly contrast with the future verbs "will be" (והיה) (5:4, 6, 7, 9), which anticipate Zion's future exaltation among the nations.

In addition to the עתה particles, notable shifts in focus distinguish our target unit even further from Micah 1:2–4:8. In the main, Micah has the transformation of human kingship in purview in this unit. Earlier, Micah

---

10. Sweeney, *Twelve Prophets*, 2:384; Smith-Christopher, *Micah*, 151.
11. Barker, "Micah," 90; Reunions, *Changing Subjects*, 158.
12. Cuffey, *Literary Coherence*, 233.
13. Fuhr and Yates, *Message of the Twelve*, 194.
14. Cuffey, *Literary Coherence*, 233–234.

indicts the leaders of Israel, its priests, judges, prophets, and rich elites for various sins which led to Zion's demise (3:12). The rich and powerful cheated the poor of their land (2:1–3), the judges rendered judgment for bribes, the priests charged a fee for their teaching, and the prophets profited from divining oracles (3:1–11). However, what is striking is that there is no indictment against Zion's present king. One can only wonder whether a competent king would allow such patent injustices in the land to take place without intervening. Perhaps the human king was incompetent. Our curiosity and speculations on the text's silence about the king are short-lived. The next section (Mic 4:9–5:14) addresses this very issue as the spotlight shines on him.

Moreover, related to the kingship motif is Micah's focus on the interesting concept of simultaneity. The concept describes the warrior deity and his human king and army both fighting on the same battlefield against a common enemy.[15] Specifically, for the first time in Micah, Yahweh fights alongside a militarized remnant to defeat the nations (Mic 4:11–13) and equips a new king for war (5:3–4). Earlier, Yahweh appeared as the sole warrior on the battlefield (e.g. 1:2–7; 3:12). In stark contrast, in the present passage, Yahweh utilizes human agency to battle the nations. Marrs concurs that Micah 5:1–5 "introduces a striking new element to the restoration of Zion. For the first time (and only time) in the book of Micah, a human agent arises to implement and exercise Yahweh's victorious sovereignty over the land."[16] Thus, the concept of simultaneity thematically demarcates Micah 4:9–5:14 from 1:2–4:8.

Another shift in focus is evident as Zion battles hostile nations. The nations do not figure prominently in the book until Micah 4. Apart from the foreign pilgrims coming peacefully to Zion to acknowledge Yahweh's sovereignty (4:1–5), Micah is silent on the role or fate of foreign nations in the earlier chapters (1–3). However, in Micah 4:9–5:14, lexical terms pointing to foreign nations are common. For instance, Micah explicitly mentions "Babylon" (בבל) and "from the hand of your enemies" (מכף איביך) (4:10), "Assyria" (אשור) (5:4, 5), "land of Nimrod" (ארץ נמרד) (5:5), and "nations" (גוים) (4:11, 13; 5:7, 14). In subsequent sections, we will demonstrate that Micah 4:9–5:14 has much

---

15. Wright, "Military Valor and Kingship," 38.
16. Marrs, "Back to the Future," 89; Bateman, Bock, and Johnston, *Jesus the Messiah*, 118–119.

to say about the fate of the nations.[17] In short, unlike Micah 1:2–4:8, where the nations are peaceful, in Micah 4:9–5:14 the nations are hostile to Zion and her king (e.g. 4:9–10, 14).

Zion/Davidic Traditions in Micah 4:9–5:14

In an effort to present the future restoration of Zion's former dominion, the prophet draws heavily on earlier biblical traditions. However, for our present needs, we will limit our discussion to motifs from the Zion/Davidic traditions. In fact, the reference to Bethlehem Ephratha also points to the Davidic traditions. Bethlehem is most likely David's place of birth and definitely the place of his anointing as Israel's next king after Saul (1 Sam 16:1–13; 17:12). Ephratha is often identified with Bethlehem (Gen 35:19; 48:7; Ruth 4:11) and with David (Ps 132:6).[18]

Another allusion to the Zion/Davidic traditions is seen in the prophet's subtle use of the birth/labor simile in Micah 4:9–10. Without being exhaustive, the twice repeated simile "like a woman in labor" (חיל כיולדה) (4:9, 10) alludes to an exact simile in Psalm 48:7. The formulaic nature of the simile is well known. It appears with some variation in several passages (e.g. Ps 48:7; Isa 13:8; 42:14; Jer 6:24; 30:6; 49:24; 50:43). For our purposes, we limit Micah's intended context to Psalm 48:7 because the two texts correspond thematically. Both passages focus on the aggression of the nations towards Zion (Mic 4:9–11; Ps 48:4–6).[19]

An additional dominant motif from the Zion/Davidic traditions is the classical *Völkerkampf* motif (Mic 4:11–13).[20] In this motif, which is a reshaped expression of the inviolability of Zion (Pss 46:6; 48:4; 76:3–6), the nations storm Zion, but they are soundly defeated (Mic 4:11–13).[21] Mays submits that 4:13 stems from a summons to a battle tradition, whereas 4:11–12 "are an

---

17. Timmer, *Non-Israelite Nations*, 96–106; Zapff, "Perspective on the Nations," 301–303.
18. Sweeney, *Twelve Prophets*, 2:387.
19. While the dating of psalms is notoriously difficult, the Zion tradition themes reflected in Ps 48:2–9 are from the pre-exilic period. See the appendix for a discussion on the origins of the Zion/Davidic traditions. Thus, it is likely that Ps 48:2–9 is earlier than Mic 4:9–11. As such, the burden of proof is upon those who would suggest otherwise.
20. Wagenaar, *Judgement and Salvation*, 287.
21. Wagenaar, 287.

expression of the motif of the 'assault of the nations/peoples' against Zion."[22] He notes:

> Motif and type are not combined elsewhere, and this is the only place where the "summons to battle" is addressed to Israel in the prophetic texts. It usually appears in oracles of doom against other nations addressed to the forces who will destroy them [Israel]. And in all the other occurrences of the "assault of Zion" motif, it is YHWH who intervenes directly and mysteriously to vanquish them.[23]

Observant readers will also notice that Micah clearly utilizes themes from the dynamic Zion tradition in articulating the present crisis of Zion at the hands of the nations. Specifically, Zion's inhabitants are exiled to Babylon, but in the future Yahweh will restore them (Mic 4:10). Most noteworthy is the transformation of Davidic kingship. Like the transformation of Zion, the transformation of Davidic kingship follows the recurring pattern of implied sin, judgment, exile, and restoration. Micah skillfully interweaves the pattern throughout this unit. As Dumbrell points out, "The prophet, in 4:9–5:15, thus has an optimistic look at current events. He does not deny the difficulty of the present but confronts it with the well-established Zion traditions. This leads to the conviction that Zion will triumph and an ideal ruler will emerge."[24]

Transformation of Davidic Kingship
Implied Sin Concerning Zion's King and Inhabitants

Mays states that there is a correlation between sin and judgment in Micah.[25] He adds that judgment falls against transgressors and fits their deeds.[26] Dempster also argues that throughout the book the assumption is that Yahweh

---

22. Mays, *Micah*, 107.
23. Mays, 107.
24. Dumbrell, *Faith of Israel*, 211.
25. Mays, *Micah*, 20. For treatments of the various models on the correspondence between sin and judgment, see Boase, *Fulfilment of Doom?*, 141–152; Miller, *Sin and Judgment*, passim; Tucker, "Sin and 'Judgment,'" 373–388; Van Henten and Houtepen, *Religious Identity*, 57–87; Barton, "Natural Law," 1–14; Westermann, *Basic Forms*, passim; Allen, *Books of Joel, Obadiah, Jonah and Micah*, 289.
26. Mays, *Micah*, 20.

will judge the covenant community for its sins.²⁷ Cuffey observes that the divine judgments in Micah 4:9–14 (e.g. exile and the king's humiliation) contain no mention of any sin which provoked them.²⁸ Both Mays's and Cuffey's seemingly contradictory conclusions are correct. Indeed, although the larger context (i.e. Mic 4:9–5:14) does not explicitly mention the specific sins of Zion's king or inhabitants, the nature of judgment implies gross sins. Dethroning Zion's king and exiling her citizen is a sign of covenant violations (Mic 4:9–10, 14), as exile represents the ultimate judgment for covenant violations (Lev 26:33).

As we have stated in chapter 2, for a covenant people to go into exile shows persistence in sin. Indisputably, the Davidic kings were obligated to obey torah and any violations would incur divine judgment (see 2 Sam 7:14; 1 Kgs 11:11–13). Moses had long warned ancient Israel that Yahweh would exile the people and their king from the land for disobedience to torah (Deut 28:15). During their exile from the land, they would have all the opportunity to serve the worthless idols that provoked deportation (Deut 28:36). Likewise, Samuel also echoed the same threat. He warned that the people and their king would perish if they persisted in rebellion against Yahweh (1 Sam 12:15, 24). Unlike Moses and Samuel, Yahweh's oracle to Solomon is even more concrete. Idolatry will cause him to cut off the nation from the land (i.e. exile), abandon his temple, and make Israel an object of ridicule (1 Kgs 9:6–7). Furthermore, Yahweh will turn the temple into a heap of ruins (v. 8).

Given the wider context of Micah, Yahweh's descent from heaven and his judgment of his covenant people were provoked by their rebellion and sins (e.g. Mic 1:5, 13; 3:8; 6:7, 13; 7:18, 19). In particular, the prophet targets both secular and religious leaders for rampant idolatry and social injustice in the land, (e.g. 1:5; 2:1–5; 3:1–11). Despite the silence about Zion's king, this does not exclude him as a possible culprit. Perhaps the king was indifferent to the sins of the leaders because they supported his court (cf. 1 Sam 8:11–17).

Even more so, idolatry incurred greater cultic and political misgivings for the king. As Yahweh's earthly vicegerent, there was a great possibility that he could easily be mistaken for an "idol," as Samuel seems to imply. Samuel

---

27. Dempster, *Micah*, 196.
28. Cuffey, *Literary Coherence*, 266.

hangs the request for a king and Israel's idolatry on the same plane of rebellion. Both are an utter repudiation of Yahweh's sovereignty (1 Sam 8:7–9). Perhaps Josiah became a model king, surpassing even David and Hezekiah, because of his sweeping reforms on idolatry (2 Kgs 23:25).[29] Similarly, unbridled injustice in the land also reflected negatively on Yahweh's vicegerent. Both the heavenly and the earthly thrones were founded upon justice and righteousness (Pss 89:15, 29; 97:2; Mic 4:1–5). Injustice threatened the social fabric and vitality of the covenant community. In this respect, that symbiotic relationship between Yahweh and his earthly vicegerent and the congruence between heaven and earth had to be maintained in order to prevent chaos on earth.[30] Thus, the dethroning of the king strongly suggests some high-handed transgressions and sins (Mic 4:14).

Judgment upon Zion's King and Inhabitants
The literary shape of Micah 4:9–14

The three mixed oracles in Micah 4:9–14 comprise a sequence of disparate, yet related, events that converge to address the demise of Zion's kingship.[31] The three oracles (4:9–10, 11–13, 14) share a similar form, which is signaled by the temporal particle עתה (4:9, 11, 14) and a present situation of distress followed by a promise of hope. In the main, each of these oracles is addressed with a vocative "Daughter Zion" (בת־ציון) (4:10, 13) and the mysterious "Daughter of troops" (בת־גדוד) (v. 14), followed by imperatives, "writhe and groan" (חולי וגחי) (v. 10), "arise and thresh" (קומי ודושי) (v. 13), and "gather in troops" (תתגדדי) (v. 14). In fact, Waltke and Hagstrom have gone an extra mile to abstract a structure for the first two oracles.[32]

The misunderstanding concerning the relation of these mixed oracles to each other is still long standing. In essence, the thorny issues concern how the doom and hope oracles relate, as well as the apparent inconsistencies

---

29. Thelle, *Approaches*, 196.

30. Leclerc, *Yahweh Is Exalted*, 65.

31. By "mixed," we refer to the abrupt reversal of the oracles from defeat and exile to rescue (4:9–10), the siege on Zion by foreign nations to Zion's decisive victory (4:11–13), and the humiliation of Zion's king (4:14).

32. Now (9A/11B); situation of distress (9B/11A); appeal to Daughter Zion with two feminine imperatives (10A/13Aα); situation of victory (10 B/13Aαβ–B). Waltke, *Commentary on Micah*, 246; Hagstrom, *Coherence*, 62.

in the chronological order of events in the oracles. Scholars have proffered various solutions. Some redaction critics simply discard the hope oracles.[33] Others discern various structures that promote unity and coherence.[34] While these structures have much to commend them, in our judgment some of them actually obscure the theological message Micah seeks to convey. It is likely that an oral audience focused more on understanding the message than discerning the literary structure of that message. A plausible path to understand Micah's message in these three עתה oracles is to read them in light of the traditions they evoke.

While we might not understand all the finer points of the passage, we contend that the oracles in Micah 4:9–14 have a narrative substructure at their base. Micah 4:9–14 is a possible theological reflection on the events at the dawn of kingship in ancient Israel. Our target passage reshapes the traditions about the emergence of kingship in Israel to make a statement about the transition from a warrior-led nation to a dynastic monarchy. Sandwiched between Yahweh's reign (Mic 4:7–8) and the anticipation of an ideal dynastic monarchy (5:1), Micah 4:9–14 is a purposefully designed and placed passage that occasions the need for an ideal Davidic king who will defeat the nations and extend Yahweh's sovereignty among the nations (5:1–5).

---

33. For instance, Biddle points out that the juxtaposition of an exile in and exodus from Babylon (Mic 4:10), and the defeat of many nations gathered against Zion (vv. 11–13), creates a tension that defies harmonization. He resolves the tension by needlessly excising the hope materials – the exodus from Babylon (v. 10bβ) and the defeat of the nations (vv. 12–13). After expunging the hope material, he suggests that the remaining doom material in the עתה oracles communicate a coherent message: Zion is under siege from hostile nations and the earthly ruler has already been exiled. Biddle, "Dominion Comes to Jerusalem," 255.

34. Cuffey avers that a key to unlock the relation among these oracles is to recognize the symmetrical structure on which each lies. He concludes that the structure communicates a message of painful doom at the hands of foreign nations, which will receive resolution in the subsequent section (Mic 5:1–14). He goes on to delineate a five-element structure: (A) Defeat (4:9–10e); (B) God's plans (4:10f–g); (C) Hostility (4:11); (B') God's plans (4:12–13); (A') Defeat (4:14). Cuffey, *Literary Coherence*, 235. Johnston also observes an eleven-element symmetric arrangement that spans 4:1–5:14. His structure has at its center Yahweh's hidden plan for Zion and the nations (4:12–13). In his schema, Johnston commendably unravels the chiastic structure and rearranges the oracles in a linear chronological order. For him, the resultant parallel elements (A. 4:12–13; B. 4:11/4:14; C; 4:9–10/5:1–2; D. 4:7b–8/5:3–6; E. 4:6a–7a/5:6–8; F. 4:1–5/5:9–14) flow from the earliest event (4:12–13) to later events (4:1–5/5:9–14). He concludes that the historical short-term doom and hope oracles (4:6–5:8) provide an important segue for the already/not yet fulfillment of Micah's prediction of the coming ideal Davidic king (5:1–5). Bateman, Bock, and Johnston, *Jesus the Messiah*, 121–122.

Emergence of kingship traditions in Micah (4:9–14)

That Micah 4:9–14 reflects the traditions about the emergence of kingship in ancient Israel is evident from the intertextual links Micah makes to Samuel's corpus. A significant expression that supports this claim is the expression "from the hands of your enemies" (מכף איביך) (v. 10). The expression is polyvalent and evokes a network of intertextual links built around a group of texts (e.g. Judg 2:18; 8:34; 1 Sam 12:10, 11; 2 Sam 3:18; 19:10; 22:1; 2 Kgs 17:39; Pss 18:1; 31:15; 106:10). Quite importantly, the polyvalent nature of the expression should not startle us. It is common for stereotypical language that is rooted in culture and tradition to be polyvalent. Such language serves as an entry point to contextual and thematic parallels between texts belonging to the wider shared tradition an author might be evoking.[35]

The expression and its wider context have received little sustained attention. Smith-Christopher, to his credit, has perceived the parallels between Micah and some of these texts (e.g. 1 Sam 4:3; 2 Sam 19:10; Ezra 8:31; Pss 18:1; 71:4).[36] In a passing mention, he notes that the expression rarely appears in the prophets other than in Jeremiah 15:21, which seems to be drawing from knowledge of the Micah traditions.[37] Apart from this rehearsal, Smith-Christopher does not attempt to exploit the implications that might stem from his observation.[38]

In order to grasp Micah's use of the expression, we must reconstruct Micah's intended context from the wider context shown above. Without being exhaustive, syntactical and thematic correspondences clearly show that Micah's intended context is 1 Samuel 12:11.[39] Syntactically, the construction (מן prep + human body part + lexeme איב + 2nd person suffix) occurs only in Micah 4:10 and 1 Samuel 12:11. Thematically, both passages emphasize the

---

35. See discussion on pp. 77–89.
36. Smith-Christopher, *Micah*, 154.
37. Smith-Christopher, 154.
38. Smith-Christopher, 154.
39. מכף איביך (Mic 4:10) // מיד איביכם (1 Sam 12:11). Wording does not necessarily have to be precise in alluding to a common tradition which an author shares with his audience. Synonyms are applicable: כף and יד (e.g. Gen 40:11; Num 5:18). Furthermore, that the referents to the 2nd person suffixes differ is not enough to invalidate Micah's use of the tradition. Various generations encountered different enemies. Thematically, the main point is simply that the nations are hostile to God's people. See our earlier discussion on allusions to traditions pp. 75–89).

theme of kingship. Both passages recall the exodus and conquest traditions through proper naming (Mic 6:3–5; 1 Sam 12:6–12). For instance, Micah mentions Moses, Aaron, and Miriam (Mic 6:4), while Samuel mentions only the two male leaders, Moses and Aaron (1 Sam 12:6, 8). The omission of Miriam in Samuel's speech should not detract or invalidate the allusion from its significance.[40] Also, Micah 4:10 speaks of a new exodus from Babylon. In our opinion, 1 Samuel 12:11 has the closest contextual parallels to Micah 4:10, and it is in this intended context that Micah's passage finds relevance.

Another lexical parallel that demonstrates that Micah 4:9–14 reflects the traditions about the emergence of kingship in ancient Israel is the construct relationship in the expression "judge of Israel" (שפט ישראל), which occurs in several passages (Mic 4:14; Num 25:5; 1 Chron 17:6).[41] A relevant variation of the expression is "prince . . . over Israel" (נגיד . . . על־ישראל) (2 Sam 7:8). Waltke remarks that Micah 4:14 was stimulated by Yahweh's statements to David in 2 Samuel 7:8.[42] The verbal correspondence might appear dubious, since Micah 4:14 uses שפט and 2 Samuel 7:8 uses נגיד. However, on closer examination this is not the case at all. The terms in the word group (שפט, שר, נגיד) are synonyms. In fact, שפט and שר are used interchangeably (Exod 2:14).

More importantly, despite the variations, the verbal expressions provide an entry point to thematic correspondences between the contexts. As we will elaborate shortly, the passages thematically focus on kingship (Mic 4:14; 2 Sam 7:8; 1 Chr 17:6). Yahweh's oracle to Nathan (2 Sam 7:8; 1 Chr 17:6) is more relevant than Numbers 25:5.

As further motivation to our observation, Sweeney agrees that the mention of "judge" (שפט) recalls its use throughout the book of Judges.[43] Goldingay

---

40. It is not unusual for allusions that comprise a list to have some elements expunged. For instance, Nehemiah's allusion to the Abrahamic covenant is unmistaken, even though he lists only six nations (Neh 9:6–8) instead of ten (Gen 15:19–20). In addition, Psalm 78 lists only seven plagues (Ps 78:44–49) instead of ten (Exod 7–12), yet this does not invalidate the allusion to the exodus. Furthermore, in alluding to the destruction of Sodom and Gomorrah (Gen 19:24), Deuteronomy lists two additional cities besides Sodom and Gomorrah (i.e., Admah and Zeboiim). See Deut 29:23.

41. In this famous oracle, Yahweh reminds his new viceroy David, through Nathan, of a time during the Judges era when he did not burden any judge (i.e., military leader) with building him a temple.

42. Waltke, *Commentary on Micah*, 301.

43. Sweeney, *Twelve Prophets*, 2:387; Whitelam, *Just King*, 53–54; McKenzie, "Judge of Israel," 121.

acknowledges that a link between the theme of human kingship in Micah and the rise of kingship in early Israel exists.[44] As he fittingly states, "The present king is here spoken of as a 'leader' (*šōpēṭ*), the term for the leaders in the book of judges, before Israel had kings. It is more significant that Micah does not use the word *king* when speaking of a king to come."[45] Altogether, it appears that the prophet intentionally frames Micah 4:9–14 around the traditions about the origins of kingship in ancient Israel. The intertextual links open up a dialogue between Micah 4:9–14 and the traditions and allow for further explorations.

A metaleptic reading of Micah 4:9–14

The aforementioned overt links by no means address the crux of the matter. To appreciate the allusions, we must explore the contextual assumptions in the evoked passages even closer. Because of a high density of thematic correspondences between Micah 4:9–14 and 1 Samuel 12, we will focus on these two texts and explore the allusion via metalepsis.[46] Metalepsis has a basic storied feature built into it, which allows us to import more of the antecedent text. Several major themes of concern here are the ineffectiveness of Zion's present king (Mic 4:9–10), the idea of a warrior-led nation as a result of a feeble king (4:11–13), and the eventual removal of Zion's king from his throne (4:14).

Briefly, an important theme that 1 Samuel 12 wrestles with is kingship. Israel had earlier demanded to transition from a warrior-led nation to one led by a human king (1 Sam 8).[47] Recall that, at the dawn of the monarchy, following the original exodus/conquest, concerns over the security of the nation against foreign invaders gave rise to the transition from a warrior-led nation

---

44. Goldingay, *Old Testament Theology*, 2:488.

45. Goldingay, 2:488.

46. Brown understands metalepsis as a literary device, whereby a part stands for the whole. Specifically, she views a metalepsis as "an author's reference to the larger literary context when offering a citation or allusion from an earlier text. In this sense, metalepsis is the use of a part of a precursor text to evoke the whole of it." Brown, "Metalepsis," 31; Brown, *Scripture as Communication*, 227. Hays defines metalepsis as "a rhetorical and poetic device in which one text alludes to an earlier text in a way that evokes resonance of the earlier text beyond those explicitly cited. The result is that interpretation of a metalepsis requires the reader to recover unstated or suppressed correspondences between the two texts." Hays, *Conversion*, 2.

47. According to Tony W. Cartledge "The rise of kingship sets the stage for the demise of the judges, including Samuel. . . . Israel's further history in the Old Testament will be told from the perspective of its kings." Cartledge, *1 and 2 Samuel*, 110.

Divine Sovereignty and the Davidic King (Micah 4:9–5:14)   143

to a dynastic monarchy (1 Sam 12:12; cf. 8:19–20). As P. Kyle McCarter points out, "Israel's pre-monarchical institutions have become inadequate to cope with new political realities, especially the Philistine threat."[48] As a result, Israel demanded a king to lead them into battle against their enemies.[49] Samuel, in his testament, reminded Israel of their ignorance in demanding an earthly ruler over and against Yahweh's kingship (1 Sam 12:11–13; cf. 8:4–6). Despite Samuel's reservations, Israel wanted to transition from a warrior-led nation to a monarchy. Up until this point in her history, Yahweh and the warrior judges had led the nation.

Volatile times and a feckless king (Micah 4:9–10)

Micah appears to find Samuel's testament concerning the origin of kingship in ancient Israel (see 1 Sam 12) fruitful ground for theological reflection upon the crisis at hand.[50] Just as Samuel recounted the tumultuous conditions prevailing during the era of the judges (1 Sam 12:9–11), Micah's opening עתה passage evinces similar conditions prevailing in eighth-century Zion (Mic 4:9–10). Micah portrays these conditions in his variegated rhetorical style. The scene opens graphically with a sequence of four related rhetorical questions marked by למה . . . . כי . . . אם . . . ה . . .[51] The prophet inquires why Daughter Zion is crying loudly: "Why do you cry so loud?" (למה תריעי רע) (4:9a). למה functions here as an adverbial interrogative marker of cause. Mays states that

---

48. McCarter, *I Samuel*, 160.

49. For a comprehensive treatment of the emergence of kingship in Israel, see Jobling, *1 Samuel*, 43–76; Hamilton, *Handbook*, 229–253; McCarter, *I Samuel*, 159–162; Howard, *Introduction*, 158–160; Michelson, *Reconciling Violence and Kingship*.

50. See discussion on allusions to traditions (pp. 75–89).

51. "Now why do you cry so loud? Is there no king in you? Has your counselor perished, such that pain seized you like a woman in labor?" (עתה למה תריעי רע המלך אין־בך אם־יועצך אבד כי־החזיקך חיל כיולדה) (Mic 4:9). The literary shapes of these rhetorical questions are a subject of scholarly discussion. Drawing from Waltke and Regt, perhaps a plausible structure is a triple rhetorical question, in which כי expresses the result of the parallel rhetorical question introduced by למה. The synonymous rhetorical questions in the middle marked by אם/ה combine to express the reason for Daughter Zion's mourning. The two rhetorical question share a common message. Furthermore, since the second rhetorical question (i.e., the אם part) synonymously augments the first, יעץ and מלך refer to the same person. Waltke, *Commentary on Micah*, 237, 239; Regt, "Discourse Implications," 60; Arnold and Choi, *Guide to Biblical Hebrew Syntax*, 150; Williams, *Williams' Hebrew Syntax*, 158, §450; Andersen and Freedman, *Micah*, 445. For the various options to understand the syntax of this rhetorical question, see Biddle, "Dominion Comes to Jerusalem," 255–256.

the question למה does not inquire but "is a dramatic interrogatory used to depict an astonishing situation."[52]

More importantly, Micah augments his rhetorical questions with graphic imagery depicting a woman crying aloud and writhing in labor pain. In her illuminating essay on women as warriors, Claudia D. Bergmann remarks that the image of a woman giving birth appears in the Old Testament and in ANE texts to describe various types of crises. She explains that childbirth imagery, as well as other crisis moments, can cause certain sounds, laments, screaming or can bring feelings of fear, terror, distress, and loss of courage.[53] She concludes that people in distress because of an impending crisis are like "women giving birth because both stand at the crossroads between life and death."[54]

What is more, the repetition of sound in the עתה particles and the abrupt transitions from doom to hope, defeat to victory, exile to rescue create a sense of disorientation. Micah's vivid style intentionally speaks of a chillingly chaotic situation.

Besides his rhetorical style, the scenes recounted in Micah 4:9–10, 14 thematically recall the tumultuous conditions widespread in pre-monarchic Israel. In both instances, the covenant people suffered distress at the hands of hostile nations. Furthermore, ancient Israel had no king. Likewise, the ineffectiveness of Zion's king implied Zion had no king.[55] He utterly fails to thwart the impending crisis and protect Zion's citizens. Just as ancient Israel

---

52. Mays, *Micah*, 105. Broadly speaking, these rhetorical questions are vivid and they grab the audience's attention. Jack R. Lundbom concludes that rhetorical questions "function as emphatic statements and are often used to intimidate." Lundbom, *Biblical Rhetoric*, 191. Furthermore, David Rhoads et al. surmise that rhetorical questions also engage the audiences by leading them to ponder the answers to the questions for themselves or to desire to know how the rest of the text will answer those questions. Rhoads, Dewey, and Michie, *Mark as Story*, 56.

53. Bergmann, "'We Have Seen the Enemy,'" 133–134.

54. Bergmann, 134.

55. Some scholars assume that the referential ambiguity in המלך in Mic 4:9 points to Yahweh. Marrs, "Back to the Future," 87n28; Waltke, *Commentary on Micah*, 238–239; Wolff, *Micah*, 139; Goldingay, *Old Testament Theology*, 2:92–93; Van der Woude, "Micah in Dispute," 250; Ben Zvi, *Micah*, 121.

did not have a king during the judges' era, the ineffectiveness of Zion's king implies Zion was functionally kingless.⁵⁶

Micah further bolsters his case about the gravity of the chaotic conditions of his day and the ineffectiveness of Zion's king by appealing to Psalm 48:7. As stated already, the twice-repeated formulaic simile "like a woman in labor" (חיל כיולדה) (Mic 4:9, 10) alludes to an exact simile in Psalm 48:7. In this classical Zion text (Ps 48:7), the psalmist describes Yahweh the divine warrior defeating the united efforts of foreign kings seeking to storm Zion. He ridicules the kings as they panic and tremble like a woman in labor. Because of the life-threatening crisis, the warring kings tremble and are no longer able to hold their weapons.⁵⁷ Like a woman feeling birth contractions, they can only hold their abdomen and not their weapons.⁵⁸

Micah reshapes the tradition in Psalm 48 by turning the classical Zion tradition motif of Zion's inviolability upside down. Rather, than protect the city from foreign invaders, Zion's earthly king is glaringly unable to do so. Ironically, Yahweh withdraws his support for Zion's king and allows foreign invaders to exile his covenant people (Mic 4:10). Like the trembling kings in Psalm 48, fear, dread, and anxiety at the looming siege grips Daughter Zion (Mic 4:10).⁵⁹ Her pain and fear are founded. There is no military support from Zion's king. Just as ancient Israel in the judges' era suffered oppression from hostile nations, Zion's citizens go into exile. They "go out of the city" (תצאי מקריה), "dwell in the open field" (ושכנת בשדה), and "go to Babylon" (ובאת

---

56. Mays aptly comments: "The question about the king seems to imply that there is a monarchy in Jerusalem. But he is of no help; he cannot carry out the duty of the king to defend his people." Mays, *Micah*, 105. Jacobs concludes that the rhetorical questions "more likely refer to the rule of a powerless king whose inability to fight off the Babylonians results in captivity of the people." Jacobs, *Conceptual Coherence*, 151; Biddle, "Dominion Comes to Jerusalem," 256. Likewise, Sweeney infers that the first rhetorical question "calls to mind the fact that Jerusalem's king would have been removed as a result of the nation's defeat and exile." Sweeney, *Twelve Prophets*, 2:384. Andersen and Freedman surmise that the scenario "sounds more like the end of a dynasty, or at least a time when no effective ruler is present." Andersen and Freedman, *Micah*, 151.

57. Bergmann, "We Have Seen the Enemy," 131–133.

58. Bergmann, 133–134.

59. Jenson, *Obadiah, Jonah, Micah*, 152.

עד־בבל) (4:10bα).⁶⁰ These three phrases of judgment indicate the phases of distress of an impending exile.⁶¹

Despite the ineffectiveness of the present king in Zion, exile is never the end of the story. Since Zion's king could not prevent an exile, he could not achieve an exodus for the people either. Only Yahweh could. Micah expects another exodus: "There you will be delivered, there Yahweh will redeem you from the hand of your enemies" (שם תנצלי שם יגאלך יהוה מכף איביך) (Mic 4:10). The picture of Yahweh as Israel's "redeemer" (גאל) speaks of his covenant obligation to rescue a remnant.⁶² Dempster suitably reminds us that it was the duty of the immediate kinsfolk to avenge the murder of a blood relative (Num 35:10–34).⁶³ Micah goes on to emphasize that the deliverance will come from "there" (in Babylon) and not at Jerusalem. The exodus is punctuated by the formidable nature of the enemy. The stereotypical expression "from the hands of your enemies" (מכף איביך) (4:10b) points to the oppressive power or strength of Judah's enemies.⁶⁴ In using it, Micah implies that only Yahweh is more powerful than the enemy. He alone will redeem the exiled remnant from a powerful nation, just as he repeatedly rescued Israel during the judges' era (1 Sam 12:11).⁶⁵

Volatile times and a militarized remnant (Micah 4:11–13)

The second עתה passage (Mic 4:11–13) provides further evidence that Micah had the traditions about the origins of kingship in view. Thematically, just as pre-monarchic Israel was under the leadership of Yahweh the divine warrior and the militarized charismatic judges, present Zion is also being led

---

60. Until recently there was much skepticism about the authenticity of Micah's oracles beyond Mic 3. Some scholars submit that 4:10 is a later gloss because it speaks of the exile and deliverance from Babylon. Simundson, *Hosea, Joel, Amos, Obadiah, Jonah, Micah*, 290. In the main, James D. Nogalski's words capture the gist of the debate. He writes, "Indeed, for over a century, scholars have considered most of Micah 4–7 to be the work of exilic and/or postexilic editors who appended words of hope to the judgment orientation so prominent in Micah 1–3." Nogalski, *Book of the Twelve*, 560. Also see Mays, *Micah*, 105; Wolff, *Micah*, 137; Sweeney, *Twelve Prophets*, 2:342, 2:385; Biddle, "Dominion Comes to Jerusalem," 255; Wagenaar, *Judgement and Salvation*, 283.

61. Jenson, *Obadiah, Jonah, Micah*, 152.
62. Barker, "Micah," 91.
63. Dempster, *Micah*, 136.
64. The expression is present in several texts (e.g. Judg 2:18; 8:34; 1 Sam 12:10, 11; 2 Sam 3:18; 19:9; 22:1; 2 Kgs 17:39; Pss 18:1; 31:15; 106:10).
65. Waltke, *Commentary on Micah*, 244.

by Yahweh and a militarized remnant in battling the nations (Mic 4:11–13). Zion's earthly king is absent as Yahweh and the remnant battle and defeat the hostile foreign kings. As Elizabeth Boase puts it, "Daughter Zion is transformed into an instrument of her salvation."[66]

Verse 11 pictures a situation of distress. The great imperial nations address Zion as a woman, announcing their shameful intention to profane her: "Let her be profaned" (תֶּחֱנָף). Dempster thinks the imagery here suggests assault and rape of Zion by the enemy.[67] The verb (תחנף) is used of harlotry when a woman degrades herself (Jer 3:2, 9).[68] However, it appears that a military attack on the temple would also be profanity. As Barker surmises, the imagery portrays hostile nations profaning Zion and her temple by trampling sacred ground with their pagan feet.[69] Andersen and Freedman agree, "Desecrating the shrine of the enemy was one of the chief aims of attacking a capital city."[70] Unfortunately, the hostile nations mistakenly assume that their intentions control the future.[71] They do not realize that they are about to spring Yahweh's trap.

Verse 12 discloses Yahweh's grand plan. He has gathered the nations as sheaves to the threshing floor. In this agricultural metaphor, Yahweh is the harvester, while Zion is the beast treading the sheaves.[72] Jenson enlightens the imagery: "In the metaphor Yhwh is the owner of the harvest, the sheaves are the nations, the threshing floor is the field of battle and the thresher is the army of Jerusalem."[73]

Verse 13 continues the harvesting metaphor, promising to arm the remnant with iron horns and bronze hoofs so they can thresh and pulverize the invading nations. Such a scene underscores the remnant's martial superiority

---

66. Boase, *The Fulfilment of Doom?*, 62.
67. Dempster, *Micah*, 137.
68. Dempster, 137.
69. Barker, "Micah," 93.
70. Andersen and Freedman, *Micah*, 451.
71. Goldingay, *Old Testament Theology*, 2:93.
72. King, *Amos, Hosea, Micah*, 111–112.
73. Jenson, *Obadiah, Jonah, Micah*, 154.

over the nations. Yahweh will strengthen the remnant for battle.⁷⁴ He will turn their horns into iron. The "horns" (קרן) are a symbol of strength (see Deut 33:17; 1 Kgs 22:11). Yahweh will make their hoofs (פרסה) into bronze, "a metal ubiquitous to warfare in the ancient Near East (2 Sam 22:35//Ps 18:34 [35]; Isa 45:2)."⁷⁵ Clearly, the implication of the imagery and the crushing defeat of the nations is the idea of the inviolability of Zion (see Pss 2; 46:7; 48:5–7; 76:4, 6–7). As Barker cogently puts it, "Because of Yahweh's enablement, Zion will be invincible."⁷⁶ In accord with the rules of Yahweh's wars, the passage closes with a call for Israel to devote the spoils of victory to Yahweh (see Pss 68; Isa 18:7; 60:5–9). Again Barker explains, "In the Old Testament, when defeated people and things were to be devoted to the Lord, it usually meant that everything perishable or flammable should be totally destroyed (cf. Josh 6–7), while gold and silver and other precious metals should be brought to the Lord's temple and used in his service."⁷⁷ By doing so, they are acknowledging that Yahweh is the divine sovereign of the whole earth.

In sum, the second עתה passage clearly shows that Zion is under theocratic rule. Yahweh and the militarized remnant defend the city from foreign invaders. We should not miss the clear absence of the king in this battle. Often, one would expect the king, with Yahweh's help, to lead the troops into battle (e.g. 1 Sam 8:20; 11:6–11; 23:1–5; 2 Sam 5:2–10; 17–25; 1 Chr 19:17). However, in the present case, Yahweh seems to have abandoned his vicegerent and enlisted a remnant.

Volatile times and the removal of Zion's king (Micah 4:14)

The third עתה passage (Mic 4:14) provides further evidence that Micah had the traditions about the origins of kingship in view.⁷⁸ As we have al-

---

74. Jenson, 154; Barker, "Micah," 93. The Victory Stele of Naram-Sîn depicts the king wearing a horned crown in a battlefield. A horned crown is a sign of divinity. Hence, the scene suggests not only the king's military valor but also his close relationship with his god on the battlefield. See Pongratz-Leisten, *Religion and Ideology*, 84–85, fig. 12; Winter, "How Tall Was Naram-Sin's Victory Stele?," 309, fig. 8; Wright, "Military Valor and Kingship," 37n14.

75. Smith-Christopher, *Micah*, 160.

76. Barker, "Micah," 93.

77. Barker, 94.

78. Despite the apparent change of addressee from בת־ציון to בת־גדוד, this last unit is a sequel to 4:9–10; both passages stress a concern about Zion's king. This unit (4:14) also looks back to the previous unit (4:11–13); both passages focus on the siege by the hostile nations.

ready shown, the expression "judge of Israel" (שפט ישראל) provides a thematic entry point to Nathan's oracle (2 Sam 7:8) in which Yahweh reminds Nathan of his experience with ancient Israel during the judges' era. By way of reversal, Micah 4:14 and 2 Samuel 7:8 share a major theme and several motifs. Within its immediate context, 2 Samuel 7:8 inaugurates the Davidic covenant. Furthermore, it presents the election of David and his dynasty as the divine viceroys (vv. 11, 12) and promises peace and security for the Davidic dynasty. Yahweh will cut off their enemies (vv. 9, 10).

In contrast, Micah 4:14 describes a covenant travesty using a sobering tone. Essentially, the passage depicts the possible termination of the Davidic covenant as Zion's king suffers humiliation. The opening command for Zion's troops to defend the city against the siege is because the king is utterly ineffective. McComiskey and Longman correctly argue that the incipient command "marshal your troops" (תתגדדי) "is a summons to the soon-to-be beleaguered city of Jerusalem to gather troops for her defense against the siege."[79] The enemy has successfully breached the city. They strike the king with his own "scepter/rod" (שבט). Striking the king on the check is an insult that the victor metes out to a defeated and powerless victim (1 Kgs 22:24; Amos 3:30).[80] In fact, Yahweh had already anticipated using this very instrument (שבט) to punish the Davidic kings for covenant breach (Ps 89:33). Johnston's thoughtful analysis of this image is noteworthy. He writes:

> Since the scepter was a traditional emblem of royalty and kingship, this insulting act conveyed the king's loss of his throne and his subjugation to foreign rule. It also represented a reversal of traditional Davidic expectations since the royal scepter, which Jacob predicted would never depart from Judah (Gen 49:10), is now wielded by a foreign ruler and used as the instrument of the Davidic king's punishment rather than as the emblem of his royal power.[81]

Jacobs, *Conceptual Coherence*, 152. For a fuller discussion on the various proposals on the connections of 4:14 to the immediate context, see Andersen and Freedman, *Micah*, 458–459.

79. McComiskey and Longman, "Micah," 529.
80. Jenson, *Obadiah, Jonah, Micah*, 156.
81. Bateman, Bock, and Johnston, *Jesus the Messiah*, 123; Sweeney, *Twelve Prophets*, 2:387.

Synthesis of Micah 4:9–14

In our opinion, Micah paradigmatically adopts from and reshapes Samuel's testament to parallel the security threats eighth-century Zion faced. As an analogical comparison of the logical flow of the passages shows, Micah 4:9–10 depicts a threatening situation that underscores the ineffectiveness of Zion's kings. As such, the feeble king acts as a foil for the new king (Mic 5:1). Like pre-monarchic Israel in the days of Samuel, at this point in her history, Zion was under the relentless threat of foreign nations (Mic 4:9–14).

While the similarities link the two texts together, the differences allow for analogical illumination of the alluding text (i.e. Mic 4:9–10).[82] Ancient Israel in 1 Samuel 12 had no king, whereas Zion lacked an effective king (Mic 4:9, 14). Micah utilizes the ineffectiveness of Zion's king quite effectively as a rhetorical foil to imply that Zion is functionally kingless (Mic 4:9, 14). This observation puts the tradition about the origins of kingship (1 Sam 12) on par with the present need of Zion (Mic 4:9–10). In other words, both passages now share a common need because of similar fates. Both are kingless.[83] Both are under the care of Yahweh and the human warriors (1 Sam 12:11; Mic 4:11–13). Just as the evoked text quite clearly anticipates the inauguration of human kingship to replace the warrior judges (1 Sam 12:13), by analogy the alluding text implicitly anticipates the restoration of a new king in Zion to replace the militarized remnant (Mic 4:11–13).

The logic from Micah 4:9 to 4:14 creates an image of a failed kingship. Micah 4:14, as the pinnacle, presents further motivation for the need of an ideal Davidic king. As we have hinted at already, Micah 4:14 alludes to traditions about David's rise. Recall that 2 Samuel 7:8 appears within a context of the inauguration of the Davidic covenant. Similarly, by way of reversal, Micah 4:14 appears in a context whereby Yahweh rejects the present Davidic king. Given the defeat of Zion's king, it appears that Yahweh is renouncing the Davidic covenant.

Has Yahweh withdrawn his commitment to David? Quite the contrary, Yahweh will forever remain faithful to his word (Ps 89:34–38). The Davidic kings were not immune from punishment when they violated torah (Ps

---

82. Sternberg, *Poetics of Biblical Narrative*, 365; Fewell, "Introduction," 13.
83. Begerau, "Micah, Prophet of Hope," 68, 71.

89:31–33). Yahweh did not necessarily act to protect a particular king but to guarantee the continuation of the dynasty.[84] Micah 5:1 ensures such continuation as Yahweh raises up an ideal Davidic viceroy.

Restoration of Zion's Former Dominion

One of the central hopes of the promise in Micah 4:8 is that Yahweh will restore Zion's kingship or sovereignty. The realization of Yahweh's promise demands the restoration of Yahweh's vicegerent to rule in Zion on his behalf. As frequently presented in the Davidic traditions found throughout 1–2 Samuel, Yahweh's ideal vicegerent is a Davidic king (e.g. 1 Sam 2:10; 26:9–16; 2 Sam 1:14; 7:14; Pss 2:6–9). Micah 5:1–4a, 5b moves along such royal traditions as it presents the person and purpose of such a figure.

Bethlehemite figure as viceroy (Mic 5:1–4a, 5b)
Bethlehemite figure is a Davidic king

Without any royal honorific fanfare, Micah presents Zion's future king by appealing to his humble ancestry. The prophet's focus on his ancestry is a telltale sign that the coming king is Davidic. Although this passage does not explicitly mention David, it is difficult to dismiss the impression that it implies the restoration of a Davidic king. That Zion's future king will be Davidic is evident from Micah's allusion to the Davidic traditions marked by the place name, "Bethlehem Ephrathah" (בית־לחם אפרתה) (Mic 5:1). McComiskey agrees with our view. He remarks that in Micah 5:1 "the Davidic roots of the coming ruler are emphasized by the prophet Micah."[85] Bethlehem was the place of Davidic ancestry. Ephrathah is also connected with Bethlehem (Gen

---

84. Moore, *Moving Beyond Symbol and Myth*, 217.

85. McComiskey, *Covenants of Promise*, 28. As usual, some scholars contest this connection between Bethlehem and the Davidic dynasty. Mays mistakenly argues that the allusion to Bethlehem only points to the hometown of the coming ruler, not to his Davidic lineage. For him, Micah does not envision Davidic succession; instead, he is revising the Davidic covenant (2 Sam 7:4–17, especially v. 16). In our estimation, Mays's hairsplitting distinction is unnecessary. To argue that Micah is revising the Davidic covenant by choosing a non-Davidic dynasty is inconsistent with Yahweh's commitment to the Davidic covenant. Because of its eternality, it is impossible for Yahweh to abrogate this covenant. Mays, *Micah*, 113–115. Like Mays, Smith-Christopher challenges McComiskey's traditional view. He thinks Micah implies a reset or a starting over. That is to say, go back to Bethlehem and choose another antimilitary dynasty. In other words, the allusion calls "for a ruler who trusts in God rather than military might." Smith-Christopher, *Micah*, 167.

35:16, 18; 48:17; Ps 132:6; 1 Sam 16:1, 18; 17:12; Ruth 4:11).[86] Twice Jesse, David's father, is identified through the gentilic of בית־לחם (בית־הלחמי), "the Bethlehemite" (1 Sam 16:1; 17:58). It follows then that Bethlehem was most likely David's birthplace.

Bethlehem is then a place of election. There Samuel anointed David as king of Israel (1 Sam 16:1–13). Through this sacred act Yahweh adopted David as his own son and invested him with the Spirit (1 Sam 16:13; cf. Isa 11:1–2; Ps 2:2, 6–7) so he could rule as king on Yahweh's behalf (1 Sam 16:1). The important point here, for our purposes, is that the address to Bethlehem Ephrathah in Micah 5:1 points back to a place where the ideal vicegerent is elected, adopted, and invested with divine authority and power to rule on behalf of the divine sovereign. Hence, Micah 5:1 anticipates a Davidic king.

That the Bethlehemite figure is Zion's future king is not without its difficulties. Apparently, some scholars question Micah's motive for using "ruler" (משל) rather than "king" (מלך) in reference to the Bethlehemite figure. Biddle, for instance, maintains that Micah circumvents kingship language concerning future human rulers because of the miserable failures of the previous monarch.[87] He argues that Micah, by using "ruler" (משל), apparently redefines and restricts the responsibility of future human agents under Yahweh's sovereignty.[88] Biddle then concludes that the Bethlehemite figure takes "the role of a human administrator of the 'dominion' that King YHWH returns to cosmopolitan Jerusalem."[89]

Micah's characterization of the Bethlehemite figure as "the ruler in Israel" (מושל בישראל) does not mean that the Bethlehemite is not a king as Biddle would have us believe. Admittedly, "ruler" (משל) generally denotes one in authority.[90] However, Micah's use of משל should not be a cause for concern because the term could be used interchangeably for מלך (Ps 105:20). Furthermore, David utilizes משל to recount the qualities of an ideal king

---

86. Sweeney, *Twelve Prophets*, 2:387; Jenson, *Obadiah, Jonah, Micah*, 156–157; Marrs, "Back to the Future," 90; Dempster, *Micah*, 138.

87. Biddle, "Dominion Comes to Jerusalem," 264–265. Also see Jenson, *Obadiah, Jonah, Micah*, 157; Willis, "ממך לי יצא in Micah 5:1," 317–318; Soggin, "משל," 691; Redditt, "King in Haggai-Zechariah," 68.

88. Biddle, "Dominion Comes to Jerusalem," 264–265.

89. Biddle, 264.

90. Koehler, Baumgartner, and Stamm, *Hebrew and Aramaic Lexicon*, 647.

(2 Sam 23:3). It appears that Biddle and others are making a mountain out of a molehill in trying to crack why Micah uses משל instead of מלך. Biddle's observation is inconclusive. He does not clarify in what manner Micah redefines or restricts human viceregency. His concept of a human administrator lacks textual support. As we will explain shortly, the responsibility of the new ruler is consistent with the divine sovereign's demands for his vicegerent.

Bethlehemite figure is the divine viceroy

The mere fact that the Bethlehemite figure is a Davidic king suggests that he is also Yahweh's vicegerent. To this plain claim, we may add several other pieces of evidence to bolster his vicegerency. For example, the prepositional phrase, "for me" (לי) (Mic 5:1), functions like a *dativus commodi*.[91] It speaks of the Bethlehemite figure as Yahweh's viceroy. The advent of David himself as Yahweh's viceroy lends support to our claim. Yahweh describes David's election using a similar prepositional phrase, לי (1 Sam 16:1, 3). Micah's characterization of the coming ruler, we also believe, underlines the close relationship between the divine sovereign and the divine vicegerent. In addition, the prepositional phrase in Micah contextually qualifies and clarifies that the sense of משל connotes someone who exercises authority on behalf of the divine sovereign. This is actually the classical sense of a vicegerent.[92] All together, Micah's use of the prepositional phrase is consistent with the concept of Davidic vicegerency whereby the Davidic king rules in subordination to Yahweh (1 Sam 2:10, 35; 24:7–11; 26:9–16; 2 Sam 1:14; 19:22; Pss 2:6–8; 45:2–3).[93]

Another piece of evidence that shows that the anticipated Bethlehemite figure is Yahweh's vicegerent is his antiquated origins: his "coming forth is from old, from ancient days" (ומוצאתיו מקדם מימי עולם).[94] While the

---

91. Williams, *Williams' Hebrew Syntax*, §271a.

92. Beale, *New Testament Biblical Theology*, 35–37.

93. Alexander, *From Eden to the New Jerusalem*, 92; Miller, "Ruler of Zion," 187–188; Brueggemann and Bellinger, *Psalms*, 33–34, 59–60, 213–14.

94. There is considerable debate among scholars concerning this intriguing clause, especially, the phrase "from ancient days" (מימי עולם). For instance, Kaiser resolutely maintains that the phrase attests to the eternal preexistence and the origins of Jesus the Messiah. Kaiser, *Messiah in the Old Testament*, 153. Alongside Kaiser, Rydelnik believes the phrase speaks of the Bethlehemite figure's divine nature. Rydelnik, *Messianic Hope*, 160–161. Contrary to Kaiser and Rydelnik, Sweeney concludes that the expression refers to the past golden era of the Davidic kingship when Yahweh inaugurated the Davidic covenant (2 Sam 7; cf. Pss 89:29, 37; 110:4).

enigmatic phrase (i.e. from ancient days) recalls the Davidic ancestry of the Bethlehemite figure, we contend that the phrase is not only the language of great antiquity but also of preeminence. Elsewhere the phrase serves as a standard upon which other notable events or persons are measured (e.g. Amos 9:11). However, in order to clarify its sense, we must attend to Micah's intended contexts.

First, the birth imagery provides Micah's immediate context. Here the relative birth order hinted at between Micah 5:1 and v. 2 shows that Micah is depicting the Bethlehemite figure as the firstborn among his brothers.[95] In ancient Israel, the firstborn son ranked above his siblings in issues of inheritance (Deut 21:17).[96] Thus, more than a literal description of a birth order, Micah's adaptation of the birth metaphor rhetorically speaks of granting royal privileges to the Bethlehemite figure.

Second, by looking at the wider context, we can even go beyond this simple observation and claim that the Bethlehemite figure is, in essence, Yahweh's own firstborn. Support for our claim comes from the elevated language used to describe the adoptive status of Yahweh's vicegerent.[97] Just as Yahweh promised to make the Davidic king his firstborn (Ps 89:27; cf. Ps 2:7), Micah's enigmatic phrase contextually implies such status for the Bethlehemite

---

Sweeney is on the right track. Sweeney, *Twelve Prophets*, 2:388; Bateman, Bock, and Johnston, *Jesus the Messiah*, 126. Dempster believes the phrase most likely means that the emergence of the Bethlehemite figure was predicted from long ago. Dempster, *Dominion and Dynasty*, 185; Dempster, *Micah*, 138. While evangelical scholars believe that there are passages in the Hebrew Bible that speak of messianic hope, for the most part scholars interpret them not as direct predictions about Jesus. In other words, with the shift in interpretation, Jesus is viewed as the climax and not the fulfillment of the Old Testament promises. For a helpful survey on these views, see Rydelnik, *Messianic Hope*, 3–7.

95. That Mic 5:1 depicts the birth of the Bethlehemite figure is seen in that יצא is a birth metaphor (cf. Gen 25:26; 2 Sam 7:12; 1 Kgs 8:19; Job 1:21). Mic 5:2 also continues the birth metaphor, depicting Israel as a woman in labor until she gives birth to the rest of his [i.e., the Bethlehemite figure's] brothers.

96. Joshua R. Porter clarifies and hammers this point home about the firstborn. As he states, "The Old Testament appears to know nothing of a hierarchy on the basis of age. Rather, the first-born was in a unique position, depending on the fact that he was 'beginning of the father's strength,' and which seem to be almost a technical expression, and which mean that the son in question was endowed with the fullness of the father's authority and power." Porter, *Extended Family*, 10.

97. Evidently, Ps 89:27 and Mic 5:3 exhibit thematic correspondence. The second portion of the poetic colon refers to the exalted status of the Davidic king as "the highest of the kings of the earth" (עליון למלכי־ארץ). Similarly, Micah also mentions the exalted status of the Bethlehemite figure: "he shall be great to the ends of the earth" (יגדל עד־אפסי־ארץ) (Mic 5:3).

figure. In this respect, the phrase is perhaps the prophet's impression of the Bethlehemite figure's firstborn status. Micah's use of the birth metaphor likely hints at Yahweh's adoption of a new king, the Bethlehemite figure.[98]

Finally, the third piece of evidence that shows that the anticipated Bethlehemite figure is Yahweh's vicegerent is the expression "and this one will be [our] peace" (והיה זה שלום) (Mic 5:4a). Such language is reminiscent of the "Prince of Peace" (שר־שלום) pointed out in Isaiah's dynastic oracle (Isa 9:5), which indisputably describes the future Davidic king as Yahweh's viceroy (Isa 9:6). According to Shirley Lucass, dynastic oracles frequently announce the birth of the coming king in terms suggestive of divinity (Mic 5:4a; Isa 7:14; 9:5–6).[99]

Indeed, at first blush, Isaiah's promised king appears to share in Yahweh's divinity, as the other titles also suggest – "Mighty God" (אל גבור) and "Everlasting Father" (אביעד). However, such royal titles do not connote the king's divine nature. Rather, they point to the Davidic king as the divine vicegerent. Allen perceptively captures the import of these royal titles in the dynastic oracles. He notes that these titles "are throne names for the expected Davidic king, in which the divine titles are transferred to the human king. The significance of this transference is that this king's reign was to be a mirror image of God's purposes, representing the kingdom of heaven and earth."[100] In other words, the royal titles in the dynastic oracles (Mic 5:4a; Isa 7:14; 9:5–6) do not ontologically connote divinity, they merely suggest that the Davidic king has a divine function (cf. Ps 45). The comment by A. Y. Collins and J. J. Collins is on target: "The main implication of the declaration that the king was a son of God is the implication that he is empowered to act as God's surrogate on earth."[101]

The Bethlehemite figure and the nations

The honored status of Yahweh's vicegerent carried with it certain responsibilities.[102] Having clandestinely introduced the Bethlehemite figure as a Davidic

---

98. Allen, *Theological Approach*, 109.
99. Lucass, *Concept of the Messiah*, 96–97; Rydelnik, *Messianic Hope*, 161.
100. Allen, *Theological Approach*, 109.
101. Collins and Collins, *King and Messiah*, 22.
102. See Chalmers, *Exploring the Religion*, 89–97.

king and as Yahweh's vicegerent, Micah turns to his responsibility. For Micah, the shepherd imagery, marked by the verb "to shepherd" ורעה (Mic 5:3a), frames the Bethlehemite figure's overarching responsibility.[103] The logical force of this key verb expresses a statement of purposes for the Bethlehemite figure.[104] Thus, the future hope of the nation depends on how well the new shepherd-king executes his duties.

The character of the Bethlehemite figure's rule

Following a discussion of his advent (5:1–2), the Bethlehemite figure ascends the throne and assumes his kingship (v.3). As most scholars agree, the verb "stand" (ועמד) (v. 3) in this context speaks of a king being enthroned (cf. Dan 11:2–3).[105] The enthronement of the Bethlehemite figure meant that he now shared in the divine sovereign's rule (see Pss 2:6, 110:1–2).[106] As a result, he will "shepherd" (ורעה), meaning that he will "rule" on Yahweh's behalf (Mic 5:3). John Gray aptly points out that the shepherd imagery suggests that the Bethlehemite figure "is appropriately the vicegerent of the Divine King, the Shepherd of Israel."[107]

In any case, the intransitive nature of the verb ורעה here allows Micah to stress the divine means by which the Bethlehemite figure's rule unfolds. As the divine viceroy, his association with Yahweh does not simply identify him as the legitimate viceroy commissioned to rule on Yahweh's behalf but also connotes something about how he executes his responsibilities.[108] Yahweh equips his earthly viceroy to fight for himself, which ensures his victory over enemies (Pss 45:4–6; 89:22). Micah too announces that the Bethlehemite

---

103. The literary significance of the shepherd imagery in Micah cannot be underestimated. For John Moss Painter, the imagery of shepherds appears frequently enough that it contributes to the literary coherence of the book. Painter, "Analysis," 3, 115–117; Chae, *Jesus*, 32.

104. The syntactical construction of the two perfect verbs, ועמד ורעה, shows that ורעה expresses a consequential or a logical outcome. *IBHS*, §32.1e; Arnold and Choi, *Guide to Biblical Hebrew Syntax*, 88, §3.5.2b.

105. Waltke, *Commentary on Micah*; Wolff, *Micah*, 146. Both Waltke and Jenson add that the verb also implies an undefeated and enduring reign. Jenson, *Obadiah, Jonah, Micah*, 159. Hillers notes that the sense of the verb is uncertain. Hillers, *Micah*.

106. For a cogent discussion on Yahweh's enthronement of the king, see Kraus, *Theology of the Psalms*, 112–113; Brueggemann and Bellinger, *Psalms*, 33, 479; Mays, "Theological Purpose," 19.

107. Gray, *Biblical*, 325.

108. Smith, *Christ the Ideal King*, 97.

figure will rule in Yahweh's "strength/power" (עֹז) and "majesty" (גָאוֹן) (Mic 5:3).[109] Andersen and Freedman correctly point out that strength and majesty "are more suited to the achievement of the soldier than the pastor."[110] Thus, the primary role of the Bethlehemite figure is to participate in the martial aspects of the kingdom under Yahweh's authority and power. As a warrior, his strength and majesty reflect that of the divine warrior (Ps 93:1; cf. Ps 96:6; 1 Chron 16:27).[111] In other words, the divine viceroy receives his victories through Yahweh's strength (Pss 21:2; 140:8).

An examination of the broader context suggests that the verb וְרָעָה connotes notions about the Bethlehemite figure as a mighty shepherd-warrior who aspires to worldwide dominion.[112] Such a shepherding role was a royal task common in the ANE world. In ancient Israel, the shepherd imagery is rooted in the Davidic-shepherd traditions (e.g. 1 Sam 16:11; 2 Sam 5:2; 7:7–10; Pss 23; 78:70–72).[113] A strand of these traditions speaks of David's

---

109. The two *beth instrumenti* in the parallel adverbial phrases ("in the strength of Yahweh" [בְּעֹז יהוה] // "in the majesty of the name of the Lord his God" [בִּגְאוֹן שֵׁם יהוה אֱלֹהָיו]) mark the divine means (Mic 5:3a). See *GKC*, §119o; JM, §132e; *IBHS*, §11.2.5d.

110. Andersen and Freedman, *Micah*, 469.

111. In this enthronement psalm (Ps 93), the poet celebrates the reign of Yahweh the divine warrior. The focus of the opening lines is on the victorious Warrior robed in עֹז and גָאוֹן. Brueggemann and Bellinger, *Psalms*, 403. As Roberts argues, the conquests of the Davidic kings "are simply a participation and reinstatement" of Yahweh's primeval victories. At times biblical authors describe David's battles in mythological language. For instance, the psalmist writes that וְשַׂמְתִּי בַיָּם יָדוֹ וּבַנְּהָרוֹת יְמִינוֹ ("I [Yahweh] will set his [David] hand on the sea and his right hand on the rivers") (Ps 89:26). Sea and river are Yahweh's cosmic enemies (see Isa 11:15; Hab 3:8, 15; Nah 1:4). Often, hostile kings and their nations are identified with chaotic primeval waters (see Pss 2:1; 46:3–7; 48:68; Isa 17:12–13). Roberts, "Enthronement of Yhwh and David," 679.

112. Barker, "Micah," 100. The role of the shepherd as protector of the flock surfaces the latent martial attributes behind the imagery. This martial emphasis is markedly clearer in Gen 49:24–25, where the epithet of Yahweh as shepherd appears in a context of military support (cf. Pss 48:15; 23:1; 28:9; 80:1; Isa 40:11). Apparently, the ancient epithets and divine names in Gen 49:24–25 are an exclusive expression of divine power and blessings. Sæbø, "Divine Names," 131. In addition, the shepherd's rod and the staff signify Yahweh's presence, security, and guidance (Ps 23:4). Aicha Rahmouni references various ANE sources that unambiguously demonstrate that the shepherd's staff functioned not only as a royal symbol but also as a weapon to vanquish enemies. Rahmouni, *Divine Epithets*, 104n16.

113. Sweeney, *Twelve Prophets*, 2:389; Waltke, *Commentary on Micah*, 283. The noun participle of רעה was understood as a royal title and epithet used to describe divine or human kings as protectors and benevolent providers of their subjects. Heim, "Kings and Kingship," 611; Brueggemann, *First and Second Samuel*, 237. Apparently, the shepherd-king motif was not particularly unique to Israel but was widely shared among ANE cultures. For instance, in the Creation Epic, Marduk is depicted as a shepherd following his cosmogonic victory over Tiamat: "The son, our champion, shall be the highest. His lordship shall be supreme, he shall

imperial might. Soon after Yahweh inaugurated the Davidic covenant (2 Sam 7), David embarked on an imperial military campaign (2 Sam 8:1–14). Such a move underscores the idea that a desirable quality of a shepherd-king is to extend Yahweh's dominion among the nations (Pss 2:8; 72:8–11; 89:27–28; 110). In the words of Joshua W. Jipp, "One of the central hopes of the royal psalms is that God will establish God's kingdom by extending worldwide dominion over the people through God's 'chosen,' elected king (Pss 89:3, 20; 132:11)."[114]

Just like David of old, the Bethlehemite figure's rule (i.e. the second/new David) will also extend Yahweh's sovereignty among the nations. This universal scope of his rule is implied in the stereotypical expression "to the ends of the earth" (עַד־אַפְסֵי־אָרֶץ) (Mic 5:3b). Since the Bethlehemite figure's greatness extends over the world, the nations are implicitly subordinate to him (Ps 72:8–9).[115] Thus, the Bethlehemite figure's rule is worldwide, which is a subtle sign that Zion is regaining her former dominion.

Another feature that characterizes the ideal vicegerent's rule is that his concomitant defeat of his enemies ushers in an era of security for his subjects (e.g., 2 Sam 7:8–11a; Ps 72:7; 144:11–14; Isa 9:7).[116] Expectedly, the

---

have no rival, He shall be the shepherd of the black-headed folk, his creatures. They shall tell of his ways, without forgetting, in the future." "Epic of Creation (Enūma Elish)," translated by Benjamin R. Foster (*COS* 1.111.VI). In late old Babylonian inscriptions, Hammurabi the king of Babylon refers to himself as a shepherd in providing his people with sustenance. "I turned both its banks into cultivated areas. I kept heaping up piles of grain. I provided perpetual water for the land of Sumer and Akkad (and) gathered the scattered peoples of the land of Sumer and Akkad (and) provided for them pastures and watering places. In abundance and plenty I shepherded them. I settled them in peaceful abodes." "Hammu-Rapi," translated by Douglas Frayne (*COS* 2.107B). Also see Waters, "Political Development," 17–67; Tanner, "King Yahweh," 272; Biwul, *Theological Examination*, 97–130; Laniak, *Shepherds After My Own Heart*, 42–71; Chae, *Jesus as the Eschatological Davidic Shepherd*, 19–96.

114. Jipp, *Christ Is King*, 35.

115. The shared context of the expression includes 1 Sam 2:10; Pss 2:8; 22:28; 67:8; 98:3; Isa 52:10; Zech 9:10. In our estimation, Ps 72:8 appears to be Micah's intended context. Smith-Christopher also believes that Ps 72 is the intended context for Mic 5:3b. In his own words, he writes, "Most important, however, is Ps 72 and its description of the ideal king . . . who rules to the 'ends of the earth' (v. 8) . . . in whose rule all nations are also blessed (v. 17; cf. Ps 67)." Smith-Christopher, *Micah*, 169. Sweeney also broadens the cognitive environment for the expression to include the traditions about Yahweh's (David's) kingship in Zion. He writes, "The presentation of the new monarch draws upon the traditions that Yahweh's (and David's) kingship in Zion will be recognized by all the nations of the earth (cf. Psalms 2; 46; 47; 48; 89; cf. 2 Sam 7:1; Ps 132:18; Isa 9:1–6; 11:1–16)." Sweeney, *Twelve Prophets*, 2:389.

116. Jipp, *Christ Is King*, 36–37.

Bethlehemite figure's rule exhibits these ideals. The leading verb "will live securely" (וישבו), in the second half of our text (Mic 5:3b), speaks of the nation's security (cf. Mic 4:4). The basis for the nation to dwell securely is because of the Bethlehemite figure's greatness, which reaches the ends of the earth.[117] Once again, security for the people means that the shepherd-warrior will have vanquished hostile enemies worldwide.

Furthermore, the rule of the Bethlehemite figure will also result in worldwide "peace" (שלום) (Mic 5:4a). According to Barker, שלום carries "the sense of the absence of war and hostility."[118] Indeed, the "peace" (שלום) Micah envisions comes militarily as the Bethlehemite figure delivers the nation from Assyrian invasion (Mic 5:5b). In response to a hypothetical Assyrian threat in the first והיה passage (5:4–5),[119] the Bethlehemite figure "will deliver" (והציל) the nation (Mic 5:5b). Consequently, this will result in peace on the land (Mic 5:4a). Notably, by metonymy, Assyria represents the many nations hostile to Israel (Mic 4:11–13; 7:12; cf. Isa 11:11; Zech 10:10–11).[120] What is more, the ability of the Bethlehemite figure to fend off any Assyrian attack conforms to the classical Zion/Davidic motif about the inviolability of Zion.

Hence, Assyria's defeat suggests that the Bethlehemite figure is essentially maintaining the worldwide שלום, which the divine warrior had already achieved (Mic 4:1–4, 5, 13).[121] As Julien Smiths asserts, "The ideal state of humanity is to be ruled by God, the supreme sovereign. This ideal state of peace, harmony, and virtue is enjoyed when God rules through his human agent, the king. That is to say, sharing in God's rule places the king in the position of distributing to humanity the benefits of God's rule."[122]

Israel and the nations (Micah 5:4b–8)

The participation of the ideal vicegerent in Yahweh's rule also results in the democratization of vicegerency to other human beings. In other words, other

---

117. Waltke, *Commentary on Micah*.
118. Barker, "Micah," 102.
119. Here the imperfect verbs (ידרך and יבוא v. 4) assume a hypothetical mood to describe a dependent event that is only contingent or possible. Arnold and Choi, *Guide to Biblical Hebrew Syntax*, 57. IBHS, §31.6.1. Also see Bateman, Bock, and Johnston, *Jesus the Messiah*, 127n19.
120. Wolff, *Micah*, 147; Barker, "Micah," 102.
121. Luker, "Doom and Hope in Micah," 181.
122. Smith, *Christ the Ideal King*, 175.

Israelites in their distinct manner will also share in Yahweh's rule. As T. D. Alexander helpfully argues, the reestablishment of Yahweh's sovereignty is not only the reinstatement of the Davidic king as the divine viceroy but also involves the restoration of other human beings as Yahweh's viceroys.[123] As we have previously argued, Genesis 1 already anticipated humanity's rule. Because humanity bears the divine image, Adam, Eve, and their progeny are recipients of dominion (Gen 1:26–28). M. David Litwa lends support to this argument, adding that "Adam's rule became paradigmatic for Israel's rule over the nations" (e.g. Deut 26:19; cf. Deut 15:6; Exod 7:1).[124] It is difficult to escape Litwa's observation. In Psalm 8, for example, Yahweh crowns humans with glory and honor and gives them dominion over the works of his hands (vv. 5–6). Similarly, after the Ancient of Days bestows dominion upon the son of man (Dan 7:13–14), the people of God are also granted everlasting dominion (vv. 22, 27).[125]

The extension of vicegerency to other human beings allows them to participate in the divine sovereign's rule. Their participation is another way of representing the divine sovereign's rule worldwide, thereby extending Yahweh's sovereignty among the nations. In short, the reception, participation, or exercise of dominion by other human beings speaks of their vicegerency.

Israel as vicegerent

Micah's two והיה passages (Mic 5:4–5; 6–8) extend vicegerency to other Israelites. Such a royal participatory context for reading these passages should not be a cause for concern. Throughout these two passages, the divine sovereign extends his sovereignty among the nations not only through the Bethlehemite figure but also through Israelite military commanders and a remnant. Undoubtedly, the seven "shepherds" (רעים) and eight "princes/

---

123. Alexander, *From Eden to the New Jerusalem*, 89; Roberts, "Divine King," 132–134; Eaton, *Kingship and the Psalms*, 156; Litwa, *We Are Being Transformed*, 179–182; Beetham, "From Creation to New Creation, 238–250; Gentry and Wellum, *Kingdom through Covenant*, 181–202; Dempster, *Dominion and Dynasty*, 56–62; Berry, *Glory in Romans*, 205–210; Beale, *New Testament Biblical Theology*, 37.

124. Litwa, *We Are Being Transformed*, 179.

125. McCartney, "Ecce Homo," 17.

chiefs" (נסיכי) serve as vicegerents (Mic 5:4b).[126] Young S. Chae dubs them as "the (under) shepherds" in an effort to underline their subordinate status to the Bethlehemite figure.[127] The terms used to describe these under-shepherds are clearly royal terms connoting power. Similarly, in the second והיה passage (5:6–8), "the remnant of Jacob" (שארית יעקב) also serve as human vicegerents (vv. 6, 7).

Israel's under-shepherds and the nations

Besides security and peace, another significant consequence of the Bethlehemite figure's victory against the Assyrians is the reestablishment of the vicegerent status of the under-shepherds – namely, the seven shepherds and eight princes/chiefs (Mic 5:4b–5a). Specifically, as a response to the Bethlehemite figure's deliverance (v. 5b), the nation of Israel "will raise up" (והקמנו) the under-shepherds (v. 4b). According to Andersen and Freedman, the operative verb (הקם) denotes Yahweh's act of raising up a deliverer (e.g. Judg 2:16, 18; 3:9; 2 Sam 7:12; 1 Kgs 14:14; Jer 23:5).[128] Although the nation actively raises up the human vicegerents, ultimately the Bethlehemite figure's victory is the impetus for extending vicegerency to the shepherds and princes/chiefs. His victory inspires others to take a stand as well.

As expected of human vicegerents, the under-shepherds exercise dominion among the nations. As Micah's context clearly shows, their primary role is "to rule" (רעה) (Mic 5:5). It is difficult to miss that their role is intertwined with that of the Bethlehemite figure through the verb (רעה) (vv. 3, 5). However, unlike the previous case, where the verb was used intransitively, in the present case both its object and instrument are marked. The under-shepherds will rule the "land of Assyria" (ארץ אשור) militarily with the "sword" (בחרב). The

---

126. Sweeney, *Twelve Prophets*, 2:390. The graduated numerical formula has been a subject of considerable discussion. The seven/eight formula appears also in Eccl 11:2, while the three/four formula appears in several passages (Prov 30:15, 18, 21, 29; Amos 1:3, 6, 9, 11, 13; 2:1, 4, 6). According to Jenson, the seven/eight formula "implies an indefinite but sufficient number of generals required for the necessary military action." Jenson, *Obadiah, Jonah, Micah*, 160. Here we understand the seven shepherds and eight chiefs as military commanders fighting alongside the shepherd-king. This notion of simultaneity is evident in the use of the shepherd imagery in fighting a common enemy, Assyria (Mic 5:3; 5:4–5). For the larger debate on the numerical formula, see Smith-Christopher, *Micah*, 172–174; Waltke, *Commentary on Micah*, 289–291; McComiskey and Longman, "Micah," 532.

127. Chae, *Jesus as the Eschatological Davidic Shepherd*, 36–37.

128. Andersen and Freedman, *Micah*, 477.

swords of these gallant warriors will not only push back the invaders but will also take the battle back to the Assyrian homeland (vv. 4b–5a). Worldwide dominion is clearly the emphasis of the passage. Israel will militarily subdue and rule the nations.

The remnant of Jacob and the nations

In the second והיה passage (Mic 5:6–8), Micah continues to underscore the extension of vicegerency to other human beings, in this case, the remnant of Jacob (vv. 6, 7). The prophet emphasizes the remnant's presence "in the midst of many peoples/nations" (בקרב עמים רבים) (vv. 6, 7).[129] Such emphasis is evident in the attributive adjective "many" (רבים), which expresses a relatively large quantity of countable nations.[130] Language is being stretched here; in our view, their dispersion among many nations subtly communicates the idea that the remnant of Jacob has filled and inhabits the entire earth. We should recall that even after the fall, Yahweh's intent for an exiled humanity (i.e. away from Eden) was for a restored remnant to procreate and fill the earth so that his sovereignty would spread among the nations (e.g. Gen 9:1, 7; Exod 1:12; cf. Gen 1:28).

Besides multiplying and filling the earth, Israel's commission was to bless obedient nations but to be a curse to disobedient nations (Gen 12:3). Similar dynamics are likely at play in Micah's two complementary metaphors. Micah describes the remnant's presence among the nations as both dew/showers and a lion (Mic 5:6, 7). These contrasting images in Micah remind us of similar images in Prov 19 where the king's anger is like a lion's growl, but his favor is like dew on the grass (v. 12). In their natural sense, dew and showers are associated with prosperity and abundance (Gen 27:28, 39; 1 Kgs 17:1; Hos 14:6). However, Jacobs thinks that dew and showers in Micah 5:6 suggest that the remnant's stay among the nations will be short. Perhaps Jacobs has Hoseanic passages in view. These speak of the transitory nature of dew (Hos 6:4; 13:3). Willis and Waltke believe that the dew and shower metaphors point to the profuse numerical growth of the remnant.[131] Willis goes on to state

---

129. Micah's emphasizes the remnant situation by repeating the phrase בקרב עמים רבים twice (5:6, 7), and then clarifying it by a parallel expression "among the nations" (בגוים) (v. 7).

130. Swanson, *Dictionary of Biblical Languages*, §8041.

131. Willis, "Structure, Setting, and Interrelationships," 228; Waltke, *Commentary on Micah*, 308.

that "v. 6 has nothing to do with Israel's relationship to the nations, either to bless them or destroy them. Instead, it announces that the power of Yahweh alone can deliver Israel from her hopeless circumstances."[132]

Against Willis and others, we contend that Micah employs the dew and shower metaphors to underscore the positive aspect of the remnant's presence among the nations to bless all the nations of the earth. Just as Jacob received the dew from heaven as his inheritance so that he could be a blessing to and exercise dominion over the nations (Gen 27:28–29), a future remnant of Jacob will also be as such.[133]

Micah also describes the remnant of Jacob as a lion among the nations. Israel's ancient traditions attest to the image of Israel as a lion (Gen 49:9; Num 23:24). The imagery deserves further comment. For instance, the prophet Amos parallels the lion symbol to Yahweh's sovereignty (Amos 3:8). Furthermore, several passages depict wicked foreign kings (Jer 50:17; Ezek 32:2) and Israel's kings as ravenous lions plundering God's people (Ezek 22:25). However, Micah uses the image uniquely, as Smith-Christopher notes, "Only here in Micah . . . does there appear to be an association of Judah/Israelites as a lion against their foes."

Without delaying the discussion with regard to the possible tenors of the metaphor, the context clearly makes plain that the remnant, like a lion, will militarily subdue the nations (Mic 5:7–8). Military connotations are evident in terms like "tramples down" (ורמס) and "tears into pieces" ((וטרף (v. 8b). In addition, the remnant will be so powerful that "there is no one to deliver" (ואין מציל) the nations. This speaks of absolute power over the enemy and any of their power bases.

Micah concludes his picture of the remnant's military might by clarifying and unraveling the lion/sheep imagery. The remnant's "hand" (יד), a symbol of military might and authority, will be lifted against the nations (Mic 5:9a). This speaks of war against other nations (cf. 2 Sam 20:21). Finally, Israel's enemies (i.e. all the hostile nations) will be "cut off" (כרת) (v. 9b). Thus, in a reversal of fortunes, the remnant will be like a strong ravenous lion devouring the nations who are now like defenseless sheep.

---

132. Willis, "Structure, Setting, and Interrelationships," 228.
133. Dempster, *Micah*, 140–141.

Altogether, Micah presents a vision for the restoration of Zion's former dominion. A Davidic ruler, Yahweh's vicegerent, will arise, lead Judah in the strength of Yahweh, and extend his rule to the ends of the earth (Mic 5:1–3). His universal rule will achieve peace, which he will maintain by placing other human vicegerents over the nations (vv. 4–8). It is this motif of peace that Micah concludes this section with (vv. 9–14). To this, we now turn.

Yahweh and the nations

In the third והיה passage (Mic 5:9–14), Micah introduces an oracle ascribed to Yahweh via an oracular formula. Formally, several features provide the literary integrity of the passage. These include the repetition of the first person verbs "cut off" (כרת) (vv. 9, 10, 11, 12), its synonym "destroy/uproot" (נתש) (Mic 5:14; cf. Jer 18:7), and the ringing second person pronominal suffix "you/your" (ך), used fourteen times in this unit alone. According to Jenson, the overall thrust of the repetition of the verb stresses Yahweh's resolve to eliminate objects that threaten trust in him.[134] To that, we may also add that the emphasis on Yahweh's agency shows that the Bethlehemite figure's reign is ultimately a participation in the peace that the divine sovereign will accomplish for him.[135] After all, Yahweh had emphatically promised that he would deliver a remnant from exile (Mic 4:10b).

For the most part, scholars agree on the literary integrity of Micah 5:9–14. However, the debate is enjoined over the identity of the referent to the pronominal suffix "you/your" (ך). The most popular position among scholars in recent years is that the passage unmistakably shows Yahweh's future cleansing and purification of apostate Israel.[136] Wagenaar's form-critical study is representative and offers a sustained argument for this view. According to Wagenaar, the series of oracles (Mic 5:9–13) are reminiscent of the extermination formula.[137] An important function of the formula, Wagenaar says, is to purge persons and objects that undermine Yahweh's relationship with

---

134. Jenson, *Obadiah, Jonah, Micah*, 163.

135. Roberts, "Divine King," 133.

136. Mays, *Micah*, 125; Cuffey, *Literary Coherence*, 244; Wolff, *Micah*, 157–158; Jenson, *Obadiah, Jonah, Micah*, 163; Jacobs, *Conceptual Coherence*, 155–156; Smith-Christopher, *Micah*, 181–184; Hillers, *Micah*, 72–73; Dempster, *Micah*, 141–142.

137. Wagenaar, *Judgement and Salvation*, 308. An important marker for the formula is the operative verb (כרת) (Mic 5:9, 10, 11, 12).

his covenant community (e.g. Lev 26:30; Zech 9:10; 13:2).[138] In light of these considerations, Wagenaar concludes that the formula has the same role in our target passage, and hence Israel is the addressee.

As commendable as the foregoing argument might be, we are not convinced that the passage has apostate Israel in view. The limitations of form criticism become evident as Wagenaar erroneously imposes the original *Sitz im Leben* of the extermination formula upon Micah 5:9–14 without considering Micah's own context. His approach here is analogous to the classical case of illegitimate totality transfer. While it is possible that Micah could use the formula without developing or altering its original sense, such a conclusion still demands argumentation. Micah's own intended context should be taken seriously in that argument. Only Micah's intended context informs how he uses or develops the extermination formula or the Isaianic passage.

A major weakness in Wagenaar's approach is his assumption that the extermination formula informs Micah's intended context. Micah's use of a shared form or language characteristic of the extermination formula does not necessarily mean that the formula is his intended context. In fact, Waltke acknowledges that most scholars assume that the extermination formula colors Micah 5:9–14. However, he contends that Isaiah 2:7–9 is Micah's intended context, because both passages share similar objects for destruction.[139] Ben Zvi has also shown that the particular arrangement of verbal forms, and their respective direct objects, in Micah 5:9–14 is unique and distinct from other texts related to the matter of ritual purges found in extermination formulas.[140] Waltke's and Ben Zvi's appraisals show that it is not quite correct to assume that the extermination formula provides Micah's intended context. Other factors, such as thematic coherence between the passages and the wider context, need to be taken into consideration in determining Micah's intended context.

Contrary to the popular view, Micah's intended context is still the Zion/Davidic traditions. Specifically, Micah 5:9–14 teases the traditions' motif of idyllic peace that follows divine victory. As Levenson and many others have observed, the Zion/Davidic traditions frequently depict the paradoxical consequence of victory over the nations – that is, the destruction of the weapons

---

138. Wagenaar, 305–310; Mays, *Micah*, 125.
139. Waltke, *Commentary on Micah*, 321.
140. Ben Zvi, *Micah*, 136–137.

of war and the inauguration of a reign of peace (e.g. Pss 46:10–11; 76:4; Isa 11:1–9; cf. 2 Sam 8:4; Zech 1:16–17; 9:9–10).[141] In fact, Micah has already shown that following the exaltation of Zion, the nations will accept Yahweh's sovereignty and destroy their war implements (Mic 4:3–4).

The initial use of this motif in Micah 4:3–4 preconditions the audience such that, upon its subsequent use, the audience can easily recognize it with little effort. In later uses, all Micah has to do is to guide his audience toward this intended context by providing clues – for instance, key terms, motifs, or themes. Here the prophet uses temporal markers as guides to connect Micah 5:9–14 to Micah 4:1–5: (והיה ביום־ההוא) (5:9) corresponds to (והיה באחרית הימים) (4:1; cf. 4:6) and differs markedly from the simple והיה markers (5:4, 6, 7). This is a significant observation. Micah is essentially interrupting the flow of thought and wants us to read the passage in light of Micah 4:1, 6, because of a shared motif. The two passages share the motif of idyllic peace.

Another clue is the operative verb "I will cut off" (כרת) (Mix 5:8, 9, 10, 11, 12), which links our target passage to the preceding one (5:6–8). What is more, in Micah 5:8 the operative verb has an explicit object qualified by the second person pronominal suffix "you/your" (ך). With all these clues, Micah is already guiding his audience on how to approach the following passage (i.e. Mic 5:9–14). In light of this evidence, Micah's intended context is not the extermination formulas, as Wagenaar and others would have us believe. Instead, Micah's intended context is likely the motif of idyllic peace that follows the divine warrior's or his vicegerent's victory.

As such, the addressee in our target passage is most likely the nations rather than apostate Israel. First, it is theologically inconsistent for Yahweh to extend victory to a remnant guilty of possessing their own instruments of war and of practicing idolatry in the land of Israel (Mic 5:9–13). Second, the purification of the land of Israel has already been achieved in the previous judgments leading up to the transformation of Zion (1:2–4:1). Hence, the idea in our target passage (i.e. 5:9–14) is that Yahweh is purifying the land possessed by the nations as an extension of sovereign rule among them (5:11). In sum, the passage is essentially an expansion of the peace motif introduced in the previous section (4:1–2).

---

141. Levenson, "Zion Traditions," 1100-1101; Weinfeld, "Zion and Jerusalem," 102; Roberts, "Enthronement of Yhwh and David," 686; Wolff, *Micah*, 118.

What we see in our target passage is a portrait of a vision of peace (see Mic 5:4a), which the Bethlehemite figure will inaugurate through Yahweh's agency. Evidently, peace comes following the Bethlehemite figure's victory and dominion over the nations (5:1–8). Yahweh will then obliterate military implements and infrastructure (vv. 9–10). Military apparatus will be futile in an era of peace, because they are contrary to the reign of an ideal king (cf. 1 Sam 8:11–12). Ultimately, the goal here is for the nations to recognize Yahweh's sovereignty.

In addition, Micah's vision of peace will also demand an acknowledgment of the absolute sovereignty of Yahweh over false gods or pagan worship (Mic 5:12b). As we have already pointed out, idolatry in all its alluring forms was a downright rebuff of Yahweh's sovereignty (1 Sam 8:7–9). As such, Yahweh will destroy all objects associated with pagan worship – that is, the occult, false gods, idols, and cult objects (Mic 5:11–13).[142] On the other hand, Yahweh will execute "vengeance" (נקם) on the nations who do not acknowledge his sovereignty (Mic 5:14; cf. Deut 32:35, 41, 43; Isa 34:8). Dempster maintains that the term נקם relates to Yahweh's vindication of his holiness and justice in the world.[143] According to Mays, Yahweh's vengeance is related to his sovereignty. As he explains, Yahweh's vengeance "is not irrationally personal revenge to satisfy a wounded ego, but the exercise of legitimate sovereignty in a punishment which must occur if the rule of God is to be maintained."[144]

Significance of Davidic Kingship

Our focus in this chapter was on the ideal Davidic king who will serve as Yahweh's vicegerent in the reestablishment of Yahweh's sovereignty over the earth (Mic 5:1–4a). As we saw, vicegerency was not only limited to the king but was being democratized, as it were, to other human beings (vv. 4b–8). Given this backdrop, the vicegerents shared in Yahweh's rule, but each had a distinct realm in which to exercise that rule. The king will rule from Zion, the other shepherds will rule in Assyria, and the remnant of Jacob will rule among the nations. Evidently, Yahweh's vicegerents are once again subduing

---

142. Barker, "Micah," 105.
143. Dempster, *Micah*, 142.
144. Mays, *Micah*, 127.

and ruling the whole earth. Hence, the reinstatement of vicegerency and its democratization signals the arrival and spreading of Yahweh's rule on earth. In addition, the vicegerency of Israel under a Davidic king fulfills the universal aspect of Zion's universal rule (Mic 4:8; cf., Pss 2:8–9; 72:8–11; 89:25). Finally, the reinstatement of human vicegerency speaks of the realization of the original divine intent for humanity and earthly order. Restored humanity is once again exercising dominion over Yahweh's kingdom (Gen 1:27-28)!

CHAPTER 6

Divine Sovereignty and the New People of God (Micah 6:1–7:20)

Introduction

In the previous two chapters, we concluded that the reestablishment of Yahweh's sovereignty speaks of two related issues respectively: the restoration of his earthly throne centered at Zion (Mic 1:2–4:7) and the restoration of the Davidic vicegerent ruling on his behalf (4:8–5:14). Logically, two questions arise. Who are the subjects of Yahweh's universal kingdom? What is their nature? Thus, the present chapter analyzes the portrayal of Yahweh's sovereignty in relations to the transformation of a new people of God in Micah 6–7.

Such a portrayal is congruent with the Zion/Davidic traditions. As we have noted earlier, Roberts aptly argues that Yahweh's presence in Zion had at least two implications for the city's inhabitants. In the first place, only those who meet Yahweh's demands for righteousness are fit to live in Zion (Pss 15:1–5; 24:3–6; Isa 33:13–16, 24).[1] In the second place, the righteous inhabitants will enjoy the security and abundant life of living in Yahweh's presence.

Moshe Weinfeld confirms Roberts' conclusion. He observes that a typical ANE notion is that the royal capital city of a nation radiates justice.[2] Likewise, Yahweh founded his throne in Zion on justice and righteousness. Only those who abhor evil will dwell in the royal city and will inherit Yahweh's

---

1. Roberts, "Enthronement of Yhwh and David," 685; Roberts, "Zion," 342–343; Abernethy, *Book of Isaiah*, 180–198; Gowan, *Eschatology in the Old Testament*, 59–96; Durant, "Imitation of God," 224–235; Jenner, "Jerusalem," 170–171; Gregory, "Postexilic Exile," 493–495.

2. Weinfeld, "Zion and Jerusalem," 99–100; Whitelam, *Just King*, 17–37; Gowan, *Eschatology in the Old Testament*, 83–93.

blessings (Pss 97:2, 10–12). It is against such a background that Micah 6–7 makes sense. This background thematically dovetails Micah 1–5 into Micah 6–7. As we hope to clarify, Micah adapts the aforementioned motifs from the Zion/Davidic traditions to effect the transformation of a new people of God (Mic 6:1–7:20).

Towards this aim, the study will discuss the literary shape of our target passage. After that, we will highlight the presence of motifs from the Zion/Davidic traditions in our target passage. We will then devote the bulk of the chapter to the issue of the transformation of a new people of God. As we will argue, the new covenant people must reflect and imitate Yahweh's character and deeds of righteousness and justice (Mic 6:8). Thus, in order to create a new people, Yahweh will judge the wicked (6:9–7:6). Noteworthy in this particular case is that judgment will not be transformative (i.e. make the wicked righteous). Instead, its ultimate goal is to remove the wicked from the land for the last time. Only a repentant remnant will enjoy transformation (7:7–20). Upon their repentance (7:9), Yahweh will graciously forgive them (7:18–19a) and defeat sin on their behalf (7:19b). In essence, Micah envisions a future kingdom that is entirely devoid of sinners and sin. Finally, the chapter will close with a summary.

Overview of Micah 6:1–7:20

Unity of Micah 6:1–7:20

The delineation of Micah 6–7 from the rest of Micah 1–5 is clearly marked by a summons to hear (וְשִׁמְעוּ) (6:1–2). In this study, the summons to hear, which introduces legal disputes, signals the beginning of each major division (Mic 1:2 and 6:1–2).[3] Jacobs aptly argues that only in Micah 1:2 and 6:1 does the summons have a macro-syntactical function – in all the other places it signals focus (3:1, 9; 6:9).[4]

Micah 6–7 also differs from the preceding section in several respects. Hagstrom observes that Micah 6–7 has a dialogical character, whereas Micah 1–5 does not.[5] In addition, he notes that the exile motif recurs frequently in

---

3. Jacobs, *Conceptual Coherence*, 64; Hagstrom, *Coherence*, 47.

4. She states that in Mic 3:1 and 9 the two summons focus on different aspects of the leader's responsibility, while 6:9 focuses on the city. Jacobs, *Conceptual Coherence*, 64.

5. Hagstrom, *Coherence*, 203.

Divine Sovereignty and the New People of God (Micah 6:1–7:20)

Micah 1–5, whereas it is glaringly missing in Micah 6–7.[6] Wagenaar perceives that Micah 1–5 has a focus on the nation's leaders (2:1–3:12), whereas Micah 6–7 focuses on the people in general (6:1–8; 7:1–7; 7:8–20) and a city (6:9–16), and only on certain occasions speaks of leaders (7:3).[7]

We may also add other notable differences between the two major sections. For instance, religious ritualism plays a significant role in Micah 6–7, whereas Micah 1–5 emphasizes idolatry and social justice. More importantly, in Micah 1–5 transformation comes through extensive judgments without any offer for repentance. In contrast, in Micah 6–7 the transformation of a new covenant community comes through forgiveness to those who obey Yahweh's demands and repent (Mic 6:6–8; 7:9). Only the unrepentant suffer judgment (6:9–7:6).

Having isolated Micah 6–7 from Micah 1–5, establishing its coherence is an issue that needs not detain us much. Recently, Cuffey and others have convincingly demonstrated that various levels of coherence bind the passage together.[8] Of interest to us at this point is discerning an overarching theme that holds the various literary forms in Micah 6–7 together. Apparently, Micah 6–7 comprises a variety of genres, which include "covenant lawsuit" (ריב) (6:1–5; 9–16), a lament (7:1–7), and a conclusion with four hymnic fragments (7:8–20).[9] As outlined below, the section is also replete with ancient Israelite traditions arranged in a symmetrical order. Such a symmetric presentation of the traditions promotes the coherence of the whole section.

   A Exodus (6:4)
      B Wilderness/Conquest (6:5)
         C Monarchic Era (6:16a)
         C' Monarchic Era (7:12)
      B' Wilderness/Conquest (7:14)
   A' Exodus (7:15, 18–19)
   Patriarchal Traditions (7:20)

---

6. Hagstrom, 203.

7. Wagenaar, *Judgement and Salvation*, 50.

8. Cuffey, *Literary Coherence*, 123–133; Jacobs, *Conceptual Coherence*, 60–96; Jenson, *Obadiah, Jonah, Micah*, 166.

9. Barker, "Micah," 34; Jenson, *Obadiah, Jonah, Micah*, 166–167; Sweeney, *Twelve Prophets*, 2:343.

What message do these variegated forms and traditions communicate? How does that message relate to the message in Micah 1–5? Cuffey appropriately argues that Micah 6–7 speaks of Yahweh restoring a remnant to covenant fidelity.[10] Yahweh will do so "by forgiving their transgressions and iniquities absolutely."[11] For the most part, we agree with Cuffey that the book of Micah centers on Yahweh who restores,[12] but we differ largely on what exactly are the objects of Yahweh's restoration and how those objects relate to Yahweh's faithfulness to the Abrahamic promises (7:20).

In our case, we take a holistic approach. We believe that the overall divine intent in Micah is to fulfill the Abrahamic promises contingent upon the people's repentance (Mic 7:18–20). Therefore, in our target section (i.e. Micah 6–7), Yahweh is not only restoring a remnant from Israel but also from the nations. Yahweh will restore a remnant from both groups, and these will comprise the new people of God. In this regard, our view is consistent with Yahweh's overall plan for humanity (Gen 12:3b). A relationship between the two major sections is that Micah 6–7 is concerned with the subjects fit to dwell in the restored kingdom, which Yahweh established in Micah 1–5.

Zion/Davidic Traditions in Micah 6:1–7:20

Before we analyze our target passage in detail, we need to show that it reflects motifs from the Zion/Davidic traditions. In our introductory remarks, we claimed that a relevant background to understanding Micah 6–7 is the Zion/Davidic traditions. Such a bold claim demands argumentation. A vast majority of scholars has challenged such a claim.[13] Wagenaar seems to be their foremost representative. In line with the analysis of older studies by such scholars as H. Wald (1867), and especially Van der Woude's seven pillars,[14]

---

10. Cuffey, *Literary Coherence*, 252; Wagenaar, *Judgement and Salvation*, 50.

11. Cuffey, *Literary Coherence*, 252.

12. Cuffey, 217–218.

13. Although Marrs limits his theological reading of Zion in the book of Micah to Micah 1–5, he does not explicitly reject the presence of motifs from the Zion/Davidic traditions per se. It appears his focus is on the most prominent Zion motifs in Micah and not on the subsidiary ones. These include Zion as the divine mountain, the defeat of the nation, and the pilgrimage of the nations. Marrs, "Back to the Future," 82nn13, 94. Interestingly, for Bob Becking, Micah 6–7 presupposes the time of King Josiah. He thus concludes that the passage speaks of "hope for the restoration of the Davidic dream of unity and for the return of the exiled Samarians." Becking, "Micah in Neo-Assyrian Light," 125.

14. For the seven pillars, see Wagenaar, *Judgement and Salvation*, 49–51.

Wagenaar unambiguously contends, "Whereas the extant text of Micah 1–5 time and again attests to theological traditions of Judah, Micah 6–7 is dominated by the Northern Israelite traditions of Exodus, Wilderness Wandering and Conquest. The theology of Zion is conspicuously lacking in Micah 6–7."[15] Wagenaar substantiates his conclusion by noting that Micah 6–7 does not mention any vocabulary or ideas associated with the Southern Kingdom (e.g. Zion, Jerusalem, Judah, or David).[16] His most important argument is that the language in Micah 6–7 is indicative of liturgy and wisdom literature, which is markedly analogous to that in Hosea, Jeremiah, and the Deuteronomistic texts.[17] Here Wagenaar is hinting at some parallelism between the entrance liturgy in Hos 6:4–6 and Micah 6:6–8.[18]

Undeniably, there are strong formal similarities between Hos 6:4–6 and Micah 6:6–8, but that by itself does not invalidate the presence of the Zion/Davidic traditions in Micah 6–7. In fact, what Wagenaar does not relate is that Hos 6:4–6 has both Israel and Judah in view. There is, therefore, no reason why Micah 6:6–8 could not also be addressed to Judah, as is Hos 6:4–6.

More importantly, the entrance liturgies in both Hos 6:4–6 and Micah 6:6–8 are actually imitations of the motifs contained in the Zion/Davidic traditions (Pss 15:1–2; 24:3–4; Isa 33:14b–16).[19] Classical expositions of the entrance liturgies understand them as questions and answers performed by the worshiper and priest, respectively, at the temple gate, concerning who may enter Zion's sacred space.[20] These entrance liturgies exhibit formal and thematic similarities with Micah 6:6–8. Formally, the liturgies have a consistent pattern: (a) a double question of who may visit Yahweh's temple (Pss 15:1; 24:3; Isa 33:14b; cf. Mic 6:6a), (b) a response concerning the qualifications required of the visitors (Pss 15:2–3; 24:4; Isa 33:15; cf. Mic 6:8), and (c) a promise (Pss 15:5; 24:5; Isa 33:16).[21]

---

15. Wagenaar, 52.
16. Wagenaar, 50.
17. Wagenaar, 51.
18. Wagenaar, 50, especially note 6.
19. Sweeney, *Twelve Prophets*, 2:398.
20. Brueggemann and Bellinger, *Psalms*, 82; Limburg, *Hosea-Micah*, 190.
21. Broyles, "Psalms," 248; Weinfeld, "Instruction," 224–225.

Thematically, the liturgies underscore justice and righteousness as major demands for covenant renewal (Pss 15:2; 24:5; Isa 33:15; Mic 6:8).[22] Only those who observe righteousness may dwell in Yahweh's presence and worship at his temple in Zion. Gowan also reaches a similar conclusion and confirms our findings. He comments, "The text [Mic 6:6–8], with its emphasis on justice (*mishpaṭ*) and kindness (*ḥesed*), thus lies in two lines of tradition; the cultic, represented by Psalms 15 and 24, and the prophetic, in which righteousness is exalted above sacrifice (Amos 5:21–24; Hos 6:5 [6])."[23] Wagenaar's dismissal of the presence of Zion theology in Micah 6:1–7:20 is premature. In sum, it is apparent that Micah 6:1–7:20 contains allusions to the Zion/Davidic traditions' subsidiary motifs.

Without being exhaustive, we can cite more evidence to cement our claim that Micah 6–7 contains motifs from the Zion/Davidic traditions. ANE cultures conceived cosmic mountains as places where the high god issued effective decrees and as places for the meeting of the gods (e.g. Ps 82).[24] The Zion/Davidic traditions also conceive of Mount Zion as a cosmic mountain from where Yahweh issues righteous decrees (Pss 96:10–13; 97:8–9; cf. 46:2–5; 48:2–3; Mic 4:1–2). However, in contrast to the ANE conception (patron gods or deified natural elements gathered in assembly), in the Zion/Davidic traditions personified natural or geographical elements (e.g. heaven and earth, mountains, and rivers) served as witnesses at these divine assemblies (Isa 1:2a; cf. Ezek 6:3; 36:4, 6; Deut 32:1).[25] Functionally, the cosmic mountains were involved in the rule and maintenance of cosmic order.[26]

With the foregoing backdrop in mind, the cosmic geography described in Micah's covenant lawsuit presupposes the two subsidiary motifs from the Zion/Davidic traditions (Mic 6:1–2). In fact, analyzing our target passage in light of Psalm 50 validates our claim.[27] Contextually, there are close formal and thematic parallels between Micah 6:1–2 and Psalm 50. Both texts are

---

22. Broyles, "Psalms," 251.
23. Gowan, *Theology of the Prophetic Books*, 57.
24. Clifford, *Cosmic Mountain*, 5, 180–181.
25. Cross, *Canaanite Myth and Hebrew Epic*, 188.
26. Clifford, *Cosmic Mountain*, 3.
27. Brueggemann and Bellinger characterize this Asaphite psalm as a covenant renewal text (see Ps 50:4). Brueggemann and Bellinger, *Psalms*, 232.

Divine Sovereignty and the New People of God (Micah 6:1–7:20)

covenant lawsuits for breach of covenant.[28] Both texts include a summons (Mic 6:1; Ps 50:1), natural elements serve as witnesses (Mic 6:1, 2; Ps 50:1, 4), and the accusations against the people involve insincere sacrificial ritualism rather than social justice (Mic 6:6–8; Ps 50:8–14, 17–20).

Cross perceptively remarks that the covenant lawsuit "had its origins in conceptions of Yahweh's divine assembly as a court."[29] It is no surprise then that in both passages the setting of the covenant lawsuit is the cosmic mountain. This is the locale for Yahweh's cosmic court.[30] In Psalm 50, Mount Zion is the indisputable cosmic mountain in view (vv. 1–2).[31] In Micah's covenant lawsuit, the cosmic character of the mountains is embedded in the expression "the enduring foundations of the earth" (האתנים מסדי ארץ) (Mic 6:2).[32] Just as the cosmic court in Psalm 50 is located at Mount Zion, it is not a stretch to surmise that Micah's covenant lawsuit is likely situated at Mount Zion as well. After all, Micah has already hinted that Mount Zion will be established as the highest of all the mountains and hills (Mic 4:1). Hence, consistent with the Zion/Davidic traditions, Micah's covenant lawsuit portrays Yahweh issuing universal decrees from his cosmic court at Mount Zion (6:1–2).[33]

Consequently, since Micah 6–7 convincingly reflects theological motifs associated with the Zion/Davidic traditions, Wagenaar's conclusion that the anonymous "city" (עיר) (Mic 6:9) should be Samaria is open for challenge.[34] By extension, the sacred temple/palace or royal city is located on the cosmic mountain. In our target passage, the juxtaposition of a lawsuit and sacrifices supports the idea that the legal proceedings took place at a temple precinct (6:1–7). Micah 4:3 has already established the temple/court nexus. In this verse (Mic 4:3), Yahweh presides over international disputes at the

---

28. Levenson, *Sinai and Zion*, 207.
29. Cross, *Canaanite Myth and Hebrew Epic*, 188–189.
30. Sweeney, *Twelve Prophets*, 2:396.
31. Levenson, *Sinai and Zion*, 207. Among other things, the expression "perfection of beauty" (מכלל־יפי) accentuates the psalm's cosmic character (Ps 50:2; cf., Job 38:19; Ezek 1:22).
32. The expression evokes the idea of a cosmic mountain whose height reaches the heavens and whose depth is in the earth's foundations (Pss 18:7, 15; 104:5; Prov 8:29). Waltke, *Commentary on Micah*, 347; Walton, *Ancient Near Eastern Thought*, 174–175; Cohn, *Shape of Sacred Space*, 30.
33. Levenson, "Zion Traditions," 1099.
34. Wagenaar, *Judgement and Salvation*, 53. F. C. Burkett even thinks the place of worship is at Gilgal and not at Zion. Burkitt, "Micah 6 and 7," 159–161.

royal temple in Zion. There is no evidence in Micah of Yahweh's court taking place at another place other than Zion. Samaria's reversion to a vineyard field declassed it of its royal status (Mic 1:6–7), which meant that Zion was now the only royal city in the land. Thus, it is not plausible that such a tense national lawsuit as in Micah 6:1–8 would take place at another court other than the one at Zion (cf. Deut 17:8). Zion is the only place where the legitimate royal court stands.

What is more, traditions about the royal capital city also imply that the anonymous city should be identified with Zion (Mic 6:9).[35] First, it is well known that ANE cultures conceived of the cosmic mountain and its associated temple as constituting the center of the cosmos (e.g. Ps 46; Mic 4:1–2).[36] As Walton notes, "The temple is considered the center of the cosmos, and itself a microcosmos."[37] By extension, this meant that the royal capital city in which the temple was situated also became the center of the universe. For our present purposes, the centeredness of the royal city aids us to understand Micah 7:11–12. The idea in Micah 7:11–12 of building walls and extending boundaries draws on the motif of the capital city as the center of the kingdom with borders reaching to the ends of the world (see Mic 5:3–4; Pss 2:8; 48:10; 72:8).[38] In other words, Yahweh's kingdom is universal, but it is centered on a particular place.

Second, since the royal city is the center of the universe, it will attract people from all over the world (Mic 7:12; cf. Isa 60:6–9).[39] Third, the royal capital is a city of righteousness because of Yahweh's presence (Mic 6:8; cf. Pss 5:5–8; 16; 24:3–5; Isa 1:21–27).[40] It is not farfetched that Zion is the unidentified city in Micah 6:9. In sum, a major theme threading Micah 6–7 is Yahweh's demand for Zion's future inhabitants to observe righteousness and justice. To this, we now turn.

---

35. Weinfeld, "Zion and Jerusalem," 104–115.
36. Lundquist, *Temple of Jerusalem*, 1, 7.
37. Walton, *Ancient Near Eastern Thought*, 123.
38. Weinfeld, "Zion and Jerusalem," 92, 102.
39. Weinfeld, 107, 110.
40. Weinfeld, 111.

Transformation of the New People of God
Yahweh Demands Covenant Recommitment
Literary form of Yahweh's rîb

The traditional classification of Micah 6:1–8 as a "covenant lawsuit" (ריב) has now been questioned and become a debated issue.[41] Andersen and Freedman contend, "This is not a transcript of a trial conducted according to the established procedures."[42] In our estimation, to reject the presence of the lawsuit form is not being forthright with the words of the texts. Three times in two verses the text mentions the term ריב (6:1, 2). We agree with Andersen and Freedman that form critics at times rigidly categorize literary genres. However, despite its truncated form, the general pattern of the lawsuit is present.[43]

Without engaging that larger debate, it is sounder to say that the passage at hand is of a mixed genre. Building on the lawsuit form, the prophet adapts and reshapes it for his own ends. Specifically, Micah essentially strings together a number of literary forms from different traditions to shape his literary piece. The passage comprises at least three literary forms – namely, a lawsuit (6:1–5) with affinities to 1 Samuel 12; an entrance liturgy (Mic 6:6–7) reminiscent of Psalms 15, 24 and Isaiah 33:14a–16; and a character sketch in didactic form (Mic 6:8) from Deuteronomy 10:12.[44] Together, the three units spell out what Yahweh expects of Israel. Each passage in its own hue blends into the others to produce a portrait of the justice and righteousness that Yahweh demands of his people. Juan I. Alfaro concurs. He comments that Micah 6:1–8 is "an

---

41. For a cogent survey of the various proposals, see Schaefer, "Genre Considerations," 18–21; Ramsey, "Speech-Forms," 45–46; Daniels, "Is There a 'Prophetic Lawsuit' Genre?," 350–354; Weinfeld, *Normative and Sectarian Judaism*, 21–24.

42. Andersen and Freedman, *Micah*, 506. Andersen and Freedman surmise that the passage is a dramatic dialogue.

43. According to Richard M. Davidson, the Israelite lawsuit for covenant breach was a mirror image of the covenant-making pattern. His pattern for Mic 6:1–8 includes: Summons and list of witnesses (6:1b); preamble (6:1a, 2); historical prologue (6:3, 5); indictment (6:6–8); verdict (6:13). Davidson, "Divine Covenant Lawsuit Motif," 65; Shaw, *Speeches of Micah*, 165; Alfaro, *Justice and Loyalty*, 64.

44. Owens, *Portraits of the Righteous*, 34; Wolff, *Micah*, 166–169. Cuffey comments, "The initial unit [Mic] (6:1–8) is a dialogue in the form of a lawsuit that includes the Lord (vv. 1–5), a representative of the people (vv. 6–7) and the prophet (v. 8). Yahweh is portrayed as bringing charges against the people. The presentation of the case is done in vocabulary reminiscent of legal proceedings in a court." Cuffey, *Literary Coherence*, 246–247.

urgent and intense appeal to a change of behaviour followed by an implicit recognition of sin and sincere attempt at expiation."[45]

Yahweh takes Israel to court

Mic 6:1–5 opens with a summons addressed to all Israel to convene for a divine legal proceeding with the mountains and hills serving as witnesses (vv. 1–2). While the court gathers to deliberate Israel's breach of covenant, a key point to note is that the intent of the lawsuit is didactic. The verb "to contend" (יכח) qualifies this pedagogical sense (v. 2b). G. Liedke postulates, "The basic meaning of *ykḥ* is 'to determine what is right.'"[46] He goes on to note that in order to determine what is right the litigants tend towards "proving, disproving, justifying."[47] Following Paul R. Gilchrist's study, Jacobs concludes that the underlying goal of the verb is to discipline or educate.[48]

That the intent of the passage is didactic finds further support in the ensuing questions in Yahweh's speech: "Oh my people, what have I done to you? How have I wearied you?" (עמי מה־עשיתי לך ומה הלאתיך) (Mic 6:3). An important observation here is that the questions open with a vocative, "my people" (עמי), in the coveted clause-initial position. Ernest J. Revell makes a strong case that the vocatives (and their placement in the speech) often provide unambiguous hints of the social relationships between speakers and addresses and reflect the speaker's attitude towards the addressee as polite, urgent, or brusque.[49] In our target verse, the use of עמי indicates the existence of a personal relationship between Yahweh and Israel. By placing the vocative as the *casus pendens*,[50] Micah shows that "Yahweh's own commitment to Israel remains valid as the unconditional basis for the lawsuit."[51] The vocative serves as an appeal to persuade Israel to undertake action that she has rejected up to this point.

Accordingly, the vocative sets the tone for the subsequent two questions, marked by the interrogatives "what . . . and how" (מה . . . ומה). Over the

---

45. Alfaro, *Justice and Loyalty*, 64.
46. Liedke, "יכח," 542.
47. Liedke, 543.
48. Jacobs, *Conceptual Coherence*, 161.
49. Revell, *Designation of the Individual*, 325.
50. Waltke, *Commentary on Micah*, 349; Miller, "Vocative Syntax," 355, 359.
51. Wolff, *Micah*, 174.

Divine Sovereignty and the New People of God (Micah 6:1–7:20) 179

years, scholars have offered divergent views on the nature of these questions.[52] Others focus on how the questions relate to the conventional covenant lawsuit pattern. George W. Ramsey holds that such formulaic questions introduce the first stage – the pre-trial encounter – of a legal proceeding.[53] While we applaud Ramsey's observations, other traditions that may provide a relevant background to Micah 6:1–5 have received little scholarly attention. Unfortunately, scholars have emphasized the lawsuit pattern in Micah 6:1–8 to the exclusion of its content – in particular, the traditions that inform the passages.

As we hope to defend, a relevant backdrop to understanding Micah 6:1–5 is Samuel's farewell testament (1 Sam 12). To his credit, Jan Joosten, following the Jewish scholar Moshe Seidel, convincingly highlights several striking parallels between Micah 6:2–5 and 1 Sam 12.[54] For instance, he observes that the expression "testify against me or answer me" (ענה בי) occurs in 1 Samuel 12:3 and Micah 6:3.[55] The syntactical construction (ענה imperative *qal* followed by בי and a first person singular suffix) is unique to these two passages. Joosten also notes that the reference to Moses and Aaron is extremely rare outside the Pentateuch but appears in Joshua 24:5, 1 Samuel 12:8, and Micah

---

52. For instance, Schaefer regards the questions as rhetorical, since God knows that he is in the right and has done nothing to weary or burden Israel. For him, the questions call Israel's attention to God's love and care. Schaefer, "Genre Considerations," 23. Cruz also thinks the questions are rhetorical. In his words, "Yahweh appears to be asking rhetorical questions in order to establish his ethos and demand recognition of his righteous deeds, preparing the ground for him to bring the charges against Israel." Cruz, "*Who Is Like Yahweh?,*" 132. Contrary to Schaefer and Cruz, Waltke maintains that the questions are not rhetorical because Yahweh demands an answer from Israel. He sees the questions as both defensive and accusatory. Yahweh defends his innocence, while at the same time accusing Israel of distrust. He conjectures that Israel has been complaining that Yahweh has exacted unbearable burdens upon them. Waltke, *Commentary on Micah*, 378–379.

53. According to Ramsey, in a customary legal proceeding the aggrieved party frequently asks the accused party (Judg 8:1, 2; 2 Sam 12:21; cf. 1 Sam 26:15; 2 Sam 16:10). He further points out that the accusation is either spelled out in the question itself (Jer 26:9) or stated in the accompanying statement (Judg 8:1). However, there are significant differences between Ramsey's legal process and Mic 6:1–8. Foremost is that Yahweh calls himself into question in Mic 6:3. In addition, our target passage lacks accusations. Ramsey, "Speech-Forms," 49–50. Perhaps the lack of explicit accusations suggests that reconciliation rather than hostility is the ultimate goal. Andersen and Freedman, *Micah*, 531.

54. Joosten, "YHWH's Farewell," 452–454. At a passing glance, several scholars have also observed the close resemblance between Micah 6:1–8 and 1 Samuel 12. For instance, Wolff, *Micah*, 170–172; Shaw, *Speeches of Micah*, 168; Waltke, *Commentary on Micah*, 350; Jacobs, *Conceptual Coherence*, 167.

55. Joosten, "YHWH's Farewell," 453.

6:4 (which adds Miriam).⁵⁶ These three texts share a unique expression not found elsewhere in the Hebrew Bible: "He sent Moses and Aaron" (וישלח יהוה את־משה ואת־אהרן) (Josh 12:5; 1 Sam 12:8) // "I sent Moses, Aaron, and Miriam" (ואשלח לפניך את־משה אהרן ומרים) (Mic 6:4).⁵⁷ Furthermore, Joosten observes that the expression "the saving acts of Yahweh" (צדקות יהוה) occurs only in Judges 5:11, 1 Samuel 12:7, and Micah 6:5.⁵⁸

Besides these verbal parallels, 1 Samuel 12 and Micah 6:2–5 share similar content and themes.⁵⁹ Both passages share a judicial setting (1 Sam 12:7; Mic 6:1–2). Both passages extensively recount the ancient Israelite traditions, the exodus, wilderness wanderings, and the conquest period (1 Sam 12:8–12; Mic 6:4–5). Perhaps more arresting is the protestation of innocence by the accusers via questions (1 Sam 12:3; Mic 6:3).

Testify against me!	Oh my people, what have I done to you?
Whose ox have I taken?	How have I wearied you
Who have I defrauded?⁶⁰	Testify against me!⁶¹

The present study affirms Joosten's literary allusions. Clearly, the parallels he adduces show a striking connection between 1 Samuel 12 and Micah 6:2–5. However, we do not share his metaleptic interpretation of the literary allusion. Joosten assumes that the historical setting of Micah 6:1–8 is the fall of Samaria in 722/721 BC.⁶² Consequently, he concludes that Micah 6:1–8, like 1 Samuel 12, speaks of divine abandonment because of Israel's unrestrained lifestyle.⁶³ Joosten's conclusion is mistaken. As Samuel makes plain, despite

---

56. Joosten, 453.
57. Joosten, 453.
58. Joosten, 453.
59. Joosten, 453.
60. 1 Sam 12:3.
61. Mic 6:3.
62. Joosten, "YHWH's Farewell," 457.
63. In his own words, Joosten writes, "An analogy is established between Samuel at the very end of the period of the judges and YHWH in the period addressed in Mic 6. As Samuel once decided to leave the Israelites to their own devices, because they had chosen a road in which he didn't feel he could be of further service, so YHWH himself, in the period evoked in the oracle, bade his people farewell because their behaviour had become incompatible with his demands. When they are understood in this way, the words attributed to YHWH in verses 3–5 imply not only an accusation of Israel, as demanded by the controversy pattern. Much more

Israel's hubris in prematurely requesting a king, "Yahweh will not abandon his people" (לֹא־יִטֹּשׁ יהוה אֶת־עַמּוֹ) (1 Sam 12:22).

Contrary to Joosten, an important theme in 1 Samuel 12 is "to motivate the people to keep the covenant sanctions which Samuel had just delivered to them" (1 Sam 12:14–15).[64] As such, Micah 6:1–8 is best understood as a covenant renewal text. Yahweh is presenting before Israel a path to restore covenantal relations. Just as Samuel succeeded in convincing Israel to repent (1 Sam 12:4, 19), the questions in Micah 6:3 are an attempt on Yahweh's part to get Israel to recognize her own sins and to motivate repentance. Such an interpretation finds support by taking a closer look at the context.

In the ensuing verses, Yahweh reminds Israel of his providential care for them during the exodus, wilderness wanderings, and conquest periods (Mic 6:4–5a). The significance of the flashback to the ancient traditions lays in its motive in the final clause. According to W. Zimmerli, the recognition formula – "that you may know" (לְמַעַן דַּעַת) (v. 5b) – always follows an account of Yahweh's action.[65] Micah expands the formula with an object clause, "the righteous acts of Yahweh" (צִדְקוֹת יהוה). Without context, ידע connotes both cognitive and effective knowledge of an object.[66]

However, in this context, Yahweh describes his acts as righteous in the sense that he delivered the weak (Israel) from powerful kings or threatening situations (perhaps the miraculous crossing [Josh 3–5]). Evidently, the exodus/conquest event was a concrete divine action aimed at revealing a specific divine attribute; an attribute Israel must imitate in dealing with the widows and orphans in her midst. From Micah's perspective, knowledge of Yahweh's righteous acts involved an intuitive awareness of Yahweh's character and nature, "and it was precisely because the people lacked such an awareness that they had failed in their social obligations."[67] Despite such failure, our present passage is "implicitly asking Israel to repent and to accept God's past acts and so renew the covenant."[68]

---

concretely, they announce a decision on the part of the divine speaker: after a long period of being Israel's God, YHWH is taking leave of his people." Joosten, 10.

64. Longman, "1 Sam 12:16-19," 169; Vannoy, *Covenant Renewal*, 160-169.
65. Zimmerli, "Knowledge of God," 30-35.
66. Waltke, *Commentary on Micah*, 383.
67. Davies, "Walking in God's Ways," 106.
68. Waltke, *Commentary on Micah*, 384.

Israel's response

Besides the opening questions (in the pre-trial encounter), Ramsey surmises that the accused would frequently respond to his accuser either by asking about his specific offense or by offering to settle the matter out of court.[69] A similar situation develops in Israel's response to Yahweh's speech (Mic 6:6–7). In this passage, Israel offers to settle the matter by asking a series of questions whose intent is to restore covenant relations with Yahweh. Essentially, the questions imply Israel's recognition of her guilt.

As we have already stated previously, most scholars agree that Micah 6:6–7 is "an example of the generic form of the temple-entrace liturgy (cf. Pss 15; 24; Isa 33:14–16)."[70] With this background in mind, Israel or their representative (note the first person verb forms in Micah 6:6: אקדם, אכף) begins by asking the customary question, "With what shall I come before Yahweh?" (במה אקדם יהוה) (v. 6a). The initial question suggests the need to bring something before Yahweh. As the context makes evident, offerings are customary when one approaches Yahweh (e.g. Exod 23:14–15; Deut 16:16–17). In fact, it should not be shocking that Israel immediately responds by offering sacrifices. A raison d'être behind the exodus event was that, following Yahweh's deliverance of Israel from Egyptian bondage, the nation would offer sacrifice to their God in the wilderness (Exod 3:12, 18; 5:3; 10:9, 25–26). Such a scenario seems to be in play here. Perhaps by being reminded of the exodus event (Mic 6:3–5), Israel instinctively reasons that Yahweh's requirements were cultic sacrifices as in the original exodus.

In any case, besides the conventional double מה-questions as in the entrance liturgies (Ps 15:1; 24:3; Isa 33:14b), in Micah Israel's representative follows up with three sets of questions (Mic 6:6b–7). In some sense, these follow-up questions are specific answers to the double מה-questions (v. 6a). The answers enumerate Israel's presentation of various offerings, which they hope are adequate to restore covenant relations with Yahweh. Foremost among these sacrifices are the "whole burnt offerings" (עולות) of year old "calves" (עגלים) (v. 6b). As Sweeney aptly points out, "The whole burnt offering was the standard daily offering at the Temple that is designed to maintain

---

69. Ramsey, "Speech-Forms," 50.
70. Sweeney, *Twelve Prophets*, 2:398.

Divine Sovereignty and the New People of God (Micah 6:1–7:20)

the relationship between the people and YHWH and to ensure the stability of the created world."[71] Besides the burnt offerings, Israel suggests other offerings as a means to "please" (רצה) Yahweh (v. 7). These include "thousands of rams" (אלפי אילים) or "ten thousand rivers of oil" (רבבות נחלי־שמן) (v. 7a), and "my firstborn" (בכורי) (v. 7b). Again, we should also recall that the sacrifice of a firstborn male animal was intended to reflect Yahweh slaying the firstborn sons of the Egyptians.[72] Likewise, the goal of the redemption of Israel's firstborn was to reflect Yahweh's redemption of Israel from bondage (Exod 13:14–15).[73]

Also noteworthy is the "ascending intensity of number and value" of the offerings.[74] Paul L. Redditt's comment captures well the full import of this progression. He notes, "In Mic 6:6–7 the worshipper start with customary offerings, but fearful of God's rejection they keep upping the offer until they ask whether they should offer the most precious thing they have: their children."[75] However, Yahweh does not approve of Israel's means for mending their strained relationship as the next verse suggests (v. 8).

Yahweh's demands

Undoubtedly, most scholars agree that Micah 6:8 is the high-water mark of the prophet's entire book. Despite this virtual consensus, scholars disagree as to its background. Obviously, an understanding of the background of a passage aids in its interpretation. As we have seen earlier, some maintain that it has roots in the temple-entrance liturgies.[76] Davidson believes that Micah 6:8 constitutes part of a review of the general stipulations or indictments in a covenant lawsuit.[77] Andersen and Freedman disagree with both of these suggestions. They believe that our target verse has affinities with wisdom ethics rather than with torah or covenant stipulations.[78] The foregoing proposals

---

71. Sweeney, 2:399.
72. Davies, "Walking in God's Ways," 102.
73. Davies, 102.
74. Mays, *Micah*, 139.
75. Redditt, *Introduction to the Prophets*, 270.
76. Sweeney, *Twelve Prophets*, 2:400; Gowan, *Theology of the Prophetic Books*, 57; Broyles, "Psalms," 287; Roberts, "Enthronement of Yhwh and David," 685.
77. Davidson, "Divine Covenant Lawsuit Motif," 65.
78. Andersen and Freedman, *Micah*, 510.

attest to the complexities involved in ascertaining the role of Micah 6:8 in its larger context. Because Micah 6:1–8 does not follow the lawsuit pattern fully, its logical flow is difficult to grasp.

However, Micah 6:8 fits the entrance liturgy pattern. Most likely, this verse essentially constitutes the answer portion of the entrance liturgy, which spells out the qualifications for a worshipper to approach Yahweh. Actually, the ritual activities in Micah 6:6–7 are not separate from the didactic material in Micah 6:8. In other words, cultic requirements were also necessary for entering the temple (e.g. Pss 20:4; 26:6; 50:23; 96:8; 116:17–19; cf. 2 Chron 23:19). Broyles's comments on the symbiotic relations between ritual activities and the didactic aspects of the entrance liturgies deserve mention. He writes:

> In these psalms we see an integral connection between worship and daily social life, especially treatment of the neighbor. They warn against both ritualism and privatized piety. There must be a concrete social reality behind one's claims to spirituality. Worshipers' character must be appropriate to the character of the God they claim to worship. The ritual for Temple entry goes to both matter of heart (private) and matters of the concrete social life (public).[79]

In any case, Micah 6:8 should be best understood in light of the entrance liturgy pattern. Karen E. Durant has effectively demonstrated that Deuteronomy 10:12–13 is the wellhead for most ethical norms found in the Old Testament, particularly in the entrance liturgies (e.g. Ps 15) and many other psalms (e.g. Pss 25; 33; 111; 112).[80] As we are about to show shortly, Micah 6:8 also draws from the same wellhead as the other entrance liturgies.[81] Thus, contrary to Andersen and Freedman, Micah 6:8 is an integral part of the entrance liturgy (vv. 6–8).

That Micah 6:8 alludes to Deuteronomy 10:12 is evident from a shared context and verbal parallels. In the first place, both texts utilize a question and a character sketch.[82] In particular, Yahweh is the model for the worshipper

---

79. Broyles, "Psalms," 286–287.
80. Durant, "Imitation of God," 122.
81. Merrill, *Deuteronomy*, 201; Barker, "Micah," 114; Owens, *Portraits of the Righteous*, 34.
82. Owens, *Portraits of the Righteous*, 34.

Divine Sovereignty and the New People of God (Micah 6:1–7:20)

as the latter adopts the divine character. Moreover, both passages are cast as part of a covenant renewal ceremony.[83]

In the second place, the two passages share a remarkable verbal correspondence. The question "and what does Yahweh require from you?" (ומה־יהוה דורש ממך) (Mic 6:8) parallels "what does Yahweh your God require from you?" (מה יהוה אלהיך שאל מעמך) (Deut 10:12). The three obligations "to promote justice" (עשות משפט), "to love" (ואהבת)), and "to walk" (הלך) (Mic 6:8) have their respective parallels עשה משפט (Deut 10:18), ואהב, and הלך (Deut 10:12). Some differences between the two passages are evident. Deuteronomy 10:12–13 enumerates five requirements in its list of Yahweh's demand, whereas Micah 6:8 only lists three. Furthermore, Deuteronomy 10:12 expands on the divine name (יהוה אלהיך) and uses a synonym verb (שאל). Apart from these differences, the literary allusion is unmistakable.

In this quintessential passage, Deuteronomy 10:12–22 presents Yahweh's attributes and deeds as the model that should characterize his people (cf. Pss 111; 112).[84] Using five infinitives, Moses exhorts Israel to fear the Lord, to walk in all his ways, to love him, to serve him, and to observe his commands (Deut 10:12–13). As the center attribute in the list, love is the essence of Yahweh and it becomes the basis for maintaining the covenant relations (v. 15). Moses then firmly anchors Yahweh's sovereignty in justice for the marginalized in society (vv. 17–18). It is here that Yahweh challenges Israel to love the marginalized because they (Israel) once lived on the margins in Egypt and Yahweh had delivered them (v. 19). As Merrill summarizes, "What God does in the social realm his people are to imitate (cf. Exod 22:22–24)."[85] That Deuteronomy 10:12–22 has a didactic purpose is beyond doubt.

A significant analogy that is established between Micah 6:8 and Deuteronomy 10:12 is that worshipers should imitate the character of the God whom they worship. In Micah 6:8, Yahweh reminds Israel "to promote justice" (עשות משפט), "to love kindness" (ואהבת חסד), "to walk wisely with your God" (והצנע לכת עם־אלהיך). As in the wider ANE context, משפט in Micah's immediate context ultimately connotes the proper ordering of society

---

83. Toombs, "Love and Justice," 405.
84. Owens, *Portraits of the Righteous*, 35.
85. Merrill, *Deuteronomy*, 204; Patterson, "Widow, the Orphan, and the Poor," 223–234; Fensham, "Widow, Orphan, and the Poor," 184.

(cf. Mic 6:10–12; 7:2–6).[86] Every "man" (אדם) had the responsibility to promote justice in society (cf. Gen 18:19). Katharine D. Sakenfeld's analysis of the term חסד led her to conclude that it refers to "an action performed for the weak party by the powerful one . . . it normally provides deliverance from dire straits."[87] The powerful party is obligated to deliver or protect the weaker party. Likewise, in Micah 6:8 the term calls on Israel to freely and willingly extend kindness or mercy to those in need.[88]

According to Waltke, the infinitive absolute והצנע, traditionally rendered "humbly," means "'circumspectly' in the sense of behaving discerningly, wisely, prudently."[89] Hillers holds that the expression "to walk wisely with your God" (Mic 6:8) involves living wisely according to Yahweh's character.[90] In an influential article, Davies discusses the metaphor of "walking in the ways of the Lord" as implying *imitatio Dei*.[91] Weinfeld's effective synthesis of the divine requirements in Micah 6:8 is informative and underscores the ideals of a community of covenanters. He comments:

> When Micah presents the demands of the divine ideal . . . he is not referring to the proper execution of justice in court, since (a) the demand is made of every "man", and not every man is a judge who is responsible for legal rulings, and (b) the two demands of loving חסד and walking humbly imply that the demands are general and moral in nature, referring to good deeds, and thus doing משפט refers to actions of social justice.[92]

Seen in this way, Micah makes plain that Yahweh demands Israel to imitate and promote the ethical norms of משפט and חסד in the land (Mic 6:8) precisely because these norms are Yahweh's essence (cf. Pss 33:5; 89:15–16;

---

86. Toombs, "Love and Justice," 408; Fensham, "Widow, Orphan, and the Poor," 178–187.
87. Sakenfeld, *Meaning of Hesed*, 233.
88. McComiskey and Longman, "Micah," 540.
89. Waltke, *Commentary on Micah*, 394.
90. Hillers, *Micah*, 78.
91. Davies, "Walking in God's Ways," 101, 103. According to Davies, such a metaphor "implies that Israel was destined to travel on a journey in which Yahweh was to lead the way as a guide and an example for the people to follow. It also suggests that the moral requirements demanded by God were those which he himself had evinced in an exemplary manner in his dealings with his people."
92. Weinfeld, *Social Justice*, 36; Leclerc, *Yahweh Is Exalted*, 7–15.

101:1–2; Jer 9:23). In this respect, Micah's call "was a summons for Israel to take seriously its special vocation as *imitator Dei*, for . . . it was the duty of the people to embody in their daily lives the very character of the God whom they worshipped."[93] So why does Micah 6:8 draw from Deuteronomy 10:12, instead of the entrance liturgies (Pss 15:1–5; 24:3–5; Isa 33:14b–16)? Most likely, Micah's concern was no longer about entering the temple but the temple city, Zion. The concern for Micah is who can dwell in Zion?

Altogether, Micah 6:1–8 is not necessarily a legal proceeding whose ultimate intent is to punish the whole nation. Rather, the proceedings are reconciliatory in intent. Gratitude for Yahweh's gracious deeds in the historical past and his character are the impetus for future ethical conduct within the covenant community (Mic 6:3–5). Yahweh's contention with and his reminder to Israel was that the people had not reflected fully on the divine compassion in their own actions towards the weak.[94] This ethical concern becomes a key litmus test for entry into Yahweh's presence. A righteous remnant will enter, but the wicked will not, and they will suffer the consequences. These two groups, the wicked and the righteous, are the concern of Micah 6:9–7:20.

Judgment upon the Wicked

Micah's prophecy against the city

Following the presentation of Yahweh's ethical demands (Mic 6:8), the next passage opens by confronting those who do not embody what the covenant community ought to be (6:9–7:6). Unlike the initial summons (שמע), which addressed the whole nation of Israel (6:1), in the present case, the summons focuses exclusively on a particular segment of the nation (6:9). In this case, the addressee is the "city" (עיר), which is clarified as the "tribe" (מטה) and as the "assembly of the city" (ומועד העיר) (v. 9).[95] Moreover, the feminine pronominal suffixes, "her rich men" (עשיריה) (v. 12) and "her inhabitants"

---

93. Davies, "Walking in God's Ways," 105; Leclerc, *Introduction to the Prophets*, 194–195.

94. Davies, "Walking in God's Ways," 105. Waltke also states that "memory entails faith and actualizes the past into the present. If Israel remembers God's saving acts, it will entail that by faith they also accept them and participate in them." Waltke, *Commentary on Micah*, 383.

95. The study is cognizant of the textual issues involved in Mic 6:9–10, and there is no need to rehearse them at this time. Here we retain the emendation by Waltke and others: "Listen, O tribe and the assembly of the city" (שמעו מטה ומועד העיר) (v. 9). Waltke, *Commentary on Micah*, 396–397, 408; Smith, *Micah-Malachi*, 52–53; Mays, *Micah*, 143; Allen, *Books of Joel, Obadiah, Jonah and Micah*, 375.

(vv. 12, 16), point to the city. Apparently, the city is a metonymy for its leaders and its common citizens.

Micah's prophecy about the city (which we argued is Zion) in this passage deserves attention. Within the broader ANE world, temple cities were often viewed as centers where social justice and righteousness should be time-honored.[96] In a Hymn to Enlil, the poet celebrates the city of Nippur as a harbinger of justice and righteousness; a place where wickedness and evil cannot escape.[97] Similarly, Zion is frequently described in glorious language as the "holy city" (עיר הקדש) (Isa 48:2; 52:1), "righteous city" (עיר הצדק) (Isa 1:26), "abode of righteousness" (נוה־צדק) (Jer 31:23), and the "city of truth" (עיר־האמת) (Zech 8:3).[98] Unfortunately, at many turns, Zion utterly failed to live up to this ideal, which led the prophets to denounce it in stinging terms. For Isaiah, the faithful and righteous city had become a whore and full of murderers (Isa 1:21).[99] Ezekiel unflinchingly calls it a "city of bloodshed" (עיר הדמים) (Ezek 22:2; 24:6, 9).[100] Apparently, the city cannot endure injustice within her boundaries and therefore the wicked had to be destroyed (Ps 101:7–8).

Therefore, it is not surprising to hear of the repugnant social conditions that had polluted Zion in Micah's day (Mic 6:10–12), for which Yahweh will judge. A point that needs clarification is that, since Yahweh had already given Israel the terms to restore the covenant relationship (6:8), the ensuing judgments are not necessarily to cleanse the unjust in order to make them righteous. Rather, Yahweh's judgments will annihilate the wicked from the land (6:13–16) but preserve the repentant righteous (7:7–9).

In any case, Zion has become a "house of the wicked" (בית רשע) because the merchants are cheating in weights by using a "short ephah/measure"

---

96. Smith, *Fate of Justice*, 60–62; Leclerc, *Yahweh Is Exalted*, 84–85; Bergsma, *Jubilee from Leviticus*, 27–28; Abernethy, *Book of Isaiah*, 181–182; Weinfeld, "Instruction for Temple Visitors," 229–230; Weinfeld, "Zion and Jerusalem," 104–106.

97. "Hymn to Enlil, the All-Beneficent," translated by S. N. Kramer (*ANET*, 573–574). "*Hypocrisy*, distortion, abuse, malice, unseemliness, Insolence, enmity, oppression . . . arrogance, violation of agreement, breach of contract, *abuse* of (a court) *verdict*, (All these) evils the city does not tolerate . . . the wicked and evil cannot escape; The city endowed with, Where righteousness (and) justice are perpetuated" (lines 20–30).

98. Smith, *Fate of the Jerusalem Temple*, 61.

99. Leclerc, *Yahweh Is Exalted*, 41–42.

100. Smith, *Fate of Justice*, 61.

Divine Sovereignty and the New People of God (Micah 6:1–7:20)

(ואיפת רזון) (Mic 6:10–11; cf. Lev 19:35–36; Deut 25:13; Hos 12:7; Amos 8:5).[101] Moreover, Zion has become a city of "violence" (חמס), "falsehood" (שקר), and "deceit" (רמיה) (Mic 6:12). As expected, the temple-entrance liturgies reference economic abuse (Ps 15:5; Isa 33:15) and deceit (Ps 24:4) to characterize those who are unfit to come before Yahweh.[102] Even more odious is that the wicked "keep" (שמר) and "walk" (הלך) in the "statutes" (חקה) of the Omride dynasty (Mic 6:16) instead of obeying Yahweh's demands (Mic 6:8). In other words, Micah is implying that present Zion disobeys Yahweh's precepts just as ancient Israel did during the era of the Omride dynasty (1 Kgs 16:24–34).

Consequently, Yahweh will not push aside the issue of wealth unjustly gained nor "acquit" (זכה) dishonest merchants who fraudulently enrich themselves (Mic 6:10–11). Instead, he will unleash covenant curses upon the wicked in Zion (vv. 13–15). Signaled by the correlative particle "and so, on [my] part" (וגם),[103] Yahweh emphatically states that he will "strike" (נכה) and "desolate" (שמם) the city (v. 13). The subsequent verses explain the nature of the desolation via five curses drawn from Leviticus 26 and Deuteronomy 28. These curses underscore the futile efforts of the wicked (Mic 6:14–15).[104]

First, the wicked will eat, but not be satisfied (Mic 6:14a; Lev 26:26b). Second, they will store up food, but they will not preserve anything (Mic 6:14b; Deut 28:51–52). An invading army will destroy or loot whatever they have stored. Third, they will sow seeds, but they will not reap any crops (Mic

---

101. As Barker eloquently explains, "These merchants and traders were using weights that weighed things heavier than they actually were or lighter than they really were, depending on whether they were buying or selling. They resorted to all the 'tricks of the trade.'" Barker, "Micah," 117.

102. Sweeney, *Twelve Prophets*, 2:400–401.

103. Williams, *Williams' Hebrew Syntax*, §381. Brown, Driver, and Briggs, *Hebrew and English Lexicon*, 169.

104. Hillers believes that our target verses (Mic 6:14–15) are an example of "futility curses" found in ANE treaties. A characteristic feature of such "futility curses" is the "but also" (ולא) formula (cf. Mic 6:14–15). Hillers, *Treaty-Curses*, 28–29; Wolff, *Micah*. In speaking of Mic 6:14–15, Hillers explains, "the guilty will undertake a course of action and inevitably be frustrated in it. The nearest biblical parallels are Deut 28:30–31 and 38–40, with briefer examples in Lev 26:26 and, in the prophets, Hos 4:10, 'They shall eat but not be satisfied: they shall play the harlot but not increase,' cf. 5:6; 8:7; 9:12; 9:16; and Amos 5:11: 'You have planted pleasant vineyards, but you shall not drink their wine.' Biblical curses of this pattern, and other prophetic threats, have parallels in the curses attached to Near Eastern treaties. It is clear that Micah, like other prophets, drew on a traditional stock of maledictions, and it is plausible to suppose that he meant to imply that just these evils were coming because the Israelites had broken their covenant with God." Hillers, *Micah*, 82.

6:15a; Lev 26:16; Deut 28:38). Fourth, the people will press olives, but they will not be able to use the resulting oil for anointing themselves (Mic 6:15bα; Deut 28:40). Finally, they will press the grapes, but they will not drink the wine (Mic 6:15bβ; Deut 28:30b, 39). Altogether, the covenant curses confirm that when the traditional customs of justice in business dealings no longer exist, the futility of all fundamental human efforts becomes an instrument of Yahweh's punishment.[105]

Micah's response

In Micah 7:1–6, the prophet (or perhaps someone representing a penitent, godly remnant of Zion) responds with a lament to the previous desolation of the city (6:9–16). Marked by a "woe" (אללי) interjection (Mic 7:1; cf. Job 10:15), the lament uses agricultural imagery and draws from various social strata to portray a morally bankrupt community. The city lacks a righteous people. Using an agricultural metaphor, Micah describes a poor person gleaning the fields hoping to find some leftover fruits following a harvest but finding none (Mic 7:1). Undeniably, the metaphor assumes the cultural tradition of leaving some crop for the poor to glean following a harvest (Lev 19:9–10; 23:22; Deut 24:19–21; Ruth 2:3, 7, 15–19).[106] Strikingly, the lack of fruit even for gleaning suggests that the farmers' harvesting techniques are "so ruthless that the fig trees and the vines are utterly denuded."[107] On one side, the metaphor implicitly accuses the harvesters of injustice and lack of kindness towards the poor. On the other, the metaphor "is effectively a death sentence for a hungry person awaiting a barren winter."[108]

The subsequent verses, by means of a simple analogy, develop the agricultural metaphor with literal social details from both the public square and the private homes. First, the prophet shows that injustice in society or the public square reflects the problem of power (Mic 7:2a–4a). Just as the gleaner could not find ripened figs, even so, the prophet looks in vain for the "godly" (חסיד) and "upright" (ישר) in the land (7:2a). Supposedly, this group of people – the godly and upright persons – imitate God and practices mercy

---

105. Wolff, *Micah*, 197.

106. Jacobs, *Conceptual Coherence*, 187; Jenson, *Obadiah, Jonah, Micah*, 179; Hillers, *Micah*, 85.

107. Jenson, *Obadiah, Jonah, Micah*, 179.

108. Jesnon, 179.

and justice toward their fellow humanity (cf. Mic 6:8; Pss 11:7; 19:9; 33:14; 111:8).[109] Unfortunately, this pious group has perished. Only violent and evil people remain (Mic 7:2b–3a).

Another powerful group comprises the corrupt leaders of the land (princes, a judge, and the great man). These are skilled in corruption; specifically, they obstruct justice by accepting bribes (Mic 7:3b). Micah underscores the utter corruptness of the nation as he compares the best among the powerful to injurious briers and thorny hedges which entangle and hurt their victims (v. 4a).[110] In short, crime and lawlessness are rampant in the villainous city.

Second, Micah turns away from the corruption in the public square and gives us a glimpse of the disintegration of morals in the private homes (7:5–6). However, before he makes the transition, Micah abruptly interrupts his description of the moral decay of the nation as he briefly points to a coming judgment (7:4b). The judgment will result in confusion – that is, a state of social anarchy and distress.[111] Following this brief announcement of judgment, Micah concludes this section with another description of his society in the private homes. Unlike the public square, where those who wield power corrupt justice, here the issue is disloyalty and disdain for those in authority in the home. One can no longer trust one's neighbor or intimate friend (7:5a). Actually, one must be careful of what one even confides to one's wife for fear of disloyalty (v. 5b). Some reasons for the social and religious collapse are that a son dishonors his father by treating him as inferior, a daughter rebels against her mother, and a daughter-in-law rises up against her mother-in-law (Mic 7:6a; cf. Exod 20:12; Deut 5:26; 21:18–21; Lev 19:3a). Lastly, one's enemies are the people of one's own household (Mic 7:6b).

Overall, Micah 7:1–6 shows a wicked society which has utterly failed to imitate Yahweh's righteousness and justice in all its institutions. Their deeds are essentially the opposite of what Yahweh expects of his covenant community. In the end, Yahweh will destroy the wicked. Having described the character and deeds of the wicked, we now turn to examine the nature of the righteous remnant.

---

109. Jacobs, *Conceptual Coherence*, 188; Hillers, *Micah*, 85.
110. Barker, "Micah," 123.
111. Swanson, *Dictionary of Biblical Languages*, §4428.

Transformation of the Righteous
Literary shape of Micah 7:7-20
Since Gunkel's influential analysis, there is a virtual consent among scholars that Micah 7:7-20 is a prophetic liturgy.[112] The liturgy comprises an introduction and four distinct units. Rhetorically, the introduction is a Janus passage (7:1-7). Moving beyond the simple doom-hope schema, Libby Ballard has credibly shown the transitional nature of the Janus passage by attending to the placement of the ancient traditions in the larger unit (Mic 6:1-7:20).[113] Apparently, beyond the Janus passage, the ancient traditions are in reverse order.[114] Such ordering has an important hermeneutical implication. It allows us to assume an exilic perspective for the unit (7:8-20). As such, the unit incorporates an underlying new exodus motif whose ultimate goal is the fulfillment of the Abrahamic promises for a righteous remnant. Without a doubt, that the fulfillment of the Abrahamic covenant is by means of an exodus-like event is a long-standing tradition anchored in the inauguration of the covenant itself (Gen 15:13-14).

At any rate, the incipient disjunctive marker "but I" (וַאֲנִי) (Mic 7:7) emphatically distinguishes the wicked in the preceding unit (6:9-7:6) and the righteous remnant in the subsequent unit (7:8-20). Hence, the liturgy proper opens with a psalm of trust (7:8-10), followed by a prophetic voice affirming the restoration of the Gentile nations (vv. 11-13), then a prayer (vv. 14-17), and concluding with a hymn of praise (vv. 18-20). These passages build upon

---

112. While scholars may differ in how to describe the liturgical character of this passage (Mic 7:7-20), the presence of liturgical elements is nonetheless widely acknowledged. Furthermore, scholars debate whether Mic 7:7 belongs with the preceding (7:1-6) or subsequent verses (7:8-20). Gunkel, "Close of Micah," passim; Smith, *Micah-Malachi*, 58; Wolff, *Micah*, 215; Hillers, *Micah*, 89; Barker, "Micah," 125; Sweeney, *Twelve Prophets*, 2:408; Mays, *Micah*, 152-153; Waltke, *Commentary on Micah*, 449; Redditt, *Introduction to the Prophets*, 270. Nogalski's liturgical framework has three units (Mic 7:8-13; 14-15; 16-20). Nogalski, "Micah 7:8-20," 63, 70, 79-81.

113. Libby Ballard has shown that the allusions to ancient tradition are arranged in an unbalanced chiastic structure with Mic 7:1-7 serving as the central element: Exodus (6:4) → Wilderness (6:5) → Monarchy (6:16) ↔ Lament (7:1-7) ↔ Monarchy (7:12) → Wilderness (7:14) → Exodus (7:15, 18-19) → Patriarchs (7:20). Ballard, "Intertextuality," passim.

114. The movement is from the mention of Egypt, Assyria, Euphrates (Mic 7:12), the crossing of the Jordan and wilderness wandering (v. 14), the exodus (vv. 15, 18-19), to the patriarchs (v. 20).

each other to effect a new exodus for a righteous remnant.[115] While we keep in mind the liturgical framework, the storyline is the exodus. The exodus provides an interpretative lens for reading our target unit (Mic 7:7–20).

The remnant waits for Yahweh

Since the introduction to the liturgy is set off by the adversative conjunction "but I" (ואני) (7:7), it contrasts the mood in Micah 6:9–7:6 to that in 7:8–20.[116] Unlike the wicked and those who put their confidence in neighbors (7:5), Micah (or a righteous remnant) hopes completely in Yahweh (Mic 7:7; cf. Ps 118:7–8). His express confidence in Yahweh is evident in the phrase, "I will repeatedly look out to Yahweh" (ביהוה אצפה) (Mic 7:7aα).[117] As the next clause clarifies, the prophet's confidence is that Yahweh will deliver him: "I will wait for the God of my deliverance" (אוחילה לאלהי ישעי) (v. 7aβ).[118] Already in veiled form, the expression "God of my deliverance" (לאלהי ישעי) subtly sets off the foundational motif of the exodus tradition. While the concept of God as "deliverer" (ישע) appears in various contexts of deliverance (Pss 25:5; 27:9; Hab 3:18), its first and prominent use appears in relation to the original exodus event (Exod 14:13; 15:2). Thus, Micah 7:7 introduces the motif of deliverance, which later passages develop.

---

115. Cuffey somewhat affirms our conclusion. As he notes, the four passages "are all tied together by the common development of a strand of thought and by the ever-intensifying tones of relief and celebration of God's forgiveness." Cuffey, *Literary Coherence*, 250.

116. The use of the first person is this verse likely suggests that Micah is a representative of a righteous remnant (cf. 7:1).

117. Koehler, Baumgartner, and Stamm, *Hebrew and Aramaic Lexicon*, 1044. The Piel yiqtol verb (אצפה) is iterative, which suggests that Micah is frequently putting his confidence in Yahweh. Williams, *Williams' Hebrew Syntax*, 60, §143.

118. Most scholars agree that the verb "hope/wait" (יחל) fits into the semantic class of verbs like "trust" and "believe." Gilchrist, "יחל," 374. Even more pointedly, Mays surmises that "waiting" is a typical attitude of the godly person: "He watches the future for an act of God (Ps. 5:4) as besieged men watch the horizon for the appearance of relief. He does not give up and surrender to depression, but 'waits,' the most powerful form of action by the helpless (Pss 38:15; 42:5, 11; 43:5; 130:5) who express in their waiting the knowledge that God comes to them in the form of salvation (Pss. 18:46; 25:5)." Mays, *Micah*, 157; Waltke, *Commentary on Micah*, 310, 429; Barker, "Micah," 125. Jacobs notes that "wait" (יחל) typically points to "a time of outcry and prayer, not a time of silent passivity or apathy towards the desolation." Jacobs, *Conceptual Coherence*, 188–189.

A remnant repents of sin

As Micah opens the psalm of trust (7:8–10), personified Zion addresses an unidentified enemy and warns her not to rejoice over her calamity (vv. 8a, 10a).[119] Micah utilizes the dual metaphors of darkness and light to picture Zion's calamitous situation. Scholars differ on the background informing Micah's metaphor. Smith believes that the mention of Yahweh as the light for Zion suggests a liturgical background (Ps 27:1).[120] To his credit, his characterization that Zion's calamity communicates a possible exile is on target. Indeed, that Zion's citizens "sit in the darkness of prison" implies an exile.[121] Unfortunately, his observations overlook the bigger picture. A liturgical backdrop is not comprehensive enough to cohere all the data.

Instead, an appropriate background for Micah's metaphors is the exodus tradition (Mic 7:8a). At the original exodus, Yahweh's deliverance of Israel involved the struggle between light and darkness (Exod 10:21–23; 13:21; 14:19–20). Similarly, the Isaianic new exodus also reflects the triumph of light shining in the darkness (Isa 9:2; 42:6–7, 16; 60:1–3). Chisholm agrees that the "background for the imagery may be release from a dark prison (cf. Isa 42:7)."[122] The reference Chisholm notes appears in the Isaianic new exodus context (Isa 40–55). Unlike the liturgical traditions, the new exodus tradition offers a comprehensive background that accounts for most of the material in Micah 7:8–20.

---

119. The first-person feminine speaker in this passage is most likely personified Zion representing a remnant (Mic 7:8a). The immediate and wider contexts reveal that the speaker is a city (7:11; cf. 1:16; 4:9–10; 6:9; Isa 60–62; Zeph 3:11–20; Ezek 16; 23). The difficulty in discerning the exact identity of the enemy in this passage has occasioned divergent proposals. The dominate proposals are Babylon, Edom, Philistia, and Assyria. Sweeney, *Twelve Prophets*, 2:409; Jenson, *Obadiah, Jonah, Micah*, 183; Wolff, *Micah*, 220; Mays, *Micah*, 159. For a sustained argument for Assyria (i.e., personified Nineveh) as the intended enemy, see Nogalski, "Micah 7:8–20," 64–71; Waltke, *Commentary on Micah*, 433, 451–455. Smith-Christopher suggests an internal rather than a foreign enemy is in view. He cites Ahab's address to Elijah as "my enemy" (2 Kgs 21:20) as support. While it is an attractive idea, Smith-Christopher is not attentive to gender concern. Smith-Christopher, *Micah*, 216. In the Old Testament, only foreign warriors/enemies are described using the feminine gender. Wright, "Military Valor and Kingship," 141–142. Note the feminine subject and object pronouns in the verbs: "she will rejoice" (Mic 7:8); "she will see" (v. 10), and "shame will cover her" (v. 10).

120. Smith, *Micah-Malachi*, 58; Mays, *Micah*, 159.

121. Smith, *Micah-Malachi*, 58.

122. Chisholm, *Interpreting the Minor Prophets*, 158.

The metaphors of darkness and light simply speak of Yahweh's judgment and deliverance. Seen from Zion's point of view, the divine judgments are necessary "because I [Zion's citizens] have sinned against him [Yahweh]" (כי חטאתי לו) (Mic 7:9a). Furthermore, the divine judgments are transformative in that they present Zion with an opportunity to recognize, acknowledge, and confess her own sin (Mic 7:9). Repentance is the key to deliverance. Within the broader sweep of the Old Testament, Yahweh's plan for restoration is contingent upon the people's repentance (Lev 26:40–45; Deut 30:1–10; Isa 59:20; Jer 18:7–8; Jonah 3:10).

Micah is walking within this new exodus tradition as he speaks of Zion's repentance (Mic 7:9a). As Smith notes, "Now for the first time in Micah we read of the people's confession of sin (7a [9a]), and a willingness to suffer because of it."[123] Zion must repent before Yahweh delivers her. We should note though that Micah does not describe the movement of his new exodus at this point in his oracles in spatial terms. Rather, he rhetorically dramatizes it as a movement from judgment to deliverance. In any case, textual evidence for the exodus motif comes from the terms "bring out" (יצא) to the light (7:9bγ) and the expression of seeing Yahweh's "righteousness" (צדקה) (v. 9bδ). Such language speaks of an exodus like deliverance (cf. Mic 2:13; 6:5; Exod 3:10, 11; 6:6, 7).[124] Unlike the wicked (Mic 6:9–16), Zion's judgment is not a retribution but chastisement because she confesses her sin. According to Barrick, retribution is terminal (Lev 26:25, 38), but chastisement results in restoration (Lev 26:39–45).[125]

Because Zion has repented, the path is now open for her vindication. In keeping with his righteous and just character (Mic 6:8), Yahweh will "contend my [Zion's] case" ((יריב ריבי) (v. 9bα) and "execute justice for me [Zion]" (ועשה משפטי) (v. 9bβ). All this suggests that Yahweh will act to vindicate Zion. Without belaboring the point, another way Yahweh will vindicate or execute justice for Zion is by punishing Zion's enemies (v. 10). In a reversal of fortunes, Yahweh will shame those who mocked Zion in her time of judgment.

In summary, what we observe is that the initial litmus test for belonging to the new people of God depends on Zion's response to Yahweh's judgments. In

---

123. Chisholm, 158.
124. Waltke, *Commentary on Micah*, 435; Jenson, *Obadiah, Jonah, Micah*, 184.
125. Barrick, "Inter-Covenantal Truth," 97.

the preceding section (Mic 6:9–7:1), the wicked perished because they failed to repent. In contrast, the present passage makes apparent that repentance reverses judgment to deliverance. Thus, repentance is the first step towards God's deliverance of a remnant.

Yahweh restores a remnant from the nations

Another allusion to the new exodus motif involves Yahweh's worldwide deliverance of a remnant from the nations (Mic 7:11–13). It is not shocking that the inclusion of the nations as part of God's people is a motif at home in the exodus tradition. The language of "a mixed multitude" (ערב רב) confirms that the original exodus included other nations alongside Israel (Exod 12:38; cf. Lev 24:10; Num 11:4; Josh 2; 6:25). Scholars are divided on whether the plural subject pronoun in Micah 7:12a – "and they will come as far as" (ועדיך יבוא) – refers to the Gentile nations or to the Judean exiles coming to Zion. Wolff takes the latter view based on Targum Micah, which mentions "the Golah" (גלותא) (7:12).[126] Mays also concludes that Judah's exiles are in view. He appeals to several biblical texts that reference an exodus from Assyria and Egypt (Isa 11:11–16; 27:12; Zech 10:8–12).[127] In contrast to Mays and Wolff, McComiskey and Longman believe the Gentile nations, symbolized by Assyria and Egypt, are in view.[128]

Contextual considerations lead us to affirm the view of McComiskey and Longman. Micah 7:17 speaks of the nations turning to Yahweh in obedience following their defeat (vv. 15–17). Earlier, Yahweh had threatened to punish the disobedient nations (5:15). Conversely, an apparent implication is that Yahweh will restore a remnant from the obedient nations. As such, Micah 7:15–17 speak of universal judgment, which is purgative in that Yahweh will restore those who come to him in obedience (7:17b). Since the nations undergo the same purgative judgments as Israel, their coming implies repentance.[129] Such a view is consistent with Yahweh's universal sovereignty.

---

126. Wolff, *Micah*, 224.
127. Mays, *Micah*, 162.
128. McComiskey and Longman, "Micah," 548; Jenson, *Obadiah, Jonah, Micah*, 185.
129. Contrary to Waltke, here the stative verb (ירא) implies a "fear" (Mic 7:17b), which results in repentance (cf. Exod 14:31; Josh 2:10–13). Waltke's interpretive context (Gen 28:17; Amos 3:8; Job 4:12–15) is mistaken. None of his passages share any thematic or contextual correspondence to Mic 7:14–17. Rather, Exod 14:31 shares thematic affinities to Mic 7:14–17. Both appear in an exodus context. Both are the people's response after they "see" (ראה) (Exod

As J. M. P. Smith notes, "Yahweh will be satisfied with nothing less than a world-wide kingdom."[130]

In this respect, Zion will be rebuilt and her borders extended to accommodate the influx of the new people of God (Mic 7:11). As we have stated earlier, the extension of Zion's boundaries evokes the cultural traditions of the royal city as the center of the universe. According to Jacobs, Zion "will be central to the nations who will come to it."[131] Andersen and Freedman add, "The theme of the wide extension of Israel's territory is not new. It is a restatement of the hope of recovering the ancient glory of David's kingdom."[132] Thus, the exodus of a remnant from the nations to Zion will result in the desolation of the whole earth (Mic 7:13; cf. Isa 24:1–6; Zeph 1:18; 3:8). D. J. Clark and N. Mundhenk appropriately capture the image of a vibrant Zion in the midst of a desolate earth: "In 6:16 Jerusalem was an island of ruin amidst a sea of scornful enemies. Here the picture is reversed, and it is an island of blessing amidst a sea of desolation."[133]

Yahweh leads the remnant

An additional allusion to the exodus event is present in Micah's use of the royal shepherd imagery (Mic 7:14-17). The imagery in Micah's prayer dramatizes the wilderness/conquest events as Yahweh led and protected his people on the journey to the promised land. As the poet reflects on the original wilderness trek, Yahweh led his people like a flock by the hand of Moses and Aaron (Pss 77:19–20; 78:51–54; cf. 95:7–8; also Joshua in Num 27:15–18). In the Isaianic new exodus, Yahweh will tend his flock like a shepherd (Isa

---

14:31, Mic 7:15) Yahweh's "great power" (היד הגדלה) (Exod 14:31) or "miracle" (פלה) (Mic 7:15). Waltke also rejects the idea of repentance by appealing to Exod 15:15, which speaks of the fear gripping the nations. For him, this is not godly fear which instills repentance. Once again, Waltke is mistaken. Just because the nations mentioned in Exod 15:15 tremble upon hearing of Yahweh's great deliverance does not suggest or even imply that some did not repent. On the contrary, Rahab is an example of those who heard of the exodus deliverance and turned to the sovereign God (Josh 2:10–14; 6:17, 22–23, 25). Waltke, *Commentary on Micah*, 462. Also, see Barker for a brief discussion on the nature of "fear" here. Barker, "Micah," 132.

130. Smith, "Critical and Exegetical Commentary," 117.
131. Jacobs, *Conceptual Coherence*, 190.
132. Andersen and Freedman, *Micah*, 586.
133. Clark and Mundhenk, *Translator's Handbook*, 185.

40:10–11). Undisputedly, the exodus is the foundational event that depicts Yahweh as the shepherd.[134]

In Micah's prayer, the prophet petitions Yahweh to protect his flock and let them feed in the fertile pasturelands of Bashan and Gilead (Mic 7:14). Yahweh's flock appears to dwell alone in vulnerable conditions. As Jenson states, "Bashan and Gilead were the paradigmatic grazing lands (Deut 13:4; Jer 50:19), situated on the other side of the Jordan and granted to the three tribes 'in the days of old,' at the beginning of the nation's conquest of the land (Num 32; Josh 22)."[135] Hence, the petition is for Yahweh to deliver the flock from their defenseless situation in a desolate forest and lead them to the pasturelands of Bashan and Gilead.

Furthermore, the following verse (Mic 7:15), explicitly recalls Yahweh's past saving acts during the days of the exodus from Egypt (cf. Exod 3:20; 14:31; Ps 78:11). Micah's allusion to Yahweh's miracles provides a transition for him to discuss the defeat of the nations (Mic 7:16–17). In response to Micah's prayer (v.14), Yahweh promises to display his mighty deeds, just as he had done during the original exodus (v. 15).[136] Using the metaphor of the cursed serpent of old (Gen 3:14), Yahweh assures the petitioner that he will decisively humiliate and defeat the nations (Mic 7:16–17a).

In summary, the underlying idea Micah envisions is that of a remnant on a perilous journey to Zion encountering various threats from the nations, just as it was in the original exodus and conquest periods.[137] Despite Yahweh's judgments against the nations, Micah 7:17 also depicts some obedient nations turning to Yahweh (cf. Josh 2:10–14). Yahweh will incorporate the latter into the new covenant community. Others have also reached a similar conclusion. For instance, Zapff pointedly states, "Mic 4:14 and 7:13 together with Micah 7:17b state that each of the nations convert to Yahweh after a final judgment."[138] Wolff holds that "the prayer also indicates an awareness that the history of

---

134. Cruz, "*Who Is Like Yahweh?*," 216.
135. Jenson, *Obadiah, Jonah, Micah*, 186.
136. Barker, "Micah," 132.
137. Sweeney, *Twelve Prophets*, 2:412–413; Hillers, *Micah*, 91; Mays, *Micah*, 165.
138. Zapff, "Book of Micah," 139.

Divine Sovereignty and the New People of God (Micah 6:1–7:20)

Israel and that of the nations, in the final analysis, are indissolubly connected with each other."[139]

Yahweh forgives and defeats sin on behalf of the remnant

Micah closes with a hymn praising Yahweh's incomparability (Mic 7:18–20). The rhetorical question, "Who is a God like you?" (מי־אל כמוך) (v. 18a) echoes, "Who is like you among the gods, O Lord?" (מי־כמכה באלם יהוה) (Exod 15:11). Evidently, these questions not only affirm Yahweh's incomparability but also recall the divine warrior's activities. The warrior delivers the repentant (Lev 26:44–45; cf. Mic 7:9, 19).

Having examined the close relationship between rhetorical questions and divine battles in various ANE texts, C. J. Labuschagne concludes that "the attribute of incomparability was originally ascribed to a limited number of gods, who had proved their supremacy through their struggle against and their victory over powers hostile to the gods, or it was originally bestowed on a few gods identified with the most conspicuous phenomena in nature, who showed unparalleled characteristics."[140] Labuschagne goes on to opine that in the Old Testament Yahweh displays his incomparability in history as the creator and redeeming God.[141] The stress is on God's redeeming aspects in his person and deeds in response to sin (see Mic 6:10–12).

The opening verse celebrates Yahweh's redeeming character in relations to his ability to forgive the remnant of their sin (Mic 7:18). To emphasize the point, the remainder of this opening verse develops further Yahweh's character. Central to Micah's understanding of Yahweh's character is Israel's ancient creed (Exod 34:6–7).[142] Notably, the creed is set within the golden calf incident (Exod 32) to underscore Yahweh's self-disclosure of his person as the God who forgives. Micah amplifies Yahweh's forgiving aspects and attenuates the creed's punitive aspects. Essentially, the divine warrior will forgive the remnant of their sin, because of his own character (Mic 7:18; cf. 1:5). As

---

139. Wolff, *Micah*, 228.
140. Labuschagne, *Incomparability of Yahweh*, 53.
141. Labuschagne, 91.
142. Jenson, *Obadiah, Jonah, Micah*, 187. The language of his attributes, his willingness to forgive – "pardoning iniquity" (נשא עון), "passing over transgression" (ועבר על־פשע), "not retain[ing] anger forever" (לא־החזיק לעד אפו), and "delight[ing] in showing kindness" (חפץ חסד) (v. 18) – recalls the affirmation in the ancient creed (Mic 7:18–19a; Exod 34:6–7). Sweeney, *Twelve Prophets*, 2:413.

Gowan insightfully puts it, "The transformation of the human person comes through forgiveness, the kind that truly erases the past and never has to be repeated ... [in order] to produce a truly new person whose most obvious improvement is the ability to obey God."[143]

More importantly, Yahweh's redeeming character is evident in his deeds as the divine warrior (Mic 7:19). The divine warrior will not only forgive the remnant, but also purify them through military-like activities. The opening verb "compassion" (רחם) emphasizes the return of Yahweh's mercy towards a helpless remnant (v. 19aα).[144] The rest of the verse develops this concept of mercy metaphorically in combat rhetoric. The divine warrior will "subdue" (כבש) Israel's iniquities under his foot (v. 19aβ) and then "cast" (שלך) sin into the depth of the sea (v. 19b). Unmistakably, Micah's combat rhetoric alludes to the battle at the Red Sea. Just as the divine warrior hurled pharaoh's army into the sea, and they sank to the depths (Exod 15:4–5), so he will hurl Israel's sins into the depths of the sea (Mic 7:19b).

It appears that Micah views sin as an enemy on par with pharaoh's armies that must be subdued and conquered (Mic 7:10; cf. 2 Sam 8:11).[145] In addition, within the ANE worldview, the "sea" (ים) often represents a chaotic force.[146] While mythic overtones are evident, there is no hint that Micah personifies the sea or that it is battling the divine warrior. Rather, it is the divine warrior's instrument, a repository to confine sin. The sea is at times viewed as a monster whose body must be split to release life (e.g. Exod 14:21; Pss 74:15).[147] Ironically, for Micah, the monstrous sea annihilates sin! The divine warrior will not simply ignore his people's sin or forgive them, but he will subdue sin and annihilate it.

Micah views Israel's sin like an enemy that Yahweh defeats and disposes of. If such a view is accepted, perhaps a viable reason why Micah does not explicitly identify Zion's enemy (Mic 7:8a, 10a) is because the ultimate enemy is not a historical nation per se but sin itself. Like pharaoh who sought to

---

143. Gowan, *Eschatology in the Old Testament*, 2.

144. As Swanson points out, רחם connotes "feelings and actions of kindness and concern for one in difficulty, regardless of one's state of guilt for an offense, usually based in a relationship or association." Swanson, *Dictionary of Biblical Languages*, §8163.

145. Barker, "Micah," 134.

146. McComiskey and Longman, "Micah," 551.

147. Wakeman, *God's Battle*, 126–128.

prevent ancient Israel from possessing the promised land, sin is the reason why Israel cannot keep covenant, maintain order, and dwell in their land. Because of his faithfulness, Yahweh annihilates sin completely on behalf of the people and confines it to the depth of the sea where evil belongs (7:19a). Micah's destruction of sin is a fitting conclusion given that, for the most part, the book persistently deals with rampant sin among Yahweh's people. Finally, Micah closes with a statement that emphasizes Yahweh's fidelity to the Abrahamic covenant (v. 20). This verse will be discussed shortly in the concluding chapter.

Conclusion

In this chapter, we discussed Yahweh's sovereignty in relation to the transformation of a new people of God. We began by asking two questions: Who are the subjects of Yahweh's universal kingdom? What is the nature of that new covenant community or people of God? From the foregoing discussion, the subjects of Yahweh's universal kingdom will comprise a righteous remnant from both Israel (Mic 7:9) and the nations (7:17b). In essence, Yahweh is extending vicegerency to all nations.

With regard to their nature, the transformed community will reflect their sovereign's character. They will be a worshipping community, which promotes justice rather than relying on cultic rituals (Mic 6:8). As a repentant community, they will reflect Yahweh's holiness. Yahweh will decisively purify them by purging sin from the land (7:19). In summary, the new covenant people will reflect their sovereign Lord, who loves justice, who is holy, and who maintains covenant fidelity for the sake of all nations.[148]

---

148. Abernethy, *Book of Isaiah*, 198.

CHAPTER 7

Covenantal Implications of Divine Sovereignty in Micah

Introduction

As we come to the close of our study, it is unnecessary to recapitulate all of our findings from the previous chapters. Instead, we find it profitable to synthesize the overall covenantal implications of the concept of Yahweh's sovereignty. In this concluding chapter, we ask: What does the concept of divine sovereignty in Micah reveal about Yahweh's character? Here we will show that Yahweh's sovereignty unequivocally speaks of his covenantal faithfulness to Abraham (Mic 7:20). The answer to our question involves two steps.

First, we will show how the Zion/Davidic traditions and the Abrahamic traditions relate. This is necessary because some scholars assume that the future hope Micah envisions lies in the Zion/Davidic traditions. According to Marrs, Micah "effectively utilizes the Zion tradition to offer comfort and hope to the disposed and disadvantaged."[1] Unfortunately, Marrs limits the substance of that future hope to those elements connected directly to the Zion/Davidic traditions, namely, the restoration of Zion and the Davidic king. This is partially correct. Marrs does not consider Micah's intentional allusion to the Abrahamic tradition at the close of Micah as the source of future hope (7:20). Because of Yahweh's faithfulness to Abraham, Micah's future hope essentially resides in the Abrahamic promises and not in the Zion/Davidic traditions. As we will demonstrate, the Zion/Davidic traditions are

---

1. Marrs, "Back to the Future," 95n55.

merely the script that informs how Yahweh fulfills the Abrahamic covenant for Micah's audience.

Second, since the future hope lies in the Abrahamic promises, we will discern the specific promises or blessings that find fulfillment in the book of Micah. As Sweeney correctly observes, "the entire book of Micah, emphasizes YHWH's faithfulness to the covenant with Israel [and the promises to the ancestors] as the basis for the claim that Yahweh will intervene to turn the present situation of punishment and calamity into one of restoration, power, and security."[2] To his credit, Sweeney mentions that Yahweh will fulfill the promises of land and Israel's status of honor. However, the promises fulfilled go beyond just these two. As we argued in the three previous chapters, each major institution in Zion (e.g. Zion, the temple, kingship), including the people, undergo a transformation. This suggests that Yahweh intends to fulfill more than just two promises, as Sweeney believes. Hence, we will build on and extend Sweeney's conclusions. We will discern the particular promises Yahweh fulfills in the book of Micah.

Zion/Davidic Traditions and the Abrahamic Traditions

In defending our thesis, we found that the Zion/Davidic traditions were an indispensable tool for our theology in Micah. The traditions provided us with an overarching framework for discussing the concept of Yahweh's sovereignty. As most scholars would agree, after the Babylonian exile Zion became a symbol of eschatological hope for future Israel and the nations.[3] According to Ezra Jin, "Zion is the eschatological symbol of hope that reinterprets all the Old Testament traditions, such as the Exodus tradition, the Abraham-Sarah tradition, the Noah tradition and the Creation tradition."[4] In fact, Zion tradition integrates all the major Israelite traditions. As Abraham Sung Ho Oh claims, "the eschatological Zion is the fulfillment of the covenant traditions

---

2. Sweeney, *Twelve Prophets*, 2:414.

3. Like most biblical scholars, we understand eschatology not as a study of the "end of time, of the world, or of history," but as referring to any historical time in the future in which Yahweh radically transforms historical realities. For instance, see Petersen, "Eschatology (OT)," 575–579; Gowan, *Eschatology in the Old Testament*, 1–3.

4. Jin, *Back to Jerusalem*, 42.

(especially, Abrahamic, Mosaic, and Davidic covenants)."[5] To these three traditions, Jin adds the creation and Noah traditions.[6]

Equally important is the earlier precedence of that eschatological hope even before the Babylonian exile in 586/7 BC. In Micah, the Zion/Davidic traditions effectively are the script that spells out how the Abrahamic covenant will be fulfilled. Towards this fulfillment, the unfolding script is the new exodus motif, the agent of that script is the divine warrior, and the destination of that new exodus is the reconstituted Zion. Therein lays the connection between the three biblical traditions (Abrahamic, exodus, and Zion/Davidic) in the book of Micah. Let us elucidate how the exodus motif binds together the Abrahamic traditions and the Zion/Davidic traditions in Micah.

In several places, biblical authors intentionally cast Abraham's story as an exodus story (e.g. Isa 29:22; Josh 24:2–3). While the Isaianic passage lacks historical or geographical references, the expression that Yahweh "delivered Abraham" (פדה את־אברהם) (Isa 29:22a) echoes typical terminology used in the constitutive exodus: "Yahweh delivered you [Israel]" (יפדך יהוה) (Deut 15:15; 24:18). Interestingly, the context of Joshua's testament reveals that Abraham's call was, in fact, an exodus-like event. Apparently, Yahweh delivered Abraham from serving false gods (Josh 24:2–3).[7] Moreover, the terms used of Abraham's call, "took" (לקח) and "led" (הלך) (Josh 24:3), also evoke a concept of the exodus. Parallel terms are common in the original exodus, "bring out" (יצא) and "led" (הלך) (Deut 8:14b–15a; cf. Amos 2:10; Ezek 20:10).

Most importantly, a close reading of the book of Genesis reveals that Abraham's escape from Egypt animates an exodus event. Specifically, Abraham's encounters in Egypt prefigure Israel's later experiences.[8] Thematic and verbal parallels support the claim. Both parties "descend" (ירד) to Egypt because of "a heavy famine" (כבד הרעב) in Canaan (Gen 12:10; 47:4). An initially warm relationship with Pharaoh (Gen 12:15–16; 47:5–6a) turns sour (Gen 12:18–19; Exod 1:8–11). Yahweh brings "plagues" (נגע) against Pharaoh (Gen 12:17; Exod 11:1). The plagues result in the "release" (שלח)

---

5. Oh, *Oh, That You Would Rend the Heavens*, 175.

6. Jin, *Back to Jerusalem*, 42.

7. Daube, *Exodus Pattern*, 45.

8. Geoghegan, "Abrahamic Passover," 47–48; Geoghegan, "Exodus of Abraham," 20–21; Daube, *Exodus Pattern*, 22–38.

(Gen 12:18–20; Exod 12:31–33). Finally, both Abraham and Israel depart Egypt with great substance (Gen 13:2; Exod 12:35–38).

An immediate consequence of our discussion is that, for the most part, Yahweh's blessings flow through an exodus experience. This should not surprise us because Abraham himself had to go out from Ur for Yahweh to fulfill the promises (Gen 12:1–3). Later on, Yahweh promised to fulfill the Abrahamic covenant for ancient Israel via the exodus event (Gen 15:13–14). As Jeffrey C. Geoghegan notes, "Given the centrality of the exodus for ancient Israel, it is understandable that the biblical authors would want to prefigure this event in the life of Israel's ancestors."[9]

Another consequence of our prefiguration of the exodus is that each Israelite generation that violated the covenant with Yahweh would undergo their own exodus experience. As we have already stated in chapter 3, Moses laid out how this exodus would work out. Persistent sin in the land would result in an exile, but repentance would result in a new exodus to the land (Lev 26:40–41). Yahweh would then fulfill the Abrahamic covenant (Lev 26:42) and renew the Mosaic covenant (v. 45).

However, in contrast to the original exodus whose destination was the promised land in general, the destination for any future exodus would be a reconstituted Zion. Because Zion is the focal point for future returnees, this is what we have described earlier in chapter 2 as the dynamic Zion tradition. In this respect, a nexus between the Abrahamic covenant and the Zion/Davidic traditions is the exodus motif. More importantly, just as Yahweh intends to fulfill the Abrahamic covenant following a covenant breach (Lev 26: 40–41), he will do the same in the book of Micah (Mic 7:20). Hence, contrary to Marrs, Micah's future hope lies not in the Zion/Davidic traditions per se, but in the fulfillment of the Abrahamic promises.

It is fitting then that Micah concludes his book by recounting the divine warrior casting sin into the sea (Mic 7:19) and Yahweh's faithfulness to the Abrahamic covenant (v. 20). First, the divine warrior intends to renew the covenant relationship with the new covenant community. This is evident in that the ancient creed behind Yahweh's attributes and deeds (Mic 7:18–19; Exod 34:6–7) is set within a covenant renewal ceremony (Exod 34:1–5,

---

9. Geoghegan, "Abrahamic Passover," 49.

10). Second, and more importantly, the divine warrior intends to fulfill the Abrahamic promise for the new people of God. Apparently, the parallel terms "loyalty" (אמת) and "kindness" (חסד), together with Yahweh's oath (Mic 7:20), not only speak of Yahweh's fidelity and loyalty to the Abrahamic covenant but also imply that he will act accordingly in order to fulfill the covenant promises.

Thus, what we observe in the book of Micah is that the divine warrior appears and radically transforms Zion in order to reestablish his sovereignty. Essentially, the reestablishment of Yahweh's sovereignty is a significant aspect of the grand program towards the fulfillment of the Abrahamic promises. Specifically, Yahweh's ultimate intent for Zion is to fulfill the four pillar promises of the Abrahamic covenant – land, kingship, Israel's status of honor as a great nation, and a new covenant community.

Restoration of the Abrahamic Promises

Yahweh Restores the Land

Many scholars agree that it is a foregone conclusion in the Old Testament that Zion assumes the place of the promised land.[10] In the first place, there are intimations that Zion, in particular Zion's temple, was the ultimate destination in the constitutive exodus (Exod 15:17). While the language of "mountain" (הר) and "place" (מכון) may refer to the promised land in general, the mention of the "sanctuary ... your hands have established" (מקדש ... כוננו ידיך) implies the temple (15:17). In essence, the reestablishment of the temple on the cosmic mountain directly connects to possessing the promised land (Exod 15:17–18).[11] Strikingly, there are verbal correspondences between the Exodus 15:17–18 and Micah 4:1–7.[12] Just as in the original exodus, the return of the remnant to Zion implies the return to the land (Mic 2:12–13; 4:6–7). Following the devastation by the divine warrior, Zion was the only inhabitable place on earth; the rest was "desolate" (שממה) (1:7; 7:13).

---

10. Isaac, *From Land to Lands*, 66–68; Gowan, *Eschatology in the Old Testament*, 9–20; Weinfeld, *Promise of the Land*, 202–220; McConville, "Jerusalem in the Old Testament," 44–49.

11. As Douglas K. Stuart comments, "Zion is envisioned here as the place of God's inheritance, that is, permanent personal real property. It is from this sort of language that one begins to trace the biblical theme of heaven as the ultimate Jerusalem." Stuart, *Exodus*, 361.

12. For instance, the terms in Exod 15:17, (כון) and (הר), also appear in Micah to describe the restored Temple (Mic 4:1). In addition, the two passages share a similar expression: "Yahweh will reign ... forever" (ועד ... ימלך יהוה) (Exod 15:18) // (ומלך יהוה ... ועד) (Mic 4:7).

In the second place, that Zion assumes the place of the promised land is evident in Moses's restoration pattern. In Moses's pattern, Yahweh threatens to desolate the land and exile the people for covenant breach (Lev 26:32–33). However, because of his commitment to the Abrahamic covenant, Yahweh will ultimately remember the land and restore a remnant back to the land upon genuine repentance (vv. 40, 42, 44).

The contours of Micah's new exodus script typify a recurrence of Moses's restoration pattern. Micah exploits the transformative nature of the divine warrior's advent. The divine warrior purifies (Mic 1:2–3:11), restores the land (4:1–5), and cleanses a repentant remnant (7:9, 17b–19). By analogy, the divine warrior's activities imply the restoration of the land. Specifically, the reestablishment of Zion (Mic 4:1), the rebuilding of walls (7:11a), and the increase in land area (7:11b) in essence re-actualize Yahweh's promise of land to the patriarchs (cf. Gen. 12:7; 13:14–15; 28:14).

A similar pattern as in the first exodus, and in Micah's new exodus, will also prevail in the second exodus from Babylon. The return to the land is a return to Zion (Isa 35:10; Jer 50:4–5; Neh 2:5; 7:7). In sum, Yahweh's sovereignty depends on his ability to (re)possess the land. Thus, the restoration of Zion assumes the restoration of the land. All this reveals Yahweh's faithfulness to the Abrahamic covenant (Mic 7:20). In addition, the restoration of Zion signals the fulfillment of Yahweh's original intent for the whole earth.

Yahweh Restores Kingship

The restoration of land also includes the restoration of a new king, presumably of Davidic origin, to rule in Zion as Yahweh's vicegerent. Although Micah's expectations of the restoration of human vicegerency looks back to the Davidic traditions (Mic 4:8; 5:1), it is nevertheless coupled to the divine promises to the patriarchs (Gen 17:6, 16; 35:11). As McCartney cogently puts it, "In the Davidic theocracy, a typological and imperfect human vicegerency was reinstated as partial fulfillment of the promise to Abraham."[13] Indeed, Micah has the promises to the patriarchs in view. The common birth motif anticipating the birth of a new king, "from you shall come forth for me" (ממך לי יצא) (5:1), alludes to the constitutive divine promise of kingship to Abraham, "from you they [kings] shall come forth" (ממך יצאו) (Gen 17:6; 35:11). In addition,

---

13. McCartney, "Ecce Homo," 2.

the reference to "Bethlehem Ephrata" (בית־לחם אפרתה) (Mic 5:1) alludes to Genesis 35:19. The immediate context of Genesis 35:19 includes Yahweh's confirmation of the Abrahamic promises to Jacob. Included in those promises is kingship (Gen 35:11). Thus, in Micah, the promise of Yahweh's vicegerent looks back beyond the Davidic traditions to the patriarchal traditions. It is also possible that that the promise anticipates the hope for the future Messiah (Mic 5:1). As Chalmers opines, the Davidic vicegerent became the basis for messianic hope.[14]

Yahweh Restores Israel's Status as a Great Nation

Micah's prophecy also anticipates the divine promise that Abraham's descendants would become a great nation (Gen 12:3). Although he does not offer textual support, Sweeney intuitively perceives that the reference to the patriarchs (Mic 7:20) includes the promise of a great nation.[15] The notions of a great nation suggest a kingdom which serves as the center of divine blessings for all other nations (Gen 12:2–3; 17:4–6; 18:18). Goldingay has well said, "Abraham is called out of the world for the world's sake"[16] . . . and "[God] intends to have the whole world seek the blessings it sees in Israel."[17] Micah animates these concepts as he anticipates the restoration of Zion's former dominion (Mic 4:8). Clearly, Zion will be a center of blessings for the nations (4:1b–4).

In addition, the notion of a great nation relates to Israel's obedience to Yahweh's laws (Deut 4:5–8).[18] By observing the law, "God's people would also display before the nations what it means to be the people of the Lord." Israel's obedience to the law serves to reveal Yahweh's character to the nations. As a result, this would attract and motivate other nations to seek Yahweh. Israel failed to live out this missionary guideline (Mic 2:1–11; 3:1–11). Fortunately, Yahweh will accomplish this mission. Nations will flock to Zion to learn *torah* from Yahweh himself (Mic 4:2), just as Yahweh intended (Deut 4:5–8). In

---

14. Chalmers, *Exploring the Religion*, 84; Bateman, Bock, and Johnston, *Jesus the Messiah*, 65.
15. Sweeney, *Twelve Prophets*, 2:413.
16. Goldingay, *Theological Diversity*, 61.
17. Goldingay, *Old Testament Theology*, 2:85.
18. Merrill, *Deuteronomy*, 116.

sum, Yahweh's sovereignty means that Zion will regain her status of honor as a great nation.

Yahweh Restores a New Covenant Community

Finally, Yahweh's intent for Zion is to form a new covenant community in line with his promises to Abraham. In accordance with the Abrahamic covenant, the new community will comprise both Israel and the nations (Gen 12:1–3). The two peoples come into focus when we contrast Genesis 15 and 17. Whereas Genesis 15 solely focuses on future Israel as beneficiaries of the covenant blessings (vv. 13, 18–21), Genesis 17 has in view the multitude of nations who will also inherit the promises (vv. 4–6).

In Micah, the new exodus motif involves both a remnant (2:12–13; 4:7; 5:7–8) and the obedient nations returning to Zion (7:12, 17b, 18). Shaw comments that Micah 7:12 utilizes various geographical places in order to emphasize the "belief about the diversity of the population that will inherit the land."[19] As we have already argued in chapter 6, we understand the wedding of Israel and the nations as the formation of a new people of God. The formation of a new people from all nations essentially fulfills the original divine intent for all nations (Gen 12:1–3). Moreover, by restoring people from all nations, Yahweh is extending his sovereignty throughout the whole earth. Yahweh's sovereignty will be universally acknowledged. As Routledge perceptively observes, "The inclusion of the nations is not an addendum to God's purpose with Israel: it is implicit from the start of the OT."[20]

Conclusion

Questions about the redaction of Micah have made it difficult to discern how the different sections in the book relate to each other. In particular, the relationship between hope and doom oracles has led some studies to conclude that Micah's book has no apparent structure. In addition, some studies have challenged the authenticity of Micah 6–7. For some, Micah 6–7 does not fit Micah's time but fits the Maccabean period. However, as we reflect on our study of Micah, the book exhibits an impressive thematic coherence. While

---

19. Shaw, *The Speeches of Micah*, 205.
20. Routledge, *Old Testament Theology*, 334.

the minute cohesive links might elude us, the book is a theological reflection on the reestablishment of Yahweh's sovereignty on earth. Sin defies and undercuts Yahweh's sovereignty on earth. It has upturned the earthly structures that mediate Yahweh's sovereignty.

Hence, the book of Micah is a vision about the transformation of Zion. It explicates how Yahweh reestablishes each of Zion's mediatorial structures via a radical battle and victory over sin. First, Yahweh will defeat sin on the mountains and on the land (Mic 1:2–2:11; 3:1–12; 4:9–14; 5:9–14; 6:9–7:6). Then he will progressively restore and elevate Zion as the earthly throne of his reign (4:1–5) and the Davidic line as his earthly vicegerent (5:1), as well as extending human vicegerency to a new covenant people (7:8–20). Finally, he will subdue and confine sin into the depth of the sea and put an end to evil (7:19). The reinstatement of Zion's mediatorial structures, with humanity properly ordered, heralds the advent of Yahweh's sovereignty on earth. Yahweh will once again mount his imperial throne at Zion (4:7).

APPENDIX

Origins of the Zion/Davidic Traditions

Introduction

For the sake of completeness, the appendix surveys and summarizes the debate on the origins of the Zion/Davidic traditions.[1] While the symbol of Zion maintained its centrality even through the vicissitudes of Israel's history, the question of the origins of the traditions it gave rise to is still a debatable issue and no scholarly consensus is in sight. For the most part, scholars propose three different views concerning the origins of the Zion/Davidic traditions: the Jebusite theory, the Shiloh ark theory, and the Davidic court theory.

The Jebusite Theory

An important and dominant theory that provides an impetus for the origins of the Zion traditions is the Jebusite theory. The Jebusite theory posits that various motifs of the Zion tradition were adopted from Jebusite cultic traditions. According to Hans-Joachim Kraus, these Jebusite cultic traditions are rooted in ancient Canaan and Syrian cultic motifs.[2] For instance, he argues that the topographical note in Psalm 48:3 describing Jerusalem as "Mount Zion in the remote part of Zaphon" (הר־ציון ירכתי צפון) stems from Ugaritic cultic traditions regarding Mount Zaphon as the mountain of the high god, Baal of Heaven.[3] Without any provable or unprovable argumentation, he

---

1. Roberts, "Davidic Origin," 313–330; Levenson, "Zion Traditions," 1101–1102; Ollenburger, *Zion*, 17–18; Poulsen, *Representing Zion*, 6–8.
2. Kraus, *Theology of the Psalms*, 83.
3. Kraus, 78–79.

concludes that most concepts associated with Mount Zaphon transferred to Jerusalem and, secondarily, to Mount Zion after having gone a development during the Jebusite era.[4]

John H. Hayes, another proponent of the Jebusite theory, explores the origin of the belief in the inviolability of Zion and its relationship to Isaiah.[5] His main argument is that the traditions about Zion's inviolability in the early Zion psalms (e.g. Pss 46, 48, 76) have priority over those in Isaiah.[6] Hayes observes that these Psalms "emphasize the impregnability of the city protected by God."[7] In his words, "These hymns could have been part of a Jebusite cult which utilized elements from a common Ugaritic-Canaanite background that viewed the gods as dwelling upon some mythological mountain which was thus divinely protected."[8] A basis for his conclusion is that the Jebusites themselves, in trying to avert David's assault on the city, believed in the inviolability of their city (2 Sam 5:6–8; cf. 1 Chr 11:4–7).[9]

Further support for the Jebusite theory probably comes from the traditions concerning Zadok.[10] H. H. Rowley maintains that Zadok was a pre-Israelite priest at the Jebusite shrine in Jerusalem.[11] His name, צָדוֹק, recalls the ancient king-priest of Salem, מלכי־צדק, in the time of Abraham (Gen 14:18–20; Ps 110:4) and אדני־צדק, king of Jerusalem during the conquest.[12] For Rowley, the evidence from Genesis 14 suggests that there was an ancient shrine in Jerusalem. He reasons that since David did not destroy this shrine upon his capture of Jerusalem, he did not also dismiss its priesthood because of its link

---

4. For instance, Mount Zaphon as the mountain of Baal was regarded as the center of the universe. Thus, if Yahweh is the creator God, then the place of his throne is the center of creation, the joy of the world marked by splendor and beauty (Ps 48:3). In glorifying Jerusalem, Ps 46:4 mentions a river that "makes glad the city of God." For Kraus, this is an adaptation of the abode of El, whose dwelling was at the source of two rivers in the middle of the two primeval oceans. Kraus, 79–80.

5. Hayes, "Tradition of Zion's Inviolability," 419.

6. Hayes, 421–422.

7. For instance, these songs ascribe praise to God for his strength (Pss 46:2–4; 76:2–3). The nations seek to destroy the city (46:7; 48:5), but God protects his valued possession (46:9–10; 48:6–9; 76:4–10). Hayes, 422.

8. Hayes, 424.

9. Hayes, 424n32; Albrektson, *Studies in the Text*, 222.

10. Rowley, "Zadok and Nehushtan," passim; Vaux, *Ancient Israel*, 374.

11. Rowley, "Zadok and Nehushtan," 123.

12. Vaux, *Ancient Israel*, 374; Rowley, "Zadok and Nehushtan," 124.

to Abraham.[13] More to the point, David did not build a shrine either. Hence, Rowley ingeniously surmises that David placed the ark of the covenant in an already existing shrine.[14] As a result, he retained the services of Zadok as a priest for Yahweh to care for the ark of the covenant. It is no surprise then that after Absalom's revolt, Zadok brought the ark back to Jerusalem – that is, to "Zadok's sanctuary" (2 Sam 15:24).[15]

Levenson also adds that David's purchase of the threshing floor of Araunah the Jebusite for an altar, following the appearance of the angel of Yahweh, provides a secure argument for the Jebusite theory (2 Sam 24:15–25).[16] Interestingly, Gary A. Rendsburg even believes that Zadok the priest and Araunah were historically the same person.[17] Lester L. Grabbe presents another hypothesis. He claims that Araunah is not a personal name but rather a Hittite or Hurrian title meaning "the Lord."[18] In this respect, Zadok was the personal name of the priest and Araunah his royal title. As such, David is seen as conforming to and continuing the Canaanite worship traditions stemming from the priesthood of מלכי־צדק by stripping Zadok of his kingship but maintaining his priesthood.[19]

Hayes's presentation of the Jebusite theory provides a reasonable theological explanation for the inviolability of Mount Zion. However, Kraus makes unprovable claims. Having argued for a connection between El and the Jebusites, he somehow assigns concepts about Baal to the Jebusites. Obviously, we lack Canaanite evidence that proves that El assumed Baal's activities.[20] Unfortunately, Rowley's analysis is a cause for concern. At several places, he seems to dismiss evidence that suggests that David erected a tent for the ark (2 Sam 6:17; cf. 2 Sam 7:2) or that the ark was moved from a tent to Solomon's

---

13. Rowley, "Zadok and Nehushtan," 124.
14. Rowley, 126.
15. Rowley, 128.
16. Levenson, "Zion Traditions," 1101; Also see Cross, *Canaanite Myth and Hebrew Epic*, 209–212.
17. Rendsburg, "Reading David," 25–26.
18. Grabbe, "Ethnic Groups in Jerusalem," 153.
19. Gordon and Rendsburg, *Bible and the Ancient Near East*, 206.
20. Roberts, "Davidic Origin," 321.

temple (1 Kgs 8:4).[21] For him, these references are later scribal interpolations, unhistorical, or the ark did not remain in a tent throughout David's reign.[22]

The Shiloh Ark Theory

Another proposal concerning the origin of the Zion tradition is the Shiloh ark or ark of the covenant theory.[23] Martin Noth, an ardent advocate of the theory, posits that the theory is inseparably connected to the rise of Jerusalem. According to Noth's reconstruction, Jerusalem lacks explicit mention in the Pentateuch, and its scanty mention (e.g. Josh 10 and Judg 1:5–8) shows that Jerusalem was detached from early Israelite traditions.[24] The once Jebusite city only became prominent after David had made it his royal capital city and transferred the ark of the covenant from Shiloh (1 Sam 4–6; 2 Sam 6). By transferring the ark from Shiloh to Jerusalem, and then enshrining it in Solomon's temple, Jerusalem became a prominent cultic center for the twelve tribes of Israel.[25]

Noth proceeds to emphasize that it was the cultic dimension rather than the political aspect that made Jerusalem prominent. He aptly argues that the defiance or rebellion of Jeroboam I in setting up royal sanctuaries in competition with Jerusalem (1 Kgs 12:28–31) was more of a religious apostasy than a political issue. Jeroboam's actions are the grounds for divine judgment upon him and his household (1 Kgs 12:26). Thus, Noth reasons that the "reference to the downfall of Jeroboam's house . . . therefore condemns the cultic schism of the tribes of Israel from Jerusalem, whereas it regards the political detachment from the Davidic monarchy as legitimate and justified."[26]

In addition, Noth argues that in spite of the deaths of David and Solomon, the reputation of Jerusalem as the shrine of Yahweh's presence (the ark and

---

21. Rowley, "Zadok and Nehushtan," 126–27.

22. Advocates of the Jebusite theory include Cross, *Canaanite Myth and Hebrew Epic*, 209–211; Clements, *God and Temple*, 40–48; Rendsburg, "Reading David in Genesis," 25–26. For its critics, see Dekker, *Zion's Rock-Solid Foundations*; Roberts, "Davidic Origin," 315–322.

23. For helpful surveys on the ark theory, see Dekker, *Zion's Rock-Solid Foundations*, 286–288, 303–308; Ollenburger, *Zion*, 37–41; Cross, *Canaanite Myth and Hebrew Epic*, 229–234; Levenson, "Zion Traditions," 1101.

24. Noth, *Laws in the Pentateuch*, 132–133.

25. Noth, 134–135.

26. Noth, 137.

the temple) continued.²⁷ The ark itself became a central holy place, and at some point it was called by the epithet "the Ark of the Covenant of Yahweh of Hosts, who dwells on the Cherubim" (ארון ברית־יהוה צבאות ישב הכרבים) (1 Sam 4:4).²⁸ In the pre-exilic prophets, the divine title "Yahweh of Hosts" (יהוה צבאות) became "he who dwells on Mount Zion" (Isa 8:18; cf. Mic 3:12; Isa 2:3).²⁹ In essence, Zion became the mountain of Yahweh. Hence, after the catastrophe of Solomon's temple in 586/7 BC, and even after the disappearance of the ark of the covenant, Jerusalem with its sacred mountain maintained its focal point as the center for Israelite hope.³⁰

Three years after the English publication of Noth's book, David Lemoine Eiler took Noth's thesis as the point of departure in his unpublished dissertation. Eiler argues that Zion theology is rooted in the theological "development of holy war and theophany themes associated with the ark and cherubim at the beginning of the monarchic period."³¹ For him, the cherubim covering the ark depicted a theophany. Here he appeals to Canaanite evidence, which portrays El as enthroned on a throne flanked by cherubim.³²

Eiler goes on to argue that in early Israel the ark served as a symbol of Yahweh's victorious presence in holy war (e.g. Num 10:36–36; Judg 3–6; 1 Sam 4–6; cf. 2 Sam 5:19; 23–24).³³ He believes that the divine title יהוה צבאות, together with its attached epithet ישב הכרבים (1 Sam 4:2; cf. 15:2; 17:45), represent an assimilation of Canaanite ideas and symbols of the storm god imagery (see Deut 32–33; Pss 47; 68; 82; 97).³⁴ Specifically, he notes that the epithet ישב הכרבי is reminiscent of Baal's epithet as the rider on clouds (see Pss 18:11; 80:2).³⁵ Apparently, this epithet (ישב הכרבים) parallels יהוה מלך and thus speaks of Yahweh's kingship in Zion (Ps 99:1).³⁶ Just like Noth, Eiler states that despite the loss of the ark and the temple, "Zion itself is the

---

27. Noth, 142.
28. Noth, 142.
29. Noth, 142.
30. Noth, 143.
31. Eiler, "Origin and History," 23.
32. Ollenburger, *Zion*, 42.
33. Eiler, "Origin and History," 59–60.
34. Eiler, 60–61, 107–110; 121–124; 130–134.
35. Ollenburger, *Zion*, 42.
36. Ollenburger, 43.

symbol of Yahweh exercising universal sovereignty by means of his holy war theophany power."[37]

Altogether, the earliest roots of the Zion tradition, according to Noth, Eiler, and others, lies in the transfer of the ark of the covenant from Shiloh to Jerusalem. Tan, Ollenburger, and Eiler give fitting conclusions to this theory. In his words, Tan writes, "Although one may not be certain about the origins of the Zion traditions, it is incontrovertible that the introduction of the ark into the Jebusite city (i.e. Jerusalem) and its being chosen as the capital city by David gave the impetus, if not the origin, for its importance in Jewish eschatological and theological thought."[38] Likewise, Ollenburger states, "these examples [Ps 18:11; 80:2; 99:1] illustrate quite clearly that Shiloh was a prime site for the integration of Canaanite and Israelite religion."[39] Eiler sees the earliest form of the Zion tradition as an exposition of the Shiloh ark tradition. He writes,

> The whole story [2 Sam 6] indicates that David was simply re-establishing the Shiloh ark cult and sanctuary at a new place which had had no previous sacral significance at all for Israel. The holiness of Zion as a Yahwistic cult place derived first of all from this act and from the ark itself rather than from any pre-existing Jebusite cult place of tradition. The assimilation of Jebusite traditions must be regarded as a later stage in the development, even if this began to take place already during the reign of David.[40]

The Davidic Court Theory

The third theory regarding the origins of the Zion tradition is the Davidic court theory. This theory posits that the tradition is wholly Israelite and is a creation of the Davidic court. Its ardent advocate is J. J. M. Roberts. For Roberts, the Zion traditions originated in the Davidic court to reflect the rise

---

37. Eiler, "Origin and History," 222.
38. Tan, *Zion Traditions*, 25.
39. Ollenburger, *Zion*, 43.
40. Eiler, "Origin and History," 69–70, 117.

of David's empire and Yahweh's sovereign power.⁴¹ In an effort to dethrone the popular Jebusite theory, Roberts unmistakably surmises that all the elements of the Zion traditions originally have a *Sitz im Leben* in the era of the Davidic-Solomonic empire.⁴²

The first element in the Zion traditions that Roberts discusses is the identification of Yahweh with El, which he surmises is earlier than the Davidic empire.⁴³ However, the rise of David and his imperial pursuits provided the needed momentum for this identification. According to Roberts, the purpose of identifying Yahweh with the imperial El, the supreme head of the Canaanite pantheon, was not only to make Yahweh the supreme deity but also to provide a theological basis for David's imperialism.⁴⁴ In other words, Yahweh as the supreme deity has the right to dethrone unfit gods who rule over the nations and grant world dominion to his viceroy in Jerusalem (contrast Deut 32 and Ps 82).⁴⁵ In addition, Yahweh also identified with Baal. Such a move exalted Yahweh as the supreme deity and validated David's rule over the nations even further. It is well acknowledged that in Canaanite religious thought, Baal played a more significant role in the actual exercise of divine rule than El, the head of the pantheon.⁴⁶ As a result, Roberts conjectures that Israel absorbed the traits and activities of Baal and attributed them to Yahweh to accord him full supremacy.⁴⁷

Furthermore, Roberts hypothesizes that to give Yahweh full supremacy was not enough. What Israel really needed was Yahweh's absolute supremacy. To underscore this concern, Israel simply identified Yahweh with Elyon, the cosmogonic deity.⁴⁸ Such a move, Roberts believes, was "an Israelite innovation, analogous to the Assyrian identification of Asshur and Anshar, motivated by an attempt to elevate Yahweh still higher than the simple

---

41. Roberts, "Davidic Origin," 342–344. Ollenburger doubts whether the Zion tradition as formulated in Pss 46, 48, and 76 actually arose in the time of the royal court. Ollenburger, *Zion*, 17–18, 60.

42. Roberts, "Davidic Origin," 324.

43. Roberts, 324.

44. Roberts, 324–326.

45. Roberts, 327.

46. Roberts, 327.

47. Roberts, 327.

48. Roberts, 327.

identification with the enfeebled Canaanite El could."[49] Although Yahweh's pre-monarchical identification with Elyon was a response to Yahweh's victory over the Canaanite gods during the conquest era, Yahweh's rise reached its apex alongside the rise of the Davidic-Solomonic empire.[50] In his words, Roberts writes, "It is precisely in the monarchical period, after the creation of David's empire gave new relevance and added credence to the imperial claims always implicit in the use of the epithet Elyon, that the epithet enjoyed its greatest popularity."[51]

Besides the identification of Yahweh with the Canaanites deities, another central element of the Zion tradition with roots in the Davidic-Solomonic era is the glorification of Jerusalem as Yahweh's abode.[52] In line with Noth's general thesis, Roberts views David's capture of Jerusalem and transformation of it into his capital city as the watershed event that brought prominence to the city.[53] David's resolute attempts and eventual success in transporting the ark of the covenant to Jerusalem was a political maneuver to transform Jerusalem into the cultic and political center of the nation.[54] According to Roberts, this maneuver required some legitimation. For him, this legitimation finds expression in Psalm 132:13–14, a passage which essentially lays the foundational belief that Yahweh chose Zion as his dwelling place and David as his viceroy (v. 17).[55] Furthermore, Roberts observes that, by the time Solomon assumed the Davidic throne, the concept of Zion as Yahweh's sacred mountain was already fixed.[56] Obviously, the building of the temple presupposes the choice of Zion as Yahweh's place of abode. At any rate, Roberts unhesitatingly speculates that the choice of Zion was more broadly acknowledged in the northern kingdom (Israel) than the traditions about the election of David and his dynasty.[57]

---

49. Roberts, 327.
50. Roberts, 327.
51. Roberts, 341–342.
52. Roberts, 328.
53. Roberts, 328.
54. Roberts, 328.
55. Roberts, 328.
56. Roberts, 328.
57. Roberts, 328.

Lastly, Roberts engages the motif of Zion's security against enemy attack. Roberts suggests that the hubris and activities of enemy kings in the Davidic-Solomonic era, and Yahweh's response to their wicked plots, best explain the origins of this motif.[58] For Roberts, most of the surrounding states were Israel's vassals, and any rebellion on their part was viewed from Israel's standpoint as a challenge to Yahweh's sovereignty.[59] Although he notes that there were no such revolts during David's reign, Roberts believes the revolts instigated by Hadad the Edomite (1 Kgs 11:14–22) and Rezon of Damascus (11:23–25) provided the impetus for the motif of the nations plotting against Yahweh and his earthly viceroy.[60] Roberts's argument thus far is hardly convincing. Perhaps sensing the inadequacy of his initial suggestions, Roberts goes on to offer a second proposal. He appeals to David's defensive wars against the Philistines in the Valley of Rephaim following David's capture of Zion (2 Sam 5:17–25).[61] In his view, the victories signal the crystallization point from which the tradition about the security of Zion would develop.[62]

Roberts's proposals are tenuous, especially since neither has clear-cut biblical support. Moreover, neither of his proposals makes adequate sense of the context. For example, he does not take into consideration that the three revolts in 1 Kings 11:14–40 were not really instigated by those foreign kings or by Jeroboam I. Instead, it was Yahweh himself who raised these rebels against the Davidic empire because of Solomon's idolatrous tendencies (vv. 9, 14). Another inconsistency with his argument is that these revolts were not an attack on Zion per se, but rather foreign vassals were asserting their own independence. As the text makes certain, Yahweh was bent on tearing down the extent of the Davidic kingdom but leaving Zion and Judah intact (v. 13). Jeroboam I would also revolt and assert his authority on the Northern tribes (vv. 26–40). Less problematic in our opinion is the Jebusite view that David cannot capture Zion.

---

58. Roberts, 328.
59. Roberts, 328–329.
60. Roberts, 329.
61. Roberts, 329. It is important to note that the narratives in 2 Sam 5 are arranged thematically, rather than in absolute chronological order. As a result, the likely date for the first Philistine battle (vv. 17–21) is before David's capture of Zion.
62. Roberts, 329.

In sum, regardless of one's conclusions on this debate, the origins of the Zion traditions were "not a *creatio ex nihilo*, but rather the creation of a focal point and integrating moment in Zion from a variety of pre-existing motifs and traditions."[63]

---

63. Renz, "Use of the Zion Tradition," 83.

Bibliography

Abernethy, Andrew. *The Book of Isaiah and God's Kingdom: A Thematic-Theological Approach*. New Studies in Biblical Theology 40. Downers Grove, IL: InterVarsity, 2016.

Adamczewski, Bartosz. *Retelling the Law: Genesis, Exodus-Numbers, and Samuel-Kings as Sequential Hypertextual Reworkings of Deuteronomy*. European Studies in Theology, Philosophy and History of Religions. Frankfurt: Peter Lang, 2012.

Aḥituv, Shmuel. *Echoes from the Past: Hebrew and Cognate Inscriptions from the Biblical Period*. Jerusalem: Carta, 2008.

Aḥituv, Shmuel, Esther Eshel, and Ze'ev Meshel. "The Inscriptions." In *Kuntillet Ajrud (Horvat Teman): An Iron Age II Religious Site on the Judah Sinai Border*, edited by Liora Freud, translated by John H. Tresman, 72–142. Jerusalem: Israel Exploration Society, 2012.

Albertz, Rainer. "Exile as Purification. Reconstructing the 'Book of the Four.'" In *Thematic Threads in the Book of the Twelve*, edited by Paul L. Redditt and Aaron Schart, 232–251. Beihefte zur Zeitschrift für die alttestamentliche Wissenschaft 325. Berlin: Walter de Gruyter, 2003.

Albrektson, Bertil. *Studies in the Text and Theology of the Book of Lamentations: With a Critical Edition of the Peshitta Text*. Studia Theologica Lundensia 21. Lund: CWK Gleerup, 1963.

Alexander, T. Desmond. *From Eden to the New Jerusalem: An Introduction to Biblical Theology*. Grand Rapids: Kregel Academic, 2009.

———. *From Paradise to the Promised Land: An Introduction to the Pentateuch*. 3rd ed. Grand Rapids: Baker Academic, 2012.

Alfaro, Juan I. *Justice and Loyalty: A Commentary on the Book of Micah*. International Theological Commentary. Grand Rapids: Eerdmans, 1989.

Allen, Graham. *Intertextuality*. The New Critical Idiom. New York: Routledge, 2000.

Allen, Leslie C. *The Books of Joel, Obadiah, Jonah and Micah*. New International Commentary on the Old Testament. Grand Rapids: Eerdmans, 1976.

———. *A Theological Approach to the Old Testament: Major Themes and New Testament Connections*. Eugene, OR: Wipf and Stock, 2014.

Alter, Robert. *The Art of Biblical Poetry*. Rev. and updated ed. New York: Basic Books, 2011.

Altman, Amnon. *The Historical Prologue of the Hittite Vassal Treaties: An Inquiry into the Concepts of Hittite Interstate Law*. Bar-Ilan Studies in Near Eastern Languages and Culture. Ramat-Gan: Bar-Ilan University Press, 2004.

Amsler, S. "היה." In *Theological Lexicon of the Old Testament*, edited by Ernst Jenni and Claus Westermann, 359–365. Peabody, MA: Hendrickson, 1997.

Andersen, Francis I., and David Noel Freedman. *Micah: A New Translation with Introduction and Commentary*. Anchor Bible 24E. New York: Doubleday, 2000.

Anderson, Jeff S. *The Blessing and the Curse: Trajectories in the Theology of the Old Testament*. Eugene, OR: Cascade Books, 2014.

Arnold, Bill T., and John H. Choi. *A Guide to Biblical Hebrew Syntax*. Cambridge: Cambridge University Press, 2003.

Attridge, Harold W., and Robert A. Oden Jr. *Philo of Byblos: The Phoenician History*. Catholic Biblical Quarterly: Monograph Series 9. Washington, DC: Catholic Biblical Association of America, 1981.

Avioz, Michael. *Nathan's Oracle (2 Samuel 7) and Its Interpreters*. Bible in History. New York: Peter Lang, 2005.

Ballard, Libby. "Intertextuality and the Coherence of Micah 6–7." In *Society of Biblical Literature Annual Meeting*. Chicago, 2012.

Barker, Kenneth L. "Micah." In *Micah, Nahum, Habakkuk, Zephaniah*, 21–136. Vol. 20 of *The New American Commentary*. Nashville, TN: Broadman and Holman, 1998.

Barr, James. *The Concept of Biblical Theology: An Old Testament Perspective*. Minneapolis: Fortress, 1999.

Barrick, W. Boyd. *BMH as Body Language: A Lexical and Iconographical Study of the Word BMH When Not a Reference to Cultic Phenomena in Biblical and Post-Biblical Hebrew*. Library of Biblical Studies/Old Testament 477. New York: T and T Clark, 2008.

Barrick, William D. "Inter-Covenantal Truth and Relevance: Leviticus 26 and the Biblical Covenants." *Master's Seminary Journal* 21, no. 1 (2010): 81–102.

———. "The Mosaic Covenant." *Master's Seminary Journal* 10, no. 2 (1999): 213–232.

Barton, John. "Déjà Lu: Intertextuality, Method or Theory." In *Reading Job Intertextually*, edited by Katharine Dell and Will Kynes, 1–16. Library of Biblical Studies. New York: Bloomsbury, 2012.

———. "Natural Law and Poetic Justice in the Old Testament." *Journal of Theological Studies* 30, no. 1 (1979): 1–14.

Bateman, Herbert W., Darrell L. Bock, and Gordon H. Johnston. *Jesus the Messiah: Tracing the Promises, Expectations, and Coming of Israel's King*. Grand Rapids: Kregel, 2012.

Batto, Bernard F. "The Combat Myth in Israelite Tradition Revisited." In *Creation and Chaos: A Reconsideration of Hermann Gunkel's Chaoskampf Hypothesis*, edited by Jo Ann Scurlock and Richard H. Beal, 217–236. Winona Lake, IN: Eisenbrauns, 2013.

―――. "The Divine Sovereign: The Image of God in the Priestly Creation Account." In *David and Zion: Biblical Studies in Honor of J. J. M. Roberts*, edited by Bernard F. Batto and Kathryn L. Roberts, 143–186. Winona Lake, IN: Eisenbrauns, 2004.

Baumgarten, Albert I. *The Phoenician History of Philo of Byblos: A Commentary*. Études préliminaires aux religions Orientales dans l'Empire romain. Leiden: Brill, 1981.

Beale, G. K. *A New Testament Biblical Theology: The Unfolding of the Old Testament in the New*. Grand Rapids: Baker Academic, 2011.

Becking, Bob. "Micah in Neo-Assyrian Light." In *"Thus Speaks Ishtar of Arbela": Prophecy in Israel, Assyria, and Egypt in the Neo-Assyrian Period*, edited by Robert P. Gordon and Hans M. Barstad, 111–128. Winona Lake, IN: Eisenbrauns, 2013.

Beckman, Gary M. *Hittite Diplomatic Texts*. 2nd ed. Society of Biblical Literature Writings from the Ancient World Series 7. Atlanta: Scholars Press, 1999.

Beetham, Christopher A. "From Creation to New Creation: The Biblical Epic of King, Vicegerency, and Kingdom." In *From Creation to New Creation: Biblical Theology and Exegesis*, edited by Daniel M. Gurtner and Benjamin L. Gladd, 237–254. Peabody, MA: Hendrickson, 2013.

Begerau, Gunnar. "Micah, Prophet of Hope through Judgment." In *The Lion Has Roared: Theological Themes in the Prophetic Literature of the Old Testament*, edited by H. G. L. Peels and Stephanus Daniel Snyman, 65–75. Eugene, OR: Pickwick, 2012.

Ben-Porat, Ziva. "The Poetics of Literary Allusion." *PTL: Journal for Descriptive Poetics and Theory of Literature* 1 (1976): 105–128.

Ben Zvi, Ehud. *Micah*. Forms of the Old Testament Literature 21B. Grand Rapids: Eerdmans, 2000.

Bergen, Robert D. *1, 2 Samuel*. Vol. 7 of *The New American Commentary*. Nashville, TN: Broadman and Holman, 1996.

Bergmann, Claudia D. "We Have Seen the Enemy, and He Is Only a 'She': The Portrayal of Warriors as Women." In *Writing and Reading War: Rhetoric, Gender, and Ethics in Biblical and Modern Contexts*, edited by Brad E. Kelle and Frank Ritchel Ames, 129–142. Society of Biblical Literature: Symposium Series 42. Atlanta: Society of Biblical Literature, 2008.

Bergsma, John Sietze. *The Jubilee from Leviticus to Qumran: A History of Interpretation*. Supplements to Vetus Testamentum 115. Leiden: Brill, 2007.

Bernat, David A. *Sign of the Covenant: Circumcision in the Priestly Tradition*. Edited by Benjamin D. Sommer. Society of Biblical Literature: Ancient Israel and Its Literature 3. Atlanta: Society of Biblical Literature, 2009.

Berrett, LaMar C., and D. Kelly Ogden. *Discovering the World of the Bible*. 3rd ed. Provo, UT: Grandin, 1996.

Berry, Donald L. *Glory in Romans and the Unified Purpose of God in Redemptive History*. Eugene, OR: Pickwick, 2016.

Bicknell, Belinda Jean. "Passives in Biblical Hebrew." PhD diss., University of Michigan, 1984.

Biddle, Mark E. "Dominion Comes to Jerusalem: An Examination of Developments in the Kingship and Zion Traditions as Reflected in the Book of the Twelve with Particular Attention to Micah 4–5." In *Perspectives on the Formation of the Book of the Twelve: Methodological Foundations, Redactional Processes, Historical Insights*, edited by Rainer Albertz, James D. Nogalski, and Jakob Wöhrle, 238–253. Beihefte zur Zeitschrift für die alttestamentliche Wissenschaft 433. Boston: Walter de Gruyter, 2012.

Biwul, Joel K. T. *A Theological Examination of Symbolism in Ezekiel with Emphasis on the Shepherd Metaphor*. Carlisle: Langham, 2013.

Black, Jeremy, and Anthony Green. *Gods, Demons and Symbols of Ancient Mesopotamia: An Illustrated Dictionary*. Austin: University of Texas Press, 1992.

Blenkinsopp, Joseph. "What Happened at Sinai? Structure and Meaning in the Sinai-Horeb Narrative (Exodus 19–34)." In *Treasures Old and New: Essays in the Theology of the Pentateuch*, 155–174. Grand Rapids: Eerdmans, 2004.

Block, Daniel I. *The Gods of the Nations: Studies in Ancient Near Eastern National Theology*. 2nd ed. Evangelical Theological Society Studies 2. Grand Rapids: Baker Academic, 2000.

Boadt, L. E. "Mythological Themes and Unity of Ezekiel." In *Literary Structure and Rhetorical Strategies in the Hebrew Bible*, edited by L. J. de Regt, Jan de Waard, and J. P. Fokkelman, 211–231. Assen: Van Gorcum, 1996.

Boase, Elizabeth. *The Fulfilment of Doom?: The Dialogic Interaction between the Book of Lamentations and the Pre-Exilic/Early Exilic Prophetic Literature*. Library of Biblical Studies/Old Testament Studies 437. New York: T and T Clark, 2006.

Boyd, B. "Lachish." *The Interpreter's Dictionary of the Bible*. Edited by George Arthur Buttrick. New York: Abingdon, 1962.

Brettler, Marc Zvi. *God Is King: Understanding an Israelite Metaphor*. Journal for the Study of Old Testament: Supplement Series 76. Sheffield: Sheffield Academic, 1989.

Bright, John. *Covenant and Promise: The Prophetic Understanding of the Future in Pre-Exilic Israel*. Philadelphia: Westminster, 1976.

———. *A History of Israel*. Philadelphia: Westminster, 1959.

Brown, F., S. R. Driver, and C. A. Briggs. *A Hebrew and English Lexicon of the Old Testament*. Oxford, 1907.

Brown, Jeannine K. "Metalepsis." In *Exploring Intertextuality: Diverse Strategies for New Testament Interpretation of Texts*, edited by B. J. Oropeza and Steve Moyise, 29–41. Eugene, OR: Cascade Books, 2016.

———. *Scripture as Communication: Introducing Biblical Hermeneutics*. Grand Rapids: Baker Academic, 2007.

Brown, William P. *The Seven Pillars of Creation: The Bible, Science, and the Ecology of Wonder*. Oxford: Oxford University Press, 2010.

———. "Theological Interpretation: A Proposal." In *Method Matters: Essays on the Interpretation of the Hebrew Bible in Honor of David L. Petersen*, edited by Joel M. LeMon and Kent Harold Richards, 387–405. Society of Biblical Literature: Resources for Biblical Study 56. Atlanta: Society of Biblical Literature, 2009.

Broyles, Craig C. "Interpreting the Old Testament: Principles and Steps." In *Interpreting the Old Testament: A Guide for Exegesis*, edited by Craig C. Broyles, 13–62. Grand Rapids: Baker Academic, 2001.

———. "Psalms Concerning the Liturgies of Temple Entry." In *The Book of Psalms: Composition and Reception*, edited by Peter W. Flint and Patrick D. Miller Jr., 248–87. Supplements to Vetus Testamentum 99. Leiden: Brill, 2005.

———. "Traditions, Intertextuality, and Canon." In *Interpreting the Old Testament: A Guide for Exegesis*, edited by Craig C. Broyles, 157–175. Grand Rapids: Baker Academic, 2001.

Bruckner, James K. *Implied Law in the Abraham Narrative: A Literary and Theological Analysis*. Journal for the Study of Old Testament: Supplement Series 335. London: Sheffield Academic Press, 2001.

Brueggemann, Walter. *First and Second Samuel*. Interpretation: A Bible Commentary for Teaching and Preaching. Louisville, KY: John Knox, 1990.

Brueggemann, Walter, and William H. Bellinger Jr. *Psalms*. New Cambridge Bible Commentary. New York: Cambridge University Press, 2014.

Bullock, C. H. "Ethics." In *Dictionary of the Old Testament: Wisdom, Poetry & Writings: A Compendium of Contemporary Biblical Scholarship*, edited by Tremper Longman III and Peter Enns, 193–200. Downers Grove, IL: InterVarsity, 2008.

Burkitt, F. C. "Micah 6 and 7 a Northern Prophecy." *Journal of Biblical Literature* 45, no. 1/2 (1926): 159–61.

Busenitz, Irvin A. "Introduction to the Biblical Covenants: The Noahic Covenant and the Priestly Covenant." *Master's Seminary Journal* 10, no. 2 (1999): 173–189.

Carmichael, Calum M. *Law and Narrative in the Bible: The Evidence of the Deuteronomic Laws and the Decalogue.* Eugene, OR: Wipf and Stock, 2008.

———. *The Origins of Biblical Law: The Decalogues and the Book of the Covenant.* Ithaca, NY: Cornell University Press, 1992.

———. *The Spirit of Biblical Law.* Athens, GA: University of Georgia Press, 1996.

Carr, David M. *The Formation of the Hebrew Bible: A New Reconstruction.* Oxford: Oxford University Press, 2011.

Carson, D. A. "Systematic Theology and Biblical Theology." In *New Dictionary of Biblical Theology: Exploring the Unity of Scripture*, edited by T. Desmond Alexander and Brian S. Rosner, 89–104. Downers Grove, IL: InterVarsity, 2000.

Cartledge, Tony W. *1 and 2 Samuel.* Smith and Helwys Bible Commentary 7. Macon, GA: Smyth and Helwys, 2001.

Cate, Robert L. *An Introduction to the Old Testament and Its Study.* Nashville, TN: Broadman, 1987.

Chae, Young S. *Jesus as the Eschatological Davidic Shepherd: Studies in the Old Testament, Second Temple Judaism, and in the Gospel of Matthew.* Wissenschaftliche Untersuchungen zum Neuen Testament 216. Tübingen: Mohr Siebeck, 2006.

Chalmers, Aaron. *Exploring the Religion of Ancient Israel: Prophet, Priest, Sage and People.* Downers Grove, IL: InterVarsity, 2013.

———. *Interpreting the Prophets: Reading, Understanding and Preaching from the Worlds of the Prophets.* Downers Grove, IL: InterVarsity, 2015.

Chisholm, Robert B., Jr. "Divine Uncertainty and Discovery: Anatomy of an Anthromorphism." *Bibliotheca Sacra* 164, no. 653 (2007): 3–20.

———. *Handbook on the Prophets: Isaiah, Jeremiah, Lamentations, Ezekiel, Daniel, Minor Prophets.* Grand Rapids: Baker Academic, 2002.

———. *Interpreting the Minor Prophets.* Grand Rapids: Zondervan, 1990.

———. "'To Whom Shall You Compare Me?' Yahweh's Polemic against Baal and Babylonian Idol-Gods in Prophetic Literature." In *Christianity and the Religions: A Biblical Theology of World Religions*, edited by Edward Rommen and Harold Netland, 56–71. Evangelical Missiological Society Series 2. Pasadena, CA: William Carey Library, 1995.

Chou, Abner. *The Hermeneutics of the Biblical Writers: Learning to Interpret Scripture from the Prophets and Apostles.* Grand Rapids: Kregel, 2018.

Ciampa, Roy E. "The History of Redemption." In *Central Themes in Biblical Theology: Mapping Unity in Diversity*, edited by Scott J. Hafemann and Paul R. House, 254–308. Grand Rapids: Baker, 2007.

Clark, David J., and Norm Mundhenk. *A Translator's Handbook on the Books of Obadiah and Micah.* New York: United Bible Societies, 1982.

Clayton, Jay, and Eric Rothstein, eds. *Influence and Intertextuality in Literary History*. Contraversions: Jews and Other Differences. Madison, WI: University of Wisconsin Press, 1991.

Clements, R. E. *Abraham and David: Genesis XV and Its Meaning for Israelite Tradition*. Studies in Biblical Theology: Second Series 5. Naperville, IL: Allenson, 1967.

———. *God and Temple: The Idea of the Divine Presence in Ancient Israel*. Eugene, OR: Fortress, 1965.

———. *Prophecy and Covenant*. Studies in Biblical Theology: First Series 43. London: SCM, 1965.

———. *Prophecy and Tradition*. Atlanta: John Knox, 1975.

Clifford, Richard J. *The Cosmic Mountain in Canaan and the Old Testament*. Harvard Semitic Monographs 4. Cambridge, MA: Harvard University Press, 1972.

———. "The Roots of Apocalypticism in Near Eastern Myth." In *The Continuum History of Apocalypticism*, edited by Bernard McGinn, John J. Collins, and Stephen J. Stein, 3–38. New York: Continuum, 2003.

Cogan, Mordechai. *Imperialism and Religion: Assyria, Judah, and Israel in the Eighth and Seventh Centuries BCE*. Society of Biblical Literature: Monograph Series 19. Missoula, MT: Scholars Press, 1974.

Cohn, Robert L. *The Shape of Sacred Space: Four Biblical Studies*. Edited by James O. Duke. American Academy of Religion Studies in Religion 23. Chico, CA: Scholars Press, 1981.

Collins, Adela Yarbro, and John Joseph Collins. *King and Messiah as Son of God: Divine, Human, and Angelic Messianic Figures in Biblical and Related Literature*. Grand Rapids: Eerdmans, 2008.

Crenshaw, James L. "Wedōrēk ʿal-Bāmŏtê ʾāreṣ." *Catholic Biblical Quarterly* 34, no. 1 (1972): 39–53.

Cross, Frank Moore. *Canaanite Myth and Hebrew Epic: Essays in the History of the Religion of Israel*. Cambridge, MA: Harvard University Press, 1973.

———. *From Epic to Canon: History and Literature in Ancient Israel*. Baltimore, MD: Johns Hopkins University Press, 2000.

Cruz, Juan. *"Who Is Like Yahweh?": A Study of Divine Metaphors in the Book of Micah*. Forschungen zur Religion und Literatur des Alten und Neuen Testaments 263. Göttingen: Vandenhoeck and Ruprecht, 2016.

Cuffey, Kenneth H. *The Literary Coherence of the Book of Micah: Remnant, Restoration, and Promise*. Library of Biblical Studies/Old Testament 611. New York: T and T Clark, 2015.

Culler, Jonathan D. *The Pursuit of Signs: Semiotics, Literature, Deconstruction*. Ithaca, NY: Cornell University Press, 2002.

Dalley, Stephanie, ed. *Myths from Mesopotamia: Creation, the Flood, Gilgamesh, and Others*. Rev. ed. Oxford: Oxford University Press, 2000.

Daniels, Dwight R. "Is There a 'Prophetic Lawsuit' Genre." *Zeitschrift für die alttestamentliche Wissenschaft* 99, no. 3 (1987): 339–360.

Daube, David. *The Exodus Pattern in the Bible*. All Souls Studies 2. London: Faber and Faber, 1963.

Davidson, Jo Ann. "The Decalogue Predates Mount Sinai: Indicators from the Book of Genesis." *Journal of the Adventist Theological Society* 19, no. 1/2 (2008): 61–81.

Davidson, Richard M. "The Divine Covenant Lawsuit Motif in Canonical Perspective." *Journal of the Adventist Theological Society* 21, no. 1–2 (2010): 45–84.

Davies, Eryl W. *Prophecy and Ethics: Isaiah and the Ethical Traditions of Israel*. Journal for the Study of the Old Testament: Supplement Series 16. Sheffield: Sheffield Academic Press, 1981.

———. "Walking in God's Ways: The Concept of Imitatio Dei in the Old Testament." In *In Search of True Wisdom: Essays in Old Testament Interpretation in Honour of Ronald E. Clements*, edited by Edward Ball, 99–115. Journal for the Study of the Old Testament: Supplement Series 300. Sheffield: Sheffield Academic, 1999.

Day, John. "Inner-Biblical Interpretation in the Prophets." In *"The Place Is Too Small for Us": The Israelite Prophets in Recent Scholarship*, edited by R. P. Gordon, 230–246. Sources for Biblical and Theological Study 5. Winona Lake, IN: Eisenbrauns, 1995.

Dekker, Jaap. *Zion's Rock-Solid Foundations: An Exegetical Study of the Zion Text in Isaiah 28:16*. Oudtestamentische Studiën 54. Leiden: Brill, 2007.

Dempsey, Carol J. *Amos, Hosea, Micah, Nahum, Zephaniah, Habakkuk*. Vol. 15 of The New Collegeville Bible Commentary: Old Testament. Collegeville, MN: Liturgical, 2013.

Dempster, Stephen G. *Dominion and Dynasty: A Theology of the Hebrew Bible*. New Studies in Biblical Theology 15. Downers Grove, IL: InterVarsity, 2014.

———. *Micah*. Two Horizons Old Testament Commentary. Grand Rapids: Eerdmans, 2017.

DeVries, LaMoine F. *Cities of the Biblical World: An Introduction to the Archaeology, Geography, and History of Biblical Sites*. Eugene, OR: Wipf and Stock, 2006.

Dick, Michael Brennan. *Reading the Old Testament: An Inductive Introduction*. Peabody, MA: Hendrickson, 2008.

Dobbs-Allsopp, F. W. *Weep, O Daughter of Zion: A Study of the City-Lament Genre in the Hebrew Bible*. Biblica et Orientalia 44. Roma: Editrice Pontificio Istituto Biblico, 1993.

Dow, Lois K. Fuller. *Images of Zion: Biblical Antecedents for the New Jerusalem*. New Testament Monographs 26. Sheffield: Sheffield Phoenix, 2010.

Dumbrell, William J. *The Faith of Israel: A Theological Survey of the Old Testament*. 2nd ed. Grand Rapids: Baker, 2002.

Dunn, Steven. *The Sanctuary in the Psalms: Exploring the Paradox of God's Transcendence and Immanence*. Lanham, MD: Lexington Books, 2016.

Durant, Karen Elizabeth. "Imitation of God as a Principle for Ethics Today: A Study of Selected Psalms." PhD diss., University of Birmingham, 2010.

Eaton, J. H. *Kingship and the Psalms*. Studies in Biblical Theology: Second Series 32. London: SCM, 1976.

Eiler, David Lemoine. "The Origin and History of Zion as a Theological Symbol in Ancient Israel." PhD diss., Princeton Theological Seminary, 1968.

Elliger, Karl. "Die Heimat Des Propheten Micha." In *Kleine Schriften Zum Alten Testament; Zu Seinem 65ten Geburtstag*, 9–71. Theologische Bücherei 3. Munich: Kaiser, 1966.

Engnell, Ivan. *Studies in Divine Kingship in the Ancient Near East*. Oxford: Basil Blackwell, 1967.

Fensham, F. Charles. "Clauses of Protection in Hittite Vassal-Treaties and the Old Testament." *Vetus Testamentum* 13, no. 2 (1963): 133–43.

———. "Widow, Orphan, and the Poor in Ancient Near Eastern Legal and Wisdom Literature." In *Essential Papers on Israel and the Ancient Near East*, edited by Frederick E. Greenspahn, 176–192. New York: New York University Press, 1991.

Fewell, Danna Nolan. "Introduction." In *Reading between Texts: Intertextuality and the Hebrew Bible*, edited by Danna Nolan Fewell, 11–20. Literary Currents in Biblical Interpretation. Louisville, KY: Westminster John Knox, 1992.

———, ed. *Reading Between Texts: Intertextuality and the Hebrew Bible*. Literary Currents in Biblical Interpretation. Louisville, KY: Westminster John Knox, 1992.

Fishbane, Michael A. *Biblical Interpretation in Ancient Israel*. Oxford: Clarendon, 1985.

Fitzgerald, Aloysius. *The Lord of the East Wind*. Catholic Biblical Quarterly Monograph Series 34. Washington: Catholic Biblical Association of America, 2002.

Fohrer, Georg. "Micha 1." In *Das Ferne Und Nahe Wort: Festschrift Leonard Rost*, 65–88. Beihefte zur Zeitschrift für die alttestamentliche Wissenschaft 105. Berlin: A. Töpelmann, 1967.

———. "Remarks on Modern Interpretation of the Prophets." *Journal of Biblical Literature* 80, no. 4 (1961): 309–19.

Foster, Benjamin R. *From Distant Days: Myths, Tales, and Poetry of Ancient Mesopotamia*. Bethesda, MD: Capital Decisions, 1995.

Fox, R. Michael, ed. *Reverberations of the Exodus in Scripture*. Eugene, OR: Wipf and Stock, 2014.

Frankfort, Henri. *Kingship and the Gods: A Study of Ancient Near Eastern Religion as the Integration of Society and Nature*. Chicago: University of Chicago Press, 1948.

Freedman, David Noel. "Divine Commitment and Human Obligation, the Covenant Theme." *Interpretation* 18, no. 4 (1964): 419–31.

Freedman, David Noel, and David Miano. "People of the New Covenant." In *The Concept of the Covenant in the Second Temple Period*, edited by Stanley E. Porter and Jacqueline C. R. De Roo, 7–26. Supplements to the Journal for the Study of Judaism 72. Leiden: Brill, 2003.

Fretheim, Terence E. "The Book of Genesis." In *General and Old Testament Articles, Genesis, Exodus, Leviticus*, 321–674. Vol 1 of *New Interpreter's Bible: A Commentary in Twelve Volumes*. Nashville, TN: Abingdon, 1994.

———. *God and World in the Old Testament: A Relational Theology of Creation*. Nashville, TN: Abingdon, 2005.

———. "Suffering God and Sovereign God in Exodus: A Collision of Images." *Horizons in Biblical Theology* 11, no. 2 (1989): 31–56.

Friebel, Kelvin G. "A Hermeneutical Paradigm for Interpreting Prophetic Sign-Actions." *Didaskalia* 12, no. 2 (2001): 25–45.

Fritz, Volkmar. "Das Wort Gegen Samaria Mi 1:2–7." *Zeitschrift für die alttestamentliche Wissenschaft* 86, no. 3 (1974): 316–31.

Fuhr, Richard Alan, Jr., and Gary E. Yates. *The Message of the Twelve: Hearing the Voice of the Minor Prophets*. Nashville, TN: Broadman and Holman Academic, 2016.

Furlong, Anne. "Relevance Theory and Literary Interpretation." PhD diss., University College of London, 1995.

Gakuru, Griphus. *An Inner Biblical Exegetical Study of the Davidic Covenant and the Dynastic Oracle*. Mellen Biblical Press 58. Lewiston, NY: Mellen, 2000.

Gentry, Peter J., and Stephen J. Wellum. *Kingdom through Covenant: A Biblical Theological Understanding of the Covenants*. Wheaton, IL: Crossway, 2012.

Geoghegan, Jeffrey C. "The Abrahamic Passover." In *Le-David Maskil: A Birthday Tribute for David Noel Freedman*, edited by Richard Elliott Friedman and William Henry Propp, 47–62. Biblical and Judaic Studies from the University of California, San Diego 9. Winona Lake, IN: Eisenbrauns, 2004.

———. "The Exodus of Abraham." *Bible Review* 21, no. 2 (2005): 16–25, 43–46.

George, A. R. *Babylonian Topographical Texts*. Orientalia Lovaniensia Analecta 40. Leuven: Peeters, 1992.

Gesenius, Friedrich H. W. *Gesenius's Hebrew and Chaldee Lexicon to the Old Testament*. Translated by Samuel Prideaux Tregelles. Bellingham, WA: Logos Bible Software, 2003.

Gibson, John C. L. *Language and Imagery in the Old Testament*. Peabody, MA: Hendrickson, 1998.

Gibson, McGuire, and Robert D. Biggs, eds. *The Organization of Power: Aspects of Bureaucracy in the Ancient Near East*. Studies in Ancient Oriental Civilization 46. Chicago: Oriental Institute of the University of Chicago, 1987.

Gilchrist, Paul R. "יחל." In *Theological Wordbook of the Old Testament*, edited by R. Laird Harris, Gleason L. Archer Jr., and Bruce K. Waltke, 373–374. Chicago: Moody, 1997.

———. "יער." In *Theological Wordbook of the Old Testament*, edited by R. Laird Harris, Gleason L. Archer Jr., and Bruce K. Waltke, 391. Rev. ed. Chicago: Moody, 1980.

Gileadi, Avraham. "The Davidic Covenant: A Theological Basis for Corporate Protection." In *Israel's Apostasy and Restoration: Essays in Honor of Roland K. Harrison*, edited by Avraham Gileadi, 157–163. Grand Rapids: Baker, 1988.

Goldingay, John. *Israel's Faith*. Vol. 2 of *Old Testament Theology*. Downers Grove, IL: InterVarsity, 2010.

———. *Israel's Gospel*. Vol. 1 of *Old Testament Theology*. Downers Grove, IL: InterVarsity, 2003.

———. *Theological Diversity and the Authority of the Old Testament*. Grand Rapids: Eerdmans, 1987.

———. *The Theology of the Book of Isaiah*. Downers Grove, IL: InterVarsity, 2014.

Gordon, Cyrus H., and Gary A. Rendsburg. *The Bible and the Ancient Near East*. New York: Norton, 1997.

Gowan, Donald E. *Eschatology in the Old Testament*. 2nd ed. London: T and T Clark, 2000.

———. *Theology of the Prophetic Books: The Death and Resurrection of Israel*. Louisville, KY: Westminster, 1998.

Grabbe, Lester L. "Ethnic Groups in Jerusalem." In *Jerusalem in Ancient History and Tradition*, edited by Thomas L. Thompson, 145–163. Journal for the Study of Old Testament: Supplement Series 381. London: T and T Clark, 2003.

Grant, Jamie A. "The Psalms and the King." In *Interpreting the Psalms: Issues and Approaches*, edited by Philip S. Johnston and David G. Firth, 101–118. Downers Grove, IL: InterVarsity, 2013.

Gray, John. *The Biblical Doctrine of the Reign of God*. London: T and T Clark, 1979.

Green, Alberto R. W. *The Storm-God in the Ancient Near East*. Edited by William Henry Propp. Biblical and Judaic Studies from the University of California, San Diego 8. Winona Lake, IN: Eisenbrauns, 2003.

Greenstein, Edward L. "Lamentation and Lament in the Hebrew Bible." In *The Oxford Handbook of the Elegy*, edited by Karen Weisman, 67–84. Oxford Handbooks. Oxford: Oxford University Press, 2010.

Gregory, Bradley C. "The Postexilic Exile in Third Isaiah: Isaiah 61:1–3 in Light of Second Temple Hermeneutics." *Journal of Biblical Literature* 126, no. 3 (2007): 475–496.

Grisanti, Michael A. "The Davidic Covenant." *Master's Seminary Journal* 10, no. 2 (1999): 233–250.

Groves, J. A. "Zion Traditions." In *Dictionary of the Old Testament: Historical Books*, edited by Bill T. Arnold and H. G. M. Williamson, 1019–1025. Downers Grove, IL: InterVarsity, 2005.

Grüneberg, Keith N. *Abraham, Blessing and the Nations: A Philological and Exegetical Study of Genesis 12:3 in Its Narrative Context*. Berlin: Walter de Gruyter, 2003.

Gudme, Anne Katrine de Hemmer, and Ingrid Hjelm. "Introduction." In *Myths of Exile: History and Metaphor in the Hebrew Bible*, edited by Anne Katrine de Hemmer Gudme and Ingrid Hjelm, 1–10. London: Routledge, 2015.

Gunkel, Hermann. "The Close of Micah: A Prophetical Liturgy." In *What Remains of the Old Testament and Other Essays*, translated by Alexander K. Dallas, 115–150. London: Allen and Unwin, 1928.

Habel, Norman. "The Silence of the Lands: The Ecojustice Implications of Ezekiel's Judgment Oracles." In *Ezekiel's Hierarchical World: Wrestling with a Tiered Reality*, edited by Stephen L. Cook and Corrine Patton, 127–140. Society of Biblical Literature: Symposium Series 31. Atlanta: Society of Biblical Literature, 2004.

Hagstrom, David Gerald. *The Coherence of the Book of Micah: A Literary Analysis*. Society of Biblical Literature Dissertation Series 89. Atlanta: Scholars Press, 1988.

Hahn, Scott. *Kinship by Covenant: A Canonical Approach to the Fulfillment of God's Saving Promises*. Anchor Yale Bible Reference Library. New Haven, CT: Yale University Press, 2009.

Hallo, William W., ed. *The Context of Scripture*, 3 vols. Leiden: Brill, 1997–2002.

Hamilton, James M., Jr. *God's Glory in Salvation through Judgment: A Biblical Theology*. Wheaton, IL: Crossway, 2010.

Hamilton, Victor P. *Handbook on the Historical Books: Joshua, Judges, Ruth, Samuel, Kings, Chronicles, Ezra-Nehemiah, Esther*. Grand Rapids: Baker Academic, 2008.

Handy, Lowell K. *Among the Host of Heaven: The Syro-Palestinian Pantheon as Bureaucracy*. Winona Lake, IN: Eisenbrauns, 1994.

Harrison, R. K. *Introduction to the Old Testament: With a Comprehensive Review of Old Testament Studies and a Special Supplement on the Apocrypha*. Grand Rapids: Eerdmans, 1969.

Hauer, Christian E. "Jerusalem, the Stronghold and Rephaim." *Catholic Biblical Quarterly* 32, no. 4 (1970): 571–578.

Hayes, John H. "The Tradition of Zion's Inviolability." *Journal of Biblical Literature* 82, no. 4 (1963): 419–426.

Hays, J. Daniel. *The Message of the Prophets: A Survey of the Prophetic and Apocalyptic Books of the Old Testament*. Grand Rapids: Zondervan, 2010.

Hays, Richard B. *The Conversion of the Imagination: Paul as Interpreter of Israel's Scripture*. Grand Rapids: Eerdmans, 2005.

———. *Echoes of Scripture in the Letters of Paul*. New Haven: Yale University Press, 1989.

Heideman, Daniel MacArthur. "Promissory and Obligatory Features of the Davidic Covenant in Samuel-Kings." PhD diss., Dallas Theological Seminary, 2015.

Heim, K. M. "Kings and Kingship." In *Dictionary of the Old Testament: Historical Books*, edited by Bill T. Arnold and H. G. M. Williamson, 610–623. Downers Grove, IL: InterVarsity, 2005.

Herdner, Andrée, ed. *Corpus des tablettes en cunéiformes alphabétiques découvertes à Ras Shamra-Ugarit de 1929 à 1939*. Paris: Geuthner, 1963.

Hess, Richard S., and Gordon J. Wenham, eds. *Zion, City of Our God*. Grand Rapids: Eerdmans, 1999.

Hill, Harriet. *The Bible at Cultural Crossroads: From Translation to Communication*. Manchester: Saint Jerome, 2006.

Hillers, Delbert R. *Micah: A Commentary on the Book of the Prophet Micah*. Edited by Paul D. Hanson and Loren R. Fisher. Hermeneia: A Critical and Historical Commentary on the Bible. Philadelphia: Fortress, 1984.

———. *Treaty-Curses and the Old Testament Prophets*. Biblica et Orientalia 16. Rome: Pontifical Biblical Institute, 1964.

Hjelm, Ingrid. *Jerusalem's Rise to Sovereignty: Zion and Gerizim in Competition*. Library of Biblical Studies/Old Testament 404. London: T and T Clark, 2004.

Holloway, Steven Winford. *Aššur Is King! Aššur Is King!: Religion in the Exercise of Power in the Neo-Assyrian Empire*. Culture and History of the Ancient Near East 10. Leiden: Brill, 2002.

Hoppe, Leslie J. *The Holy City: Jerusalem in the Theology of the Old Testament*. Collegeville, MN: Liturgical, 2000.

Hossfeld, Frank-Lothar, and Erich Zenger. *Psalms 2: A Commentary on Psalms 51–100*. Translated by Linda M. Maloney. Hermenia: A Critical and Historical Commentary on the Bible. Minneapolis: Fortress, 2005.

House, Paul R. *Old Testament Theology*. Downers Grove, IL: InterVarsity, 1998.

———. *1, 2 Kings*. Vol. 8 of *The New American Commentary*. Nashville, TN: Broadman and Holman, 1995.

Howard, David M., Jr. *An Introduction to the Old Testament Historical Books*. Chicago: Moody, 2007.

———. *The Structure of Psalms 93–100*. Edited by William H. Propp. Biblical and Judaic Studies from the University of California, San Diego 5. Winona Lake, IN: Eisenbrauns, 1997.

Hugenberger, Gordon Paul. *Marriage as a Covenant: A Study of Biblical Law and Ethics Governing Marriage, Developed from the Perspective of Malachi*. Supplements to Vetus Testamentum 52. Leiden: Brill, 1994.

Hughes, Julie A. *Scriptural Allusions and Exegesis in the Hodayot*. Studies on the Texts of the Desert of Judah 59. Leiden: Brill, 2006.

Hultgren, Stephen. *From the Damascus Covenant to the Covenant of the Community: Literary, Historical, and Theological Studies in the Dead Sea Scrolls*. Studies on the Texts of the Desert of Judah 66. Leiden: Brill, 2007.

Humphreys, W. Lee. *Crisis and Story: An Introduction to the Old Testament*. Palo Alto, CA: Mayfield, 1979.

Hundley, Michael B. *Gods in Dwellings: Temples and Divine Presence in the Ancient Near East*. Society of Biblical Literature: Writings from the Ancient World Supplement Series 3. Atlanta: Society of Biblical Literature, 2013.

Hurowitz, Victor. *I Have Built You an Exalted House: Temple Building in the Bible in the Light of Mesopotamian and North-West Semitic Writings*. Continuum, 1992.

Hutton, Jeremy M. "Isaiah 51:9–11 and the Rhetorical Appropriation and Subversion of Hostile Theologies." *Journal of Biblical Literature* 126, no. 2 (2007): 271–303.

Hwang, Sunwoo. *The Hope for the Restoration of the Davidic Kingdom in the Light of the Davidic Covenant in Chronicles*. Lewiston, NY: Mellen, 2014.

Isaac, Munther. *From Land to Lands; from Eden to the Renewed Earth: A Christ-Centred Biblical Theology of the Promised Land*. Carlisle: Langham, 2015.

Jacobs, Mignon R. *The Conceptual Coherence of the Book of Micah*. Journal for the Study of the Old Testament: Supplement Series 322. Sheffield: Sheffield Academic, 2001.

Jacobsen, Thorkild. *The Treasures of Darkness: A History of Mesopotamian Religion*. New Haven, CT: Yale University Press, 1976.

Jael, Roy R. "Sociorhetorical Intertexture." In *Exploring Intertextuality: Diverse Strategies for New Testament Interpretation of Texts*, edited by B. J. Oropeza and Steve Moyise, 151–164. Eugene, OR: Cascade Books, 2016.

Janzen, J. Gerald. *Abraham and All the Families of the Earth: A Commentary on the Book of Genesis 12–50*. International Theological Commentary. Grand Rapids: Eerdmans, 1993.

Jauhiainen, Marko. "'Behold, I Am Coming': The Use of Zechariah in Revelation." *Tyndale Bulletin* 56, no. 1 (2005): 157–60.

———. *The Use of Zechariah in Revelation*. Wissenschaftliche Untersuchungen zum Neuen Testament 199. Tubingen: Mohr Siebeck, 2005.

Jenner, K. A. D. "Jerusalem, Zion and the Unique Servant of Yhwh in the New Heaven and the New Earth: A Study on Recovering Identity versus Lamenting Faded Glory (Isaiah 1–5 and 65–66)." In *"Enlarge the Site of Your Tent": The City as Unifying Theme in Isaiah: The Isaiah Workshop – De Jesaja Werkplaats*, edited by Archibald L. H. M. van Wieringen and Annemarieke van der Woude, 169–90. Old Testament Studies 58. Leiden: Brill, 2011.

Jenson, Philip Peter. *Obadiah, Jonah, Micah: A Theological Commentary*. New York: T and T Clark, 2008.

Jeppesen, Knud. "How the Book of Micah Lost Its Integrity: Outline of the History of the Criticism of the Book of Micah with Emphasis on the 19th Cent." *Studia Theologica* 33, no. 2 (1979): 101–31.

Jin, Ezra. *Back to Jerusalem with All Nations: A Biblical Foundation*. Eugene, OR: Wipf and Stock, 2016.

Jipp, Joshua W. *Christ Is King: Paul's Royal Ideology*. Minneapolis: Fortress, 2015.

Jobling, David. *1 Samuel*. Edited by David W. Cotter. Berit Olam: Studies in Hebrew Narrative and Poetry. Collegeville, MN: Liturgical, 1998.

Jodłowiec, Maria. *The Challenges of Explicit and Implicit Communication: A Relevance-Theoretic Approach*. Text-Meaning-Context: Cracow Studies in English Language, Literature and Culture 11. Frankfurt: Peter Lang, 2015.

Johnston, Gordon H. "A Critical Evaluation of Moshe Weinfeld's Approach to the Davidic Covenant in the Light of Ancient Near Eastern Royal Grants: What Did He Get Right and What Did He Get Wrong?" Paper presented at the National Meeting of the Evangelical Theological Society, San Francisco, 2011.

———. "The Oven and Torch Passing between the Pieces (Gen 15:17): Unilateral Covenant Ritual or Prophetic Symbol Dream?" Paper presented at the Southwest Regional Meeting of the Evangelical Theological Society, New Orleans, 2005.

———. "The 'Unconditional' and 'Conditional' Passages in the Abrahamic Covenant in the Light of Ancient Near Eastern Royal Land Grants and Grant Treaties." Paper presented at the National Meeting of the Society of Biblical Literature, Boston, 2008.

Joosten, Jan. "YHWH's Farewell to Northern Israel: (Micah 6, 1-8)." *Zeitschrift für die alttestamentliche Wissenschaft* 125, no. 3 (2013): 448–62.

Joüon, Paul, and T. Muraoka. *A Grammar of Biblical Hebrew*. Rev. ed. Subsidia Biblica 27. Rome: Editrice Pontificio Istituto biblico, 2006.

Juvan, Marko. *History and Poetics of Intertextuality*. Translated by Timothy Pogačar. Comparative Cultural Studies. West Lafayette, IN: Purdue University Press, 2008.

Kaiser, Walter C., Jr. "Images for Today: The Torah Speaks Today." In *Studies in Old Testament Theology: Historical and Contemporary Images of God and God's*

People, edited by Robert L. Hubbard, Robert K. Johnston, and Robert P. Meye, 117–132. Dallas: Word, 1992.

———. *The Messiah in the Old Testament*. Studies in Old Testament Biblical Theology. Grand Rapids: Zondervan, 1995.

———. *Toward Rediscovering the Old Testament: Biblical Exegesis for Preaching and Teaching*. Grand Rapids: Baker Books, 1981.

Kalluveettil, Paul. *Declaration and Covenant: A Comprehensive Review of Covenant Formulae from the Old Testament and the Ancient Near East*. Analecta Biblica 88. Rome: Biblical Institute Press, 1982.

Kaminski, Carol M. *From Noah to Israel: Realization of the Primaeval Blessing After the Flood*. New York: T and T Clark, 2005.

———. *Was Noah Good? Finding Favour in the Flood Narrative*. Library of Hebrew Bible/Old Testament Studies. New York: T and T Clark, 2014.

Kasari, Petri. *Nathan's Promise in 2 Samuel 7 and Related Texts*. Finnish Exegetical Society 97. Helsinki: Finnish Exegetical Society, 2009.

Kautzsch, Emil, ed. *Gesenius' Hebrew Grammar*. Translated by Arther E. Cowley. 2nd ed. Oxford:Clarendon, 1910.

Keel, Othmar. *The Symbolism of the Biblical World: Ancient Near Eastern Iconography and the Book of Psalms*. Translated by Timothy J. Hallett. Winona Lake, IN: Eisenbrauns, 1997.

Keil, Carl Friedrich, and Franz Delitzsch. *The Twelve Minor Prophets*. Vol. 1. Clark's Foreign Theological Library: Fourth Series 17. Edinburgh: T and T Clark, 1871.

Kelly, Joseph Ryan. "Intertextuality and Allusion in the Study of the Hebrew Bible." PhD diss., Southern Baptist Theological Seminary, 2014.

Kim, Hyun Chul Paul. "An Intertextual Reading of 'A Crushed Reed' and 'A Dim Wick' in Isaiah 42.3." *Journal for the Study of the Old Testament* 83 (1999): 113–24.

King, Philip J. *Amos, Hosea, Micah: An Archaeological Commentary*. Philadelphia: Westminster, 1988.

Kitchen, K. A., and Paul Lawrence. *Treaty, Law and Covenant in the Ancient Near East*. 3 vols. Wiesbaden: Harrassowitz, 2012.

Kline, Jonathan G. *Allusive Soundplay in the Hebrew Bible*. Ancient Israel and Its Literature 28. Atlanta: Society of Biblical Literature, 2016.

Kline, Meredith G. *Treaty of the Great King: The Covenant Structure of Deuteronomy: Studies and Commentary*. Grand Rapids: Eerdmans, 1963.

Klingbeil, Martin. *Yahweh Fighting from Heaven: God as Warrior and as God of Heaven in the Hebrew Psalter and Ancient Near Eastern Iconography*. Orbis Biblicus et Orientalis 169. Göttingen: Vandenhoeck and Ruprecht, 1999.

Klingler, David Ryan. "Validity in the Identification and Interpretation of a Literary Allusion in the Hebrew Bible." PhD diss., Dallas Theological Seminary, 2010.

Klink, Edward W., III, and Darian R. Lockett. *Understanding Biblical Theology: A Comparison of Theory and Practice*. Grand Rapids: Zondervan, 2012.

Knight, Douglas A., ed. *Tradition and Theology in the Old Testament*. Philadelphia: Fortress, 1977.

Knoppers, Gary N. "Ancient Near Eastern Royal Grants and the Davidic Covenant: A Parallel?" *Journal of the American Oriental Society* 116, no. 4 (1996): 670–97.

Koehler, L., W. Baumgartner, and J. J. Stamm, *The Hebrew and Aramaic Lexicon of the Old Testament*. Translated and edited under the supervision of M. E. J. Richardson. 4 vols. Leiden, 1994–1999.

Köhler, Ludwig. *Old Testament Theology*. Translated by A. S. Todd. Library of Theological Translation. Philadelphia: Westminster, 1957.

Kraus, Hans-Joachim. *Theology of the Psalms*. Translated by Keith Crim. Continental Commentary. Minneapolis: Fortress, 1992.

Laato, Antti. "Psalm 132 and the Development of the Jerusalemite/Israelite Royal Ideology." *Catholic Biblical Quarterly* 54, no. 1 (1992): 49–66.

———. "Second Samuel 7 and Ancient Near Eastern Royal Ideology." *Catholic Biblical Quarterly* 59, no. 2 (1997): 244–69.

Labuschagne, C. J. *The Incomparability of Yahweh in the Old Testament*. Leiden: Brill, 1966.

Laniak, Timothy S. *Shepherds After My Own Heart: Pastoral Traditions and Leadership in the Bible*. New Studies in Biblical Theology 15. Downers Grove, IL: InterVarsity, 2006.

Leclerc, Thomas L. *Introduction to the Prophets: Their Stories, Sayings and Scrolls*. New York: Paulist, 2007.

———. *Yahweh Is Exalted in Justice: Solidarity and Conflict in Isaiah*. Minneapolis: Fortress, 2001.

Lee, Suk Yee. *An Intertextual Analysis of Zechariah 9–10: The Earlier Restoration Expectations of Second Zechariah*. Library of Hebrew Bible/Old Testament Studies 599. London: T and T Clark, 2015.

Leonard, Jeffery M. "Identifying Inner-Biblical Allusions: Psalm 78 as a Test Case." *Journal of Biblical Literature* 127, no. 2 (2008): 241–65.

Levenson, Jon D. *Creation and the Persistence of Evil: The Jewish Drama of Divine Omnipotence*. Princeton, NJ: Princeton University Press, 1994.

———. *The Death and Resurrection of the Beloved Son: The Transformation of Child Sacrifice in Judaism and Christianity*. New Haven, CT: Yale University Press, 1993.

———. *Sinai and Zion: An Entry into the Jewish Bible*. New Voices in Biblical Studies. Minneapolis: Winston, 1985.

———. "Zion Traditions." In *The Anchor Bible Dictionary*, edited by David N. Freedman, 6:1098–1102. New York: Doubleday, 1992.

L'Heureux, Conrad E. *Rank among the Canaanite Gods: El, Ba'al, and the Repha'im*. Harvard Semitic Monographs 21. Missoula, MT: Scholars Press, 1979.

Liedke, G. "יכח." In *Theological Lexicon of the Old Testament*, edited by Ernst Jenni and Claus Westermann, 542–543. Peabody, MA: Hendrickson, 1997.

Limburg, James. *Hosea-Micah*. Interpretation: A Bible Commentary for Teaching and Preaching. Louisville, KY: Westminster, 2011.

Litwa, M. David. *We Are Being Transformed: Deification in Paul's Soteriology*. Beihefte zur Zeitschrift für die neutestamentliche Wissenschaft 187. Berlin: Walter de Gruyter, 2012.

Longman, Tremper, III. "1 Sam 12:16–19: Divine Omnipotence or Covenant Curse?" *Westminster Theological Journal* 45, no. 1 (1983): 168–71.

———. "Micah." In *Evangelical Commentary of the Bible*, edited by Walter A. Elwell, 3:650–658. Baker Reference Library. Grand Rapids: Baker, 1996.

———. "Psalm 98: A divine warrior Victory Song." *Journal of the Evangelical Theological Society* 27, no. 3 (1984): 267–274.

Lucass, Shirley. *The Concept of the Messiah in the Scriptures of Judaism and Christianity*. Library of Second Temple Studies. London: T and T Clark, 2011.

Luker, Lamontte M. "Doom and Hope in Micah: The Redaction of the Oracles Attributed to an Eighth-Century Prophet." PhD diss., Vanderbilt University, 1985.

Lundbom, Jack R. *Biblical Rhetoric and Rhetorical Criticism*. Hebrew Bible Monographs 45. Sheffield: Sheffield Phoenix, 2013.

Lundquist, John M. *The Temple of Jerusalem: Past, Present, and Future*. Westport, CT: Praeger, 2008.

Lyons, Michael A. "Marking Innerbiblical Allusion in the Book of Ezekiel." *Biblica* 88, no. 2 (2007): 245–250.

Maier, Christl M. *Daughter Zion, Mother Zion: Gender, Space, and the Sacred in Ancient Israel*. Minneapolis: Fortress, 2008.

Marrs, Rick R. "'Back to the Future': Zion in the Book of Micah." In *David and Zion: Biblical Studies in Honor of J. J. M. Roberts*, edited by Bernard F. Batto and Kathryn L. Roberts, 77–96. Winona Lake, IN: Eisenbrauns, 2004.

———. "Micah and a Theological Critique of Worship." In *Worship and the Hebrew Bible: Essays in Honor of John T. Willis*, edited by M. Patrick Graham, Rick R. Marrs, and Steven L. McKenzie, 184–203. Journal for the Study of Old Testament: Supplement Series 284. Sheffield: Sheffield Academic Press, 1999.

Mathews, Kenneth A. *Genesis 1–11:26*. Vol. 1A of *The New American Commentary*. Nashville, TN: Broadman and Holman, 1996.

———. *Genesis 11:27–50:26*. Vol. 1B of *The New American Commentary*. Nashville, TN: Broadman and Holman, 2005.

Mays, James L. *Amos: A Commentary*. Old Testament Library. Philadelphia: Westminster, 1969.

———. *The Lord Reigns: A Theological Handbook to the Psalms*. Louisville, KY: Westminster John Knox, 1994.

———. *Micah: A Commentary*. Old Testament Library. Philadelphia: Westminster, 1976.

———. "The Theological Purpose of the Book of Micah." In *Beiträge zur alttestamentlichen Theologie: Festschrift für Walther Zimmerli zum 70.Geburtstag*, edited by Herbert Donner, Robert Hanhart, and Rudolf Smend, 276–287. Göttingen: Vandenhoeck and Ruprecht, 1977.

McCann, Hugh J. *Creation and the Sovereignty of God*. Indiana Series in the Philosophy of Religion. Bloomington, IN: Indiana University Press, 2012.

McCann, J. Clinton, Jr. *A Theological Introduction to the Book of Psalms: The Psalms as Torah*. Nashville, TN: Abingdon, 2011.

McCarter, P. Kyle, Jr. *I Samuel: A New Translation with Introduction, Notes, and Commentary*. Anchor Bible 8. Garden City, NY: Doubleday, 1995.

———. *II Samuel: A New Translation with Introduction, Notes, and Commentary*. Anchor Bible 9. New York: Doubleday, 1984.

McCarthy, Dennis J. *Old Testament Covenant: As Survey of Current Opinions*. Growing Points in Theology. Richmond, VA: John Knox, 1972.

———. *Treaty and Covenant: A Study in Form in the Ancient Oriental Documents and in the Old Testament*. New ed. Analecta Biblica: Investigationes scientificae in res biblicas 21A. Rome: Biblical Institute Press, 1978.

McCartney, D. G. "Ecce Homo: The Coming of the Kingdom as the Restoration of Human Vicegerency." *Westminster Theological Journal* 56, no. 1 (1994): 1–21.

McComiskey, Thomas E. *The Covenants of Promise: A Theology of the Old Testament Covenants*. Eugene, OR: Wipf and Stock, 2000.

McComiskey, Thomas E., and Tremper Longman III. "Micah." In *Daniel-Malachi*, edited by Tremper Longman III and David E. Garland, 491–552. Vol. 8 of *The Expositor's Bible Commentary*. Rev. ed. Grand Rapids: Zondervan, 2008.

McConville, Gordon. "Jerusalem in the Old Testament." In *Jerusalem Past and Present in the Purposes of God*, edited by Peter W. L. Walker, 21–51. Cambridge: Tyndale House, 1992.

McFadden, W. Robert. "Micah and the Problem of Continuities and Discontinuities in Prophecy." In *Scripture in Context II: More Essays on the Comparative Method*, edited by William W. Hallo, James C. Moyer, and Leo G. Perdue, 127–146. Winona Lake, IN: Eisenbrauns, 1983.

McKane, William. *The Book of Micah: Introduction and Commentary*. Edinburgh: T and T Clark, 1998.

McKenzie, Donald A. "Judge of Israel." *Vetus Testamentum* 17, no. 1 (1967): 118–121.

McKenzie, John L. *A Theology of the Old Testament*. Eugene, OR: Wipf and Stock, 1974.

McKenzie, Steven L. *Covenant*. Understanding Biblical Themes. St. Louis, MO: Chalice, 2000.

Mead, James K. *Biblical Theology: Issues, Methods, and Themes*. Louisville, KY: Westminster John Knox, 2007.

Mendenhall, George E. "Covenant Forms in Israelite Tradition." *Biblical Archaeologist* 17, no. 3 (1954): 50–76.

Merrill, Eugene H. *Deuteronomy*. Vol. 4 of *The New American Commentary*. Nashville, TN: Broadman and Holman, 1994.

———. *Everlasting Dominion: A Theology of the Old Testament*. Nashville, TN: Broadman and Holman, 2006.

Mettinger, Tryggve N. D. *In Search of God: The Meaning and Message of the Everlasting Names*. Translated by Frederick Cryer H. Philadelphia: Fortress, 2005.

Michelson, Marty Alan. *Reconciling Violence and Kingship: A Study of Judges and 1 Samuel*. Eugene, OR: Pickwick, 2011.

Middlemas, Jill. *The Divine Image: Prophetic Aniconic Rhetoric and Its Contribution to the Aniconism Debate*. Forschungen zum Alten Testament 2.Reihe 74. Tübingen: Mohr Siebeck, 2014.

Middleton, J. Richard. *The Liberating Image: The Imago Dei in Genesis 1*. Grand Rapids: Brazos, 2005.

Miller, Cynthia L. "Vocative Syntax in Biblical Hebrew Prose and Poetry: A Preliminary Analysis." *Journal of Semitic Studies* 55, no. 2 (2010): 347–364.

Miller, Dane Eric. "Micah and Its Literary Environment: Rhetorical Critical Case Studies." PhD diss., University of Arizona, 1991.

Miller, Geoffrey D. "Intertextuality in Old Testament Research." *Currents in Biblical Research* 9, no. 3 (2011): 283–309.

Miller, Patrick D., Jr. "The Ruler of Zion and the Hope of the Poor: Psalms 9–10 in the Context of the Psalter." In *David and Zion: Biblical Studies in Honor of J. J. M. Roberts*, edited by Bernard F. Batto and Kathryn L. Roberts, 187–97. Winona Lake, IN: Eisenbrauns, 2004.

———. *Sin and Judgment in the Prophets: A Stylistic and Theological Analysis*. Chico, CA: Scholars Press, 1982.

———. "The Sovereignty of God." In *The Hermeneutical Quest: Essays in Honor of James Luther Mays on His Sixty-Fifth Birthday*, edited by Donald G. Miller, 129–144. Eugene, OR: Wipf and Stock, 1986.

Miner, Earl. "Allusion." In *Encyclopedia of Poetry and Poetics*, edited by Alex Preminger, 18. Princeton, NJ: Princeton University Press, 1965.

Mitchell, John J. "Abram's Understanding of the Lord's Covenant." *Westminster Theological Journal* 32, no. 1 (1969): 24–48.

Monson, John M. "The Temple of Solomon: Heart of Jerusalem." In *Zion, City of Our God*, edited by Richard S. Hess and Gordon J. Wenham, 1–22. Grand Rapids: Eerdmans, 1999.

Moore, Anne. *Moving Beyond Symbol and Myth: Understanding the Kingship of God of the Hebrew Bible Through Metaphor*. Studies in Biblical Literature 99. Frankfurt: Peter Lang, 2009.

Moore, Stephen D., and Yvonne Sherwood. *The Invention of the Biblical Scholar: A Critical Manifesto*. Minneapolis: Fortress, 2011.

Morrow, William S. *An Introduction to Biblical Law*. Grand Rapids: Eerdmans, 2017.

Mullen, E. Theodore. *The Assembly of the Gods: The Divine Council in Canaanite and Early Hebrew Literature*. Harvard Semitic Monographs 24. Chico, CA: Scholars, 1986.

Na'aman, Nadav. "'The House-of-No-Shade Shall Take Away Its Tax from You' (Micah 1:11)." In *Ancient Israel's History and Historiography the First Temple Period*, 291–302. Collected Essays 3. Winona Lake, IN: Eisenbrauns, 2006.

———. "The Inscriptions of Kuntillet 'Ajrud through the Lens of Historical Research." *Ugarit-Forschungen* 43 (2011): 299–324.

———. "Sennacherib's Campaign to Judah and the Date of Lmlk Stamps." *Vetus Testamentum* 29 (1976): 61–86.

Niehaus, Jeffrey J. *Ancient Near Eastern Themes in Biblical Theology*. Grand Rapids: Kregel Academic, 2008.

———. *God at Sinai: Covenant and Theophany in the Bible and Ancient Near East*. Studies in Old Testament Biblical Theology. Grand Rapids: Zondervan, 1995.

Nogalski, James D. *The Book of the Twelve: Micah-Malachi*. Smyth and Helwys Bible Commentary. Macon, GA: Smyth and Helwys, 2011.

———. "Micah 7:8–20: A Reevaluation of the Identity of the Enemy." In *The Book of the Twelve and Beyond: Collected Essays of James D. Nogalski*, 63–81. Ancient Israel and Its Literature 29. Atlanta: Society in Biblical Literature, 2017.

Noth, Martin. *The Laws in the Pentateuch and Other Essays*. Translated by D. R. Thomas. Edinburgh: Oliver and Boyd, 1966.

O'Brien, Julia M. *Micah*. Wisdom Commentary 37. Collegeville, MN: Liturgical, 2015.

O'Brien, Mark. *Restoring the Right Relationship: The Bible on Divine Righteousness*. Hindmarsh: ATF Theology, 2014.

Oh, Abraham Sung-Ho. *Oh, That You Would Rend the Heavens and Come Down!: The Eschatological Theology of Third Isaiah (Isaiah 56–66)*. Eugene, OR: Pickwick, 2014.

Ollenburger, Ben C. *Zion: The City of the Great King; A Theological Symbol of the Jerusalem Cult*. Journal for the Study of Old Testament: Supplement Series 41. Sheffield: Sheffield Academic Press, 1987.

Ortlund, Eric. "An Intertextual Reading of the Theophany of Psalm 97." *Scandinavian Journal of the Old Testament* 20, no. 2 (2006): 273–285.

———. *Theophany and Chaoskampf: The Interpretation of Theophanic Imagery in the Baal Epic, Isaiah, and the Twelve*. Gorgias Ugaritic Studies 5. Piscataway, NJ: Gorgias, 2010.

Oshima, Takayoshi. *Babylonian Poems of Pious Sufferers: Ludlul Bel Nemeqi and the Babylonian Theodicy*. Orientalische Religionen in der Antike 14. Tübingen: Mohr Siebeck, 2015.

Owens, Daniel C. *Portraits of the Righteous in the Psalms: An Exploration of the Ethics of Book I*. Eugene, OR: Pickwick, 2013.

Paas, Stefan. *Creation and Judgement: Creation Texts in Some Eighth Century Prophets*. Leiden: Brill, 2003.

Painter, John Moss. "An Analysis of the Nature and Function of Motif in Micah." PhD diss., Southern Baptist Theological Seminary, 1997.

Parker, Simon B., ed. "The Baal Cycle." In *Ugaritic Narrative Poetry*, translated by Mark S. Smith, 81–180. Society of Biblical Literature: Writings from the Ancient World 9. Atlanta: Scholars Press, 1997.

———, ed. "Kirta." In *Ugaritic Narrative Poetry*, translated by Edward L. Greenstein, 9–48. Society of Biblical Literature: Writings from the Ancient World 9. Atlanta: Scholars Press, 1997.

Pate, C. Marvin, J. Scott Duvall, J. Daniel Hays, E. Randolph Richards, W. Dennis Tucker, and Preben Vang. *The Story of Israel: A Biblical Theology*. Downers Grove, IL: InterVarsity, 2004.

Pattemore, Stephen. "Relevance Theory, Intertextuality, and the Book of Revelation." In *Current Trends in Scripture Translation*, edited by Philip A Noss, 43–60. United Bible Society Bulletin. Ann Arbor, MI: United Bible Societies, 2003.

Patterson, Richard D. "The Widow, the Orphan, and the Poor in the Old Testament and Extra-Biblical Literature." *Bibliotheca sacra* 130, no. 519 (1973): 223–234.

Paulien, Jon. "Elusive Allusions: The Problematic Use of the Old Testament in Revelation." *Biblical Research* 33 (2005): 37–53.

Perri, Carmela. "On Alluding." *Poetics* 7 (1978): 289–307.

Perry, Peter S. "Relevance Theory and Intertextuality." In *Exploring Intertextuality: Diverse Strategies for New Testament Interpretation of Texts*, edited by B. J. Oropeza and Steve Moyise, 207–221. Eugene, OR: Cascade Books, 2016.

Petersen, Allan Rosengren. *The Royal God: Enthronement Festivals in Ancient Israel and Ugarit?* Journal for the Study of Old Testament: Supplement Series 259, Copenhagen International Seminar 5. Sheffield: Sheffield Academic, 1998.

Petersen, David L. "Eschatology (OT)." In *Anchor Yale Bible Dictionary*, edited by David Noel Freedman and Gary A. Herion, 2:575–579. New York: Doubleday, 1992.

———. *The Prophetic Literature: An Introduction*. Louisville, KY: Westminster John Knox, 2002.

Peterson, Brian Neil. *Genesis as Torah: Reading Narrative as Legal Instruction*. Eugene, OR: Cascade, 2018.

Pfeiffer, Robert Henry. "The Polemic against Idolatry in the Old Testament." *Journal of Biblical Literature* 43, no. 3–4 (1924): 229–240.

Phillips, Anthony. *Essays on Biblical Law*. Journal for the Study of the Old Testament: Supplement Series 344. Sheffield: Sheffield Academic Press, 2002.

Plett, Heinrich F. "Intertextualities." In *Intertextuality*, edited by Heinrich F. Plett, 3–29. Research in Text Theory 15. Berlin: Walter de Gruyter, 1991.

Pongratz-Leisten, Beate. *Religion and Ideology in Assyria*. Berlin: Walter de Gruyter, 2015.

Porter, Joshua Roy. *The Extended Family in the Old Testament*. London: Edutext, 1967.

Poulsen, Frederik. *Representing Zion: Judgement and Salvation in the Old Testament*. Copenhagen International Seminar. London: Routledge, 2015.

Preuss, Horst Dietrich. *Old Testament Theology*. Translated by Leo G. Perdue. Vol. 2. Old Testament Library. Louisville, KY: Westminster John Knox, 1996.

Rad, Gerhard von. *Old Testament Theology: The Theology of Israel's Prophetic Traditions*. Translated by D. M. G. Stalker. Vol. 2. New York: Harper and Row, 1965.

Rahmouni, Aïcha. *Divine Epithets in the Ugaritic Alphabetic Texts*. Translated by J. N. Ford. Handbook of Oriental Studies: The Near and Middle East 93. Leiden: Brill, 2008.

Ramsey, George W. "Speech-Forms in Hebrew Law and Prophetic Oracles." *Journal of Biblical Literature* 96, no. 1 (1977): 45–58.

Redditt, Paul L. *Introduction to the Prophets*. Grand Rapids: Eerdmans, 2008.

———. "The King in Haggai–Zechariah 1–8 and the Book of the Twelve." In *Tradition in Transition: Haggai and Zechariah 1-8 in the Trajectory of Hebrew Theology*, edited by Mark J. Boda and Michael H. Floyd, 56–82. Library of Biblical Studies/Old Testament 475. New York: T and T Clark, 2008.

Regt, L. J. de. "Discourse Implications of Rhetorical Questions in Job, Deuteronomy and the Minor Prophets." In *Literary Structure and Rhetorical Strategies in the Hebrew Bible*, edited by L. J. de Regt, Jan de Waard, and J. P. Fokkelman, 51–78. Assen: Van Gorcum, 1996.

Reimer, David J. "The Prophet Micah and Political Society." In *"Thus Speaks Ishtar of Arbela": Prophecy in Israel, Assyria, and Egypt in the Neo-Assyrian Period*, edited by Robert P. Gordon and Hans M. Barstad, 203–224. Winona Lake, IN: Eisenbrauns, 2013.

Renaud, Bernard. *La formation du Livre de Michée: Tradition et Actualisation*. Etudes bibliques. Paris: Gabalda, 1977.

Rendsburg, Gary A. "Reading David in Genesis: How We Know the Torah Was Written in the Tenth Century BCE." *Bible Review* 17, no. 1 (2001): 20–33, 46.

Rendtorff, Rolf. "'Covenant' as a Structuring Concept in Genesis and Exodus." *Journal of Biblical Literature* 108, no. 3 (1989): 385–393.

———. *The Covenant Formula: An Exegetical and Theological Investigation*. Translated by Margaret Kohl. Old Testament Studies. Edinburgh: T and T Clark, 1998.

Renz, Thomas. "The Use of the Zion Tradition in the Book of Ezekiel." In *Zion, City of Our God*, edited by Richard S. Hess and Gordon J. Wenham, 78–84. Grand Rapids: Eerdmans, 1999.

Reunions, Erin. *Changing Subjects: Gender, Nation and Future in Micah*. London: Sheffield Academic, 2001.

Revell, Ernest John. *The Designation of the Individual: Expressive Usage in Biblical Narrative*. Contributions to Biblical Exegesis and Theology 14. Kampen: Kok Pharos, 1996.

Rhoads, David, Joanna Dewey, and Donald Michie. *Mark as Story: An Introduction to the Narrative of a Gospel*. 2nd. ed. Minneapolis: Fortress, 2012.

Richard, Pablo. "Biblical Theology of Confrontation with Idols." In *The Idols of Death and the God of Life: A Theology*, edited by Pablo Richard, translated by Barbara E. Campbell and Bonnie Shepard, 3–25. Eugene, OR: Wipf and Stock, 2008.

Roberts, J. J. M. "Davidic Covenant." Edited by Bill T. Arnold and H. G. M. Williamson. *Dictionary of the Old Testament: Historical Books*. Downers Grove, IL: InterVarsity, 2011.

———. "The Davidic Origin of the Zion Tradition." *Journal of Biblical Literature* 92 (1973): 329–344.

———. "The Divine King and the Human Community in Isaiah's Vision of the Future." In *The Quest for the Kingdom of God: Studies in Honor of George E. Mendenhall*, edited by H. B. Huffmon, F. A. Spina, and Alberto Ravinell Whitney Green. Winona Lake, IN: Eisenbrauns, 1983.

———. "The Enthronement of Yhwh and David: The Abiding Theological Significance of the Kingship Language of the Psalms." *Catholic Biblical Quarterly* 64, no. 4 (2002): 675–686.

———. "Solomon's Jerusalem and the Zion Tradition." In *Jerusalem in Bible and Archaeology: The First Temple Period*, edited by Andrew G. Vaughn and Ann

E. Killebrew, 163–170. Society of Biblical Literature: Symposium Series. Atlanta: Society of Biblical Literature, 2003.

———. "Zion in the Theology of the Davidic-Solomonic Empire." In *The Bible and the Ancient Near East: Collected Essays*, 331–347. Winona Lake, IN: Eisenbrauns, 2002.

Rohland, Edzard. "Die Bedeutung der Erwählungstradition Israels für die Eschatologie der alttestamentlichen Propheten." ThD diss., University of Heidelberg, 1956.

Rooker, Mark F. *Leviticus*. Vol. 3A of *The New American Commentary*. Nashville, TN: Broadman and Holman, 2000.

Rosner, Brian S. "Biblical Theology." In *New Dictionary of Biblical Theology: Exploring the Unity and Diversity of Scripture*, edited by T. Desmond Alexander and Brian S. Rosner, 3–11. Downers Grove, IL: InterVarsity, 2000.

Routledge, Robin. "Is There A Narrative Substructure Underlying the Book of Isaiah?" *Tyndale Bulletin* 55, no. 2 (2004): 183–204.

———. *Old Testament Theology: A Thematic Approach*. Downers Grove, IL: InterVarsity, 2008.

Rowley, H. H. "Zadok and Nehushtan." *Journal of Biblical Literature* 58, no. 2 (1939): 113–141.

Rydelnik, Michael. *The Messianic Hope: Is the Hebrew Bible Really Messianic?* NAC Studies in Bible and Theology 9. Nashville, TN: Broadman and Holman, 2010.

Sæbø, Magne. "Divine Names and Epithets in Genesis 49:24b–25a: Some Methodological and Traditio-Historical Remarks." In *History and Traditions of Early Israel: Studies Presented to Eduard Nielsen*, edited by André Lemaire and Benedikt Otzen, 115–132. Supplements to Vetus Testamentum 50. Brill, 1993.

Sakenfeld, Katharine D. *The Meaning of Hesed in the Hebrew Bible*. Harvard Semitic Monographs 17. Missoula, MT: Scholars Press, 1978.

Sarna, Nahum M. "Psalm 89: A Study in Inner Biblical Exegesis." In *Biblical and Other Studies*, edited by Alexander Altmann, 29–46. Studies and Texts 1. Cambridge, MA: Harvard University Press, 1963.

Schaefer, Nancy A. "Genre Considerations for Micah 6:1–8." *Journal of Translation and Textlinguistics* 17 (2004): 18–35.

Schneider, Tammi J. *An Introduction to Ancient Mesopotamian Religion*. Grand Rapids: Eerdmans, 2011.

Schniedewind, William M. *Society and the Promise to David: The Reception History of 2 Samuel 7:1–17*. Oxford: Oxford University Press, 1999.

Scobie, Charles H. H. *The Ways of Our God: An Approach to Biblical Theology*. Grand Rapids: Eerdmans, 2003.

Segal, Alan F. *Rebecca's Children: Judaism and Christianity in the Roman World*. Cambridge, MA: Harvard University Press, 1986.

Seow, C. L. "The Rule of God in the Book of Daniel." In *David and Zion: Biblical Studies in Honor of J. J. M. Roberts*, edited by Bernard F. Batto and Kathryn L. Roberts, 219–246. Winona Lake, IN: Eisenbrauns, 2004.

Shaw, Charles S. "Micah 1:10–16 Reconsidered." *Journal of Biblical Literature* 106, no. 2 (1987): 223–229.

———. *The Speeches of Micah: A Rhetorical-Historical Analysis*. Journal for the Study of the Old Testament: Supplement Series 145. Sheffield: Sheffield Academic Press, 1993.

Simundson, Daniel J. *Hosea, Joel, Amos, Obadiah, Jonah, Micah*. Abingdon Old Testament Commentaries. Nashville, TN: Abingdon, 2005.

Smith-Christopher, Daniel L. *Micah: A Commentary*. Old Testament Library. Louisville, KY: Westminster John Knox, 2015.

———. *The Religion of the Landless: The Social Context of the Babylonian Exile*. Eugene, OR: Wipf and Stock, 2015.

Smith, John M. P. "A Critical and Exegetical Commentary on the Books of Micah, Zephaniah, and Nahum." In *A Critical and Exegetical Commentary on Micah, Zephaniah, Nahum, Habakkuk, Obadiah and Joel*, 5–363. International Critical Commentary. Edinburgh: T and T Clark, 1911.

Smith, Julien. *Christ the Ideal King: Cultural Context, Rhetorical Strategy, and the Power of Divine Monarchy in Ephesians*. Wissenschaftliche Untersuchungen zum Neuen Testament 313. Tübingen: Mohr Siebeck, 2011.

Smith, Ralph L. *Micah-Malachi*. Word Biblical Commentary 32. Waco, TX: Word Books, 1984.

Smith, Richard G. *The Fate of Justice and Righteousness during David's Reign: Narrative Ethics and Rereading the Court History According to 2 Samuel 8:15–20:26*. Library of Biblical Studies: Old Testament Studies 508. New York: T and T Clark, 2009.

Smith, Steve. *The Fate of the Jerusalem Temple in Luke-Acts: An Intertextual Approach to Jesus' Laments over Jerusalem and Stephen's Speech*. Library of New Testament Studies 553. London: Bloomsbury, 2017.

Smoak, Jeremy D. "Building Houses and Planting Vineyards: The Early Inner-Biblical Discourse on an Ancient Israelite Wartime Curse." *Journal of Biblical Literature* 127, no. 1 (2008): 19–35.

Soggin, J. A. "משׁל." In *Theological Lexicon of the Old Testament*, edited by Ernst Jenni and Claus Westermann, 689–691. Vol. 2. Peabody, MA: Hendrickson, 1997.

Sommer, Benjamin D. *A Prophet Reads Scripture: Allusion in Isaiah 40–66*. Contraversions. Stanford, CA: Stanford University Press, 1998.

Sparks, Kenton L. *Ancient Texts for the Study of the Hebrew Bible: A Guide to the Background Literature*. Peabody, MA: Hendrickson, 2005.

Stansell, Gary. *Micah and Isaiah: A Form and Tradition Historical Comparison.* Society of Biblical Literature: Dissertation Series 85. Atlanta: Scholars Press, 1988.

Steinmann, Andrew E. "What Did David Understand about the Promises in the Davidic Covenant?" *Bibliotheca Sacra* 171 (2014): 19–29.

Sternberg, Meir. *The Poetics of Biblical Narrative: Ideological Literature and the Drama of Reading.* Indiana Studies in Biblical Literature. Bloomington, IN: Indiana University Press, 1987.

Still, Judith, and Michael Worton. "Introduction." In *Intertextuality: Theories and Practices*, edited by Michael Worton and Judith Still, 1–45. Manchester: Manchester University Press, 1991.

Stohlmann, Stephen. "The Judean Exile After 701 BCE." In *Scripture in Context II: More Essays on the Comparative Method*, edited by William W. Hallo, James C. Moyer, and Leo G. Perdue, 147–175. Winona Lake, IN: Eisenbrauns, 1983.

Strong, James T. "Zion." Edited by Willem VanGemeren. *New International Dictionary of Old Testament Theology and Exegesis.* Grand Rapids: Zondervan, 1997.

Stuart, Douglas K. *Exodus.* Vol. 2 of *The New American Commentary.* Nashville, TN: Broadman and Holman, 2006.

Stulman, Louis. *Jeremiah.* Abingdon Old Testament Commentaries. Nashville, TN: Abingdon, 2005.

Swanson, James. *Dictionary of Biblical Languages with Semantic Domains: Hebrew (Old Testament).* Logos Bible Software. Oak Harbor, WA: Logos Research Systems, 1997.

Sweeney, Marvin A. *The Prophetic Literature.* Interpreting Biblical Texts. Nashville, TN: Abingdon, 2005.

———. *The Twelve Prophets.* Edited by David W. Cotter. Vol. 2, *Micah, Nahum, Habakkuk, Zephaniah, Haggai, Zechariah, Malachi.* Berit Olam: Studies in Hebrew Narrative and Poetry. Collegeville, MN: Liturgical, 2000.

Tan, Kim Huat. *The Zion Traditions and the Aims of Jesus.* Society for New Testament Study: Monograph Series 91. Cambridge: Cambridge University Press, 1997.

Tanner, Beth LaNeel. *The Book of Psalms through the Lens of Intertextuality.* Studies in Biblical Literature 26. New York: Peter Lang, 2001.

———. "King Yahweh as the Good Shepherd: Taking Another Look at the Image of God in Psalm 23." In *David and Zion: Biblical Studies in Honor of J. J. M. Roberts*, edited by Bernard F. Batto and Kathryn L. Roberts, 267–284. Winona Lake, IN: Eisenbrauns, 2004.

Tate, Marvin E. *Psalms 51–100.* Word Biblical Commentary 20. Dallas: Word, 1990.

Terrien, Samuel. *The Psalms: Strophic Structure and Theological Commentary.* Grand Rapids: Eerdmans, 2003.

Thelle, Rannfrid I. *Approaches to the "Chosen Place": Accessing a Biblical Concept.* Library of Hebrew Bible/Old Testament Studies 564. London: T and T Clark, 2012.

Thiessen, Matthew. *Contesting Conversion: Genealogy, Circumcision, and Identity in Ancient Judaism and Christianity.* Oxford: Oxford University Press, 2011.

Thompson, Michael B. *Clothed with Christ: The Example and Teaching of Jesus in Romans 12.1–15.13.* Journal for the Study of the New Testament: Supplement Series 59. Sheffield: Sheffield Academic Press, 1991.

Timmer, Daniel. *The Non-Israelite Nations in the Book of the Twelve: Thematic Coherence and the Diachronic-Synchronic Relationship in the Minor Prophets.* Biblical Interpretation Series 135. Leiden: Brill, 2015.

Toombs, Lawrence E. "Love and Justice in Deuteronomy: A Third Approach to the Law." *Interpretation* 19, no. 4 (1965): 399–411.

Trimm, Charlie. *"YHWH Fights for Them!": The divine warrior in the Exodus Narrative.* Gorgias Biblical Studies 58. Piscataway, NJ: Gorgias, 2014.

Tucker, Gene M. "Prophecy and Prophetic Literature." In *The Hebrew Bible and Its Modern Interpreters*, edited by Douglas A. Knight and Gene M. Tucker, 325–368. Chico, CA: Scholars Press, 1985.

———. "Sin and 'Judgment' in the Prophets." In *Problems in Biblical Theology: Essays in Honor of Rolf Knierim*, edited by Henry T. C. Sun, Keith L. Eades, and G. I. Muller, 373–388. Grand Rapids: Eerdmans, 1997.

Tull, Patricia. "Intertextuality and the Hebrew Scriptures." *Currents in Research: Biblical Studies* 8 (2000): 59–90.

———. *Remember the Former Things: The Recollection of Previous Texts in Second Isaiah.* Society of Biblical Literature: Dissertation Series 161. Atlanta: Scholars Press, 1997.

Turner, Kenneth J. *The Death of Deaths in the Death of Israel: Deuteronomy's Theology of Exile.* Eugene, OR: Wipf and Stock, 2010.

Van der Woude, Adam S. "Micah in Dispute with the Pseudo-Prophets." *Vetus Testamentum* 19, no. 2 (1969): 244–260.

VanDrunen, David. *Divine Covenants and Moral Order: A Biblical Theology of Natural Law.* Emory University Studies in Law and Religion. Grand Rapids: Eerdmans, 2014.

Van Henten, Jan Willem, and Anton Houtepen, eds. *Religious Identity and the Invention of Tradition: Papers Read at a NOSTER Conference in Soesterberg, January 4–6, 1999.* Studies in Theology and Religion 3. Assen: Van Gorcum, 2001.

Vanhoozer, Kevin J. "Introduction: What Is Theological Interpretation of the Bible?" In *Theological Interpretation of the Old Testament: A Book-by-Book*

Survey, edited by Kevin J. Vanhoozer, 15–28. Grand Rapids: Baker Academic, 2008.

Vannoy, J. Robert. *Covenant Renewal at Gilgal: A Study of 1 Samuel 11:14–12:25*. Eugene, OR: Wipf and Stock, 1978.

Vaughan, Patrick H. *The Meaning of "Bāmâ" in the Old Testament: A Study of Etymological, Textual and Archaeological Evidence*. Society for Old Testament Study: Monograph Series 3. London: Cambridge University Press, 1974.

Vaughn, Andrew G., and Ann E. Killebrew, eds. *Jerusalem in Bible and Archaeology: The First Temple Period*. Society of Biblical Literature: Symposium Series 18. Atlanta: Society of Biblical Literature, 2003.

Vaux, Roland de. *Ancient Israel: Its Life and Institutions*. Biblical Resource Series. Grand Rapids: Eerdmans, 1997.

Vriezen, Th. C. *An Outline of Old Testament Theology*. Translated by S. Neuijen. Oxford: Blackwell, 1958.

Wagenaar, Jan A. "The Hillside of Samaria: Interpretation and Meaning of Micah 1:6." *Biblische Notizen* 85 (1996): 26–30.

———. *Judgement and Salvation: The Composition and Redaction of Micah 2–5*. Supplements to Vetus Testamentum 85. Leiden: Brill, 2001.

Wakeman, Mary K. *God's Battle with the Monster: A Study in Biblical Imagery*. Leiden: Brill, 1973.

Walsh, Carey. *The Fruit of the Vine: Viticulture in Ancient Israel*. Harvard Semitic Museum Publications 60. Winona Lake, IN: Eisenbrauns, 2000.

Waltke, Bruce K. *A Commentary on Micah*. Grand Rapids: Eerdmans, 2007.

———. *An Old Testament Theology: An Exegetical, Canonical, and Thematic Approach*. Grand Rapids: Zondervan, 2011.

———. "The Phenomenon of Conditionality within Unconditional Covenants." In *Israel's Apostasy and Restoration: Essays in Honor of Roland K. Harrison*, edited by Avraham Gileadi, 123–139. Grand Rapids: Baker, 1988.

Walton, John H. *Ancient Near Eastern Thought and the Old Testament: Introducing the Conceptual World of the Hebrew Bible*. Grand Rapids: Baker Academic, 2006.

Waters, John W. "The Political Development and Significance of the Shepherd-King Symbol in the Ancient Near East and in the Old Testament." PhD diss., Boston University, 1970.

Weinfeld, Moshe. "בְּרִית Berîth." In *Theological Dictionary of the Old Testament*, edited by G. Johannes Botterweck and Helmer Ringgren, translated by John T. Willis, 2:253–279. Rev. ed. Grand Rapids: Eerdmans, 1977.

———. "The Covenant of Grant in the Old Testament and in the Ancient Near East." *Journal of the American Oriental Society* 90, no. 2 (1970): 184–203.

———. *Deuteronomy and the Deuteronomic School*. Winona Lake, IN: Eisenbrauns, 1992.

———. "Instruction for Temple Visitors in the Bible and in Ancient Egypt." In *Egyptological Studies*, edited by Sarah Israelit-Groll, 224–250. Scripta Hierosolymitana 28. Jerusalem: Magnes, 1982.

———. "Kuntillet 'Ajrud Inscriptions and Their Significance." *Studi epigrafici e linguistia* 1 (1984): 121–130.

———. *Normative and Sectarian Judaism in the Second Temple Period*. Library of Second Temple Studies 54. London: T and T Clark, 2005.

———. *The Promise of the Land: The Inheritance of the Land of Canaan by the Israelites*. Taubman Lectures in Jewish Studies. Berkeley: University of California Press, 1993.

———. *Social Justice in Ancient Israel and in the Ancient Near East*. Minneapolis: Fortress, 1995.

———. "Zion and Jerusalem as Religious and Political Capital: Ideology and Utopia." In *The Poet and the Historian: Essays in Literary and Historical Biblical Criticism*, edited by Richard Elliot Friedman, 75–115. Harvard Semitic Studies 26. Chico, CA: Scholars Press, 1983.

Wellhausen, Julius. *Prolegomena to the History of Israel*. Translated by J. Sutherland Black and Allan Menzies. Cleveland, OH: World, 1957.

Wenham, Gordon J. *Genesis 16–50*. Word Biblical Commentary 2. Dallas: Word, 1994.

Westermann, Claus. *Basic Forms of Prophetic Speech*. Translated by Hugh Clayton White. Philadelphia: Westminster, 1991.

———. *Genesis 12–36*. Translated by John Scullion J. Continental Commentary. Minneapolis: Augsburg, 1985.

Whitelam, Keith W. *The Just King: Monarchical Judicial Authority in Ancient Israel*. Journal for the Study of Old Testament: Supplement Series 12. Sheffield: Journal for the Study of Old Testament, 1979.

Wildberger, Hans. "Die Volkerwallfahrt zum Zion: Jes. II 1–5." *Vetus Testamentum* 7, no. 1 (1957).

Williams, Ronald J. *Williams' Hebrew Syntax*. 3rd ed. Toronto: University of Toronto Press, 2007.

Williamson, Paul R. *Sealed with an Oath: Covenant in God's Unfolding Purpose*. New Studies in Biblical Theology 23. Downers Grove, IL: InterVarsity, 2007.

Willis, Amy C. Merrill. *Dissonance and the Drama of Divine Sovereignty in the Book of Daniel*. Library of Hebrew Bible/Old Testament Studies 520. New York: T and T Clark, 2010.

Willis, John T. "David and Zion in the Theology of the Deuteronomic History: Theological Ideas in 2 Samuel 5–7." In *David and Zion: Biblical Studies in Honor of J. J. M. Roberts*, edited by Bernard F. Batto and Kathryn L. Roberts, 125–140. Winona Lake, IN: Eisenbrauns, 2004.

———. "Fundamental Issues in Contemporary Micah Studies." *Restoration Quarterly* 13, no. 2 (1970): 77–90.

———. "The Structure, Setting, and Interrelationships of the Pericope in the Book of Micah." PhD diss., Vanderbilt University, 1966.

———. "ממך לי יצא in Micah 5:1." *Jewish Quarterly Review* 58, no. 4 (1968): 317–322.

Winkel, Hetty Lalleman-de. *Jeremiah in Prophetic Tradition: An Examination of the Book of Jeremiah in the Light of Israel's Prophetic Traditions*. Contributions to Biblical Exegesis and Theology 26. Leuven: Peeters, 2000.

Winter, Irene J. "How Tall Was Naram-Sin's Victory Stele? Speculations on the Broken Bottom." In *Leaving No Stones Unturned: Essays on the Ancient Near East and Egypt in Honor of Donald P. Hansen*, edited by Erica Ehrenberg, 301–311. Winona Lake, IN: Eisenbrauns, 2002.

Wiseman, D. J. "The Vassal-Treaties of Esarhaddon." *Iraq* 20, no. 1 (1958): 1–99.

Wolff, Hans Walter. *Micah: A Commentary*. Minneapolis: Fortress, 1990.

Won, Young-Sam. "An Examination of the Relationship between the Abrahamic and Mosaic Covenants in Light of Psalm 105." PhD diss., Dallas Theological Seminary, 2017.

Wright, Christopher J. H. *The Mission of God: Unlocking the Bible's Grand Narrative*. Downers Grove, IL: InterVarsity, 2013.

Wright, Jacob L. "Military Valor and Kingship: A Book Oriented Approach to the Study of a Major War Theme." In *Writing and Reading War: Rhetoric, Gender, and Ethics in Biblical and Modern Contexts*, edited by Brad E. Kelle and Frank Ritchel Ames, 33–56. Society of Biblical Literature: Symposium Series 42. Atlanta: Society of Biblical Literature, 2008.

Young, Ian, Robert Rezetko, and Martin Ehrensvärd. *An Introduction to Approaches and Problems*. Vol. 1 of *Linguistic Dating of Biblical Texts*. Bible World 1. London: Equinox, 2008.

Youngblood, Ronald F. "The Abrahamic Covenant: Conditional or Unconditional." In *The Living and Active Word of God: Studies in Honor of Samuel J. Schultz*, edited by Morris A. Inch and Ronald F. Youngblood, 31–46. Winona Lake, IN: Eisenbrauns, 1983.

Zapff, Burkard M. "The Book of Micah: The Theological Center of the Book of the Twelve." In *Perspectives on the Formation of the Book of the Twelve: Methodological Foundations – Redactional Processes – Historical Insights*, edited by Rainer Albertz, James D. Nogalski, and Jakob Wöhrle, 129–146. Beihefte zur Zeitschrift für die alttestamentliche Wissenschaft 433. Berlin: Walter de Gruyter, 2012.

———. "The Perspective on the Nations in the Book of Micah as a 'Systematization' of the Nations' Role in Joel, Jonah, and Nahum? Reflections on a Context-Oriented Exegesis." In *Thematic Threads in the Book of the*

Twelve, edited by Paul L. Redditt and Aaron Schart, 292–312. Berlin: Walter de Gruyter, 2003.

Zimmerli, Walther. "Knowledge of God according to the Book of Ezekiel." In *I Am Yahweh*, edited by Walter Brueggemann, translated by Douglas W. Stott, 29–98. Atlanta: John Knox, 1982.

Langham Literature, with its publishing work, is a ministry of Langham Partnership.

Langham Partnership is a global fellowship working in pursuit of the vision God entrusted to its founder John Stott –

> *to facilitate the growth of the church in maturity and Christ-likeness through raising the standards of biblical preaching and teaching.*

Our vision is to see churches in the majority world equipped for mission and growing to maturity in Christ through the ministry of pastors and leaders who believe, teach and live by the Word of God.

Our mission is to strengthen the ministry of the Word of God through:
- nurturing national movements for biblical preaching
- fostering the creation and distribution of evangelical literature
- enhancing evangelical theological education

especially in countries where churches are under-resourced.

Our ministry

Langham Preaching partners with national leaders to nurture indigenous biblical preaching movements for pastors and lay preachers all around the world. With the support of a team of trainers from many countries, a multi-level programme of seminars provides practical training, and is followed by a programme for training local facilitators. Local preachers' groups and national and regional networks ensure continuity and ongoing development, seeking to build vigorous movements committed to Bible exposition.

Langham Literature provides majority world preachers, scholars and seminary libraries with evangelical books and electronic resources through publishing and distribution, grants and discounts. The programme also fosters the creation of indigenous evangelical books in many languages, through writer's grants, strengthening local evangelical publishing houses, and investment in major regional literature projects, such as one volume Bible commentaries like the *Africa Bible Commentary* and the *South Asia Bible Commentary*.

Langham Scholars provides financial support for evangelical doctoral students from the majority world so that, when they return home, they may train pastors and other Christian leaders with sound, biblical and theological teaching. This programme equips those who equip others. Langham Scholars also works in partnership with majority world seminaries in strengthening evangelical theological education. A growing number of Langham Scholars study in high quality doctoral programmes in the majority world itself. As well as teaching the next generation of pastors, graduated Langham Scholars exercise significant influence through their writing and leadership.

To learn more about Langham Partnership and the work we do visit **langham.org**

www.ingramcontent.com/pod-product-compliance
Lightning Source LLC
Chambersburg PA
CBHW051538230426
43669CB00015B/2644

Interpreters have struggled to discern literary-theological unity in the book of Micah, leading some to deny it exists. Colin Semwayo rightly challenges such scepticism. He argues that the central theological theme of Micah is the reestablishment of Yahweh's sovereignty in the face of the covenant community's rebellion. Yahweh accomplishes this through the restoration of Zion and the Davidic dynasty. In the process Yahweh fulfills his promises to Abraham. Semwayo's most valuable contribution to our understanding of Micah is showing how the Zion/Davidic and Abrahamic promises intersect.

Robert B. Chisholm, Jr, ThD
Chair and Senior Professor of Old Testament Studies,
Dallas Theological Seminary, Dallas, Texas, USA

In this scholarly exegesis of the book of Micah, the reader is guided step by step through a careful analysis to the conclusion. There is a sense of honesty in the use of the evidence which gives the reader a glimpse of scholarship at its best, and there is much here which will be of value to both the layperson and academic in their studies of the minor prophets.

William Domeris, PhD
Senior Academic in Biblical Studies,
South African Theological Seminary, Bryanston, South Africa

Biblical theology is a well-worn subject area, and the study of the theology of Micah is no exception in this regard. But Dr Semwayo brings a fresh voice to the conversation. Methodologically, he applies relevance theory, a linguistic model of communication that has been underutilized in biblical studies. This validates his search for intertextual allusions that are necessary to link various motifs in Micah and unify the theme of divine sovereignty with the Zion traditions and the Abrahamic covenant. Semwayo's discussion of covenants is also refreshing, being informed by recent developments in our understanding of ancient Near Eastern covenants and the Old Testament. On the whole, this is biblical theology at its best.

John W. Hilber, PhD
Professor of Old Testament,
Grand Rapids Theological Seminary, Grand Rapids, Michigan, USA

This biblical-theological study examines the thematic coherence of the book of Micah in relation to the theme of divine sovereignty, specifically with regard to the Lord's action on and for Mt Zion in fulfilment of the Abrahamic promise. It argues that the vision of the Lord's rule on Zion, through the Davidic king, unto the blessing of all creation, is the means by which Micah uses Zion/David themes to apply the Abrahamic promise to his own generation and stands as the theme uniting the apparently disparate texts making up his book. The discussion ranges over divine sovereignty in the ancient Near East and the Old Testament and previous scholarship on Micah's unity or perceived lack thereof (ch. 1); scholarly understanding of covenants, arguing for varying dimensions of symmetry and asymmetry in promise and obligation as the best model for relating and distinguishing them (ch. 2); and Zion traditions and motifs of divine combat (ch. 3). The thesis is then cogently applied to the book of Micah in three final chapters.

The level of scholarship is high and the dissertation successfully challenges previous studies which regard Micah's oracles as only superficially connected and/or reject the authenticity of Micah 6–7. The author's examination of divine sovereignty as expressed in the Zion traditions cogently demonstrate the conceptual coherence and structure of the book of Micah.

Eric Ortland, PhD
Lecturer in Old Testament and Biblical Hebrew,
Oak Hill College, London, UK